KHODASEVICH

Khodasevich———

HIS LIFE AND ART

DAVID M. BETHEA

Princeton University Press | Princeton, New Jersey

Published by Princeton University Press, 41 William Street,
Princeton, New Jersey 08540
In the United Kingdom: Princeton University Press, Guildford, Surrey

Library of Congress Cataloging in Publication Data will be found
on the last printed page of this book

ISBN 0-691-06559-4

Publication of this book has been aided by a grant from the
Publications Program of the National Endowment for the Humanities

This book has been composed in Linotron Trump

Clothbound editions of Princeton University Press books are printed
on acid-free paper, and binding materials are chosen for strength
and durability. Paperbacks, although satisfactory for personal
collections, are not usually suitable for library rebinding.

Printed in the United States of America by Princeton University
Press, Princeton, New Jersey

To my father
and to the memory of my mother

С пожелтевших страниц поднималась ушедшая жизнь,
Уходила во тьму, бормоча и рыдая.
Ты поденщиком был, ты наемником был, и рабом,
И я шла за тобою, доверчивая, молодая.

Раздавили тебя. Раздробили узоры костей.
Надорвали рисунок твоих кружевных сухожилий,
И, собрав, что могли, из почти невесомых частей,
В легкий гроб, в мягкий мох уложили.

Перед тем, как уйти, эти тени ласкают меня,
И кидаются снова, и снова на грудь и на шею,
Обнимают, и молят, и ищут ушедшего дня,
Но ответить я им, и утешить я их не умею.
—Нина Берберова, "Гуверовский архив"

From the yellowed pages there rose a life that was gone;
it left into the darkness, muttering and sobbing.
You were a day-laborer, a hireling, a slave,
and I, young and trusting, followed you.

They crushed you, they shattered the fretwork of your bones.
They ripped to pieces the picture of your lace-like tendons,
and, gathering what we could from your almost weightless remains,
we placed you in a light coffin, in the soft moss of your grave.

Now, before leaving, these shadows begin to caress me,
again and again they cling to my neck and my breast,
embracing, beseeching, looking for the day that's no more,
but to answer them, to console them, I have no way.
—Nina Berberova, "The Hoover Archive"

"My poor boy, take a seat and listen." This is merely showing
off with words. The sounds—well, I remove them as easily from
my "bag" as the conjurer catches his rouble notes from the
thin air. . . . You speak of the significant, of the profound, and
it comes out small; I speak of the small, and the profound is
revealed. You speak of the beautiful so that it comes out drab;
I speak of someone ugly in such a way that—oh my! Why is this?
Well, I'm not quite sure. One has to suffer a lot—in the name
of a word, under the sign of a word. . . . And still more. . . . And
more after that. . . . One has to live not only *here*. . . . In me the
main thing is not the citizen, or the worker, or the lover. . . . In
me the main thing is the poet.
—*Ars poetica*, from Khodasevich's notebook

CONTENTS _____

ILLUSTRATIONS _____

xi

PREFACE _____

I suspect my introduction to the name Vladislav Khodasevich was not much different from that of many other
American graduate students interested in modern Russian
literature. One day our class on Nabokov was to begin discussion of *The Gift*; sifting my way through the "Foreword,"
looking for hints and disclaimers of what was to follow (with
Nabokov I had discovered that the two were often one and
the same), I came upon this paragraph:

> The tremendous outflow of intellectuals that formed such a
> prominent part of the general exodus from Soviet Russia in the
> first years of the Bolshevist Revolution seems today [in March 1962]
> like the wanderings of some mythical tribe whose bird-signs and
> moon-signs I now retrieve from the desert dust. We remained un-
> known to American intellectuals (who, bewitched by Communist
> propaganda, saw us merely as villainous generals, oil magnates, and
> gaunt ladies with lorgnettes). That world is now gone. Gone are
> Bunin, Aldanov, Remizov. Gone is Vladislav Khodasevich, the
> greatest Russian poet that the twentieth century has yet produced.
> The old intellectuals are now dying out and have not found suc-
> cessors in the so-called Displaced Persons of the last two decades
> who have carried abroad the provincialism and Philistinism of their
> Soviet homeland.

The paragraph suggests a good deal more to me now than it
did then. Nabokov was trying in his opening remarks, as
perhaps he was in the text of *The Gift* itself, to jolt the
Western reader into the realization that under the ocean of
our smugness and too easily received views of Soviet Russian
literature an Atlantis of forgotten poetry and prose was waiting to be discovered. What better way than in a first-rate
novel to rout the ghost of Western "self-censorship," to lay
to rest "the conviction," as Simon Karlinsky put it some
years later, "that a Russian writer who resides outside the
Soviet Union cannot be of any interest to the Western reader"?

xiii

Such ghosts continue to haunt us, however, and the one bright exception of Nabokov, dazzling though it may be, has not been enough to attract more than the eye of the specialist to that "other" Russian literature. The names Bunin (a 1933 Nobel laureate), Aldanov, Remizov, and Khodasevich are not, to state it mildly, household words in the West. Perhaps the most fitting irony in all this, one that Khodasevich, a consummate ironist, would have appreciated, is that I—and presumably other students of Russian literature—was learning of Khodasevich's existence not by reading his verse but by reading Nabokov's novel, especially those passages describing the shadow colloquies between Koncheev, the genuine poet that the young hero wishes to become, and the young hero Fyodor himself. That Koncheev, whose source was Khodasevich, should have a ghostly presence in the novel and that the colloquies should turn out to be will-o'-the-wisps seems to add to the air of unreality and "otherness" that has pursued Khodasevich the artist right up to the present.

But this, the bigger picture, went over my head at the time. I was startled by Nabokov's categorical praise of Khodasevich: "Gone is Vladislav Khodasevich, the greatest Russian poet that the twentieth century has yet produced." Who was this Khodasevich? Blok, Mandelshtam, Mayakovsky, Pasternak—yes; but Khodasevich? Here was Nabokov, a writer nobody could ignore, invoking the name of a writer that everybody, or what seemed like everybody, had managed to ignore. Soon I discovered that Nabokov's declaration was not a case of temporary insanity and that he had repeated himself in the commentaries to his famous translation of *Eugene Onegin*: "This century has not yet produced any Russian poet surpassing Vladislav Hodasevich." The bur, so to speak, was under my saddle, and the chase was on.

At the same time I was discovering the haunting charm of Khodasevich's poetry, I was discovering that Nabokov had in fact not been speaking into a void. When Khodasevich emigrated from the Soviet Union in June 1922, he already had quite a reputation as a poet. Andrey Bely helped to make that reputation with important articles on Khodasevich in 1922 and 1923. Thereafter, into the late 1920s, Khodasevich's art was spoken of in glowing terms by some of the most distinguished Soviet and Russian émigré critics and belletrists: Gorky raved that "Khodasevich writes utterly amazing verse," and that "Khodasevich, to my mind, is modern-day Russia's best poet"; Mandelshtam complained that Khodasevich was one of those poets toward whom contemporaries had shown "monstrous ingratitude"; Wladimir Weidlé, in a long article written in 1928 shortly after the appearance of Khodasevich's *Collected Verse*, expressed the view that Khodasevich was now, after the death of Blok, Russia's leading poet. The émigré press was dotted with warm articles and reviews written by, among others, Gleb Struve, Konstantin Mochulsky, Yuly Aikhenvald, Alfred Bem, and Nabokov. To all appearances, Khodasevich the poet had clearly arrived.

Then at some point in the late 1920s, for reasons that were implicitly related to life in exile, Khodasevich began to write less and less poetry. Apparently he had, as the Russian captures it in one neat verb form, "written himself out" (*ispisalsia*). By the early 1930s (if not in fact sooner) Khodasevich had turned exclusively to the tasks of biographer, memoirist, Pushkinist, critic, and shaper of poetic taste. Due to many things, including Khodasevich's ensuing silence as a poet, his prickly personality in and out of print, and literary politics in emigration as well as in the Soviet Union, his artistic reputation was already in sharp decline when he died of cancer in 1939. People seemed to have forgotten that he was, in the first place, a poet.

And it is precisely this cloud of oblivion that Nabokov was trying to disperse when he wrote, in a beautiful necrology that appeared in *Contemporary Annals*: "I find it odd myself that in this article, in this rapid inventory of thoughts prompted by Khodasevich's death, I seem to imply a vague nonrecognition of his genius and engage in vague polemics with such phantoms as would question the enchantment and importance of his poetry." Unfortunately, Nabokov had good reason to engage in polemics with phantoms that doubted the importance of Khodasevich's poetry. The eloquent efforts of those such as Nabokov, Nina Berberova, and Wladimir Weidlé notwithstanding, Khodasevich has yet to be discovered by many Slavists (not to speak of the generalist Western reader). Rarely has an artist, at one time so highly regarded—and not by the popularizers (Khodasevich was never widely read in this sense), but by those whose authority we respect—been so thoroughly forgotten by later generations. From the late 1920s to the present day there exist only a handful of scholarly articles devoted to Khodasevich's poetry. Finally, in the last decade, as new dissertations are being written about him, as he is being widely reprinted for the first time, as his best works are being collected in an impressive five-volume edition, the situation appears to be changing. The phantoms of which Nabokov spoke may at last be on the run. The present study is an attempt, however imperfect and "introductory," to jar our collective memory into a recognition of what it has lost, to search for *temps perdu* not in a biographical so much as in an aesthetic sense, and—if the attempt is successful—to scatter the phantoms of forgetfulness once and for all. Not a modest undertaking, but then Khodasevich's was no modest poetic accomplishment.

There are, I believe, many good reasons for studying the life and work of Khodasevich. On the plane of biography, he knew many of the writers seminal to the modern period in Russian literature and was on intimate terms with at least two of them—Bely and Gorky. As *littérateur*, he is the author of *Nekropol'* (Necropolis), a superb collection of memoirs devoted to the leading figures of Symbolism; *Derzhavin*, the finest "artistic" biography in the Russian language; two elab-

orate studies of Pushkin; numerous translations—especially
of the Polish classics and modern Hebrew poets—into Russian; and hundreds of essays and feuilletons on a multitude
of topics. But as Nabokov has pointed out, if Khodasevich
is to attract and hold our attention, it is because he is a poet.
Thus my intention while researching and writing this study
has not been to ignore Khodasevich's numerous other ac-
complishments (quite the contrary), but to keep the accent
where possible on the one accomplishment, his verse, out
of which the others grew. When Khodasevich swore in 1903,
at the age of seventeen, that he was dedicating himself to
"poetry forever," he was not speaking idly. There is a sense
in which he saw everything he did through the eyes of a
poet. Even in the 1930s, when he had begun to speak more
retrospectively, to study the past glories of Russian poetry
(Pushkin, Derzhavin, Symbolist colleagues), to admonish,
sometimes peevishly, the younger generation of émigré poets
for losing sight of tradition, the creative personality was
never far below the surface.

What sort of poetry did Khodasevich write? What, in a few
words, is its secret? The uniqueness of Khodasevich's poetic
manner resides in his startling fusion of Symbolism and post-
Symbolism, "idealism" and "realism," Pushkinian lapidary
form and ever-questioning irony. Indeed, in Khodasevich's
finest work an improbable balance—a sort of "moving
stasis"—is struck between a private, ulterior sense of beauty
and the process of "living down" that beauty. Though Khodasevich may have some distinguished relatives in the Western poetic tradition (the names of Laforgue, Hardy, and Auden come first to mind), there is virtually no one, particularly
if we consider his application of the principles of modern
"unstable" (the term is Wayne Booth's) irony in lyric form,
with whom he might be compared in Russia. In a study such
as this it is essential to demonstrate both how Khodasevich's
mature aesthetic operates in isolation, how his ironic speaker,
for instance, produces a remarkable interplay of voices and

rhetorical tension in a certain poem, *and* how that aesthetic was "programmed" to operate in a larger context, how Khodasevich arrived at it through internal necessity, via personal experience and the history of his time. I found, in trying to arrive at a balanced reading of Khodasevich's mature verse, that the one point of view does not exclude the other, which brings me to a question that gave me some pause, that is, the question of biography.

Critical biographies of writers often imply a certain causal approach to the material, a "first this, then that" attitude that can be seen to surface even in the titles of such studies: *Khodasevich: His Life* and *Art*. Does the conjunction insert a synchronic link or a diachronic wedge between the concepts it straddles? If it were not so clumsy, I would prefer another title in this case: *Khodasevich: His Life in his Art and his Art in his Life*. Rather than write a separate, self-enclosed biography followed by a separate, self-enclosed analysis of the poetry, I have tried to demonstrate to the reader that there exists between the biography and the poetry of each period a genuine symbiotic relationship. There are, to be sure, impressive examples of the-life-then-the-art approach (Karlinsky's fine study of Tsvetaeva), but I am convinced that the reasons for taking an "integrated" approach to the study of Khodasevich are valid and compelling ones.

One of the great Pushkinists of his generation, Khodasevich liked to search for the biographical facts of Pushkin's life that shed light on the poet's art. And to Khodasevich's mind there was no detail too small or insignificant to pass by. Typical, for instance, might be Khodasevich's attempt to show how the various details surrounding Pushkin's affair with Baroness Ficquelmont are transformed into the scene of the old woman's boudoir in "The Queen of Spades." It would be a mistake to think that Khodasevich was interested in simple identification; he was interested in the way Pushkin objectified or "masked" (to use Yeats's term) all that was crudely autobiographical, how the "real" became the "artistic" through a process that was organic, unsponsored, internally motivated. Khodasevich wanted to capture the psychic metabolism of the artist in the act of creation. Thus those approaches that ignored either the poet's life (the Formalists) or the poet's art (the pure biographer Veresaev) could never do justice to Pushkin's dimensionality. If one were to give a name to Khodasevich's approach to Pushkin, it would be "stereoscopic," simultaneously aware of the life and the art and the mysterious link that binds them. I do not purport to read Khodasevich as well as Khodasevich reads Pushkin. But I do believe that a similar relation exists between the life and the art of Khodasevich, and I have tried to focus on those aspects of his biography that best show his becoming an artist and his transformation of life into art.

This study is the first critical biography of Khodasevich to appear in any language. Although its format suggests a certain comprehensiveness, it would be foolish to claim that what I say exhausts the subject. Obviously, with the focus on Khodasevich the poet, Khodasevich the critic and publicist gets short shrift. But works such as this can never be all things to all people; if I had devoted equal space to each aspect of Khodasevich's career as professional man of letters, the text would have soon become unwieldy. So my assumption (and sincere hope) has been that interest in Khodasevich is only just beginning and that what I have not managed to say others will.

There are seven chapters in all, the first being purely biographical and the last six combining the biography and the work of a given period. Chapters 2 through 6 have alternating sections of biography and analysis of poetry; chapters 2 and 3 begin with discussions of the two phenomena, Symbolism (or more precisely "Bryusovism") and Pushkin, that were seminal to Khodasevich's early development as a poet; chapter 4 opens with a discussion of Khodasevich's "poetics of irony" and introduces the poetry of the major period; chapters 4 through 6 (those dealing with the major period) conclude with a final section giving a detailed exegesis of a major text (or texts) in that collection. The largely "literal" translations of Khodasevich's poetry appearing throughout the text are my own.

Any work such as this is in a real sense a joint undertaking. To begin with, had the Graduate School at the University of Kansas not supported my initial project ("Irony in the Poetry of Vladislav Khodasevich") with a Dissertation Fellowship in 1976 and had the National Endowment for the Humanities not underwritten the expanded version with a Fellowship in Category B in 1979, it is difficult to imagine what still unborn state the present study would be in. I might sum up my debt of gratitude to former teachers, who so carefully wrote in the margins of my schoolboy consciousness, with lines from the verse letter that Keats once sent to his favorite teacher Cowden Clarke: "Ah! had I never seen, / Or known your kindness, what might I have been?" Here I should like to mention Mr. Thomas Donovan, who guided my first struggling steps in the art of self-expression; Professor James Boatwright and Mr. Henry Sloss, who did so much to bring English and American literature alive for me; Professors J. Theodore Johnson and Harold Orel, both amazingly perceptive and generous experts on modern European literature; and the Department of Slavic Languages at the University of Kansas, especially Professors Joseph Conrad, Gerald Mikkelson, Stephen Parker, and Heinrich Stammler. The Russian language, which I have so grown to admire and marvel at, first became known to me through the efforts of my teachers at the Defense Language Institute (none, as I recall, were gaunt ladies with lorgnettes, but tended to be full of body, with full-bodied voices) and thereafter became an intimate ally through the efforts of Professor Robert Lager, Mrs. Eugenia Felton, and others.

Those colleagues, some Khodasevich aficionados and other experts on the period, who have shared insights or material, or both, with me include: Mr. Alexandre Bacherac, Professors Sergei Davydov, Roger Hagglund, Robert Hughes, Lev Loseff, Jane Miller, Gleb Struve, Richard Sylvester, and Mr. Martin Sixsmith. I would like to thank especially Miss N. B. Nidermiller, Khodasevich's niece, for providing needed information on the poet's background, as well as the families of the late Professor M. M. Karpovich and the late I. I. Bernshtein for granting me access to Khodasevich's papers in their possession. Research at Watson Library (University of Kansas), Widener Library (Harvard), Sterling Library (Yale), and New York Public Library and archival work at the Hoover Institute (Stanford), Beinecke Library (Yale), the Central State Literary Archive (TsGALI) (Moscow), and the Gorky Institute of World Literature (IMLI) (Moscow) were made simpler by the pleasant staffs at each. Typing of the text was ably handled by Ms. Mary Longey. And warm thanks are due to Ms. Tam Curry, my copyeditor, who did her difficult job superbly and who taught me much about language, especially my own.

Finally (or almost), my debt to Nina Berberova, who read the manuscript, offered valuable suggestions, and generally encouraged me along the way, is incalculable: just as it would have been impossible to retrieve much of Mandelshtam's literary estate without the constant vigilance of his widow, Nadezhda Yakovlevna, so would it have been impossible to keep Khodasevich's memory alive without the ongoing efforts of this woman, his wife of ten years and his closest companion in the hard years of exile; it was she alone, an important émigré writer in her own right, who took pains to preserve Khodasevich's papers in her archives and who published what were until recently the only editions of his poetry and prose to appear either in the Soviet Union or in the West since the 1930s.

The appreciation that goes with my last acknowledgment is as precise as any dead reckoning of this sort: thank you, Kim, in what must have at times seemed our "star-crossed" years, for steering a straight course.

Parts of chapters 4, 5, and 6 have appeared, respectively, in *Topic* (Fall 1979), *Slavic and East European Journal* (Fall 1981), and *Slavic Review* (May 1980). The passage from Nina Berberova's *The Italics Are Mine* that is quoted on pp. 342-345 of this book is reprinted courtesy of Harcourt Brace Jovanovich, Inc. Mrs. Vera Nabokov has kindly granted me permission to cite in full Nabokov's translation of "Ballada."

Madison, Wisconsin, August 1982 DMB

A NOTE ON THE TRANSLITERATION

The system of transliteration I have used is that recommended by Professor J. Thomas Shaw in his *The Transliteration of Modern Russian for English-Language Publications* (Madison, 1967). In the text itself and in the expository sections of the notes, I have used Shaw's "System I," which is a modified version of the Library of Congress system for the purpose of "normalizing" (making more pronounceable) personal and place names for the generalist Western reader. In all citations of bibliographical material and in transliterations of words as words I have used "System II," which is the unmodified Library of Congress system, with the diacritical marks omitted. It is hoped that any confusion that might arise from the combination of these two systems (e.g., the reader will find "Valery Bryusov" in the text but "Valerii Briusov" in a citation) will be compensated for by the increased readability afforded the nonspecialist and the greater precision afforded the specialist.

ABBREVIATIONS _____

Italics	Nina Berberova, *The Italics Are Mine*, trans. Philippe Radley (New York, 1969).
Kursiv	Nina Berberova, *Kursiv moi* (The Italics Are Mine). Munich, 1972.
Nekropol'	V. Khodasevich, *Nekropol'* (Necropolis). Brussels, 1939; rpt. Paris, 1976.
PN	*Poslednie novosti* (The Latest News).
Stat'i	V. Khodasevich, *Literaturnye stat'i i vospominaniia* (Literary Articles and Memoirs). New York, 1954.
SS	V. Khodasevich, *Sobranie stikhov* (Collected Verse). Ed. Nina Berberova. Munich, 1961.
SZ	*Sovremennye zapiski* (Contemporary Annals).
Voz	*Vozrozhdenie* (The Renaissance).

KHODASEVICH

1

ORIGINS: 1886-1896

Oh! Blessed rage for order, pale Ramon,
The maker's rage to order words of the sea,
Words of the fragrant portals, dimly-starred,
And of ourselves and of our origins,
In ghostlier demarcations, keener sounds.
—Wallace Stevens, "The Idea of Order at Key West"

In a hundred years or so some young scholar, or poet, or
maybe just a snob, some long-nosed chatterbox . . . will
turn up a book of my verse and create (for a month or two)
a literary fad of Khodasevich.
—from Khodasevich's notebook

Other than what is given in "Mladenchestvo" (Infancy), Khodasevich's short autobiographical fragment, and in retrospective asides that dot his later memoirs and critical prose,
we know relatively little about the early life of the poet. To
proceed with the modest inventory of these beginnings is to
proceed as well with the following assumption: Khodasevich
saw the past somewhat differently than did many contemporaries; his relation to personal history was neither so "lyrical" as that of Irina Odoevtseva, nor so "metaphysical" as
that of Fyodor Stepun, nor so resiliently forward-looking as
that of Nina Berberova, nor so capriciously revisionist as
that of Andrey Bely. Nor were his memories from childhood
on like Nabokov's, suspended in a sort of amniotic fluid, "a
radiant and mobile medium that was none other than the
pure element of time."[1] Khodasevich might have remarked
instead, not unlike Joyce's Stephen Dedalus, "History is a
nightmare from which I am trying to awake";[2] and thus he

[1] Vladimir Nabokov, *Speak, Memory* (New York, 1970), p. 21.
[2] James Joyce, *Ulysses* (New York, 1961), p. 34.

3

never had the internal equilibrium, never was "awake" from personal history long enough to write a volume about himself. Unfortunately, all we have is the first installment; but if a little under twenty pages of economical prose, wrought from what seems a prehensile memory by the blade of self-analysis, is any indication of promise, then such a volume would have been remarkable indeed.

Vladislav Felitsianovich Khodasevich was born in Moscow on 28 May 1886 (16 May, old style) into a family of modest means whose ties with Russia were more geographical than genealogical. His father, Felitsian Ivanovich (1834?-1911[3]), was the son of a disenfranchised Polish nobleman who had fled with his family into Russia (from his native Lithuania) during the Polish rebellion of 1833. What we can say further about Felitsian Ivanovich is quite sketchy, his son giving us little in his autobiographical prose to flesh out the paternal portrait. He decided as a young man on a career in painting and studied under the famous F. A. Bruni at the Imperial Academy in St. Petersburg; he had at one point painted frescoes in the churches of Vilnius. But then with time he abandoned this first love, either because he doubted his talent or his ability to support a family (he had married Vladislav's mother while still a fledgling painter). At the time of Vladislav's birth, he was Moscow's first Kodak dealer, the proprietor of a photographic supply shop centrally located on Bolshaya Dmitrovka Street. Felitsian Ivanovich, then, seems to hover somewhere slightly beyond the threshold of impressions that Khodasevich recalls in his autobiographical fragment: perhaps he was too old (he was going on fifty-two when Vladislav was born); more likely he was simply too busy making ends meet to be a chief attraction in the fanciful

---

[3] We know the precise dates of few members of Khodasevich's immediate family. The year of F. I. Khodasevich's birth can be reconstructed from "Infancy": "When I was born my father was going on fifty-two, my mother forty-two." (Khodasevich, "Mladenchestvo" [Infancy], *Vozdushnye puti* [Aerial Ways], 4 [1965], 100.)

world of his youngest child. Still, as Khodasevich suggests elsewhere, his father appears to have been quiet and kindly, happy during the evening to play an occasional game of *soroka-vorovka* (something like "This Little Piggy") with his son.[4] It would be wrong, I think, to interpret Khodasevich's relative silence as resentment of his father's absence, while much closer to the truth to take it at face value: as the lack of strong influence, either positive or negative. Generally speaking, a father's domestic role during this late Victorian period was not nearly so intimate as it is today. Like Blok, Khodasevich would be growing up mainly in the presence of women, or as he puts it, in a "gynaeceum."[5] What in fact the poet finally does have to say about his father, the artist *manqué*, comes not in prose but in the *sub specie aeternitatis* of poetry, as Blok used to call the artistic transformations of his affair with Volokhova: over forty years later Khodasevich would, with some fine dactylic strokes, provide the image of an artist-become-father whose gift to his son-become-artist was, ironically, the will and talent he did not have. The sixth child of a six-fingered father, Khodasevich would find a use for the extra little finger that, like the unfulfilled aspirations of a young painter, his father had kept hidden in his left hand:

> Был мой отец шестипалым. А сын? Ни смиренного
>   сердца,
>   Ни многодетной семьи, ни шестипалой руки
> Не унаследовал он. Как игрок на неверную карту
>   Ставит на слово, на звук—душу свою и судьбу . . .
> Ныне, в январьскую ночь, во хмелю, шестипалым
>   размером
>   И шестипалой строфой сын поминает отца.[6]

> My father was six-fingered. And his son? Neither a
>   humble heart,
>   nor a family of many children, nor a six-fingered hand

[4] See *SS*, p. 196.
[5] Khodasevich, "Infancy," p. 109.
[6] *SS*, p. 197.

5

did he inherit. As does a gambler on a risky card,
    so does he on a word, on a sound, bet his soul and
    fate . . .
Now, this January night, a little in his cups, with a six-
    fingered meter
and a six-fingered strophe the son remembers the
    father.

Vladislav's mother, Sophia Yakovlevna (née Brafman) (1844?-1911), assumes a greater, though by no means dominant, presence in the writings of her son. Her father was Ya. A. Brafman (c. 1825-1879), the Jewish author of the notorious *Book of the Kahal* (1869) and *Jewish Communes: Local and International* (1888).[7] The *Book of the Kahal*, which discusses the oppression in southwest Russia of poor Jews by rich Jews, was interpreted as a justification for pogroms. As his daughter after him, Ya. A. Brafman was converted from Judaism to Christianity—first Protestantism, then Catholicism—and under Alexandr II became something rare for his time, a nobleman of Jewish origin. The maternal grandparents of the poet must have separated at an early date, since Sophia Yakovlevna was soon left an "orphan," having "lost" her mother; through her father's connections, she was taken in by the Radziwiłls, one of the most prominent families in Polish Lithuania.[8] The orphaning of the girl was real if not literal: her mother, whose name is found nowhere, apparently did not die, but according to family legend, ran off with another man and thereafter became a black sheep.[9] She later returned to her daughter's household,

[7] See *Encyclopaedia Judaica* (Jerusalem, 1971-1972), pp. 1,287-1,288; and Louis Bernhardt, "V. F. Khodasevich i sovremennaia evreiskaia poeziia" (V. F. Khodasevich and Contemporary Hebrew Poetry), *Russian Literature* 6 (1974), 24n.

[8] See V. Lednitskii, "Literaturnye zametki i vospominaniia" (Literary Notes and Recollections), *Opyty* (Experiments), 2 (1953), 166: "My [Khodasevich's] mother was an orphan, having lost her mother early, and was taken in . . . by the family of Prince Radziwiłl."

[9] My thanks to Miss N. B. Nidermiller (Khodasevich's niece) for providing me with this information.

however, and was to be one of the fixtures in the distaff world surrounding young Vladislav.

It was in the aristocratic Radziwiłł household that the Jewish girl Sophia seems to have found not only material shelter but cultural and spiritual largesse as well, for when she and her new husband, Felitsian Ivanovich, left Vilnius for St. Petersburg and his renewed course of study at the Imperial Academy, she had been converted to Roman Catholicism and had conceived a lasting passion for Polish literature. In an article about Mickiewicz that her son wrote much later the completely ingenuous nature of Sophia Yakovlevna's feeling for her acquired, yet nonetheless real, homeland is poignantly evident:

Several impressions, which even now I recall very clearly, relate to the earliest period of my life, to the time when I had not yet begun to go to kindergarten, after which there set in my irrevocable russification.

During the mornings, after tea, my mother would take me into her room. A picture of the Ostrobram Holy Virgin hung there in a golden frame over the bed. A little rug lay on the floor. I would kneel and read first "Our Father," then "Hail Mary," then the "Credo." After that mama would tell me about Poland and sometimes read me poetry. The poetry would be from the beginning of *Pan Tadeusz*. I learned what sort of work that was only much later, and only then understood that her reading went no further than the seventy-second verse of the first book. Every time the hero (as yet unnamed), after having just climbed out of the carriage, ran alongside of the house, caught sight of the familiar furniture and chiming clock, and with childish joy

Once again tugged the cord that let forth
the familiar surge of an old mazurka by Dąbrowski,

mother would begin to cry and let me go.[10]

Here in the child's view the traditions of Roman Catholicism and Polish national identity are magically woven into the poem's "acoustic fabric" (*zvukovaia tkan'*),[11] the result being

[10] Khodasevich, "K stoletiiu 'Pana Tadeusha' " (For the Hundredth Anniversary of *Pan Tadeusz*), *Stat'i*, p. 73.
[11] Ibid., p. 75.

7

a sort of nostalgic tinnitus, what thereafter would be a benignly recurring autosuggestion of who he was and where he had come from:

I knew these verses almost by heart, not understanding much in them, and not trying to. I knew that they were written by Mickiewicz, a poet in the same way that Pushkin, Lermontov, Maykov, and Fet were poets. But to understand Pushkin, Lermontov, Maykov, and Fet was both necessary and possible, but Mickiewicz was something else altogether: his was not just poetry, it was something inextricably bound to prayer and to Poland, that is, to the church, to that Catholic church [*kostel*] on Milyutinsky Lane where mama took us on Sundays. I never saw Mickiewicz or Poland, for they were as impossible to see as God, but they were there in the same place as God: behind the low railing covered in red velvet, in the organ's thunder, in the smoke of the incense and in the golden radiance of the slanting rays of the sun, falling sideways out of somewhere onto the altar. For me the altar was the threshold or even the beginning of "that other world" where I was before I was in this one and where I will be when I am in this one no longer.

God—Poland—Mickiewicz: invisible and incomprehensible, but my own [*rodnoe*]. And—inseparable from one another.[12]

So without getting too far ahead of ourselves, we can see in these passages, the details of which are as emotionally shaped as any in Khodasevich's autobiographical prose, the character of the maternal legacy. On the other hand, the fact that the poet was by blood half-Jewish seems to have had little significance for his childhood development. Only much later, perhaps through his close friendship during the Symbolist years with the Jewish poet Muni (Samuil Viktorovich Kissin) (who wrote in Russian), and certainly through his editing and translating of the texts of the great modern Hebrew poets (including Bialik and Tschernichowski), did the fact of his Jewish heritage begin to take on an added weight. Strangely enough, it was Khodasevich's Jewish mother who so religiously emphasized the Polish legacy that by blood issued from Felitsian Ivanovich. And stranger still, like one

[12] Ibid., p. 74.

of those infinite vagaries that pattern our lives if only there is an ironist there to see them, it would be another Jewish member of Khodasevich's family, this time the wife and ministering angel of his final years in emigration, Olga Borisovna Margolina-Khodasevich, who converted not to Roman Catholicism but to Russian Orthodoxy shortly before disappearing into a Nazi heart of darkness.

Khodasevich's "irrevocable russification," which he dates from his entrance into kindergarten and, presumably, into a world full of Russian youngsters, might have begun even earlier with the appearance of a third very important adult influence on his childhood life. Like many children of foreign-born parents committed to preserving native traditions in an alien environment, the young Vladislav grew to chafe at his mother's reminders that other Polish children living in Moscow still managed to speak their language and go to church regularly. Wacław Lednicki, the Polish scholar, who met Khodasevich only many years later as a result of a mutual love of Pushkin, was apparently just such a model child, and without even knowing him, Vladislav came to hate him like the taste of bad medicine.[13] But alongside Mickiewicz, Roman Catholicism, and maternal coaxing there was a Russian presence from the very beginning: as Khodasevich tells us in verses whose odic splendor recalls Derzhavin, the child "sucked the agonizing right . . . to love and curse"[14] Russia with the milk of his nurse, Elena Alexandrovna Kuzina (by marriage, Stepanova). More than to his mother or father, it was to this simple peasant woman, born in a village of the Tula Province, that Khodasevich traced his adopted birthright as a Russian poet. There was no need to embellish the fact of her importance. When as a newborn infant Khodasevich appeared too weak to suckle and all other wet nurses refused the task, Elena Alexandrovna managed the impos-

---

[13] Lednitskii, "Literary Notes and Recollections," pp. 166-167.

[14] Khodasevich, "Ne mater'iu, no tul'skoiu krest'iankoi" (Not by my mother, but by a peasant woman from Tula), SS, p. 66.

sible. And in suckling the little Vladya, she not only saved his life, she gave up the life of her unweaned son, Vladya's coeval: to have milk enough for one, she had to give the other to a foundling hospital, where he was bound to die, and did shortly thereafter. The debt that the future poet owed his nurse, therefore, was incalculable, and it is not curious that her example, which reads like fiction become life, should provide an important clue to the portrait of an artist *in statu nascendi*.

Yet the Russian legacy goes deeper, I think, than these perhaps too easily romanticized facts. It is not enough (though much, to be sure) that Elena Alexandrovna was Russian and the baby owed his life to her, since this does not account for her connection with the *chudotvornyi genii* (wonder-working genius)[15] of the Russian language, as Khodasevich calls it in the same poem. Unlike another famous nurse, she did not, as the poet tells us, ply her young listener with the language-rich marvels of Russian fairy tales. The answer lies in what Elena Alexandrovna came to represent, what Khodasevich made her, in his poetry. Of the three parental figures, she alone occupies a central position in the *Collected Verse*. In a sense that returns to this heavily patinated metaphor some of its original vitality, Elena Alexandrovna was Khodasevich's Muse; it is her image that will be tightly linked with that of the poet's *dusha*, his Psyche and Beautiful Lady;[16] it is for this reason that the poem invoking the old nurse comes very close to the beginning of *Tiazhelaia lira* (The Heavy Lyre), Khodasevich's finest, most "musical" collection.[17] Like Pushkin before him, whose Muse undergoes

[15] Ibid., p. 67.

[16] Khodasevich connects the notions of Psyche and *Prekrasnaia Dama* (Beautiful Lady) in "Iridion," *Stat'i*, p. 102.

[17] It is perhaps significant that Khodasevich moved the poem about Elena Alexandrovna close to the beginning of *The Heavy Lyre* in the 1927 (Paris) edition of *Collected Verse*, whereas the same poem was located in the middle of the 1922 (Moscow-Petrograd) edition of *The Heavy Lyre* published separately.

gradual mythopoesis from old nurse, Arina Rodionovna, to winsome young goddess, Khodasevich will trace his "psychic" milk to the real breasts of Elena Alexandrovna.[18]

F. I. KHODASEVICH and his bride had arrived in St. Petersburg in the early 1860s. It was not long thereafter that Felitsian Ivanovich changed his profession and the family moved to the ancient city of Tula, eighty miles south of Moscow. Tolstoy had been born on Yasnaya Polyana, his family estate nearby Tula, and one anecdote has Khodasevich's father photographing the great author.[19] Although Vladislav, born some twenty years later, does not appear at first to have been much interested in his father's (for that time) innovative profession, it is curious that the central image in *Sorrentinskie fotografii* (Sorrento Photographs), perhaps Khodasevich's greatest work, is a double-exposed snapshot.[20] Why Khodasevich, in many ways a traditionalist, would use what Susan Sontag calls an "optical-chemical process"[21] to develop the image of Russian culture in eclipse might be explained by a conviction that the photograph is an ersatz art form, catching by chance what a painting would catch by design—Felitsian Ivanovich had traded genuine art for photography, a mechanical substitute.[22]

In Tula the Khodasevich family began to grow. After the first child, a son, died within a few months of birth, there

[18] See V. Khodasevich: "Arina Rodionovna," *Voz*, no. 1314 (6 January 1929); and "Iavlenie Muzy" (The Appearance of the Muse), *O Pushkine* (On Pushkin) (Berlin, 1937), pp. 8-38.

[19] Lednitskii, "Literary Notes and Recollections," p. 166.

[20] A provocative "photography" shows up as an entry in Khodasevich's "calendar" for the year 1897. The calendar was a list of brief, diaristic entries for the years 1886-1921; it was given to Nina Berberova at the time she and Khodasevich left the Soviet Union in June 1922. See *Kursiv*, pp. 168-170.

[21] Susan Sontag, *On Photography* (New York, 1977), p. 158.

[22] Although Khodasevich never criticized photography as an art form, he did have negative things to say about the cinema. See V. Khodasevich, "O kinematografe" (On the Cinematograph), *PN*, no. 2045 (28 October 1926).

followed over the next eleven years (1864-1875) Mikhail, Maria, Viktor, Konstantin, and Evgenia.[23] Except for Evgenia

[23] Of Khodasevich's brothers and sisters we know very little, and there is not much likelihood of discovering more. Mikhail (Misha) (1865-1925) was a Moscow lawyer known for his Ciceronian eloquence and sartorial flair. He followed the arts enthusiastically (along with Vladislav's, his name shows up on the list of subscribers to *Vesy* [The Scales], the Symbolist journal *par excellence*). His daughter was Valentina Khodasevich (1894-1970), the portrait painter and set designer. For brief portraits of Mikhail Khodasevich, see Lednitskii,"Literary Notes and Recollections," pp. 156-159; and Richard D. Sylvester, ed., *Valentina Khodasevich and Olga Margolina-Khodasevich: Unpublished Letters to Nina Berberova* (Berkeley, 1979), pp. 13-14. An excellent portrait of Valentina Khodasevich is also found in Sylvester, pp. 13-49. The other children, with the exception of Evgenia, went their separate, sketchy ways: Maria (Manya) married Mikhail Antonovich Voyshitsky, a tax collector with musical inclinations, and moved to Petersburg; Viktor chose to work in his father's store, but apparently he died early; Konstantin (Stasya) was the black sheep—unlucky in school and in marriage, he was shot by the Bolsheviks. Evgenia (Zhenya) (1876-1960) is portrayed in "Infancy" as an attractive older sister: "well-dressed, slender, and graceful, . . . [with] pretty hands and legs, [so that] even a brown gymnasium dress with black apron look[ed] very good on her" (p. 109). (Mikhail, Evgenia, and Vladislav all shared a penchant for elegant clothes.) Like her younger brother, Evgenia eventually took up permanent residence in Paris following the Revolution. It is to her daughter, Miss N. B. Nidermiller, that I owe thanks for much of this information.

Vladislav Khodasevich as a little boy with his sister Evgenia (Zhenya), c. 1890.

(Zhenya), we know almost nothing about the others as children, for by the time the family had moved to Moscow (sometime after Evgenia's birth in 1875) and Vladislav was born and had his first childhood impressions, the older children had already begun to leave the household: Mikhail to become a lawyer, Maria to get married, Viktor to work in his father's store, and Konstantin to enter medical school. From little Vladya's point of view they appear as adults who drop in to visit.

The birth of the last child, the future poet, was premature by two weeks. Impatience, in some ways characteristic of the modern period for which Khodasevich was to write,[24] was even in this initial setting forth a salient quality:

An important trait in me is impatience, which has furnished me in life with many an unpleasantness and has tormented me constantly. Perhaps it comes from the fact that I was, as it were, born too late and ever since it seems as though I have been trying unconsciously to make up the loss. . . . In our family I came to be a Benjamin, a "leftover" [poskrebysh], a favorite. I was watched over, pampered, and everything taken together had a rather bad effect on my health, my character, even on several of my habits.[25]

In later feuilleton-length sallies against Vladimir Mayakovsky, Maxim Gorky, Ilya Ehrenburg, A. I. Kuprin, Modest Gofman, Zinaida Gippius, Georgy Adamovich, and many

---

[24] In May 1885, just a year before Khodasevich's birth, Victor Hugo, a literary colossus spanning most of the century, was buried in a massive state funeral unlike any Paris had ever seen. "The twentieth century," as Roger Shattuck formulates it, "could not wait fifteen years for a round number; it was born, yelling, in 1885. . . . By this orgiastic ceremony [Hugo's wake and funeral] France unburdened itself of a man, a literary movement, and a century." (Roger Shattuck, *The Banquet Years* [New York, 1968], pp. 4-5.) Though it would be difficult to find such a watershed year in the Russian context, the deaths of the great Realists—Dostoevsky and Pisemsky in 1881, Turgenev in 1883—along with Tolstoy's radical renunciation of the self that authored *War and Peace* and *Anna Karenina* suggest that by the mid-1880s Realism (at least in literature) had spent itself and the transition (perhaps most easily identifiable with the onset of Chekhov's mature period in 1886-1888) to Symbolism and "Modernism" had begun.

[25] Khodasevich, "Infancy," p. 100.

13

others it is not difficult to see the markings of this impatience. Khodasevich could not brook, particularly in discussions of Pushkin, an opponent whose theories were founded on less than precise knowledge. And more than once, he plunged headlong into an attack before considering the consequences.[26] One of the most impressive aspects of Khodasevich's biography is his record in matters of literary conscience; an aspect much more controversial is his record in matters of literary tact and forbearance. While it would be far too simple to see in the polemical essays that Khodasevich launched from *Vozrozhdenie* (The Renaissance) and targeted to Adamovich at *Poslednie novosti* (The Latest News) the behavior of a spoiled child (what was at stake was infinitely more important than one's personal feelings), there remains a sense in which his fierce individualism, his rejection of any compromise, his isolation from all the "isms" of modern Russian poetry can be traced to his role as the last, or in a way only, child, the Benjamin of a doting Rachel and Jacob.[27] Indeed, as Khodasevich explains almost in the same breath, the fact that he was as if an only child, with few playmates his own age and primarily his own fancy and the world of adults with which to occupy himself, led naturally, though no less profoundly, to his personality as a poet:

[26] See, for example, as described in M. Vishniak, *Sovremennye zapiski: Vospominaniia redaktora* (*Contemporary Annals*: Memoirs of the Editor) (Bloomington, IN, 1957), pp. 140-149, 205-206, Khodasevich's virulent criticism of the pro-Soviet *Versty* (Versts) group (Svyatopolk-Mirsky, Sergey Efron, P. Suvchinsky, Artur Lourié) and his charge that the Pushkinist Modest Gofman committed plagiarism. The editorial board position at *Versts* is found in Simon Karlinsky, *Marina Cvetaeva: Her Life and Art* (Berkeley, 1966), pp. 68-69. The articles on *Versts* and Gofman are V. Khodasevich: "O 'Verstakh'" (On *Versts*), *SZ* 29 (1926), 433-441; and "Konets odnoi polemiki" (The End of One Polemic), *Voz*, no. 1318 (10 January 1929).

[27] "Khodasevich could be capricious and stubborn like a child. He would establish his truth on irrational bases, and in order to defend it, once having taken the bit, and ignoring everyone and everything, he would charge ahead—usually at a loss to himself and to his truth." (Vishniak, *"Contemporary Annals": Memoirs of the Editor*, p. 206.)

My late arrival hindered me even in literature. Had I been born ten years earlier, I would have been a contemporary of the Decadents and Symbolists: three years younger than Bryusov, four years older than Blok. But I made my appearance in poetry precisely when the most significant of all modern trends [i.e., Symbolism] had begun to exhaust itself, yet the time for something new to appear had still not set in. Gorodetsky and Gumilyov, my coevals, felt this just as I did. They attempted to create Acmeism, from which, in essence, nothing came and of which nothing, save a name, has remained. But Tsvetaeva (who is, however, younger than I) and I, having emerged from Symbolism, attached ourselves to nothing and to no one, and remained forever solitary, "wild." Literary classifiers and compilers of anthologies don't know where to stick us.[28]

There is something very touching about Khodasevich looking to his origins and linking his independent spirit and his loneliness to the same qualities in Marina Tsvetaeva. Though their poetry could not be more different, they were united, as Simon Karlinsky describes the mood of Tsvetaeva's last letter to Khodasevich, by "the closeness of two great poets who had no place in Soviet literature and who by the mid-thirties remained alone in émigré literature as well."[29] Perhaps no one understood the tragedy of emigration better than these two; perhaps no one's art bore the scars of that tragedy with greater force.

Khodasevich's role as coddled child had, as he suggests, a rather significant effect on his physical development as well. Not only would the *mal du siècle* provide a historical mood for growth into later childhood and adolescence; there would also be real illnesses, with threats more immediate and physical, to punctuate the flow of early impressions. Khodasevich would have bad health his entire life; he would be thin, prone to illness, his complexion sallow; he would smoke with a passion, surrounding himself (and, if present, his interlocutor) in billows of smoke, "his long fingers," in Nabokov's

[28] Khodasevich, "Infancy," pp. 200-201.
[29] S. Karlinskii, ed., "Pis'ma M. Tsvetaevoi k V. Khodasevichu" (Letters of M. Tsvetaeva to V. Khodasevich), *Novyi zhurnal* (New Review), 89 (1967), 107-108.

15

words, "screwing into a holder the half of a *Corporal Vert* cigarette";[30] and he would complain, with a similarity to Tolstoy's famous cancer victim, Ivan Ilyich, that seems prophetic, of an ashen taste in his mouth. Because his health from birth was perilous, his family fed him only the blandest diet, which so took hold that Vladislav developed a sort of "gustatory infantilism" (*vkusovoi infantalizm*)[31]—till the end of his life he would avoid fish, fruit, and greens, preferring instead pap and chicken fricassee. The delights of Gogolian and Chekhovian gastronomical *poshlost'* (a uniquely Russian "philistinism") would be lost on him: "Fish makes me sick, I don't know the taste of caviar, oysters, lobster—I've never tried them."[32]

A host of later major and minor illnesses—measles, bronchitis, smallpox, bad teeth, tuberculosis of the spine, furunculosis, eczema, catarrh, cancer—were probably caused by a combination of factors, including bad luck (Khodasevich's back problems began in 1915 when he fell and injured his spine at a friend's name-day party) and exceedingly poor living conditions ("hunger" appears often in the "calendar" of his early manhood).[33] But there is little doubt that a major factor was the dietary habits that threatened to shatter the child's health from the beginning. The abdominal discomfort that the solicitous parents feared would result from a normal diet was not avoided. Indeed, it returned with a vengeance in the last years of Khodasevich's life and culminated in the gallstones and hepatic cancer that killed him, prematurely, at fifty-three. The theories of Hippocrates and Galen would have found a prime example in Khodasevich, for the "bil-

---

[30] Nabokov, *Speak, Memory*, p. 285. See the portraits of Khodasevich by his niece Valentina Khodasevich and by Yury Annenkov in Sylvester, *Valentina Khodasevich and Olga Margolina–Khodasevich: Unpublished Letters to Nina Berberova*, pp. 34-35 (insert no. 2); and Iurii Annenkov, *Dnevnik moikh vstrech* (Diary of My Encounters) (New York, 1966), I, 29.

[31] Khodasevich, "Infancy," p. 100.

[32] Ibid.

[33] *Kursiv*, p. 169.

ious" temperament that later made him notorious seems to have had as analogue a real anatomical imbalance.[34]

Khodasevich's health was further endangered when he was an infant by an ominous swelling that appeared on his tongue, which resulted in his refusing to take food. But Dr. Smith, a kindly pediatrician, successfully cauterized the tumor, and Elena Alexandrovna was soon nursing the sickly child back to health. Here instead of Galen a popular Russian expression suggests an analogue: *tipun tebe na iazyk* (freely: "Bite your tongue!") is literally rendered "May you get a blister on your tongue!" and is meant as a riposte to a particularly nasty remark. That Khodasevich, perhaps the most ironic of all modern Russian poets and, as the occasion demanded, one of the most sarcastic of émigré critics, should be born with a lingual blister appears almost prefigured.

Despite his frail constitution, the poet's early childhood seems to have passed in a state of happiness, one governed by a proprietary vigilance and concern on the part of parents and siblings. His first home, a two-storied house of brick construction, was located on Kamergersky Lane, a few blocks north of the Kremlin and directly across from what is today the Moscow Art Theater. But in the autumn of 1886 the family moved two blocks north to 14 Bolshaya Dmitrovka Street, where they were closer to Felitsian Ivanovich's place of business. Here the Khodaseviches rented rooms from a certain A. B. Neidgardt, a gentleman of the bedchamber and a dandy in beaver cap and greatcoat, whose aristocratic hauteur appears to have struck fear into Anton the yardman and a spirit of flight into the neighborhood children. It is from the period of life at Neidgardt's house that Khodasevich dates his first conscious moments.

[34] See, for example, Viktor Shklovsky's later description (c. 1920) of Khodasevich: "The skin on his face is taut, and he has formic acid in his veins instead of blood. . . . When he writes, a dry, bitter sandstorm whirls him along. Microbes can't live in his blood: they curl up and die." (Viktor Shklovsky, *A Sentimental Journey*, trans. Richard Sheldon [Ithaca, 1970], pp. 236-237.)

One special charm of Khodasevich's autobiographical fragment is the tone he strikes with the reader. Written in 1933 when he had entered a period of poetic silence more profound than that of Fet or Valéry—that is, one from which there would be no return—his descriptions of himself and of his environment are both "lyrical" (young Vladislav's) and "ironic" (Khodasevich's). In them we see the world of turn-of-the-century Moscow through the eyes of a child; we see that world in vivid detail, spontaneously glimpsed particularity, and there is the sense that we are seeing it as if for the first time (in fact, Vladislav's perceptions of his first trip to the Bolshoi Theater suggest an obvious parallel to Natasha Rostova's impressions of her first visit to the opera—one of Shklovsky's most famous illustrations of "making strange"). Yet there is present as well in this romance of the new a gentle but real sense of self-irony (absent, of course, in Tolstoy's Jamesian approach), one cultivated by a consciousness, as Harry Levin remarks in another context, of having "lived down" certain ideals.[35] When Khodasevich tells us that according to family legend his first words, pronounced at age one, were "Kitty, kitty!" he quickly counters with the example of Derzhavin, one of his favorite poets, whose first word was much grander: "God."[36] The detail seems to be as revealing as it is humorous: Derzhavin, a great odist of the eighteenth century and a panegyrist of deity, began by looking to heaven; Khodasevich, a great ironist of the twentieth century and an expert on the domestic and quotidian, begins by shrinking his vistas and looking close to home (cats were his favorite animal). But the juxtaposition, of course, is made by the man, not the child. Thus the interplay of intimacy and ulteriority gives Khodasevich's text a tension and economy of means that would not be present had he chosen to use either viewpoint exclusively.

[35] Harry Levin, *The Gates of Horn* (New York, 1963), p. 85. Quoted in Donald Fanger, *Dostoevsky and Romantic Realism* (Chicago, 1967), p. 8.
[36] Khodasevich, "Infancy," p. 102.

Although it is quite absurd to speak of economy of means in the case of Proust, another writer concerned with his own childhood, there is a similar self-irony and interplay of views in his novel: in "Combray," for example, the narrator observes Mlle Vinteuil's behavior from a younger unfiltered viewpoint, then follows with an aside, obviously attributable to someone more sophisticated, on the nature of genuine versus feigned sadism. Tolstoy's *Childhood* shares with the others finely detailed recollections, a mother's protectiveness, a lyrical tone, and a child's discovery that the adult world can be fallible and inconsistent. But what is absent is another voice, older and wiser, coming, as it were, from somewhere offstage. The tension that emerges as a mature Khodasevich relates the enthusiasms of his childhood self appears in this regard to be important. It will surface again when the mature poet begins to "live down," though never completely and never without some pain, the legacy of his Symbolist youth.

SUPPLIED with books by his brother Misha, Vladislav began reading at age three. Yershov's Russian children's classic, "The Hunchbacked Little Horse," was his first favorite, and remained a favorite for years afterwards. But soon he passed to Pushkin's fairy tales, which he thought unimpressive next to Yershov. Little did he know that Pushkin was to become one of his great loves, a countersign by which "to hail [friends] in the mounting gloom."[37] He avoided Lermontov, however, almost as if in anticipation of later skirmishes with Georgy Adamovich over the priority of the classical versus the romantic in Russian poetry. The book of Lermontov's work that was given to him as a boy, *The Boyar Orsha*, had a reclining skeleton depicted on its cover, and this ghoulish illustration caused Vladislav nightmares, being joined in his fantasy with devils, corpses, and a Joycean fear of hell. Other

---

[37] Khodasevich, "Koleblemyi trenozhnik" (The Shaken Tripod), in *Stat'i o russkoi poezii* (Articles on Russian Poetry) (Petersburg, 1922), p. 121.

favorite childhood authors included the now forgotten Alexandr Kruglov, whose children's verse was "excellent [and], . . . most important, not sickly sweet,"[38] and Apollon Maykov, one of the better poets still writing in the otherwise dismal eighties.

Khodasevich in fact met the aging Maykov by chance in the summer of 1896. The ten-year-old boy had already begun to experiment with various poetic forms—first lyrical imitations of Maykov, then verse apologues in the manner of Dmitriev, and after that *serdtseshchipatel'nye* (heart-rending) gypsy romances. Then while vacationing at his uncle's *dacha* at Siverskaya outside Petersburg, he learned that his coryphaeus was also staying nearby. "I read a great deal, but I had never set eyes on a real live [*zhivoi*] poet, and in the depths of my soul was not even sure of the genuine existence of such beings. And suddenly, here he was, a real live, genuine poet! And, of all things, which one? Maykov!"[39] The young versifier waited at the outskirts of the neighboring *dacha* until the day came when Maykov was rolled out in his wheelchair and left alone to take the air. After a brief and comically awkward introduction ("I could only blurt out, 'I know you.' "), the boy declaimed "Lastochki" (The Swallows), a poem the old man had written forty years earlier. With his rather high-strung feelings of pride and *amour-propre* he was especially grateful that Maykov seemed to take him seriously and never smiled. "That encounter moved me deeply, and for a long time afterward I told no one about it. It was solemn and important: the first acquaintance with a poet. Subsequently, [though] I was to know how many other poets, including some that were more remarkable, . . . I must admit that the sense [of that encounter] . . . was there no longer."[40] Like the chance meeting between Rilke and a

---

[38] Khodasevich, "Parizhskii al'bom" (Parisian Album), *Dni* (Days), no. 1051 (11 July 1926).

[39] Ibid.

[40] Ibid.

ten-year-old Pasternak, which took place on one of those trains so symbolically rich for the latter and which appeared as an artistic awakening in *Safe Conduct*, Khodasevich's meeting Maykov had a lasting significance as well. It too was a privileged moment, an awakening into a special medium which bound a living image to its word. Indeed, it may be a poem Khodasevich wrote many years later that best confirms this: also entitled "The Swallows," it grows out of the last line from Maykov—"O, if only I too had wings!"— into one of Khodasevich's most painfully beautiful lyrics.

Though Khodasevich began writing verse at age six, he did not, it seems, come to poetry via Pushkin, Kruglov, and Maykov alone. The sense of elegant but economical movement, of classically sculptured line made possible only with great tension, that marks his early poetry to a lesser degree and his later poetry more thoroughly derives in a very real sense from his love of classical ballet. As the poet later wrote of his first glorious outing to the Bolshoi Theater:

From that day on my entire childhood was colored by a passion for ballet. . . . Ballet had a deciding influence on my entire life, on how my tastes, predilections, and interests subsequently took shape. *In the final analysis, it is through ballet that I came to art in general and poetry in particular.* The Bolshoi Theater was my spiritual homeland. I remember with reverence and gratitude its solemn splendor, its cloudy and mythological plafond, its magnificent gilding, the scarlet velvet of its stalls, the royal purple brocade of the curtains in its boxes, the majestic and severe emptiness of the Tsar's box, in the mysterious darkness of which the mirror was becoming tarnished. . . . I remember to [the tiniest] details the theater's semicircular corridors, the polished steps of its stone staircases, and the completely special, unique, slightly cloying smell of the theater hall: it seemed to me a *mélange* of chocolate, perfume, and cloth.[41]

Thus the young Vladislav (he was close to four when he first visited the Bolshoi) soaked up the pleasures of ballet with a fervor greater and more persistent than that of any ephemeral infatuation. He saw some of his epoch's greatest ballerinas

[41] Khodasevich, "Infancy," p. 107. (My emphasis.)

perform—Roslavleva, the second Fyodorova, the second Domasheva—followed their careers and personal lives with a sort of vigilant adoration, and took their various roles onto the smaller stage of his fantasy world. Light-boned and graceful himself (even in his maturity, the fluid movement of his walk would strike friends), he began to perform his own "monoballets" at home in front of the mirror. And it appears that he had considerable promise as a ballet dancer—so considerable in fact that his parents not only had their "prodigy" display his talent to friends but went so far as to discuss the possibility of professional schooling. This possibility was ruled out, however (to Khodasevich's permanent regret), because of recurrent health problems; with the appearance of bronchitis at age six, it was decided by Dr. Smith that formal training would put too great a strain on the lungs of the little "balletomane."

If classical ballet, as Khodasevich's own statements indicate, was a powerful force in shaping the poet's artistic personality, and thus presumably his art, how far can the balletic analogy be taken? Do poems written much later show, to misquote Yeats, the dancer in the dance? Nikolay Gumilyov, whose eye for new poetic talent was sharp, was the first to see the element of dance in Khodasevich's poetry. In his review of *Schastlivyi domik* (The Happy Little House), Khodasevich's second collection, he described Khodasevich's work as a mixture of the balletic and poetic media.[42] Pasternak and Tsvetaeva, in many ways Khodasevich's foils, originally came to poetry through (or at least after studying) music—the former willingly, the latter unwillingly. The tremendous impact, for example, that Scriabin had on the young Pasternak is by now critical commonplace. The fact that poetically speaking Pasternak and Tsvetaeva saw each other

[42] N. Gumilev, "Stat'i i zametki o russkoi poezii" (Articles and Notes on Russian Poetry), *Sobranie sochinenii* (Collected Works) (Washington, 1968), IV, 333-346.

as kindred spirits—Pasternak appears to have discovered *Versts I* at the same time that Tsvetaeva was becoming deeply impressed by *My Sister, Life*[43]—suggests that one thing they might have shared was an appreciation of modern musical composition. Khodasevich's poetry, however, would not be "musically" composed; it would remain very close to the prosodic canons of Pushkin and would avoid almost entirely the syntactical and metrical innovations of Pasternak and Tsvetaeva—the one's motile syntax in which we are apt to see "the extemporising pianist elated by his audience,"[44] and the other's "fusion of binary and ternary meters" recalling the major-minor "metrical harshness . . . not unlike the effect of some of Ravel's harmonies."[45] Curiously, Khodasevich did not even notice the music that was part of his first visit to the ballet. Like the Yeats of "Among School Children," Khodasevich seemed captivated by the synesthetic unity of dance. Perhaps rather than purely "musical" or "dramatic," or even "operatic" (drama set to music), a more appropriate epithet for the poetry of Khodasevich's major period is "balletic" (dance that is dramatic *and* musical). "Balletic" of course loses some of its metaphorical imprecision if it can be shown that there is a genuine sense in which Khodasevich's poetry combines drama and choreography, rhetorical tension and dancelike release:

> Да, да! В слепой и нежной страсти
> Переболей, перегори,
> Рви сердце, как письмо, на части,
> Сойди с ума, потом умри.
>
> И что ж? Могильный камень двигать
> Опять придется над собой,
> Опять любить и ножкой дрыгать
> На сцене лунно-голубой.[46]

---

[43] See Karlinsky, *Cvetaeva*, p. 56.
[44] Henry Gifford, *Pasternak* (Cambridge, England, 1977), p. 70.
[45] Karlinsky, *Cvetaeva*, p. 158.
[46] *SS*, p. 79.

23

Yes, yes! In blind and tender passion
wear out the pain, burn out the fire,
like a letter, tear your heart to pieces,
go out of your mind, and then expire.

What then? Once more will come the need
to move the gravestone over you,
to love again and flit your foot
upon a stage of lunar blue.

Not only is the poem *about* ballet—that is, it takes the story of Giselle as its subject and the "lunar blue stage"[47] of the Bolshoi as its setting—it is also its own miniature *ballet d'action*. Against the first quatrain, with the vocalically wailing *-i* of its imperatives (Giselle of Act I caught in her *danse macabre*), Khodasevich sets the second quatrain, with its vocalically closed infinitives (Giselle of Act II dancing with the Wilis in a state beyond death). Much more might be said about the poem, but one thing is clear. The idea of ballet grows out of its form: passion and madness seem both what they are *and* under control; gestures—the tearing up of a letter, the flitting of a foot—seem choreographed because they unite the precision and grace of the *mot juste* and the tension of hidden psychic musculature. Wladimir Weidlé has remarked that there is in these eight lines "more of 'Giselle'. . . . than in the ballet itself, though I saw the latter when Pavlova was Giselle."[48] Semantically modest and prosodically economical (Pushkin's favorite iambic tetrameter), the poem is versts away from the grand lexicon of Bryusov, the high lyricism of Blok, the fanciful etymologies of Khlebnikov, the dense imagery of Mandelshtam, the metrical pioneering of Tsvetaeva. Yet, as if following Noverre's *Lettres*

---

[47] "I . . . imagined myself on the *light-blue, lunar stage of the Bolshoi Theater*, dressed in tights, with a smile frozen on my face, my left arm raised and rounded, and my right arm supporting a ballerina in a white tutu studded with golden spangles." (Khodasevich, "Infancy," p. 108.) (My emphasis.)

[48] V. Veidle, "O tekh, kogo uzhe net" (About Those No Longer Here), *Novoe russkoe slovo* (New Russian Word) (6 June 1976).

sur la danse et les ballets, it tells Giselle's story with its own fragilely flexed body language.

SEEMING neither desultory nor neatly contrived, the childhood experiences described in "Infancy" show what shaped a poet's perceptions and what, in their present recollected form, could be shaped by him. While there is not space enough to discuss them all, it is important to note, in summing up, that simply by appearing in the autobiographical fragment they take on a certain weight. Not only the last child of Felitsian Ivanovich and Sophia Yakovlevna, Khodasevich was also, by his own admission, one of the last children of Symbolism. The portrait of Khodasevich that emerges from "Infancy" is both the work of a particular family life and the general atmosphere of the 1890s. There is a sheltered, potentially neurasthenic or "hothouse" quality to these early years. Vladislav was surrounded by females (his mother, nurse, grandmother, and sister Zhenya); he learned to like his sister's smart way of dressing and became himself a little dandy; though he was not fond of playing with children, when he did he preferred to play with girls; in his monoballets he always danced the role of ballerina; for him it was as interesting to observe from his nurse's window (the window will become one of his favorite poetic images) the happenings in the courtyard below as to be an active participant in those happenings; he was overly serious for his age and was duly dubbed "the little old man";[49] he took a sort of neurotic pleasure in imagining himself the victim of various family tragedies à la Dickens and in so doing saw himself in the third, rather than the first, person. These details suggest ready parallels to the biographies of famous neurasthenics, including Proust and Konstantin Somov, whose careers began in the 1890s. Somov as a child, for example, "loved to play alone . . . and very often used to play with dolls, like a

[49] Khodasevich, "Infancy," p. 114.

little girl."[50] But the conclusion we might draw from such parallels—that Khodasevich's "effeminacy," as in the cases of Proust and Somov, was a sign of homosexuality—is not borne out in any account of his later life.

What these details do confirm is that Khodasevich was a sensitive child, physically vulnerable and emotionally high-strung. While not himself endowed with an attractive physiognomy, he admired elegance and external beauty. One of his most vivid memories is the first time he experienced the "fascination of femininity":

Those childhood moments during which something is first "re-vealed" to us are remembered with indelible clarity. Thus, the fascination of femininity [obaianie zhenstvennosti] (O, to what heights does it climb!) was revealed to me on a clear frosty Sunday in the Tretyakov Gallery. How old could I have been? About ten or twelve.

It was a narrow, long canvas: a portrait of a very beautiful woman, perhaps under a veil. Her dress, it seems, was of red silk and black lace. Painting—it goes without saying I understood nothing about it. But from the graceful figure, the turn of the head, the lips, the dark eyes there suddenly wafted a delight heretofore unknown and incomprehensible to me. I read in the catalogue: "I. E. Repin. Portrait of Baroness V. I. Iskul von-Gillenband."[51]

Though Khodasevich received his first taste of feminine beauty from Repin, one of the Wanderers, he received his formal training as a poet from a later generation of artists and *littérateurs*, from a generation that staunchly rejected the realistic canons of their fathers. By the time Khodasevich saw this portrait and had begun (or was about to begin) his passage from childhood to adolescence, Merezhkovsky had published his famous essay signaling a new idealism and interest

---

[50] Quoted in John E. Bowlt, *The Silver Age: Russian Art of the Early Twentieth Century and the 'World of Art' Group* (Newtonville, Mass., 1979), p. 211.

[51] Khodasevich, "Pamiati Bar. V. I. Iskul' fon-Gillenband" (To the Memory of Baroness V. I. von-Gillenband), *Voz*, no. 995 (22 February 1928).

in literary form;[52] Bryusov and Balmont had written their first Symbolist collections and, taking the cue from Western Europe, had introduced the "poison" of so-called Modernism into a nineteenth-century culture largely raised on social issues and verisimilitude; Chekhov had entered the realm of his mature plays, with their soft and impotent heroes; and Diaghilev, Bakst, Benois, and others had transformed the "Nevsky Pickwickians," a little known *cénacle* that met to discuss the latest trends in music, art, and literature, into the influential "World of Art" group. At this point the fact should be stressed that Khodasevich did not, like Pushkin, appear at a young age "in the full armor of his originality."[53] The strong aftertaste of mannerism and *epigonstvo* (imitation) that mars his first two books of verse seems attributable in part to his own predilection for external style and elegance (many of his early poems might provide examples of a literary *Style moderne*, "illustrations in verse" of the paintings of Somov or Beardsley) and in part to the fact that Symbolism had reached the height of its influence when he first began to publish in 1905. Pushkin and Romanticism joined forces when their powers were on the rise and mutually augmentative; Khodasevich, quite to the contrary, would be overwhelmed by the poetic conventions established by Bryusov, and thus his relationship to Symbolism would be less than symbiotic. Like the Yeats of the Celtic Twilight period, the unseasoned Khodasevich would start by giving his personas the unlikely role of old man and weary lover. And only somewhere beyond Symbolism, both as an historical movement and literary method, would the poet find his true voice. Still, the poetic borrowing of these first years gradually takes the shape of originality, and should be studied as it does so.

---

[52] D. S. Merezhkovskii, "O prichinakh upadka i o novykh techeniiakh sovremennoi russkoi literatury" (On the Reasons for the Decline and on the New Trends in Modern Russian Literature), *Izbrannye stat'i* (Selected Articles) (Munich, 1972), pp. 209-305.

[53] V. Veidle, "Vladislav Khodasevich," *Voz*, no. 1766 (3 April 1930).

2

YOUTH AND *YOUTH*: 1896-1908

Tell for the power how to thunderclaps
The graves flew open, the rivers ran up-hill;
Such staged importance is at most perhaps.

Speak well of moonlight on a winding stair,
Of light-boned children under great green oaks:
The wonder, yes, but death should not be there.
—W. H. Auden,"One Circumlocution"

Словно в зеркале страшной ночи
　　И беснуется и не хочет
　　　Узнавать себя человек,
А по набережной легендарной
　　Приближался не календарный—
　　　Настоящий Двадцатый Век.
—Анна Ахматова, "Поэма без героя"

It was as if in the pier glass of terrible night
　　Man moved possessed and had no wish
　　　To recognize himself,
While along the legendary embankment
　　There approached not the calendar
　　　But the real Twentieth Century.
—Anna Akhmatova, *Poem Without A Hero*

The adolescence and early manhood of Khodasevich encompass a period in his life when Symbolism and the avuncular, even paternal, role of Valery Bryusov were the critical forces shaping the young poet's development. The "life experience" of Symbolism seems more important here for subsequent discussion than Khodasevich's own attempts to produce Symbolist verse. But these attempts still merit more than passing consideration, for as often happens, the poet's personal aesthetic changed dramatically from youth to maturity. In the poet who first imitated Zhukovsky we do not readily see the Nekrasov of later *engagé* themes and *chansonette* style, nor in the poet who first evoked Keats do we see the William Carlos Williams of the red wheelbarrow, of the clean, tense images that revolutionized post-World War II American poetry. Yet Khodasevich never denied the historical or personal significance of his novitiate years. In time he was to become one of Symbolism's most perceptive chroniclers. And even of Bryusov, the father figure against whom he would have to rise up in order to reach his own artistic maturity, he was years later to say:

That future historian of Russian literature, who will study the end of the last century and the beginning of the present one, may regard the work and personality of Bryusov either positively or negatively. . . . But one thing is beyond doubt: he will have to study Bryusov intently and at great length because, if not the work, then the influence (good or evil, warranted or unwarranted) of Bryusov was great. Bryusov was not the only, but certainly the most active leader of the most prominent movement of that era. . . . He can't be thrown out of literary history.[1]

Khodasevich's formal education dates to the fall of 1894 when he began to attend L. N. Valitskaya's grade school on Maroseyka Street. Vladislav appears to have been a model pupil—industrious and well-behaved if somewhat meek and quiet. We know little about the school's curriculum. Only during dancing lessons did he seem to stir from passivity.

In the spring of 1896 Vladislav passed the entrance examinations to Moscow's Third Gymnasium. That spring and summer must have been festive ones, filled with a holiday spirit and an insouciant air of beginnings. Vladislav donned his newly won cap with cockade to help celebrate the coronation of Nicholas II and stayed on to admire an illuminated Kremlin and to inhale the lampions' special odor. Then

---

[1] Khodasevich, "Kniga o Briusove" (The Book About Bryusov) (review of N. Ashukin, *Valery Bryusov* [Moscow, 1929]), *Voz*, no. 1682 (9 January 1930).

late in May he went to visit his sister Maria and her husband in Petersburg where he was introduced to Ozerki, the vacation spot outside the city that was to be one of Blok's favorite haunts. "The scenery of Ozerki," as Khodasevich recalled, "with its hill overgrown by a pine wood, its sandy, whitish slope to the lake, its strolling public and its multicolored *dachas*—a blend of the vulgar [*poshloe*] and the severe—was unforgettable. How fantastically and truly did Blok convey it ten years later in 'The Stranger' and 'Free Thoughts'!"[2] Finally, the summer was capped by Khodasevich's meeting with Maykov, his first encounter with a poet. That Khodasevich seems to have seen these beginnings as mutually significant suggests that life outside the home was making its overture.

The gymnasium that Khodasevich entered that fall was *klassicheskaia* (classical), and opposed the more scientifically oriented *real'noe uchilishche* (modern school). Located on Bolshaya Lubyanka (directly behind the imposing Telegraph Office), it had a curriculum based on Latin and Greek, with an impressive constellation of other subjects: scripture, logic, mathematics, physics, history, geography, French, German, and Russian. Vladislav's *attestat* (diploma) indicates that he was a better than satisfactory pupil in all subjects except German, and that his conduct was "excellent," his preparation for class "quite good," his diligence "adequate," and his eagerness to learn "developed, particularly in the subject of the Russian language."[3] We may assume that a germ of the mature poet's much-discussed classicism was first conceived under the influence of this curriculum. A close knowledge of and penchant for alluding to classical mythology probably date to such study.

---

[2] Khodasevich, "Parisian Album," *Days*, no. 1051 (11 July 1926).

[3] "Attestat zrelosti vydannyi Khodasevichu V. F. ob okonchanii 3-ei Moskovskoi gimnaziii" (Graduation certificate issued to V. F. Khodasevich on completion of the Third Moscow Gymnasium), archive (*fond*) no. 537, item no. 112, The Central State Literary Archive (TsGALI) (Moscow).

Yet "classical," at least at this early date, may cloud more than clarify the issue. The classical *topoi* present in the early work of Merezhkovsky, Vyacheslav Ivanov, and (most important for Khodasevich) Bryusov seem more revealing of Decadence, of the influence of Baudelaire and Nietzsche, than of a return to the classical manner of Pushkin. The character of Merezhkovsky's Julian (*Julian the Apostate* [1896]) is colored by a post-Dostoevskian, post-Nietzschean crisis of values; as a hero, Julian may have less to do with the actual fourth-century emperor than with his author's own anxiety over the present dangers of humanism—those same dangers that Vladimir Solovyov presents in *Three Conversations* (which Khodasevich read when it first appeared in 1900) as the imminent confrontation of East (Japan) and West (Europe) brought on by Tolstoyan Christianity without Christ. Likewise, Ivanov's poetic cycle to Dionysus in *Pilot Stars* (1903) and his later articles in *Vesy* (The Scales) show his particular mix of the philosophies of Solovyov and Nietzsche, of the one's syncretic Christianity and of the other's rediscovery of the dithyramb and renunciation of Winckelmann's post-Socratic ideal of sophrosyne. And the Medeas and Cleopatras of Bryusov share their author's Baudelairian preoccupation with erotic pain and morbid passion. As Viktor Zhirmunsky has convincingly demonstrated, neither in terms of lexicon, nor instrumentation, nor rhythm, can Bryusov's verse be claimed the work of Pushkin's "custodian, . . . the one classical poet in a modern era . . . of romanticism."[4] Hence the classical iconography that surfaces in various periods of Khodasevich's poetry need not be equated with the Pushkinian manner he came to admire and adapt to his own purposes. His first working association with classicism, as we shall be seeing shortly, was Bryusovian and nominal. It was based on little experience, either artistic or biographical.

[4] V. Zhirmunskii, *Teoriia literatury, poetika, stilistika* (Theory of Literature, Poetics, Stylistics) (Leningrad, 1977), p. 143.

It needed to be tested against some internal measure of genuineness.

Khodasevich's friends and school fellows at the gymnasium included Georgy Malitsky, to whom he wrote several early letters;[5] Viktor Gofman, soon to be a Symbolist poet and a disciple of Bryusov; and Alexandr Bryusov, the poet's younger brother. It is through Alexandr (Sasha) that Khodasevich was introduced to the Bryusov household and the rambling house on Tsvetnoy Boulevard. What these friends shared was a reverence for the elder Bryusov that bordered on idolatry. There were doubtless other adolescent interests. Khodasevich's calendar reveals that he began to attend balls in 1897 and fell in love for the first time (Zhenya Kun) the year after. Like Nabokov, Khodasevich was a collector of butterflies. It is risky, then, to speak of Khodasevich's "Bryusovism." One can overstate the obvious and reduce a jejune talent to the sum of one part. Nevertheless, Khodasevich spoke more fully of the phenomenon of Bryusov than of his own youth, which suggests that Bryusov, who "despised democracy,"[6] held tremendous sway over the mind of the young poet. And Bryusov's influence becomes particularly evident from 1903, when Khodasevich left his parent's home for his brother Misha's and declared his allegiance to "poetry forever,"[7] until the appearance of *Molodost'* (Youth) in 1908.

THOUGH Bryusov's image, both as poet and literary legislator, has tarnished considerably over the years, he was at the turn of the century a cultural phenomenon of the first magnitude. Poet, critic, editor, translator, Pushkinist, and reigning impressario of Modernism, he might be compared to Apollinaire in France—a sort of clearing house for new

[5] Khodasevich,"Iz neizdannykh pisem i stikhov" (From Unpublished Letters and Verse), *Vestnik russkogo khristianskogo dvizheniia* (Bulletin of the Russian Christian Movement), 127 (1978), 117-120.

[6] *Nekropol'*, p. 54.

[7] *Kursiv*, p. 169.

ideas and trends entering Russia. He wrote on a multitude of topics from Dante to necromancy in Reformation Germany, from the poet Konstantin Sluchevsky to the French Symbolist René Ghil. The breadth of his erudition was remarkable. An early diary entry (15 March 1897) tells us, "[at the moment] I'm reading Weber, Maeterlinck, the Bible, Sumarokov. I've got to read Kant, Novalis, Boileau."[8] His organizational talents were equally brilliant. Not only did he control S. A. Polyakov, the de jure editor of *Vesy*, one of the most prominent journals of the period,[9] he controlled as well

[8] V. Briusov, *Dnevniki, 1891-1910* (Diaries, 1891-1910) (Moscow, 1927), p. 28; quoted in Khodasevich, "O dnevnike Briusove" (On Bryusov's Diary), *Voz*, no. 765 (7 July 1927).

[9] For a full discussion of Bryusov's role in the publication of *The Scales*, see K. M. Azadovskii and D. E. Maksimov, "Briusov i 'Vesy' " (Bryusov and

Valery Bryusov's house on Tsvetnoy Boulevard where Khodasevich first met Andrey Bely.

Valery Bryusov in the
early 1900s.

the literary fortunes of many young Symbolists, including
Andrey Bely (whom he was not averse to manipulating in
attempts to keep below the horizon another rising star—
Blok). Furthermore, his poetry, along with that of Balmont,
enjoyed the adoration of the younger generation, even as (or
perhaps because) it scandalized an older generation with its
erotic themes and cult of form. To the ecstatic Bely, Bryusov
was, after Pushkin and Lermontov, one of the greatest Russian poets, on equal footing with Nekrasov, Tyutchev, and
Fet.[10] Blok's feeling for Bryusov was apparently no less en-

The Scales), in V. R. Shcherbina, chief ed., _Literaturnoe nasledstvo: Valerii
Briusov_ (Literary Heritage: Valery Bryusov) (Moscow, 1976), pp. 255-324.

[10] See A. Belyi, "Apokalipsis v russkoi poezii" (Apocalypse in Russian
Poetry), _Vesy_, no. 4 (April 1905), pp. 11-28. Bryusov, feeling that Bely's
praise of his poetry was excessive, answered in V. Briusov,"V zashchitu ot
odnoi pokhvaly: otkrytoe pis'mo Andreiu Belomu" (Defending Oneself from
One Case of Praise: An Open Letter to Andrey Bely), _Vesy_, no. 5 (May 1905),

thusiastic. After the appearance of *Urbi et Orbi* (1903) he took the occasion to inform the *maître*, "I have no hope of ever finding myself next to you. I do not purport to know if what is known to you will ever become available to the rest of us or to speculate as to how soon this is likely to happen."[11] Little wonder, then, that Bryusov enjoyed the respect, if not the awe and admiration, of Khodasevich and nearly every other promising young poet.

Yet a declaration of Bryusov's historical significance seems least of all satisfying. The encomia of Bely and Blok are excessive to be sure, but they remain intriguing if only by the fact of their existence. Something is clearly lost through time as we endeavor to translate Bryusovism into our own critical idiom. The present generation of readers has largely fallen out of touch with the Symbolist ambiance. Today important post-Symbolist names such as Mandelshtam or Wallace Stevens are apt to be invoked more readily than Blok or Yeats. In short, we seem skeptical of the "heroic" aspects of Symbolism, the mystical nationalism of Blok and Yeats, the persistent attempts within the context of Russian and Irish myth to see the Beautiful Lady and Leda in the all-too-real countenances of Lyubov Mendeleeva and Maud Gonne. Therefore, it takes an effort of considerable empathy, what Keats would call "Negative Capability," to retrieve the lost atmosphere of those years. Khodasevich gave the problem a fine distillation in "O simvolizme" (On Symbolism), an essay written in 1928:

---

pp. 37-39. Bely then had the last word in A. Belyi, "V zashchitu ot odnogo narekaniia: otkrytoe pis'mo Valeriiu Briusovu" (Defending Oneself from One Case of Censure: An Open Letter to Valery Bryusov), *Vesy*, no. 6 (June 1905), pp. 40-42. The relations between Bely and Bryusov during these years are best seen in their correspondence: see S. S. Grechishkin and A. V. Lavrov, eds., "Perepiska Valeriia Briusova s Andreem Belym, 1902-1912" (The Valery Bryusov-Andrey Bely Correspondence, 1902-1912), in *Literary Heritage: Valery Bryusov*, pp. 325-427.

[11] O. Nemerovskaia and Ts. Volpe, eds., *Sud'ba Bloka* (The Fate of Blok) (Leningrad, 1930), p. 65. Quoted in Victor Erlich, *The Double Image* (Baltimore, 1964), p. 85.

Recently I had the occasion to be at a lecture on the poetry of
Innokenty Annensky. In the first part of the talk the speaker gave
a short survey of Russian Symbolism. I experienced an unexpected
feeling. Everything that the speaker said was historically accurate,
completely conscientious in its accounting of literary facts. The
speaker succeeded in observing correctly, even perceptively, much
in Symbolism. In a word, the speaker has all my praise.

Still, while listening, I kept having the sense that, yes, it's correct,
true, but I also know that in reality it didn't occur like that. Like
that, but not like that.

The reason became clear to me instantly. The speaker knew
Symbolism according to books, I according to memories. The speaker
had studied the country of Symbolism, its landscape, but I had
managed to inhale its air before the air had dispersed and Symbolism had become a planet without atmosphere. And you see, as
it turns out, rays in that atmosphere were refracted in a way somehow special, unique to them, and objects appeared in different
contours.[12]

Khodasevich's search for the elusive spirit of lost time is
richly rewarded in *Necropolis*, his book of memoirs. In portraits of Bryusov, Bely, Nina Petrovskaya, Blok, Sologub, and
others he shows a gift for weaving telling details with sharply
focused character analysis. He unabashedly prefers a gran-
ulated surface to the glossy touch-up of romantic memoir
literature and would have strongly disapproved, for instance,
of Alexandr Bryusov's retouching of his brother's portrait.[13]
Of his memoir of Bely, Khodasevich warns the reader:

Don't expect from me an iconic, anthological portrayal. Such por-
trayals are harmful to history. . . . Truth cannot be low for there is
nothing higher than truth. I want to set *the truth that elevates us*
[*nas vozvyshaiushchaia pravda*] against Pushkin's "elevating deceit" [*vozvyshaiushchii obman*]: we must learn to honor and love
a remarkable person with all his weaknesses and sometimes even
for those very weaknesses. Such a person has no need of our em-

---

[12] *Stat'i*, p. 153.

[13] A. Briusov, "Vospominaniia o brate" (Recollections of My Brother),
Briusovskie chteniia 1962 goda (Readings in Bryusov for 1962) (Erevan,
1963), pp. 293-301.

bellishments. He demands from us something much more difficult—completeness of understanding.[14]

Bryusov, for his part, apparently had many sides to his
character. But it was the side of artistic rebel rising up against
an encrusted establishment that most likely attracted the
aspiring young poet in Khodasevich. Khodasevich first saw
Bryusov when he was eleven. Rather than the *outré* Decadent (of the lilac hair and green nose) encountered in the
cartoons of *Novosti dnia* (Daily News), he found "a modest
young man with a short mustache and crew cut, dressed in
a cotton collar and jacket of the most ordinary tailoring."[15]
Bryusov's businesslike appearance, the hint of petty bourgeois origins, is a significant gloss on Khodasevich's part. It
may have been picked up by an eleven year old; but it was
fully understood only by the memoirist writing more than
twenty-five years later.

A more revealing encounter took place some time in late
1902 or early 1903. Vladislav was now in his next to last
year at the gymnasium and wanted desperately to hear Bryusov's lecture on Fet at the Moscow Circle of Art and Literature. All Moscow was buzzing about the celebrated Tues-
days at the Circle where occasion was provided over the
years for speeches by Balmont, Bely, Vyacheslav Ivanov,
Merezhkovsky, Yuly Aikhenvald, Korney Chukovsky, Maximilian Voloshin, Georgy Chulkov, Sergey Gorodetsky, Sergey Makovsky, Nikolay Berdyaev, and many others. Since
Khodasevich was soon to finish the gymnasium, leave his

---

[14] *Nekropol'*, p. 62. See Johnson's famous remark to Edmond Malone on
the uses of biography: "If nothing but the bright side of characters should
be shewn, we would sit down in despondency, and think it utterly impossible to imitate them in *any thing*. The sacred writers (he observed) related
the vicious as well as the virtuous actions of men; which had this moral
effect, that it kept mankind from *despair*." (Boswell, *Life of Johnson*, ed.
Hill-Powell [1934-1940], IV, 53; quoted in Walter Jackson Bate, *John Keats*
[New York, 1966], p. 35.)

[15] *Nekropol'*, p. 26.

parents' home for a life on his own, and declare his eternal allegiance to poetry, the moment was pregnant with possibilities. In a word, the time was ripe for the emergence of another father figure (Khodasevich was still only sixteen), one who not only shared but was a source of new values, and one who could provide guidance at the beginning of a professional career.

In order to get into the lecture (which was forbidden to gymnasium students), Khodasevich had to sew silver buttons—those worn by university students—on his gymnasium student's double-breasted jacket. But the ruse worked. The lecture, later collected in *Dalekie i blizkie* (Those Far and Near [1912]), had a profound impact on several aspects of Khodasevich's life and art at the time:

... Persons then unknown to me sat with ponderous importance on a brightly lit stage at a long table on which pencils and sheets of paper were spread out along a dark green cloth. Bryusov stood sideways at a reading desk and spoke addressing the audience, not those on stage.

"The face is the mirror of the soul." This is certainly true. Yet it is not enough to say that so-called outward appearance, all of that human aspect subjected to polishing at the hands of the barber and tailor, is deceiving. It is false. Only Bryusov's fiery eyes and voice, the "eagle-like screech" with which he hurled out his sharp, clipped words, were wonderful. He was wholly unattractive, angular; in his shabby frock-coat and cheap necktie, he was simply insignificant by comparison to the Olympians listening to him politely and disapprovingly. But that was understandable: the literary committee consisted of prominent lawyers, doctors, and journalists who radiated prosperity, satiety, liberalism. The committee was presided over by the psychiatrist Bazhenov, chairman of the board, a fat, bald, ruddy, and snub-nosed man, looking like a teapot with its spout broken off. He was a connoisseur of wines and "of the female heart" ... "a Russian Parisian" and author of an essay on Baudelaire from the point of view of psychiatry. ... But in 1902 it was with obvious disapproval that he listened to the talk of the upstart Decadent poet, the author of "Blednye nogi" [Pale Legs], who was speaking enthusiastically about the poetry of Fet, a poet

38

who everyone knows was an advocate of serfdom and, what's more, a chamberlain. The feeling of disapproval was shared as well by the other members of the committee, and by the vast majority of the audience. When discussion began, a certain individual stood up with an appearance so poetical as to suffice for Shakespeare, Dante, Goethe, and Pushkin combined. This was Lyuboshits, a feuilletonist for *Novosti dnia*. Next to him Bryusov had a depressingly prosaic look. Lyuboshits announced straightaway that the poetry of Fet was like a cocotte who hid dirty underwear under an elegant dress. The metaphor had a smashing success. The auditorium burst out in a storm of applause. It is true that, speaking of Fet, Lyuboshits ascribed someone else's verses to him. It is also true that the young Decadent poet Boris Koyransky leaped tempestuously on stage and exposed the ignorance of Lyuboshits on the spot. But by then no one wanted to listen. Bryusov's reaction was drowned in public indignation.[16]

The liveliness of the sketch depends almost entirely on its roving-eyeball-of-the-ingénu approach. In his attempt to restore atmosphere to the planet of Symbolism, Khodasevich gives us the scandalous lecture as he saw it—according to *memory, not books*. Of course the ironic patination belongs to an older Khodasevich. Still, the general tone tilts its sympathy toward the underdog Bryusov and the reckless Koyransky, figures with whom Khodasevich would have identified at the time. Khodasevich has sharp scorn for Bazhenov, a *poshliak* (vulgarian) whose liberalism and corporation thrive in concert, and Lyuboshits, who looks the part of a poet but does not know his lines. Although his less than heroic appearance would deny it, Bryusov represents, especially for a sixteen-year-old gymnasium student, what is provocative, risky, and thus probably appealing.

What was presented in the lecture, and indeed, what was the linchpin of Bryusov's Decadent program, does not seem

---

[16] Khodasevich, "Moskovskii literaturno-khudozhestvennyi kruzhok" (Moscow Circle of Art and Literature), *Stat'i*, pp. 297-299. See Bely's account of the evening in A. Belyi, *Nachalo veka* (Beginning of the Century) (Moscow-Leningrad, 1933; rpt., Chicago, 1966), pp. 208-215.

on the face of it particularly recherché. Man, as he began, lives the majority of his life in what Fet called the *golubaia tiur'ma* (blue prison) of the phenomenal world.[17] In privileged moments, however, he finds routes of escape into a higher world of essences. "Ecstasy, intuition, inspiration give us 'strange insight,' draw us beyond the border of our 'daily lot,' free us of the ultimate fetters . . . of 'nature's slavery,' of 'iron fate,' of conditions of our normal cognition and being."[18] The average mortal frees himself from the phenomenal world and enters the realm of essences only rarely via the mystical passion of love (one of Bryusov's favorite words was *strast'*—"passion").[19] If one is an artist, on the other hand, one escapes via the "insanity" and "intoxication" of inspiration:

The objects of science are phenomena or the conditions of phenomena. The objects of art are essences. Art is found only where the artist "dares [to embark] on a forbidden path," attempts to scoop up a drop of "an alien, otherworldly element." Art is found only where there is insanity, a shining-through [*prosvet*] to "the sun of the world." The conclusions of science change and *can* change. . . . The creations of art are eternal.[20]

Yet even art, in Bryusov's analysis of Fet, is an unworthy receptacle for these essences, since the material out of which art is fashioned—words, paint, marble—belongs to the same inert labyrinth of the "blue prison" from which the artist seeks routes of escape: "How to embody the eternal in the

[17] V. Briusov, "A. A. Fet: iskusstvo ili zhizn'" (A. A. Fet: Art or Life), *Dalekie i blizkie* (Those Far and Near) (Moscow, 1912; rpt. Letchworth-Herts, 1973), p. 20. The image of the "blue prison" comes from Fet's poem, "Pamiati N. Ia. Danilevskogo" (In Memory of N. Ya. Danilevsky). A fine discussion of this lecture and its effect on Khodasevich is found in Richard D. Sylvester, "V. F. Xodasevič in Moscow and Petersburg: A Study of *Putem zerna* [Grain's Way] and *Tjaželaja lira* [The Heavy Lyre]" (Ph.D. diss., Harvard, 1976), pp. 57-69.

[18] Briusov, "A. A. Fet," p. 21.

[19] See, for example, V. Briusov, "Vekhi: strast'" (Landmarks: Passion), *Vesy*, no. 8 (August 1904), pp. 21-28.

[20] Briusov, "A. A. Fet," p. 22.

temporal, to express essence in a phenomenon, to convey the ineffable in a word?"[21]

The problem here was of course raised by Tyutchev and the German Romantics before him. The world is a welter of dualities and only in art, which itself comes perilously close to being compromised, are the dualities provisionally united. The turn taken by Bryusov at the conclusion of the lecture, however, was one that must have sent ripples of indignation through the audience and a wave of silent approval through the young Khodasevich. Since art is a rickety mansion, all that remains to the artist is to celebrate himself: "Man is for man the last 'measure of things.' In man there is everything: all life, and all beauty, and all meaning in art. No matter how great the claims made by poetry, it cannot do more than express the human soul."[22] Bryusov had suddenly veered from the realm of poetry, where his authority was great but still limited, into the realm of "creative behavior," where his authority (at that time) was unassailable. There is a way, he suggested, "to live poetically." Those who understood Fet's dilemma (that poetry is the worthiest of the unworthy) still had the ability to express their inexpressible souls, to transform the phenomenal world into a skein of moments that "shone through" to the realm of essences. From his remarks on Fet, Bryusov had built himself a "bio-aesthetic" platform. And he concluded with a call for new recruits: "We ... think that the entire goal of mankind's earthly development should be that *everyone* constantly live 'in such an aroused atmosphere' that that atmosphere become mankind's normal air."[23]

The call to live in a constantly "aroused atmosphere" was taken quite literally by the young writers surrounding Bryusov. Khodasevich's friend Viktor Gofman was by 1902-1903 a publishing poet, with poems in the miscellany *Severnye*

[21] Ibid., p. 23.
[22] Ibid., p. 24.
[23] Ibid., p. 26.

tsvety (Northern Flowers) and the yearbook *Grif* (Griffin). Khodasevich, as yet unpublished, admired Gofman for his first laurels. And strangely enough, Gofman seems in several ways to have been a slightly older version of the young Vladislav—thin arms, a light, dancer's gait, a muliebrile quality to his gestures, a childhood spent with girls, and significantly, a close attachment to and poetic apprenticeship under Bryusov.[24] Perhaps, then, in the unhappy fate that soon overtook Gofman, Khodasevich came to see a manifest danger to himself. For what began as a promising poetic career ended in paralyzing neurasthenia and suicide in 1911. "Bad luck," as Khodasevich remarked retrospectively, "brought Gofman in contact with Bryusov. Very impressionable and 'lyrical' by nature, the seventeen-year-old Gofman immediately mastered the Decadent lessons: the philosophy of 'moments' and lyrical adventurism."[25] Ignoring traditional measures of morality, Gofman devoted his young life to the random accumulation of such moments. He and his friends appeared bewitched by Bryusov's invitation to a solipsistic *Walpurgisnacht*:

The business of the poet was to "take" these moments and "destroy" them, that is, experience them as keenly as possible and then, having exhausted them, move on to the next ones. . . . The process of accumulation ran quite chaotically, and without spiritually enriching anyone, it simply wore out and undid one's nerves in the extreme. Life turned into a constant state of intoxication, a sort of gnawing of emotional sunflower seeds, the more of which are eaten, the harder it is to stop, while the hunger does not lessen, and the heartburn intensifies.[26]

The hunger for some higher fulfillment coupled with the heartburn caused by lower forms of gluttony plagued Gofman up to the time of his suicide. What promise he had as a poet faded, according to Khodasevich, when for personal

[24] See Khodasevich, "Viktor Gofman," *PN*, no. 2031 (14 October 1926).
[25] Ibid.
[26] Ibid.

reasons Bryusov had him driven out of the Decadent journals and publishing houses in Moscow.[27] After spending two aimless years in Petersburg, he arrived in Paris a helpless neurasthenic fearing for his sanity. It was there, in a hotel on Boulevard Saint-Michel, that Gofman, just twenty-seven, shot himself in August 1911.

Khodasevich met the young belletrist Nina Petrovskaya in 1902. They had occasion to see more of each other when they began collaborating at "Grif," the publishing house founded by Sergey Krechetov-Sokolov in the spring of 1903. Khodasevich and Petrovskaya grew to be good friends. In fact, he dedicated a poem in *Youth* to her and borrowed the poem's title, "Sanctus amor," from her collection of stories by the same name; she in turn later reviewed *The Heavy Lyre*. Thus through his friendship with Petrovskaya, his interest in Bryusov, and his acquaintance with Bely (whom he first met in late 1904 at one of Bryusov's famous "Wednesdays"), Khodasevich was in a uniquely privileged position to witness the unfolding of what was, after the *ménage à trois* of Blok, Bely, and Lyubov Mendeleeva, the most remarkable love triangle of the Symbolist period. The stormy relationship between Bely, Bryusov, and Petrovskaya reads like a melodramatic novel, which is what Bryusov made of it in *Ognennyi angel* (The Fiery Angel) (1907-1908). Against a background of sixteenth-century Germany, the Faust legend, necromancy, witch hunts, and *autos-da-fé*, Bryusov fashioned a plot in which the main characters—the possessed heroine Renata, the "fiery angel" Heinrich-Madiel, and the narrator Ruprecht—had transparent analogues in life. Despite an impressive historical framework, *The Fiery Angel* is primarily a fictionalization of Bely's "incandescent" charm, Petrovskaya's hysterical attempts at "self-immolation," and Bryusov's "earthly" observations in the first person. The novel may be the most striking example we have

[27] Ibid.

КНИГОИЗД
АТЕЛЬСТВО
СКОРПІОНЪ
ВѢСЫ ЕЖЕ
МѢСЯЧНЫЙ
ЖУРНАЛЪ

МОСКВА, ТЕАТРАЛЬНАЯ
ПЛ., Д. МЕТРОПОЛЬ, 23.
ТЕЛЕФОНЪ 50-89.

An invitation to an at-home given by Bryusov in 1904.
To the left is a seal of the publishing house "Skorpion."
The invitation reads:

Dear Vladislav Felitsianovich,
    This Friday evening after nine several persons from
our usual circle—that is, of those already in Moscow—
will gather at my place (Tsvetnoy B.). I would be most
pleased if you too would wish to be there that evening.
Knowing how terribly busy I am, you will forgive me for
addressing this invitation to you in writing rather than
in person.

                            Respectfully,
                            Valery Bryusov
                                            1904.

of a bio-aesthetic genre, of actual experiences caught or *em-
plotted* in what Oscar Wilde would call the clever "lie" of
art. The fatal sin of Symbolism, as Khodasevich opined, lay
in its urge "to turn art into reality and reality into art."[28]
    At the time of his affair with Petrovskaya, Bely was in fact

[28] *Nekropol'*, p. 10.

viewed by the artistic public as a sort of fiery angel: "In 1904 Andrey Bely was still young, golden-locked, blue-eyed, and extremely charming. . . . People were in raptures over him. Everything in his presence seemed to change instantly, to be displaced or lit up by his light. And, indeed, he was radiant [*svetel*]."[29] Therefore, when Petrovskaya fell in love with him, she was seen to be seducing Symbolism's crown prince, and when the "moment" of their ecstatic affair was exhausted, Bely did not simply leave his lover, he " 'escaped from temptation' . . . in order to shine still more dazzlingly before another [Lyubov Mendeleeva] . . . the precursor of the Woman Clothed in the Sun."[30]

Though Petrovskaya was deeply stung by the loss of Bely, the affair might have ended there. The bio-aesthetic plotting of their relationship had reached a certain denouement, and Petrovskaya, a writer of limited talent and a woman of limited beauty, had little chance to live out a sequel to *that* novel. But Bryusov qua necromancer[31] intervened and offered Petrovskaya, in whom he saw (or, what is more likely, affected to see) a modern witch, the chance of recovering Bely through black magic.[32] Thus the novel-in-life continued. Its plot became tangled in the extreme when Bryusov, like his double in the novel, called his rival out to a duel. Fortunately, what takes place between Ruprecht and Hein-

---

[29] Ibid., pp. 15-16.

[30] Ibid., pp. 16-17. See also, Belyi, *Beginning of the Century*, pp. 276-287; and Oleg Maslenikov, *The Frenzied Poets* (Berkeley, 1952), pp. 110-114.

[31] See K. Mochul'skii, *Valerii Briusov* (Paris, 1962), p. 17: "Bryusov bore his ineradicable materialism through all his infatuations with mysticism, god-seeking, occultism, and spiritism. The 'Great Magus,' as his admirers called him, never believed in anything."

[32] Khodasevich's antipathy for Bryusov, largely motivated by the deaths of friends, certainly colored his account of Bryusov's cynical, manipulative role at this time. Mochulsky, on the other hand, sees Bryusov in a more vulnerable position: in his account Bryusov underwent a "deep moral crisis" as a result of his uncontrollable passion for Petrovskaya and had what resembled a nervous breakdown following the suicide of Lvova (*Briusov*, pp. 102-103, 155-156). See as well Petrovskaya's memoir of Bryusov in *Literary Heritage: Valery Bryusov*, pp. 773-798.

rich never did between Bryusov and Bely. Petrovskaya, however, was not Renata: she did not die when Bryusov completed the serialization of *The Fiery Angel*.[33] After occult means failed to return Bely to her, she attempted to shoot him at a lecture in the spring of 1905, but the Browning pistol she was using misfired. And when Bryusov then left her a year later, she, like Gofman, gradually lapsed into a haunting reminder of the incinerating philosophy of moments and the mutability of *sanctus amor*. Following bouts of alcoholism and morphine addiction, an attempted suicide, and years of degrading poverty in emigration, the "lyrical improvisation" of Petrovskaya's life finally ended in February 1928 when she turned on the gas in a sordid hotel room in Paris.[34]

Gofman and Petrovskaya were not the only victims of this *carpe diem* philosophy. Some years later Nadezhda (Nadya) Lvova, a young poet and another friend of Khodasevich, came under the personal and professional guidance of Bryusov (they seemed dangerously linked). As time passed, Lvova had difficulty living with the disparity between Bryusov the magus and Bryusov the satisfied family man; not unexpectedly, she failed to lure Bryusov away from the hearth into the "aroused atmosphere" he had coached her to breathe. In 1913, after "Bryusov had systematically accustomed her to the idea . . . of suicide,"[35] she too killed herself, with the same pistol that Petrovskaya had used in her attempt to shoot Bely—a present from Bryusov. This death was particularly painful for Khodasevich, because Lvova, still young and bright but confused,

---

[33] There is no hint of the actual human drama accompanying the writing of *The Fiery Angel* in Bely's review: A. Belyi, "Ognennyi angel" (The Fiery Angel), *Vesy*, no. 9 (September 1909), pp. 91-93. Additional information on the Bely-Petrovskaya-Bryusov affair and its relation to *The Fiery Angel* is found in S. S. Grechishkin and A. V. Lavrov, "Biograficheskie istochniki romana Briusova 'Ognennyi angel'" (Biographical Sources of Bryusov's Novel *The Fiery Angel*), *Wiener Slawistischer Almanach*, no. 1 (1978), pp. 79-109.

[34] *Nekropol'*, p. 23.

[35] Ibid., p. 47.

had phoned both Bryusov and Khodasevich on the night of her suicide. Bryusov was "busy";[36] Khodasevich was not at home.

What emerges, therefore, as we try to reconstruct Khodasevich's attitude toward Bryusovism is the sense of heavy personal loss against which the older and wiser poet could not but weigh his first efforts in verse. It seems plausible that Khodasevich excluded *Youth* and *The Happy Little House* from his collected verse because they were more than just artistically "juvenile."[37] Of all the portraits in *Necropolis*, that of Bryusov is etched in the darkest colors. Khodasevich did not simply reject Bryusov as poetic mentor, though he had, judging by the poems in *Youth*, good cause to. More important, he felt compelled to reject Bryusov's bio-aesthetic platform. It would take Blok, a figure who was *prekrasnyi* ("beautiful" in ways that lead back to his essential integrity), to replace the manipulative Bryusov as the Symbolist poet *and* personality par excellence, for in Blok above all others the bio-aesthetic nexus would be raised to real heroic dimensions. Though unlikely, Khodasevich might have better understood the loss of his friends if Bryusov as controlling force had been *prekrasnyi*.[38] But just as Bryusov lacked Blok's gift as a poet, so too he lacked Blok's integrity as a personality, his gift (not a happy one) for living. To a degree that his protégés could not, Bryusov was able to separate his various roles as tame husband, *outré* poet, imperious editor, satanic lover. He loved the carrot pies baked by his wife

---

[36] Ibid.

[37] See "Predislovie" (Preface) to *SS*.

[38] Khodasevich's account of Bryusov's reaction to the deaths of Gofman and Lvova is chilling. To Gofman's words—"I've got to try to manage to shoot myself"—written in a letter to his sister prior to suicide, Bryusov reacted when told with "What an awkward sentence. But interesting" (Khodasevich, "Viktor Gofman"). After Lvova's death Bryusov spent some time in a sanatorium in Riga, struck up a new romance there, and returned to Moscow with his "spiritual wound" healed and with new verses, including the following, to offer to the Circle of Art and Literature: "Dead one, sleep calmly in the coffin, / Living one, make use of life" (*Nekropol'*, pp. 48-49).

Ioanna Matveevna, and, indeed, those pies were considered by literary Moscow to be "the symbol of Bryusov's vulgarity [*meshchanstvo*], both material and spiritual."[39] We do not know precisely when it was that Khodasevich first realized the flaw in Bryusovism. What personal notes we do have suggest that the process of discovery was gradual. Yet the *éducation peu sentimentale* eventually came full circle, ending—and righting itself—where it began, when a wiser Khodasevich subsequently noted the lack of the *prekrasnoe* in Fet. Like his famous champion, the poet of essences had his banal, phenomenal side. If the man (Shenshin) could marry for gain, then could not the artist (Fet) coldly ply the memory of an early attachment, that with a girl, Yelena Lazich, who had loved genuinely and who by burning to death may have committed suicide, to produce a cycle of lyrics thirty years later?[40] For Khodasevich the tragic residue of the Symbolist years suggested that a human life is more than source material.

To sum up, then, Khodasevich's involvement with Bryusovism did not die easily. Bryusov was the best man at Khodasevich's wedding in April 1905 and held the traditional crown over the poet and his striking bride Marina Ryndina in the church at the Rumyantsevsky Museum. Khodasevich's calendar from 1903, when he left his parents' home, to 1914, when what is generally regarded as his mature period began, is punctuated regularly with pastimes bent on seizing the moment—hard drinking, affairs of the heart, and cards (to be an ongoing passion).[41] Like Gofman, Petrovskaya, and Lvova, Khodasevich was a devotee of Bryusov and his philosophy, but unlike them, he survived to tell his—and their—story. It is intriguing to speculate that Khoda-

[39] Khodasevich, "Izbrannye stikhi Briusova" (review of *The Selected Verse of Bryusov* [Moscow, 1934]), *Voz*, no. 3228 (5 April 1934).

[40] Khodasevich, "Knigi i liudi" (People and Books), *Voz*, no. 2872 (13 April 1933).

[41] *Kursiv*, p. 169.

sevich was in some way more resilient and less erratic. Or perhaps it is more likely that he simply saw in time what they failed to see, that unconsciously he heard the voice that Bryusov used only in his diary, a voice that sounded too much like Salieri or Julien Sorel, and in hearing that voice he began to search elsewhere for appropriate models:

Talent, even genius, will honestly give only slow success, if they will give it at all. That's not enough! Not enough for me. I've got to choose another way ... to find a lodestar in the mist. And I see it: it's Decadence. Yes! Whatever one says, whether it's false or ridiculous, it's moving ahead, developing, and the future belongs to it, particularly when it finds a worthy leader. And *I* will be that leader! Yes, *I*.[42]

KHODASEVICH had ample reason to disown the personal legacy of the Symbolist years. His reasons for wanting to disown *Youth*, the artistic legacy of those years, appear equally strong. Not one to mitigate his views on art, Khodasevich could turn the blade of his criticism inward as well as outward. While he was later thankful to Krechetov-Sokolov for opening the pages of the yearbook *Grif* to him and giving him his debut in print in March 1905, he did not look fondly on the three poems—"Zimnie sumerki" (Winter Twilight), "Osennie sumerki" (Autumn Twilight), and "Skhvatil ia dymnyi fakel moi" (I gripped my smoky torch)—that gave him his start:

To my surprise (and of course to my great pride) he himself [Krechetov-Sokolov] offered to publish them. They appeared in the next number of the yearbook. I have always remained grateful to S. A. Sokolov but I think that at that moment he was too indulgent: the poems were so bad that to this day it is unpleasant for me to recall them, even though I was eighteen when I wrote them.[43]

[42] Briusov, *Diaries*, p. 12. Quoted in Khodasevich, "On Bryusov's Diary."
[43] Khodasevich, "V. F. Khodasevich," *Novaia gazeta* (New Gazette), no. 1 (1 March 1931). See also Khodasevich,"Pamiati Sergeia Krechetova" (To the Memory of Sergey Krechetov), *Voz*, no. 4012 (28 May 1936). Khodasevich's feelings about the poems of *Youth* are most evident in an unpublished preface to what (in October 1921) he thought would be (but never

There is no false modesty in this self-criticism. Khodasevich was clearly uneasy at the thought that he, a poet whose mature aesthetic rested on such notions as irony, understatement, precision, and pun, could have at one time written verse that was marked by "vagueness of thought and imprecision of lexicon."[44] The complex grafting of styles, the semantic hypercompression amid rhythmical simplicity, the rhetorical tension between speaker and reader are nowhere to be seen in *Youth*. What we find instead are the attitudinizing, the rhetoric of world-weariness, and the straining after effect of a well-studied Bryusovian curriculum.

Yet just as it would be too easy to claim that Khodasevich's life between 1903 and 1908 was influenced exclusively by Bryusovism, so would it be too easy to discover an exclusively Bryusovian aesthetic in *Youth*. In his least "Khodasevich-like" collection it should not be curious that Khodasevich is at his most eclectic. The dedications to Marina Ryndina (of the entire collection), Muni, Nina Petrovskaya, Krechetov-Sokolov, Sergey Auslender, and Bely, and the epigraphs from Pushkin, Heine, Sologub, and Bryusov suggest that Khodasevich is casting about for a voice to give authority to a voice that is not completely his own. In the poems themselves there are obvious echoes of other pre-

---

was) a new edition of the collection: "In order that no one conclude that . . . I think this book is good in its present form, I will speak plainly: no, it is a very weak book, and it is dear to me not in a literary but in a biographical sense. It is linked with dear memories. Its title, which once seemed a bitter irony to me, has now become a precise designation: yes, this was my youth, the point from which I began. In this book there are echoes of that era when Symbolism had not yet uttered its final word, when for some of us, especially those as young as I, it had still not hardened into the forms of a literary school, but was a way to feel, think, and, more than that, *live*. For me, this book is linked with memories of persons who have died, or who I have not seen for a long time and, perhaps, will not see again, or who have had to be struck from my heart." (From the papers of I. I. Bernshtein. Courtesy of the family of I. I. Bernshtein.)

[44] Khodasevich, "S. Ia. Parnok," *Voz*, no. 3026 (14 September 1933).

Symbolist and Symbolist models—Maykov, Aleksey Apu-
khtin, Annensky, Balmont, Sologub, the early Blok. Still,
one hesitates to underrate the direct influence that Bryusov's
poetry had on *Youth*. Khodasevich apparently acceded to the
theory that a novice poet should apprentice himself out to
a master; and in his case, the master was Bryusov. The young
Vladislav had an intimate knowledge of Bryusov's early verse.
He subscribed to, and presumably read avidly, *Vesy*, the journal that Bryusov's name helped raise to the heights of success
in the years immediately preceding the publication of *Youth*.[45]
But most convincing in the search for a purely formal point
of departure is the evidence of *Youth* itself, for it is the
poems—their manner, diction, "lyrical personality"—that
best show the wholly conscious nature of Khodasevich's
apprenticeship.

What precisely did Khodasevich borrow from Bryusov? He
borrowed, to begin with, the abstract principles, the intellectual skeleton, of Bryusov's *ars poetica*, beginning with
his Flaubertian respect for the station of the artist and for
art as a *métier*. "Art," as Flaubert said fifty years earlier,
"must rise above personal emotions and susceptibilities. It
is time to endow it with pitiless method, with the exactness
of the physical sciences."[46] Victor Erlich has used Khodasevich's memoirs to make the point that, *mutatis mutandis*,
Bryusov and the Moscow Symbolists ascribed to the controlled, dispassionate "making" of art, while Blok and the
Petersburg Symbolists felt their poetic role to be that of
"seers," possessed and Pythic.[47] The distinction may break
down with particular examples, yet the tendency seems true
and not unhelpful. Khodasevich felt, and would continue to
feel, that poetry writing was hard work and had little to do

[45] See Khodasevich, "Juvenilia Briusova" (Bryusov's *Juvenilia*), *Sofiia* (Sophia), 2 (February 1914), 64-67.
[46] Letter to Mlle Leroyer de Chantepie (1857), in Gustave Flaubert, *Selected Letters*, trans. Francis Steegmuller (London, 1954), p. 195.
[47] Erlich, *The Double Image*, pp. 68-119.

with flights of inspiration and the "wings of poesy." Time and again in later asides in his essays he would invoke Pushkin's formula *voobrazhenie povereno rassudkom* (imagination checked by logic) to clip the wings of a free-wheeling tyro.

Perhaps one of Bryusov's most programmatic poems, which bears a dateline (18 December 1907) close to the publication of *Youth*, shows the correlation between theory and practice in more tangible terms; my free rendering of the original is an (admittedly imperfect) attempt to "English" the fustian rhetoric of Bryusov's Russian:

Ты должен быть гордым, как знамя;
Ты должен быть острым, как меч;
Как Данту, подземное пламя
Должно тебе щеки обжечь.

Всего будь холодный свидетель,
На все устремляя свой взор.
Да будет твоя добродетель—
Готовность взойти на костер.

Быть может, все в жизни лишь средство
Для ярко-певучих стихов,
И ты с беспечального детства
Ищи сочетания слов.

В минуты любовных объятий
К бесстрастью себя приневоль,
И в час беспощадных распятий
Прославь исступленную боль.

В снах утра и в бездне вечерней
Лови, что шепнет тебе Рок,
И помни: от века из терний
Поэта заветный венок.[48]

You must be proud like a banner,
you must be sharp like a sword;
your cheeks like those of Dante
by an underground flame must be scorched.

[48] V. Briusov, *Sobranie sochinenii* (Collected Works) (Moscow, 1973), I, 447.

Cast your gaze on all that surrounds you,
coldly witness the sum of it all,
may your virtue upon the bonfire
be your urge to rise to its call.

Perhaps, after all, life is only
a poem's tuneful, luminous means,
and you from insouciant childhood
seek words in a dovetailing stream [lit: "combination"].

In moments of passion's embraces
there is a self without passion to train;
at crucifixion's merciless hour
glorify the furious pain.

In dreams of morning, in chasms of evening
catch what Fate may whisper to you
and remember: the thorns of a lifetime
crown the poet as his sacred due.

Balancing contradictory images of heat and cold, detachment and self-immolation, art and life, "Poetu" (To the Poet) is above all a glorification of the *role* of the poet, of how the latter fashions art from the stuff of experience. The speaker is not a particular sensibility dealing with a particular lyrical problem or situation (recall Mill's formulation of the lyric poet "overhearing" himself); he is a sort of poetic Wizard of Oz, dispensing the requisite talents and indicating the way down poetry's yellow brick road. The search for a lexicon hyperbolic enough to thwart any emotional middleground (the negative prefix *bez-* serves to clear away mediating nuances) and the piling up of abstract nouns ("virtue," "willingness," "passionlessness") make of language something contextless, grand, and magisterial—in short, Oz-like.[49] Language thus bent to a stylistic outer limit runs the risk of catachresis, of metaphorical fuzziness due to rhetorical hyperextension. Because Bryusov appears more concerned with maintaining nearly absolute phonetic and rhythmic paral-

[49] An excellent discussion of Bryusov's language is found in V. Zhirmunskii, *Theory of Literature, Poetics, Stylistics*, pp. 142-204.

lelism in the first two lines, the reader suffers a loss of sight: personal qualities that are bannerlike or swordlike are impossible to visualize; in each case the entire simile, both tenor and vehicle, has taken to the air, and the function of a normally reifying vehicle disappears. Hence what emerges is a poem strikingly (especially for those raised on the predominantly *visual* texture of post-Symbolist images) void of concrete detail, built up on imagery that is medieval and merely iconographic. "To the Poet" is governed by what Frank Kermode would call the "ornamental," as opposed to the "integral," image: the banner and sword appear as items "attached to discourse, the flower stuck in the sand," and not as "a unification of thought and feeling."[50]

Of the three styles—*deklamativnyi* (declamatory), *napevnyi* (melodic), and *govornoi* (conversational)—that Boris Eikhenbaum coins to deal with the history of the Russian lyric, "To the Poet" offers a blend of the first two, of Tyutchev-like declamation (N.B. the imperative mood and elevated diction) and Fet-like melodic devices (N.B. the anaphora and weakened logical emphasis of the coordinating conjunction *i*).[51] Rather than the conversational style of the later Pushkin, Akhmatova, and the mature Khodasevich, what we generally find in Bryusov (and the young Khodasevich) is a style in which

the concrete meaning of words may be masked, the logical syntax of speech may be distorted by a musical element, the optic clarity of images may recede to the background, [and] the subtle differentiation in the selection and use of words [may disappear], [so that] all these aspects yield their position to melodiousness, to the vague alternation of images that function musically to elicit an

[50] Frank Kermode, " 'Dissociation of Sensibility': Modern Symbolist Readings of Literary History," in *Modern Poetry: Essays in Criticism*, ed. John Hollander (New York, 1968), p. 323.

[51] Boris Eikhenbaum, *Melodika russkogo liricheskogo stikha* (Melodics of Russian Lyric Verse) (Petersburg, 1922; rpt. Leipzig, 1973), p. 8.

indefinite lyrical mood and to excite the emotional impressiona-
bility of the listener.[52]

The declamatory and melodic styles of Bryusov's poem suggest, paradoxically, both the presence and absence of high-
pitched emotions, since emotions cannot remain high-pitched
indefinitely without losing their edge. In the end, however,
it is the poem's emphasis on detachment, its ritualizing of
the poetic and depersonalizing of the biographical processes,
that exerts a strong influence on *Youth*. As we shall see,
Khodasevich borrows the image of crucifixion to chasten, or
affect to chasten, a creative life he is only just beginning.
Though overworked by the poseur of *Youth*, the urge for
detachment will find some remarkable analogues in the dramatic speakers of later collections.

Thematically Bryusov's poems of the period recall, among
others, Baudelaire, Poe, and Swinburne. Speakers make love
to marble-breasted heroines in moonlit crypts. Love is cultivated in dizzying combinations of pleasure and pain, virginity and perversity. In a sobering gloss on the Petrovskaya
affair Erlich describes the lines "We are high priests / We
celebrate a rite" of Bryusov's much-quoted "V Damask" (Road
to Damascus) (1903) as "terrible words," for "if what is involved is a rite, the identity of the partner does not matter.
The 'priestess of love' is Bryusov's favorite expression. But
the face of the priestess is covered. One priestess can be
easily replaced by another; the rite will remain the same."[53]
The concept of passion turned into a morbid ritual involving
angels, hetaeras, or, more likely, combinations of both, seems
to issue directly from *Les Fleurs du mal* (1857). Moreover,
as mentioned earlier, Bryusov's saturnine classicism derives
largely from the poet of "Sed Non Satiata" (Bryusov has a
poem by the same title), "De Profundis Clamavi" (Oscar

[52] Zhirmunskii, *Theory of Literature, Poetics, Stylistics*, p. 174.
[53] Erlich, *The Double Image*, p. 79.

Wilde's confessions from prison were translated in *Vesy*), and "Semper Eadem." And one of Bryusov's most notorious themes, that of necrophilia, probably traces back to Baudelaire and Poe as well. In "V sklepe" (In the Crypt) (1905), one of the poems in *Stephanos* that clearly intrigued the youthful Khodasevich, the speaker says to his Ligeia-like lover, "You are immobile, you are beautiful in a myrtle wreath. / I kiss the heavenly light on your face."[54]

In speaking of Bryusov's poetry one is hard pressed not to overgeneralize. Other poets of comparable reputation might draw our attention to what they, over time, have arrived at, what is, artistically speaking, *theirs*. And to be sure, there are those, such as Vladimir Markov, who continue to see Bryusov's lyrical gestures as unique and to find "imagination in his dryness and individuality in his eclecticism."[55] Yet, on the whole, despite impressive changes over the years in thematic venue, Bryusov's lyrical personality is remarkably uniform and monochromatic. It takes a devotion to the hard work of poetry and, more important, a consciousness hardened to the wayside's multiform reality to speak, as Bryusov did, of whipping on his bovine dream. With few exceptions Bryusov's speakers appear as masks without idiolect or idiosyncrasy. One compelling reason why Khodasevich dropped the masks he borrowed from Bryusov was that he sensed that those masks had been borrowed in the first place. So while Bryusov taught Khodasevich the not unimportant skill of good verse making, what Khodasevich learned during his apprenticeship (aside from the lessons of personal experience) was that, once behind Fet's melodic devices, Tyutchev's declamatory style, Pushkin's clitism, Gautier's lapidary finish, Baudelaire's obsession with beauty and death, and Flaubert's *impassibilité*, there was little finally to separate the master from the master apprentice.

[54] Briusov, *Collected Works*, I, 404.
[55] *Modern Russian Poetry*, ed. Vladimir Markov and Merrill Sparks (Indianapolis-New York, 1967), p. liv.

56

WHEN *Youth* was published by "Grif" in 1908 Viktor Gofman, then reviewing at *Russkaia mysl'* (Russian Thought),
had both praise and criticism for "the young poet's extraor-
dinarily subtle and quantitatively meager book of poems."[56]
Khodasevich, it is true, would never be prolific. What Gofman saw as virtues in *Youth* is revealing of the aestheticism
of the time:

It is enough to open [the book] to any poem to convince oneself
that the poet is first and foremost an exacting master of form.
External form and poetic technique are nearly everywhere beyond
reproach and often refined. Khodasevich knows the value of words,
loves them, and within his work one usually finds that their selection is strict and deliberate. His cadences are multifarious and
internally regular, consistently growing out of a poem's content
and essence, or even themselves comprising part of that essence.
Almost everywhere there is a singing melodiousness that wins one
over. Finally, among the positive aspects of the book one should
include the genuine artistic taste of the author.[57]

The allusions, as might be expected, are to a poetry of essence
and melodiousness, a Bryusovian mastery of form, and verse
making whose subject is often itself.

Gofman's reservations about *Youth* are equally illustra-
tive, however, and show that in his view favorite Decadent
devices may be by 1908 losing their appeal: "But there are
also, to be sure, negative aspects [to the poems]: such are
the author's frequent and unpleasant affectation, his self-
infatuation, and his urge to what is called *épater les bourgeois*. And with what cheap, second-rate Decadent devices
he sometimes manages this!"[58] The reviewer was also clearly
bothered by those poems in which Khodasevich's "elegant
sentimentality" crosses a dangerous border into "senile tear-

---

[56] V. Gofman, "Vladislav Khodasevich—Molodost'," *Russkaia mysl'*
(Russian Thought), no. 7 (July 1908), p. 143. See also Bryusov's lukewarm
review in V. Briusov, "Debiutanty" (Debutantes), *Vesy*, no. 3 (March 1908),
pp. 79-80.
[57] Ibid.
[58] Ibid.

jerking" (*starcheskaia slezlivost'*).[59] Even Gofman, someone
steeped in Decadent pathos, felt Khodasevich's manner in a
number of poems to be over-rich or cloying.

"V moei strane" (In My Country), the first half of *Youth*,
consists of fifteen short lyrics. The second stanza of the
opening poem gives the section its title and quickly ushers
the reader into a private landscape:

> В моей стране—ни зим, ни лет, ни весен,
> Ни дней, ни зор, ни голубых ночей.
> Там круглый год владычествует осень,
> Там—серый свет бессолнечных лучей.[60]

> My country has no summers nor no winters,
> no springs, no dawns, no sky-blue nights, no days.
> There all year round the autumn holds dominion,
> There only gray light shines in sunless rays.

Structurally the poem is arranged around an agricultural
metaphor that will be important in his later collections, but
here Khodasevich inverts the images of sowing and reaping
for Decadent shock value: the "deadly country" is peopled
by fathers that sow their barren seeds and are no better than
their cattle, by mothers that cultivate in turn their shameless sexuality, and by freakish children damned at birth. The
heavy use of anaphora and the negative prefixes *bez-* and *ne-*
give the poem a melodic-rhetorical quality, make of the
country an intangible never-never land, work against a context that is potentially ironic, and show the general stylistic
influence of Bryusov.

The title of the book itself is provided by "Net, molodost' "
(No, Youth) (1907), the second poem in the section. Here we
encounter the familiar crypt along with other Decadent
clichés:

> Нет, молодость, ты мне была верна,
> Ты не лгала, притворствуя, не льстила.

59 Ibid.
60 Khodasevich, *Molodost'* (Youth) (Moscow, 1908), p. 9.

Ты тайной ночью в склеп меня водила
И ставила у темного окна.
Нас возносила грузная волна,
Качались мы у темного провала,
И я молчал, а ты была бледна,
Ты на полу простертая стонала.
Мой ранний страх вздымался у окна,
Грозил всю жизнь безумием измерить . . .
Я видел лица, слышал имена—
И убегал, не смея знать и верить.[61]

No, youth, you were true to me,
you did not lie, or feigning, flatter.
One secret night you led me to the crypt
and stood me there beside the darkened window.
We were borne upon a ponderous wave,
pitched at the brink of a dark funnel,
and I was silent, and you were pale,
you moaned as you lay stretched upon the floor.
My early fear rose up beside the window,
threatened to make life's only measure madness . . .
I saw faces and I heard names,
and fled, not daring what to know or trust.

One is immediately struck by the way Khodasevich's language again registers a high degree of mood-inducing *napevnost'* (melodiousness) at the expense of precise visual detail. The poem makes its acoustic impression more through the use of vocalic rhyme (note the *a*-based end rhyme and the assonance in lines four, six, seven, and nine), one of Bryusov's favorite devices, than through the use of Balmontian alliteration.[62] There is not, on the other hand, a specific adjective or noun in the poem: completely ignoring the actual world of turn-of-the-century Moscow, Khodasevich seems to lift the *amor fati* theme and lunar landscape from Bryusov. Thus, taken together, the adjective-noun combinations ("secret night," "dark window," "ponderous wave," "dark funnel") add to the poem's melodic character a semantic equiv-

[61] Ibid., p. 11.
[62] See Zhirmunskii, *Theory of Literature, Poetics, Stylistics*, pp. 170-173.

alent of the eerie and indeterminate. It is difficult to take seriously the reality of Khodasevich, twenty-one at the time, writing a poem in which a terrified, old-mannish speaker looks back at youth personified as a wraithlike maiden (*molodost'* is feminine).[63]

Equally representative of "In My Country" is "Osen'" (Autumn) (1905). The solipsistic viewpoint, the language of ritual, the languorous courtship of pleasure and pain, the autumnal mood, and the symbolism of crucifixion come, almost transparently, from Bryusov:

Свет золотой в алтаре
В окнах—цветистые стекла.
Я прихожу в этот храм на заре,
Осенью сердце поблекло . . .
Вещее сердце поблекло . . .

Грустно. Осень пирует,
Осень развесила красные ткани,
Ликует . . .
Ветер—как стон запоздалых рыданий.
Листья шуршат и, взлетая, танцуют.

Светлое утро. Я в церкви. Так рано.
Зыблется золото в медленных звуках органа,
Сердце вздыхает покорней, размерней,
Изъязвленное иглами терний,
Иглами терний осенних . . .
Терний—осенних.[64]

There is a gold light on the altar,
and in the windows stained glass.
I come to this temple at dawn,
in autumn my heart has faded . . .
my prophetic heart has faded . . .

---

[63] The datelines for the poems in *Youth* did not appear in that collection but have been preserved in Khodasevich's unpublished papers. The majority of the poems, including "No, Youth," were written in 1907. See O. D. Golubeva, *Literaturno-khudozhestvennye al'manakhi i sborniki* (Literary Yearbooks and Miscellanies) (Moscow, 1957), pp. 67, 114.

[64] Khodasevich, *Youth*, pp. 15-16.

It is sad. Autumn is feasting,
autumn has spread out her red fabrics,
and is exultant . . .
The wind is like the moan of belated sobbing.
The leaves rustle and, flying up, dance.

A bright morning. I am in church. It's so early.
Gold is scudding in the slow sounds of the organ,
my heart sighs more submissively, more evenly,
like an open sore rent by thorny needles,
the thorny needles of autumn . . .
the thorns of autumn.

This short lyric is interesting precisely for its telescoping of those problems of artistic conception that Khodasevich would eventually overcome. As in the first two poems, the setting is generalized and atmospheric, the diction grandiloquent ("prophetic heart"), moody-mysterious ("the leaves rustle"), and sentimental ("my heart sighs"). Again the rarefied stage props (autumn, dawn, a temple) do not yet permit the possibility of a self-ironizing speaker. Corresponding to the setting, the short repeated phrases suggest a kind of litany. Although a mood exfoliates, nothing really "happens," hence no events can be presented to our sense of irony. If the time and space of the poem are shadowy attenuations, the means to dramatize, to bring the world of the specific and immediate into conflict with otherworldly pretensions, is lost. "Autumn," in a word, contains more pure *lyrical* devices than anything Khodasevich would write thereafter. What it lacks, however, and what makes it so unlike later work, is the counterbalancing ironic voice inserted between the speaker and his lyrical ponderings.

With minor variations, the other poems comprising the first half of *Youth* follow the examples of "In My Country," "No, Youth," and "Autumn." The debt to Decadence is only reaffirmed by correspondences between them: Baudelairian bats and spiders, more tombs, gravestones and gravediggers, mummers, devils and apparitions, fate and fortune-telling, baying hounds. The role of brooding and buskined *poète maudit* has yet to be played out.

IN THE nineteen poems of "Kuzina" (Cousin), the second half of *Youth*, Khodasevich works and reworks many of the motifs introduced in "In My Country." But several digressions from the Decadent character of "In My Country" offer new profiles of Khodasevich's as yet undefined speaker. More important, there is at least one instance of concrete, present-day imagery, which, though attached to the familiar mood of world-weariness, promises to become an essential element in Khodasevich's later verse.

The four poems of the cycle "Stikhi o kuzine" (Poems About Cousin) are, somewhat belatedly, Khodasevich's contribution to the Romantic tradition. Strangely enough, there is little trace of Decadence in them. The note of happiness struck in the poems is attributable to Khodasevich's writing of this portion of *Youth* at a time when his love for Marina Ryndina was at its height. Vladislav and Marina spent the summers of 1905-1907 at Lidino, an estate near Bologoe in Novgorod Province, and their romance, played against the background of this idyllic setting, surfaces in the mood of the poems. Hence "Ona" (She) (1907), "Starinnye druz'ia" (Old Friends) (1907), "Vospominanie" (Recollection) (1907), and "Kuzina plachet" (Cousin Weeps) (1907) give us the opportunity to see Khodasevich try his hand at nature painting à la Fet and Maykov. This is an anomalous moment in Khodasevich's apprenticeship, because once sure of his gestures, he would become almost exclusively a poet of the urban and the domestic.

But for now, at least, Khodasevich overcomes the narcissistic gloom of "In My Country" and pens amorous verses to his beautiful wife. The images of first love would be incongruous in later poems: speakers steal kisses near the jasmine, watch butterflies bob among the dodders, address cuckoos, and allow tears to replenish a flower garden. Perhaps "Recollection," the third poem in the cycle, recalls most vividly the combination of innocence and eroticism that occupies a salient place in the verse of Batyushkov and Maykov:[65]

Все помню: день и час, и миг,
И хрупкой чаши звон хрустальный,
И темный сад, и лунный лик,
И в нашем доме топот бальный.

Мы подошли из темноты
И в окна светлые следили:
Четыре пестрые черты,—
Шеренги ровные кадрили . . .

У освещенного окна
Темнея тонким силуэтом,
Ты, поцелуем смущена,
Счастливым медлила ответом.

И вдруг—ты помнишь,—блеск и гром;
И крупный ливень, чаще, чаще,
И мы таимся под окном,
А поцелуи—глубже, слаще . . .

А после—бегство в темноту,
Я за тобой, хранитель зоркий;
Мгновенный ветер на лету
Взметнул кисейные оборки.

Летим домой, быстрей, быстрей,
И двери хлопают со звоном.
В блестящей зале, средь гостей,
Немножко странно и светло нам . . .

Стоишь с улыбкой на устах,
С приветом ласково-жеманным,
И только капли в волосах
Горят созвездием нежданным.[66]

I remember all: the day, hour, and instant,
and the fragile bowl, its crystal tinkling,

[65] See Maykov's "Pod dozhdem" (In the Rain) (1856).
[66] Khodasevich, *Youth*, pp. 40-41.

and the dark garden, and the man in the moon,
and our house with its ballroom clattering.

We crept out of the dark
and peered into bright windows:
four multicolored lines
formed a quadrille of even rows.

Beside the lighted glass
silhouetted dark and slender,
you were shy about my kiss
and tarried with the happy answer.

And suddenly—remember?—thunder and flash,
and the heavy downpour faster, faster,
and we are hiding beneath the sill,
with kisses coming deeper, sweeter . . .

And then the run into the dark,
with me behind to keep the vigil;
a momentary gust of wind
played at your muslin frills.

Now faster, faster we fly home,
and there the doors slam with a banging.
In the bright hall, amid the guests,
all seems a little strange and shining . . .

You stand, a smile upon your lips,
its greeting tenderly affected,
and only in your hair the drops
shine in a star-burst unexpected.

Khodasevich's use of playful eroticism, even if borrowed
from another convention, is refreshing after the stylized sensuality of "In My Country." The lines give the sensation of
having been lived.[67] They pick up tempo (helped by the repetition of conjunctions in stanza four and the breathless
chashche, chashche, glubzhe, slashche, bystrei, bystrei) as
they move to an actual climax, the slamming of doors, then
gradually slow down until the final two lines when the stressed
a ("*kapli v volosakh,*" "*goriat . . . nezhdannym*") lingers on

[67] Formal dances indeed played a role in Khodasevich's early life. See
Kursiv, p. 168.

her beauty. Here, then, significantly, not only mood but drama is involved.

In "Infancy" an older Khodasevich caught our attention with his precise recollection of early years. Down to the pots of ficus and philodendron on the dining room window he conjured up the details that constituted the living matter, the real tissue, of his childhood. But in terms of *Youth* this passion for detail has yet to find a proper mode of expression. "Recollection" may be different, however, because the poet's powers of observation are turned on a world that, if not completely real, is still more realistic than what was seen before. While Khodasevich chooses details, such as the muslin frills and the raindrops in the hair, that enhance the impression of romance and first love, those details are specific and not generic. In terms of the bloodless world of "In My Country" this is a considerable adjustment.

Khodasevich's infatuation with the Romantic tradition is short-lived, passing with the failure of his marriage to Marina Ryndina.[68] After all, to wear the mask of nature's *pevets* (bard), a mask worn first by Zhukovsky and Pushkin, seems no less artificial than to wear the mask of Decadent cryptkeeper.[69] But before leaving this period of experimentation, of Khodasevich's youth and *Youth*, perhaps there is one other poem worthy of mention. Its theme, the irretrievable past, is not new to us, yet "Vecher kholodno-vesennii" (The cold spring evening) (1907) shows a speaker in the process of changing keys:

[68] Khodasevich separated from Ryndina on 30 December 1907 (ibid., p. 169). She subsequently married Sergey Makovsky, the editor of *Apollon* (Apollo). See Andrei Belyi, *Mezhdu dvukh revoliutsii* (Between Two Revolutions) (Leningrad, 1934; rpt. Chicago, 1966), p. 248. For a brief portrait of Ryndina, the least known of Khodasevich's four wives, see Anna Chulkova, "Vospominaniia o Vladislave Khodaseviche" (Memoirs of Vladislav Khodasevich), *Russica* (almanac) (1982), pp. 275-294.

[69] See "Poet, elegiia" (The Poet, An Elegy) in Khodasevich, *Youth*, p. 46. Khodasevich quotes, with slight variation, two lines from Pushkin's poem "Pevets" (Bard) (1816).

Вечер холодно-весенний
    Застыл в безнадежном покое.
Вспыхнули тоньше, мгновенней
    Колючки рассыпанной хвои.

Насыпи, рельсы и шпалы,
    Извивы железной дороги . . .
Я, просветленный, усталый,
    Не думаю больше о Боге.

На мост всхожу, улыбаясь,
    Мечтаю о милом, о старом . . .
Поезд, гремя и качаясь,
    Обдаст меня ветром и паром.[70]

The cold spring evening
    has frozen in hopeless calm.
Thorns of scattered needles
    have burst, more thin and fleeting, into flame.

Embankments, rails, and cross-ties,
    the railroad's windings . . .
I, lucid and tired,
    think no longer of God.

I climb on a bridge and, smiling,
    think of what's dear, of what's old,
A train, swaying and rumbling,
    will douse me with wind and steam.

It is safe to say that this poem did not make Khodasevich's reputation. Even in terms of *Youth*, it is lost in the background of those poems that are properly Decadent or Romantic. Still, the second and third stanzas represent new possibilities. With details suggesting Annensky's railroad poems, they bring the speaker out from the natural setting of pine needles and introduce him to the modern world of trains—rails, ties, embankments.[71] When it sways and rumbles past, the machine promises to douse the speaker with

[70] Khodasevich, *Youth*, p. 47.

[71] See Annensky's unique blend of Fet-like musicality and painfully concrete urban details in "Lunnaia noch' v iskhode zimy" (Lunar Night at the End of Winter) (1906) and "Toska vokzala" (Melancholy of the Station) (first appeared in *Kiparisovyi larets* [Cypress Chest] [1910]).

steam and wind, the hot and cold air of a new reality, and to wake him, a Decadent lotus-eater, from his dreams. At last Khodasevich is beginning to develop a context for irony, and with it the possibility (though still faint) of psychological drama rare in lyric form. In *The Happy Little House*, his next collection, the real and the ideal will find more opportunity to collide.

3

FINDING A HOME: 1908-1914

> Благословляю новоселье,
> Куда домашний свой кумир
> Ты перенес—а с ним веселье,
> Свободный труд и сладкий мир.
> —Пушкин, "Новоселье"

> I bless this new home,
> where you have moved
> your domestic idol, and with it joy,
> unrestricted labor and sweet tranquility.
> —Pushkin, "The New Home"

> We cannot use language maturely until we are
> spontaneously at home in irony.
> —Kenneth Burke, *Language as Symbolic Action*

In an essay that has since been the subject of some dispute, T. S. Eliot once described the seventeenth century as a time governed by a "dissociation of sensibility."[1] As his formulation suggests, at a specific point in time, namely, at the passing of Donne and the appearance of Milton, English poetry ceased being "reflective" and became forever "intellectual," that is, it ceased being a poetry of conceits, one which yokes together inconceivably disparate elements and "feel[s] . . . thought as immediately as the odour of a rose,"[2] and became instead a poetry of heady Latinate syntax. Eliot's essay has its appeal, offering a precise history of the "fall" of post-Renaissance poetic sensibility and thus a way to make sense of, even recuperate, much of the doubt and irony that

---

[1] T. S. Eliot, "The Metaphysical Poets," *Selected Essays* (New York, 1950), p. 247.
[2] Ibid.

68

eventually came in the wake of that fall (for if we can lay the blame, then we can place that doubt and irony in a discursive order). But it is probably inaccurate; indeed, Frank Kermode has traced such a dissociation through Averroes and the Aristotelian tradition of Padua as far back as Athens.[3] Perhaps, on the other hand, what the essay says about Eliot is more important than what Eliot says in the essay: like other poets looking for an ideal cultural homeland—for Yeats, it was Byzantium; for Mandelshtam, Greece—Eliot was looking for that time and space (the Renaissance) when the artistic sensibility was healthy, seamless, thoughtful *and* passionate. Whether in fact that time and space ever existed is moot. The act of enunciation itself, the urge to see a homeostatic poetic intelligence and to apply it as touchstone against the present, seems to prevail independent of the actual argument.

Russia of course had no Renaissance, and Khodasevich had no Shakespeare against which to judge the modern poetic sensibility. But he did have, as he thought, a "Renaissance" poet of undivided genius and a historical moment that provided the atmosphere necessary for the creation of poetry in an "unfallen" state:

The personal life of Pushkin was defined by the spirit of future creation, and I would say that that is the genuine spirit of the Renaissance. Yes, at the beginning of the nineteenth century, there was in Russia a moment when the greatest of its artists, in no way "stylizing" . . . revived the Renaissance itself by dint of inner necessity alone. . . . In autumn 1822, in Kishinyov, in the Bessarabian province, Russia relived the Renaissance in the person of Pushkin as creator of *The Gavriliada.*

An admiration for the "devilish" charm of the world and a paganistic *joie de vivre*, as they are applied to a treatment of Biblical-Christian themes, comprise one of the outstanding qualities of the Italian Renaissance. . . . In this regard the Venetian artists sur-

---

[3] Frank Kermode, " 'Dissociation of Sensibility': Modern Symbolist Readings of Literary History," in *Modern Poetry: Essays in Criticism*, ed. John Hollander (New York, 1968), pp. 318-339.

passed, it seems, all others—a detail lost neither on their contemporaries nor the Catholic Church. . . . Arguments about the blasphemous nature of paintings conceived mainly for churches were raised even then: such was the case with Veronese, who was forced to answer before a court of the Inquisition for his too resplendent and festive depiction of events from the Gospels. His explanation to the court was magnificent. . . . He said that he had depicted events from the Gospels just as it had seemed necessary and fitting to him, an artist, that is, just as his artistic conscience had told him. And so great was the judges' respect for the freedom of art that Veronese was vindicated by the Inquisition itself.

Yet no matter how remarkable were Veronese's explanations, he still did not say, or want to say, what was most important. Otherwise he would have informed the monks that to dress Gospel characters in the finery of Venetian patricians; to bring hunchbacked jesters, dwarfs and dogs to the marriage in Cana of Galilee; to have some soldiers, ignoring the presence of Christ, put away tasty dishes with gusto and greedily drain their pitchers; to move the moment of the Annunciation from a poor little house in Nazareth to a marble palace in Venice, and so on, and so on, was all motivated not only by the desire to employ certain artistic devices but by something rather more complex as well. He would have said that the world in which he, Veronese, was living at the moment was so dear, so beautiful to him that he did not want to part with that world even for the holiest of places and moments. And that, perhaps, even the very home of the Lord would be unappealing if that home were too unlike Venice.

Veronese was an Italian of the sixteenth century, Pushkin a Russian living in the nineteenth century. Veronese was a painter, Pushkin a poet. It is likely that Veronese considered himself a Catholic; Pushkin, at the writing of *The Gavriliada*, did not believe at all. Veronese made paintings for churches and palaces; *The Gavriliada* was written "quietly," "for oneself." All this predetermines a number of profound differences between the paintings of Veronese and the poem of Pushkin. . . . Nevertheless, their approach to the [Gospel] theme was essentially identical, inasmuch as that approach was born from one and the same feeling: a fascination with the world that surrounded them. Neither wanted to part with earthly passions.[4]

---

[4] Khodasevich, "O Gavriliade" (On *The Gavriliada*), *Stat'i o russkoi poezii* (Articles on Russian Poetry) (Petersburg, 1922), pp. 100-103.

It would be convenient for the critic if Khodasevich had written this essay about *The Gavriliada* sometime between 1908 and 1914 during the writing of *The Happy Little House*. Such a dating would simultaneously raise and answer many of the questions about life and art that must have been vexing Khodasevich in the years following the publication of *Youth*, as the high-toned lifestyle and language of Symbolism began to lose their novelty. Yet in many ways a slow developer, Khodasevich did not accommodate the massive cultural phenomenon of Pushkin to his own idiom with some study and several proleptic strokes of the pen. Although we catch glimpses of such study as early as 1908 in Khodasevich's essay on Countess Rastopchina, the process of assimilating Pushkin and his time was incremental.[5] Even after 1914, when Khodasevich began to produce his mature works, his verse can be called "Pushkinian" only with considerable distortion. On the other hand, the *departure* from Pushkin and Symbolism, or rather the unique grafting of the one's manner onto the other's thematics in the presence of a complex self-ironizing speaker, distinguishes Khodasevich's work after 1914 and makes his verse a vital missing link—one easily lost in the programmatic dicta of Gumilyov and Gorodetsky—between Symbolism and Acmeism.[6]

[5] "In our days—tense, deliberately complex, spiritually living beyond their means—there is a special joy in looking into such a soul [i.e., that of Countess Rastopchina], in admiring her feelings, simple and ancient like the earth, whose rotation, charm, and power are eternally sacred, and eternally banal. O, how old and feeble are those to whom green springs, the chirp of the nightingale, and the lunar night seem old-fashioned. At least once in a while may sacred simplicity and her sister sacred banality overshadow them with their light wings." (Khodasevich, "Grafinia E. P. Rastopchina" [The Countess E. P. Rastopchina], *Articles on Russian Poetry*, p. 42.) "Pushkin" first appears in one of Khodasevich's unpublished calendars in late 1905.

[6] The concept of stylistic grafting is vital to Khodasevich's *ars poetica*. He uses the grafting metaphor to describe his own verse (see "Petersburg," *SS*, p. 123) and applies it as well to Pushkin (from whom he undoubtedly had something to learn): "Pushkin by no means sought an identification of his works [i.e., the fairy tales] with popular ones. He did not transplant but grafted: he grafted the shoot of popular work onto the tree of bookish

Still, the comparison of Pushkin to Veronese may be rich in ways other than narrowly chronological. Written in 1917 when the world of "earthly passions" here spoken of so lovingly had run amok, this passage shows how far Khodasevich had traveled from the empyreal and chthonian essences of *Youth*. As in his experience with Symbolism, Khodasevich had to first be engulfed by the tradition of Pushkin, had to learn what for him at a particular historical and personal moment were that tradition's limitations as well as its strengths, before he could naturalize it and make it his own. Pushkin, it is true, proved a more lasting source of inspiration than Bryusov. As Weidlé has remarked, "Khodasevich is linked with Pushkin as with no other Russian poet, and no other Russian poet is linked with Pushkin as is Khodasevich."[7] But also worth keeping in mind, as we examine Khodasevich's efforts to understand and apply the tradition of Pushkin, is Weidlé's counterclaim: "The existence of Pushkin's verse presupposes a cosmos, a world that is ordered, beautiful, inviolable, that same world which, like a paper envelope covered with meaningless blue, Khodasevich must pierce to make his own poetry possible."[8]

With the study of Pushkin and his epoch that Khodasevich undertook in the years following *Youth* came a new understanding of the relation between biographical and literary fact. Bryusov's bio-aesthetic genre, his willful blurring of the boundaries separating art and life, slowly yielded to Pushkin's subtle transformation of raw experience into the finished poem, his desire to keep out of sight all that was too narrowly personal or self-regarding. While Bryusov strived

---

literature, producing a plant of a completely unique third style." (Khodasevich, "Zametki o stikhakh" [Notes on Verse], *PN*, no. 1573 [11 January 1925].)

[7] V. Veidle, "Poeziia Khodasevicha" (The Poetry of Khodasevich), *SZ* 34 (1928), 454.

[8] Ibid., p. 457.

for an apotheosis of the artistic personality in language that was rhetorical and semantically imprecise, Pushkin, particularly in the 1830s, stressed the poet's human-relatedness in language that was "nakedly simple," increasingly realistic and private, yet independent of the man who was hounded by Bulgarin, debts, and the specter of his wife's infidelity. Boris Tomashevsky has said that the only biographical data having aesthetic relevance are those that contribute to the "ideal biographical legend," which the poet constructs and embeds in his poetry.[9] Khodasevich would probably have interpreted the function of biography in terms broader than Tomashevsky's, and Tomashevsky in turn would have relegated much of Khodasevich's study of the life of Pushkin to the discipline of history, particularly his tireless search for the domestic revelation—the joking note that accidentally uncovers the strained relations of Pushkin with his sisters-in-law, the jealous reaction of Pushkin's wife that dates his affair with Baroness Ficquelmont, the personal animosity of Baroness Nesselrode that provides a logical motive for the anonymous letters provoking Pushkin's duel with D'Anthès. Some admirers of Pushkin have felt that at best Khodasevich's probings are those of a zoologist blind to all save his infusoria and that at worst the discussions of the poet's gambling and love life are simply lurid and voyeurish.[10]

Yet Khodasevich grew to have deep convictions about the intimate, irreducible details of Pushkin's life, for these details seemed to him charged, capable of shedding light in several directions at once. The affair with Baroness Fic-

---

[9] Boris Tomashevsky, "Literature and Biography," in *Readings in Russian Poetics: Formalist and Structuralist Views*, ed. Ladislav Matejka and Krystyna Pomorska (Cambridge, Mass., 1971), p. 52.

[10] See Khodasevich, "A. I. Kuprinu" (To A. I. Kuprin), *PN*, no. 1251 (22 May 1924); and A. Kuprin: "V. Khodasevichu" (To V. Khodasevich), *Russkaia gazeta* (Russian Gazette), no. 10 (3 May 1924), and "Dva iubileia" (Two Anniversaries), *Russkaia gazeta*, no. 67 (13 July 1924).

quelmont, for instance, shows the biographical fact that generates the artistic fact of a lady's boudoir in "The Queen of Spades." But Khodasevich was interested in more than simple identification. He chose the stereoscopic view of a biographer-critic who focuses on both facts simultaneously with the aim of reconstructing Pushkin's psychic metabolism in the act of creation.[11] It might be said that the characters of *The Fiery Angel* have little life outside the biographical nexus generating them because Bryusov mechanically superimposes the Petrovskaya affair on an exotic setting. The key to understanding Pushkin, however, was far from simple. In his case life and art were not sacrificed in the name of something higher but, yielding neither value nor authority, were joined in a process that was organic, unsponsored. Here, in short, was the special integrity that Bryusov lacked. Khodasevich's gradual recognition of this integrity caused him to remark that Pushkin possessed "the first Russian biography in which life is organically and consciously merged with art. . . . He was the first to live his life as a poet, and only as a poet, and for that reason perished."[12] Therefore, the older Khodasevich grew, the more he became convinced that the Formalists, on the one hand, and the pure biographers (Veresaev), on the other, had lost the stereoscopic perspective—the life illuminating the art and the art illuminating the life—that alone could do justice to the dimensionality of Pushkin: "It is impossible to write a 'naked' biography of Pushkin that is not connected with the

[11] "To a certain degree [the creative process] still becomes accessible to us in those cases when we suddenly discover a point, or a series of points, simultaneously positioned on the plane of art and on the plane of life. In other words, when we are able to glimpse the intersecting line of these two planes. It is precisely this glimpsing of the original creative process, this observing of how reality becomes art and of how the experience of a man is refracted in the creation of an artist, that the study of an author's biography puts to use." (Khodasevich, "People and Books," *Voz*, no. 2802 [2 February 1933].)

[12] Khodasevich, "Pamiati Gogolia" (To the Memory of Gogol), *Stat'i*, p. 89.

history and meaning of his art just as his art is unintelligible, impossible to decode, without the biographical link. These are two things which are inextricable."[13]

As the allusion to Veronese and the Italian Renaissance suggests, the first great lesson Khodasevich gleaned from his study of Pushkin was a respect for the phenomenal world, that "blue prison" from which Bryusov had sought routes of escape.[14] By 1913 in the later poems of *The Happy Little House* Khodasevich began, though still somewhat sparingly, to include the homely details that would have been considered too "unpoetical" for *Youth*. While he said very little about his first two books of verse, leaving the case for an unequivocal genealogy cloudy, we may assume that these details make their way into the poems thanks to the study of Pushkin and to the experiences (not to be underestimated) of life, including a trip to Veronese's Venice in 1911.

The fate of the realistic detail in Russian poetry is a complex one, and Khodasevich was certainly not the first to use what Pushkin jokingly introduced into Russian parlance as the "unnecessary prosaism."[15] In the European context it may well be that the stylistic shift down from the "grandeur of generality" advocated by Johnson to the debunking details championed in the manifestos of Champfleury and Duranty is most clearly associated with the birth of realistic and naturalistic prose—the stories and novels of Pushkin, Gogol, Stendhal, and Flaubert.[16] That, after all, is what is usually meant by "prosaic." Yet strong evidence suggests as well that, at least in Russia, the prose works of the so-called Golden and Silver Ages grew out of prior developments in

---

[13] Khodasevich, "Pushkin v zhizni" (review of V. Veresaev, *Pushkin in Life* [Moscow, 1926]), *PN*, no. 2122 (13 January 1927).

[14] See Sylvester, "V. F. Xodasevič in Moscow and Petersburg," pp. 53-94.

[15] *Nenuzhnyi prozaizm* (unnecessary prosaism) comes from Pushkin's poem "Osen'" (Autumn) (1833). See Lidiia Ginzburg, *O lirike* (On Lyric Poetry) (Leningrad, 1974), p. 215.

[16] See Donald Fanger, *Dostoevsky and Romantic Realism* (Chicago, 1967), pp. 3-27.

poetry. Thus, we might argue, the concrete detail and the specific context of the Russian lyric have a line of descent that begins with the empiricism of Derzhavin in works such as "Zhizn' zvanskaia" (Life at Zvanka) (1807), takes hold under the influence of the friendly epistle and its "domestic semantics" (Tynyanov) in the first two decades of the nineteenth century, gathers depth and seriousness in the 1820s as Pushkin mixes those domestic elements (heretofore out of bounds) with the abstract elegiac tradition of Batyushkov and Zhukovsky, and becomes fully established (for the Golden Age) in the last poems of Pushkin, those marked by "naked simplicity."[17] At the same time—and logically so—that Pushkin was turning with increasing energy to the field of prose fiction, he was, in poems such as "Osen' " (Autumn) (1833), "Vnov' ia posetil" (Again I have visited) (1835), and "Iz Pindemonti" (From Pindemonte) (1836), bringing the traditional idiom of the lyric closer to prose (at least *his* prose) than ever before.

As Khodasevich would hasten to add, however, Pushkin's language in his last poems is far from "prosaic," and it is precisely his ability to house the prosaic detail under the lofty dome of his lyrical musings that most likely impressed Khodasevich and suggested a historical rightness for the path taken from Symbolism to the utter simplicity of his own later collections. The blank verse, bare idiom, even the setting of "Again I have visited"—

[17] In an article ("On Poetic Style") written in 1828 Pushkin said, "There comes a time in mature literature when minds, wearied by monotonous works of art, by the limited compass of conventional, highbrow language, turn to the fresh inventions of the people and to quaint popular speech, heretofore despised." It was in the draft of that article that he mentioned the "charm of naked simplicity." (Aleksandr Pushkin, *Complete Works* [the 'Academy' edition] [Moscow, 1937-1959], XI, 73, 344; quoted in Ginzburg, *On Lyric Poetry*, p. 222.) Khodasevich also noticed that in his last poems "Pushkin surpasses himself in the quest for ultimate simplicity [*posledniaia prostota*], relentless truthfulness, and the most resolute realism." (Khodasevich, "Devianostaia godovshchina" [Ninetieth Anniversary], *Voz*, no. 618 [10 January 1927].)

> Вот опальный домик,
> Где жил я с бедной нянею моей.
> Уже старушки нет—уж за стеною
> Не слышу я шагов ее тяжелых,
> Ни кропотливого ее дозора.[18]

> Here's the [exile's] disgraced little house
> where I lived with my poor nurse.
> The old woman is here no longer—it's true I can
> no longer hear her heavy steps behind the wall,
> her toilsome patrol.

—are echoed in "Dom" (The House) (1919-1920), one of Khodasevich's fine efforts in an elegiac mood:

> Но вот—
> Шуршат шаги. Горбатая старуха
> С большим кулем. Морщинистой рукой
> Она со стен сдирает паклю, дранки
> Выдергивает. Молча подхожу
> И помогаю ей, и мы в согласьи добром
> Работаем для времени. Темнеет,
> Из-за стены встает зеленый месяц,
> И слабый свет его, как струйка, льется
> По кафелям обрушившейся печи.[19]

> But here's
> the rustle of steps. A hunchbacked old woman
> with a large sack. With a wrinkled hand
> she strips tow from the walls, tears loose
> laths. Silently I approach
> and help her, and we in kindly consort
> work for time. Darkness gathers,
> a green moon rises from behind a wall,
> and its faint light, like a streamlet, pours
> over the tiles of a tumbledown stove.

Here, as Khodasevich seems to conjure up the ghost of Pushkin's nurse, we find the human-relatedness and "luminous

---

[18] Pushkin, *Complete Works*, III, 399.
[19] *SS*, p. 55.

sadness" (*svetlaia pechal'*)[20] that link both poets. The question is not one of mixing "high" and "low" styles: Benediktov attempted that in poems such as "Val's" (Waltz) (1841) and failed miserably. Clearly, realistic details do not *ipso facto* enrich the language of the lyric. They have to be aesthetically shaped. As Lidia Ginzburg observes: "In the late lyrics of Pushkin traditional symbolism often draws the everyday word into its sphere, as though infecting it with the poetical character [*poetichnost'*] of the surrounding environment."[21] And with this "poeticizing of the non-poetic" the concept of *stikhotvornyi prozaizm* (verse prosaism) is born: "a stylistically unmarked [*nestilevoe*] word ... signify[ing] the unpredetermined thought of the poet, the possibility of that thought intruding into any area of material and spiritual life."[22]

Just as Pushkin's later poetry largely opposes the Batyushkov-Zhukovsky school of "harmonious precision" that gave him his start,[23] so Khodasevich's later poetry opposes the Symbolist tradition followed in *Youth*. Whether this similarity was consciously cultivated by Khodasevich is difficult to say. He himself never called his verse "Pushkinian"; such a comparison would have been immodest. Moreover, as we shall see later on, the differences between the two poets are just as striking. Of course, Khodasevich was not the only modern Russian poet to have something to learn from Pushkin. To cite just two examples, domestic details play a vital role in the work of Annensky, and an intimate, conversational style is characteristic of the poetry of Akhmatova. But of all modern Russian poets, perhaps there is no one whose

[20] Khodasevich, "Grobnitsa poeta" (The Tomb of the Poet), *Volia Rossii* (The Will of Russia), 8 (1924), 85-97. *Svetlaia pechal'* (luminous sadness) comes from Pushkin's poem "Na kholmakh Gruzii lezhit nochnaia mgla" (On the hills of Georgia there lies an evening gloom) (1829).

[21] Ginzburg, *On Lyric Poetry*, p. 212.

[22] Ibid., p. 218.

[23] Aleksandr Pushkin, "Kareliia" (review of Glinka's poem *Karelia*), *Complete Works*, XI, 110. Quoted in Ginzburg, *On Lyric Poetry*, p. 27.

work makes better use of the verse prosaism and in so doing comes closer to the "naked simplicity" of Pushkin's last poems than Khodasevich.

BEYOND the bare facts we know little about Khodasevich's life from 1908-1914, but with some ingenuity a good deal can be reconstructed. One possible source, Bely's memoirs *Mezhdu dvukh revoliutsii* (Between Two Revolutions) (1934), is strongly colored by the author's desire to recast personal history in accordance with the pressures of Soviet literary life in the 1930s. Khodasevich was one of Bely's good friends during the years of the great Symbolist's rise to prominence and notoriety, when the collections of verse *Pepel* (Ashes) (1909) and *Urna* (Urn) (1909), the novel *Serebrianyi golub'* (The Silver Dove) (1909), and the articles in *Simvolizm* (Symbolism) (1910) were being written. In fact, in the summer of 1908 Khodasevich had the unique fortune to be the first to hear Bely's pathfinding theory on the deviation of rhythm from meter.[24] Later, during Bely's turbulent years in Berlin, Khodasevich may have been his closest friend. He was well aware of the mercurial character and the duality that made a personal relationship with Bely difficult, and even came to value that duality as an essential element of Bely's genius. Yet both men could be peevish and unforgiving when a matter of pride was concerned. Their final split in 1923 has had the effect of making it doubly difficult for the biographer to separate fact from fantasy in Bely's later portrait of Khodasevich. By 1934 Khodasevich was already politically untouchable; add to that a personal score to settle, and what emerges from *Between Two Revolutions* is a venomous caricature:

I shuddered at the thought of Khodasevich. Having sprung up between Bryusov and the journal *Iskusstvo* [Art], he nipped at the

---

[24] *Nekropol'*, pp. 77-79. See A. Belyi, "Opyt kharakteristiki russkogo chetyrekhstopnogo iamba" (An Attempt at Describing Russian Iambic Tetrameter), *Simvolizm* (Symbolism) (Moscow, 1910), p. 286.

heels of Bryusov, who had not appreciated him right off. Soon he turned up in Bryusov's company, then skipped away from him again. For five years he capriciously flitted around Zaytsev, Bryusov, and Sokolov, hurling his gossip from camp to camp. Making friends with all, he would make trouble for all. He lived at the Bryusovs' and spread family secrets about the fight of the parents with the son. He inspired respect with his intelligence, taste, critical acumen edged with vinegar and bile, understanding of Pushkin, and even industriousness: in all senses Khodasevich had gone far. His capricious, overwrought, self-poisoning and biting mind developed at the expense of disintegrating ethics.

Pathetic, green, sickly, his face that of a little corpse and his expression that of a green-eyed snake, he sometimes seemed to me a youth who had fled from a crypt where he had already met with maggots. Putting on a pince-nez, combing his black hair with a tiny part, covering his proud little chest with a gray jacket, he surprised us for years with his ability to bite himself and others— a quality which recalled a little scorpion in a shell.

When I arrived at [the journal] *Pereval* [The Divide], I fell right into the clutches of Khodasevich. He could amaze you with his straightforwardness, ensnare you with it, weaving together reproof with the most subtle flattery, charming you with the boldness of his self-analysis. Who would think that this was a ruse to enter

Andrey Bely in 1904, the year Khodasevich first met him.

Khodasevich as a
young man.

each person's soul? And he did enter everyone's soul, made himself
comfortable there, did his dirty work there, and then, undetected,
left again with great ease. He spoke only the "truth." The lie was
in the breath he took before he spoke, in his tone of voice. He had
the ability to distort, not in the "what" but in the "how," to slander
you with a pause—a raise of his eyebrows and a twist of his dry,
beardless little mouth. Only much later did he reveal himself to
me completely.

As would happen, he knew how, with the quiet tenderness, the
"childish" grief of a sickly little freak, to quietly cry about the
sense of honor dying in him. He loved to pretend that out of a
feeling of depression he was crawling in his own slime before the
raiments of holiness. He even became elegant when, with twinkling
eyes, a drag of his dry cigarette, and a twitch of his snake-like little
head, he would sing in a highstrung, chesty, smoke-filled voice that
he loved Pushkin because Pushkin reveled in his slime, as did
Bryusov, and he, and even . . . I—as did all the best and doomed
people.

Many powerful people forgave him much for the role he played
everyday. Physically he inspired pity as well: at one time he would
be covered with furuncules, at another he would be writhing in
pain (tuberculosis of the spine).[25]

[25] Belyi, *Between Two Revolutions*, pp. 249-250.

How close is Bely's description to the Khodasevich of those years? Any fully rounded portrait of Khodasevich would doubtless have its bright and dark areas. What Khodasevich said about Bely applies equally well to himself: "We must learn to honor and love a remarkable person with all his weaknesses and sometimes even for those very weaknesses. Such a person has no need of our embellishments. He demands from us something much more difficult—completeness of understanding."[26] Bely's description must contain a kernel of truth: Khodasevich was secretary of *The Divide*, Krechetov-Sokolov's journal, in 1906; he did wear a pince-nez, love Pushkin, suffer from furunculosis, have a bitingly sarcastic manner, and so on. Even Bely's characterization of his friend as gossipy may possess an element of truth: Khodasevich's memoirs and his studies of Pushkin suggest that he was as capable of drawing attention to a hero's clay feet as to his bust. But was this trait motivated by an Iago-like "motiveless malignancy" or by a desire to see such heroes separated from falsifying legends and returned to the historical and biographical ambiance that first produced them?

Evidence, particularly the many later articles concerned with the role of history and tradition in poetry, tells us that the answer lies with the latter. Khodasevich's post-Symbolist development was "centripetal," leading back to the real world, which his poetry celebrated for a time, and then on to a darkening skepticism and irony when the real world made celebration an impossibility. Bely, ecstatic and "centrifugal," was a Symbolist par excellence. For him the real world was primarily a point of departure. Given the artistic and biographical personalities of the two men, their paths seemed bound to collide; and when they did, Bely exclaimed, "all his life [Khodasevich] has poisoned [my] best moments, cut short [my] most noble actions, with his skepticism."[27] Memoir literature necessarily tells something of the author

---

[26] *Nekropol'*, p. 62.
[27] Ibid., p. 95. See also *Kursiv*, pp. 186-187.

and something of the other individuals whom the author remembers. Though no such literature is perfectly reliable, that which strives in a balanced and factually accurate fashion to tell less of the author and more of the others is, at least for the biographer of one of the others, more reliable. Thus, despite its liveliness, Bely's description of Khodasevich is more Gogolian profile than rounded portrait.[28] Khodasevich never lived at the Bryusovs'.[29] The likelihood that he was personally responsible for Bryusov family secrets being bruited about Moscow is minimal. Hardly is it more likely that Bely, six years older than the unknown Khodasevich and a charmer whom Bryusov had already acknowledged as a leading poet and the most interesting man in Russia, "fell into Khodasevich's clutches" at *The Divide*.[30]

The two warmest portraits in *Necropolis* belong to Jews—those of Muni (Samuil Viktorovich Kissin), with whom Khodasevich shared the artistic failures and halting growth of the Symbolist years, and of Mikhail Gershenzon, with whom Khodasevich shared a love for Pushkin. This fact may be fortuitous or it may suggest a growing awareness of heri-

[28] "Precisely as Bely had caricatured and made demonic everyone who had surrounded the heroes of his novels, so now [in his memoirs] he caricatured and presented in a totally diabolical light his former friends. His remarkable gift made its presence felt here as well: everyone emerged looking like themselves, but looking even more like the characters of *Petersburg* or *Moscow Exposed*. I have no doubt that Bely worked with the enthusiasm of a genuine artist, and with some part of his soul believed in what was emerging from under his pen. However, if the Bolsheviks had possessed more artistic sensitivity, they could have told him that just as his quasi-historical novels were in reality fantastic, for the unreal characters in them act in an unreal atmosphere, so too was his autobiography fantastic. Moreover, they could have told him that he had finally exposed himself as an incorrigible mystic, since not only had he fabricated, distorted, and turned inside out the facts together with the individuals, but had generally presented his entire life as an otherworldly battle with demons rather than as a real battle with the hirelings of capitalism." (*Nekropol'*, pp. 98-99.)

[29] See Khodasevich, "Ot polypravdy k nepravde" (From Half-Truth to Untruth), *Voz*, no. 4133 (27 May 1938).

[30] See Briusov, *Diaries, 1891-1910*, p. 122; and Maslenikov, *The Frenzied Poets*, p. 106.

tage.[31] But more obvious, it provides a good index of Khodasevich's interest before and after 1914. Khodasevich loved both friends for their honesty in matters of literary conscience and their willingness to amicably take him to task for mistakes he made at different stages of his career as a poet and critic. What was background for these stages—Symbolism and Pushkin—would become foreground in a number of poems and articles through the inspiring examples of these friends. For Khodasevich, Muni and Gershenzon seemed to personalize and domesticate larger questions of the historicity of Symbolism and Pushkin. The words that the usually reserved Khodasevich applies to his years with Muni are unique in his memoirs: "We lived in such true brotherhood, such close love, that even now it seems miraculous to me."[32]

Like Bryusov and unlike Bely, Khodasevich was skeptical of mysticism; yet unlike Bryusov and like Bely, Khodasevich possessed (though he would probably deny it) a genuine mystical streak. His relationship with Muni, which spanned the years between 1905 and 1916, provided the special circumstances wherein mystic and skeptic could meet on equal terms. With bushy eyebrows, cavernous cheeks, a pipe in his teeth, a floppy hat on his head, and a lanky frame from which long arms gesticulated forcefully, Muni must have struck quite a figure in prerevolutionary Moscow. He and Khodasevich would walk the city streets long into the night. Their friendship was cemented during these nocturnal meanderings, when the city slept, and they, "as though lovers escorting each other home several times," could not bear

[31] Gershenzon certainly had a role in Khodasevich's growing admiration for the great Hebrew poets, including Bialik. There is evidence that Khodasevich learned much from his study and translation of Bialik that could be applied to his own poetry: see Khodasevich, "Kh. N. Bialik," *Dni* (Days), no. 65 (17 January 1923). Gershenzon, as Andrey Bely remarked (*Between Two Revolutions*, pp. 286-287), thought Bialik to be Pushkin's equal. See the discussion of Gershenzon and the Hebrew poets in chapter 4 of this study, pp. 129ff.
[32] *Nekropol'*, p. 101.

to separate.[33] Regardless of the hour or circumstance, they always met at the end of an evening to talk. Both experienced the atmosphere of those years as ominous and ineluctable. Though Muni, as Khodasevich tells us, never wrote anything of lasting value, he seems to have been a failure of genius, alive with ideas and sensations that had their effect on his best friend.

One idea shared by both was that of time and space as a series of reflecting and interpenetrating surfaces. A reflecting surface, for example, becomes the primary image in "Ishchi menia" (Look for Me), Khodasevich's beautiful lyric about his dead friend, and a stereoscopic metaphor underlies *Sorrento Photographs*, his masterpiece and swan song to pre-revolutionary Russia. It should be stressed, therefore, that in these poems the imagery does not simply function *ad hoc* but traces back to mystical notions of friendship and to the timing of that friendship in the Symbolist years:

In the hot air of those years prior to the storm it was difficult to breathe; everything seemed to us to mean and signify two things at once; the outlines of objects seemed to us unstable. Reality, dispersing in one's consciousness, became *transparent [skvoznaia]*. We lived in the real world and, at the same time, in some sort of unique, obscure and complex *reflection* of that world, where everything was "that, but not that." It was as though every thing, every step, every gesture was *reflected* by prior arrangement, *projected* onto another plane, onto a near yet intangible screen. *Occurrences became apparitions.* Every event, beyond its obvious meaning, acquired a second meaning which was necessary to interpret. Such meaning did not come easily but we knew that precisely this meaning was the genuine one.[34]

Hidden in the memoirist's language, referring here to life with Muni, are the conceits of the poet. The speaker of "Look for Me" (whose voice is that of the dead Muni) exclaims "Look for me in the *transparent [skvoznoi]* spring light";[35]

[33] Ibid., p. 110.
[34] Ibid., p. 102.
[35] *SS*, p. 40.

the speaker of *Sorrento Photographs* begins with the image of a double-exposed photograph and goes on to watch the occurrences of prerevolutionary life become apparitions as they are projected onto the negative of life in exile. Khodasevich and Muni spoke in a language of hints, gestures, and shared terminology. People had trouble understanding them, for they seemed capable of communicating without resorting to the circuitry of conventional speech. As "Look for Me" suggests, they saw their souls as the ultimate extension of a reflecting surface, as a means of penetrating three dimensional time and space and communicating from beyond the grave. Muni's death in 1916 shattered—at least in this world—the mirror of their kinship and proved to be a lasting source of guilt for Khodasevich: when, in 1911, suffering from deep depression, Khodasevich had considered shooting himself, Muni had come to save him; but when, five years later, mobilized to Minsk and suffering from similar depression, Muni considered shooting himself, Khodasevich could not come to help. "He certainly recalled that event [Khodasevich's contemplation of suicide]," as Khodasevich says, "and as he died, 'what was ours' was not forgotten."[36]

Following his separation from Marina Ryndina, Khodasevich plunged headlong into the life of Moscow literary bohemia. Later on, during the years of emigration in Paris, Berlin, and other European cities, he would be drawn out into the night to *observe* the low life in bistros and *cafés chantants*, the images of a Western world in disintegration that make his last collection *Evropeiskaia noch'* (European Night) terrifying. But to this period (roughly early 1908 to mid-1911) relates his own prolonged bout, as participant rather than observer, with a life of dissipation. He drank every evening in the cafés and restaurants of Moscow, played all-night games of chemin de fer at the Circle of Art and Lit-

[36] *Nekropol'*, p. 117.

erature (the sons of Dostoevsky and Tolstoy, themselves famous gamblers, happened at times to play with him),[37] and together with Muni, seemed to live on the oneiric atmosphere of their aimless walks and the draughts of their feverish conversations. The final stage in this dissipation was an affair with Zhenya Muratova, then the wife of Khodasevich's friend Pavel Muratov, the art historian. Khodasevich met Muratova in 1910 and parted with her the summer of the following year. She appears in several poems of *The Happy Little House* as a Carmen-like enchantress. Judging by the poems, she liked to place a large black bow in her red hair in order to accentuate her gaudy desirability.[38] Muratova cultivated the role of "infernal" woman and seemed to take sadistic pleasure in tormenting her poet-slave. Khodasevich was perhaps following a path of disenchantment similar to that of Blok.[39] Trading thesis for antithesis and, as Hart Crane describes a similar groping after insight, Parsifal's Holy Grail for a wine glass, he may have derived perverse satisfaction from trampling the image of Marina Ryndina, the innocent "cousin" of *Youth*, in the image of Zhenya Muratova, the painted "tsarevna" of *The Happy Little House*. Clearly the affair was a source of humiliation and anguish, inspiring "Materi" (To Mother) (1910), the most baldly emotional— and probably the worst—poem Khodasevich ever wrote:

Мама, все я забыл! Все куда-то исчезло,
Все растерялось, пока, палимый вином,
Бродил я по улицам, пел, кричал и шатался.
Хочешь одна узнать обо мне всю правду?
Хочешь—признаюсь? Мне нужно совсем не много:
Только бы снова изведать ее поцелуи,
(Тонкие губы с полосками рыжих румян!)

---

[37] Khodasevich, "Moscow Circle of Art and Literature," p. 305.

[38] See Khodasevich, "Portret" (Portrait), *The Happy Little House* (Moscow, 1914), pp. 55-57.

[39] The Baratynskian theme of *razuverenie* (disenchantment) is central to *The Happy Little House*. See Khodasevich, "K Muze" (To the Muse), *The Happy Little House*, pp. 36-37.

Только бы снова воскликнуть: Царевна! Царевна!—
И услышать в ответ: Навсегда.[40]

Mama, I've forgotten everything! All has disappeared,
been lost, while I, on fire with wine,
roamed the streets, sang, screamed and swayed.
Want alone to hear all the truth about me?
If you want, I'll confess? I need very little:
only to taste once more her kisses—
(the thin lips lined with red rouge!)—
Only to exclaim once more, "Tsarevna, Tsarevna!"
and hear in answer, "Forever."

But Khodasevich did not live the life of a bohemian indefinitely, and the year 1911, as far as we can tell, provided the sobering events that jolted him into taking stock of himself. It is probably these events, along with the study of Pushkin, that were responsible for the shift to the more modest idiom of several of the poems written in 1912-1913. From these poems the step to the language of *Putem zerna* (Grain's Way) is small.

Khodasevich spent the summer of 1911 in Italy. From that *preskrasnoe daleko* (beautiful afar), as Gogol called it, Khodasevich must have cleared his head of the physical and mental crapulence of the last years. In Genoa and especially in Venice he became acquainted with the Renaissance art he later praised in the essay on *The Gavriliada*. Among friends who joined him there were the journalist Mikhail Osorgin, the translator and lexicographer B. A. Griftsov, the prose writer Boris Zaytsev, and Muratov.[41] All shared a passionate interest in Italy. Muratov in particular, whose detailed *Images of Italy* began to appear in 1912, was a charming in-

[40] Khodasevich, "To Mother," *The Happy Little House*, pp. 18-19.
[41] "Khodasevich traveled to Italy alone in 1911, but once there he joined the company of old Moscow friends: Muratov, Grivtsov, Osorgin, and Zaytsev. The dates of the journey are unknown. Their itinerary included a visit to Genoa and an extended sojourn in Venice." (Private letter from N. N. Berberova to Richard D. Sylvester, 18 March 1974, in Sylvester, "V. F. Xodasevič in Moscow and Petersburg," p. 266n.)

terlocutor and an inspired guide.[42] One suspects, however, that the reason Khodasevich made this first trip abroad was not only a desire to sightsee; he seems to have followed Muratov's wife there. But his stay, happily, was more important for the effect it had on his poetry. The affair burned itself out in Venice, yet the impressions left by Veronese's paintings together with the sights and smells of the Italian summer intoxicated Khodasevich as they, ironically, brought him to his senses.[43] Stored away like fine wine, the impressions would later be uncorked and savored in the two great Venetian poems of *Grain's Way*. More than any other poems written by Khodasevich, "Polden' " (Noon) and "Vstrecha" (The Encounter), with their Renaissance perspective and remarkable dimensionality, their *sfumato* overlay of poetic free flight mediated by the clean outline of physical detail, are products of the Veronese-Pushkin connection.

Having lost Zhenya Muratova and gained an admiration for the Renaissance world, Khodasevich returned to Russia to have his eyes opened by other events. Without doubt the greatest shock was the death of his mother that autumn in a freak street accident. The horse that was drawing Sophia Yakovlevna's carriage through downtown Moscow suddenly became frightened and bolted, overturning the carriage and killing Sophia Yakovlevna when her head struck a lamppost. Added misfortune followed shortly thereafter: Felitsian Ivanovich, already quite elderly and grieving over the loss of Sophia Yakovlevna, did not survive until the end of the year. These sudden deaths, coupled with the guilt over a dissolute life that Khodasevich was already showing in "To Mother," must have had a tremendous impact. No longer a son with a benign older generation separating him from the reality of death, Khodasevich was left alone with his grief and the weight of responsibility. Though we have no way of knowing

---

[42] See *Kursiv*, p. 245.

[43] See the verse fragment about parting with Muratova in *SS*, pp. 191-192.

for sure, it seems likely that it was at this moment that Khodasevich contemplated suicide. Like the young Joyce (and his character Stephen Dedalus), who was playing the literary bohemian in Paris as his mother lay dying in Dublin, Khodasevich had the impossible task of squaring his mother's death with his riotous past. To accept his failure as a son was a mighty step in his personal and artistic coming-of-age.

The last important event in 1911 was Khodasevich's meeting Georgy Chulkov's sister Anna, or as Khodasevich came to call her, Nyura. Coming after his break with Zhenya Muratova and the devastating loss of Sophia Yakovlevna, the appearance of Nyura was almost providential. Quiet and domesticated where the "tsarevna" had been flashily erotic, the new companion offered the ideal antidote to Khodasevich's despondency. Eventually they married and, despite hard years of war, hunger, and illness, lived in relative happiness and domestic tranquility until Khodasevich's emigration in 1922. It was either in late 1911 or sometime in 1912, at 49 Pyatnitskaya Street, that they first set up house. Nyura emerges from the poems of this period as a gentle soul: baking bread, embroidering, nursing her sick husband back to health.[44] Indeed, it is doubtful that Khodasevich could have survived the war years without her.[45] But particularly in 1911 she was the ballast that Khodasevich's high-strung nature needed. In turn, Khodasevich dedicated *The Happy Little House* to her and borrowed the title, with its suggestion of housewarming, hearth, and *genius loci*, from, significantly, Pushkin.[46]

---

[44] See "O, esli b v etot chas" (O, if only in that hour), "Bez slov" (Without Words), and "Khleby" (The Loaves), in *SS*, pp. 26, 59, 60. A brief portrait of Chulkova is found in Nadezhda Mandelstam, *Hope Abandoned* (New York, 1974), pp. 140-141.

[45] See Khodasevich, "Vladislav Khodasevich," *Novaia russkaia kniga* (New Russian Book), 7 (1922), 36-37.

[46] Pushkin, "Domovomu" (To the Domestic Spirit), *Complete Works*, II, 93.

Finding a happy home, at least for the time being, meant that Khodasevich could concentrate with renewed energy on his writing career. The years immediately prior to the outbreak of war were mostly years of quiet, steady growth. Between writing poems Khodasevich found time to pose for one of his niece Valentina's portraits;[47] to collaborate at the publishing house "Musaget," the newspaper *Russkie vedomosti* (Russian Gazette), and Muratov's short-lived journal *Sophia*; to provide material for Nikita Baliev's theater of mime; and to rub shoulders with the Futurists.[48] Though his reputation, next to Blok's or Bely's, was quite modest, he had, through the study of Pushkin, the trip to Italy, the experience of his mother's death, and the support of Nyura, managed to find himself as well. It would not be long now before his career took a sharp rise.

The Happy Little House was published by "Al'tsiona" in 1914. By this time Khodasevich was attracting attention, and the reviews of his second book of verse were, if not glowing, definitely encouraging. Bryusov noticed Khodasevich's mastery of technique and his ties with Pushkin, and Gumilyov pointed out the elegant composition and dancelike character of the poems.[49] Unfortunately for Khodasevich, Gumilyov's witty summation—"The poet . . . is for now only a ballet-master, but the dances he teaches are sacred ones"[50]—which was meant as praise for a poet on the verge of maturity, would be taken up by later critics of Kho-

[47] See Sylvester, ed., *Valentina Khodasevich and Olga Margolina-Khodasevich: Unpublished Letters to Nina Berberova*, pp. 15-16.

[48] See Khodasevich, "Igor' Severianin i futurizm" (Igor Severyanin and Futurism), *Russkie vedomosti* (Russian Gazette) (29 April and 1 May 1914). A brief glimpse of Khodasevich gambling with Mayakovsky, his future *bête noire*, is found in Boris Pasternak, *Safe Conduct* (New York, 1958), p. 104.

[49] V. Briusov, "Prodolzhateli" (Continuers), *Russkaia mysl'* (Russian Thought), no. 7 (1914), pp. 19-23; and Gumilev, "Articles and Notes on Russian Poetry," *Collected Works*, IV, 333-346.

[50] Gumilev, "Articles and Notes on Russian Poetry," *Collected Works*, IV, 343-344.

dasevich's poetry as apodictic proof of his chief failure—the lack of a major Blokian key.[51] But the reviewers overlooked what was most important, namely, the subtle shift that had taken place in a number of poems written in 1913.

One need not look far to find reasons for such oversight. Prima facie the book certainly contains more that links it with *Youth* than with *Grain's Way*. We find a heavy residue of early Khodasevich: bouquets of roses, romantic shepherd's pipes, daggers, elegiac moods, *ubi sunt* themes, iconographic allusions to Orpheus, an abundance of exclamation points and imperatives, and titles such as "Uvy, ditia!" (Alas, Child!). For the most part, the cosmetic tropes remain unremoved from a pathetic context.

The three sections of *The Happy Little House*—"Plennye shumy" (Captive Sounds), "Lary" (Lares), and "Zvezda nad pal'moi" (The Star over the Palm)—conclude, not insignificantly, with poems written either in 1912 or 1913. Khodasevich's poems nearly always tell the story of "where he was" psychologically at the moment of writing. To a much lesser degree, however, particularly after 1914, do they tell where he was vis-à-vis concepts of language. This is not to say that after 1914 Khodasevich's poetic idiom does not change, for there are real shifts in usage that make it impossible, for instance, to place many of the poems from *European Night* in the context of *Grain's Way*. But qualitative changes in mood, changes that enter into the overall character of each progressive book, are accompanied by relatively subtle changes in style, diction, prosodic design. From *Grain's Way* on the mixture of prosaisms and Church Slavonicisms is an established practice, though it may, and often does, change its ratio depending on Khodasevich's psychic "temperature" at the time of writing. But the framing of sections in *The Happy Little House* offers unique opportunities for

[51] See G. Ivanov, "V zashchitu Khodasevicha" (In Defense of Khodasevich), *PN*, no. 2542 (8 March 1928).

observing Khodasevich at an emotional *and* stylistic crossroads.

"Captive Sounds" ends with "Zhemannitsy bylykh godov" (Affected ones of bygone years) (1912), a poem that, following poems of quiet disenchantment—"Elegiia" (Elegy) (1908), "Ushcherb" (Loss) (1911), "Kogda pochti blagogoveino" (When almost reverently) (1913), "V tikhom serdtse" (In a quiet heart) (1908)—and poems of urgent anguish—"To Mother" (1910), "Dusha" (Soul) (1909), and "Vozvrashchenie Orfeia" (The Return of Orpheus) (1909)—confronts a convention whose hollowness the sober speaker now acknowledges:

> Жеманницы былых годов,
> Читательницы Ричардсона!
> Я посетил ваш ветхий кров,
> Взглянул с высокого балкона
>
> На дальние луга, на лес,
> И сладко было мне сознанье,
> Что мир ваш навсегда исчез,
> И с ним его очарованье.
>
> Что больше нет в саду цветов,
> В гостиной—нот на клавесине
> И вечных вздохов стариков
> О матушке—Екатерине.[52]

> Affected ones of bygone years,
> readers of Richardson!
> I visited your ancient abode
> and looked out from its high balcony
>
> at the distant meadows, the forest,
> and the realization was sweet to me
> that your world has vanished forever,
> and with it its charm.
>
> That no longer are there flowers in the garden,
> or in the drawing room music on the harpsichord

---

[52] Khodasevich, "Affected ones of bygone years," *The Happy Little House*, p. 30.

and the eternal sighs of old men
about the Empress Catherine.

These lines show us a newer, plainer point of view. Despite
some rhetorical tics, the diction and meter of "Affected ones
of bygone years" do not draw attention to themselves: one
senses that the simple iambic tetrameter is a pleasant return
to some middle ground, particularly in the wake of the highly
modulated dactyls of "To Mother."

More important, the title and movement of the poem indicate that by the time of its writing Khodasevich is no
longer satisfied with poetic poses. He is looking for some
degree of detachment ("I visited your ancient abode / and
looked out from its high balcony"), and thus, not surprisingly, in the witty cataloguing of flower gardens and drawing
rooms there is a spark of irony. The harpsichord music, the
Empress Catherine, and Richardson's sentimental novels
(which in the Russian context evoke characters such as Tatyana Larina [*Evgeny Onegin*] and Liza Muromskaya ["The
Lady Peasant"], at whom Pushkin gently pokes fun for reading *Pamela* and *Clarissa*) all belong to a former age. It is not
unlikely that Khodasevich at first viewed Marina Ryndina,
especially in the setting of Lidino, as one of the *uezdnye
baryshni* (provincial maidens) idealized by Pushkin.[53] But by
now he is capable of looking beyond (or through) that sentimental world and deflating its trappings.

The poems of "Lares," as the Latin title tells us, center
on the theme of the domestic spirits that protect the poet's
"happy little house." A playful affection for *genii loci* is not
new to Russian poetry. Batyushkov, in "Moi penaty" (My
Penates) (c. 1811-1812), an epistle to Zhukovsky and Vyazemsky, steps down for a moment from the elegiac tradition
and takes a charming look at the domestic front. But in
"Lares," as in so much else, the obvious source is Pushkin:

---

[53] See Khodasevich, "To the Muse," *The Happy Little House,* pp. 36-37.

Поместья мирного незримый покровитель,
   Тебя молю, мой добрый домовой,
Храни селенье, лес и дикий садик мой
   И скромную семьи моей обитель!
Да не вредят полям опасный хлад дождей
   И ветра позднего осенние набеги;
      Да в пору благотворны снеги
      Покроют влажный тук полей!
Останься, тайный страж, в наследственной сени,
Постигни робостью полунощного вора
      И от недружеского взора
      Счастливый домик охрани!
Ходи вокруг его заботливым дозором,
Люби мой малый сад и берег сонных вод,
      И сей укромный огород
С калиткой ветхою, с обрушенным забором!
      Люби зеленый скат холмов,
Луга, измятые моей бродящей ленью,
Прохладу лип и кленов шумный кров—
      Они знакомы вдохновенью.[54]

Invisible guardian of my peaceful estate,
   I entreat you, my kind domestic spirit,
guard my grounds, my forest and wild garden,
   and the humble dwelling of my family!
May the dangerous chill of the rains and the autumnal
   forays of the late winds not harm my fields;
      may the salutary snows cover on time
      the rich wet soil of my fields.
Remain, secret guardian, in my hereditary home,
strike with fear the midnight robber
      and guard from hostile glance
      my happy little house!
Keep around it with a careful patrol,
love my little garden and the shore of my sleepy waters,
      and this cozy kitchen-garden
with its dilapidated gate and tumbledown fence!
      Love the green slope of the hills,
the meadows, flattened by my wanderer's idleness,

---

[54] See note 46 above.

> the coolness of the lindens and the loud shelter of the
> maples—
> they have known inspiration.

Khodasevich had, as he remarked several years later, a special admiration for this poem, and that admiration might be seen to bear directly on his design in "Lares":

In this lyric, whose meaning is the blessing of peaceful, domestic, workaday life, the kindly domestic spirit, to whom the poem is addressed, and the prayerful humility of the house's inhabitant, and, finally, the estate itself, with its forest, garden, tumbledown fence, noisy maples, and green slope of its hills, are all depicted with equal attention. The task of the lyric poet, conveying his spontaneous feeling, and that of the folklorist, and that of the nature painter are all resolved separately, with utter completeness. Three different feelings, simultaneously and with equal force, are sounded in the reader. The three-tiered nature of the picture gives it a stereoscopic depth.[55]

Thus Khodasevich felt the three-tiered nature (including, most importantly, the domestic details) of Pushkin's poem to be the secret of its charm. And he was probably trying (though still with limited success) to impart a similar multi-tiered character to his poems about domestic spirits.

In a twist of the theme as it is presented in Batyushkov and Pushkin, Khodasevich gives the domestic spirits a bizarrely realized identity in "Myshi" (The Mice), the cycle of three poems that concludes "Lares." Coming, as in "Captive Sounds," on the heels of several poems—including "To the Muse" (1910), "Stansy" (Stanzas) (1908), "Poetu" (To the Poet) (1908), and "Dozhd'" (The Rain) (1908)—that mourn the passing of innocence and the loss of the "cousin," these poems—"Vorozhba" (Sorcery) (1913), "Syrniku" (To Curd Fritter) (1913), and "Molitva" (Prayer) (1913)—shift to a minor key as they assert their ties with the world of experience and with the wisdom of having outlived certain romantic ideals. Written in the important year 1913, they present a

---

[55] Khodasevich, "The Shaken Tripod," *Articles on Russian Poetry*, p. 108.

speaker who is half-whimsical, half-ironic. The Decadent speaker of *Youth* might have identified the mice that come to receive offerings of cheese every evening with the lares merely for shock value. Here in "Sorcery," as his home-loving companion (an image of Nyura) playfully stamps her foot to summon the nocturnal confidantes, the speaker introduces instead the less-than-sublime tradition of the popular charm:[56]

Догорел закат за речкой.
Загорелись три свечи.
Стань, подруженька, за печкой,
Трижды ножкой постучи.

Пусть опять на зов твой мыши
Придут вечер коротать.
Только нужно жить потише,
Не шуметь и не роптать.

Есть предел земным томленьям,
Не горюй и слез не лей.
С чистым сердцем, с умиленьем
Дорогих встречай гостей.[57]

The sunset has burned down beyond the river.
Three candles have begun to burn.
Stand, little friend, behind the stove,
stamp your foot three times.

Once again let the mice come
to while away the evening at your call.
All one needs is to live more quietly,
not to make noise and not to grumble.

There is a limit to earthly torments,
do not grieve and shed tears.
With a pure heart, with tenderness
greet our dear guests.

[56] Khodasevich affectionately called Nyura "Mysh' " (Mouse) in his letters to her. See "Pis'ma Khodasevicha V. F. Khodasevich Anne Ivanovne" (Unpublished letters of V. F. Khodasevich to Anna Ivanovna Khodasevich), archive (*fond*) no. 537, item no. 45, TsGALI (Moscow).

[57] Khodasevich, "Sorcery," *The Happy Little House*, p. 47.

"Sorcery" was by no means intended to be taken merely as
a piece of light verse. Khodasevich was feeling his way toward that ideal middle ground (his model was the poem by
Pushkin) between the homely and the sublime. But what is
immediately noticeable is the deliberate undercutting of a
former grand style with diminutives (*podruzhen'ka*—"little
friend"), folk rhymes (*trizhdy nozhkoi postuchi*—"stamp your
foot three times"), substandard stress (*prídut vécher koro-
tát'*—"come to while away the evening"), and popular
expressions (*ne goriui i slez ne lei*—"do not grieve and shed
tears"). This is certainly not the Khodasevich of "No, Youth."

The speaker calls one of the mice by name in "To Curd
Fritter," a poem whose title is hardly appropriate for a conventional poem in the odic or elegiac tradition. Refusing in
his solitude to be self-indulgent, the speaker watches the
mouse's activities and comments ironically on their meaning:

Ты не разделяешь слишком пылких бредней,
Любишь только сыр, швейцарский и простой,
Редко ходишь дальше кладовой соседней,
Учишь жизни ясной, бедной и святой.

Заведу ли речь я о Любви, о Мире—
Ты свернешь искусно на любимый путь:
О делах подпольных, о насущном сыре,—
А в окно струится голубая ртуть . . .

Друг и покровитель, честный собеседник,
Стереги мой домик до рассвета дня . . .
Дорогой учитель, мирный проповедник,
Обожатель сыра,—не оставь меня![58]

You don't share my too hot-spirited ravings,
you love only cheese, Swiss and plain,
rarely do you go beyond the neighbor's pantry,
you teach a life that's holy, poor and sane.

[58] Khodasevich, "Syrniku" (To Curd Fritter), *The Happy Little House*, pp.
49-50. The name "Syrnik," as letters to Chulkova suggest, probably refers
to Khodasevich's stepson Garik. See note 56 above.

> If I begin to speak about Love, about the World,
> you artfully turn back onto your favorite path:
> about underground affairs, about daily cheese,
> while blue quicksilver streams through the window . . .
>
> Friend and protector, honest interlocutor,
> guard my little house until the break of day . . .
> Dear teacher, peaceful preacher,
> worshipper of cheese—don't abandon me!

Simple, perhaps rhetorically still a little forced, this may be the most significant poem Khodasevich wrote before 1914. To begin with, it is not an idyllic or moody-mysterious landscape but a domestic scene, a description of living quarters that Khodasevich will return to often in later verse. Next, the speaker is a willing *observer*, ready to make statements about life based on what he sees in the industry of an otherwise insignificant creature. A similar projection of animal "values" into the world of humans will create a delicate ironic equipoise in later poems such as "Obez'iana" (The Monkey). The more modest focus is beginning to turn up the specific details of the *réalistes*—the mouse does not eat just any cheese or cheese "in general" but Swiss cheese. "Swiss" functions in the poem as (what Ginzburg calls) a "verse prosaism": that is, not a deliberately *unpoetic* word, but "a stylistically *unmarked* word . . . signify[ing] the unpredetermined thought of the poet, the possibility of that thought intruding into any area of material and spiritual life." The mouse's lesson, furthermore, is to wean his poetic friend from emotional outpourings and abstract discussions on upper case verities. And last, as in "Sorcery," the potential seriousness of the speaker's utterance is offset by the sprightliness of the mouse's activity: the "o delakh podpol'nykh, o nasushchnom syre" (about underground affairs, about daily cheese), with its Biblical allusion to daily bread, is plainly funny, and the appositional ordering of the last stanza, leading triumphantly to *obozhatel' syra* (worshipper of cheese), is not completely on the level. The play of viewpoints and the mediation of domestic details make this Khodasevich's first attempt at what he termed the "stereoscopic depth" of Pushkin's poem.

"The Star over the Palm" is the last section of *The Happy Little House*, and, composed mainly between 1911 and 1913, its poems fall rather neatly into two groups: those, such as "Portret" (Portrait) (1911), "Progulka" (Stroll) (1910), "Dosada" (Disappointment) (1911), "Uspokoenie" (Calm) (1911), and "Zavet" (Testament) (1912), unified by the presence of the sultry "tsarevna"; and those, such as "Vecher" (Evening) (1913) and "Rai" (Paradise) (1913), that accord with Khodasevich's more modest, self-deflecting mood following the break with Muratova. "Begstvo" (Flight) (1911) is transitional because it reveals a speaker that has (as had Khodasevich in the aftermath of the Muratova affair) laid down his armor and settled on the simple pleasures offered by a Derzhavinian Chloe (another realization of Anna Chulkova).

"Evening" is a poetic encapsulation of the Christmas story. The speaker first strikes a grand note with an opening allusion to Mars and pagan heavenly alliances based on strength and war and then, winding down to a disarmingly humble level, discovers an "objective correlative" to the holy family's flight in a Genoese donkey:

> Не в такой ли час, когда впервые
> Небеса синели надо всем,
> На таком же ослике Мария
> Покидала тесный Вифлеем?
>
> Топотали частые копыта,
> Отставал Иосиф, весь в пыли . . .
> Что еврейке бедной до Египта
> До чужих овец, чужой земли?
>
> Плачет мать. Дитя под черной тальмой
> Сонными губами ищет грудь,
> А вдали, вдали звезда над пальмой
> Беглецам указывает путь.[59]

[59] Khodasevich, "Evening," *The Happy Little House*, pp. 66–67.

Wasn't it at such an hour, when first the
heavens were turning blue above it all,
wasn't it on such a little donkey that Mary
abandoned crowded Bethlehem?

The quick hooves clattered,
Joseph, all dirty, lagged behind . . .
What does a poor Jewess have to do with Egypt,
with alien sheep, with an alien land?

The mother cries. Beneath her talma the child
seeks her breast with sleepy lips,
while far, far in the distance a star over a palm
shows the fugitives the way.

The poem has no "I," no self-absorption. Instead, the cy-
nosure is located in the human traits of the holy family.
Mary's view—"chto evreike bednoi do Egipta, / do chuzhikh
ovets, chuzhoi zemli" (what does a poor Jewess have to do
with Egypt, / with alien sheep, with an alien land)—is given
in the elliptical idiom of speech. Khodasevich is now operating under a new set of aesthetic principles: descriptions of
emotions are unemotional; diction is sparse and tightly knit;
momentous, even apocalyptic events are controlled by homely
details. The section gets its title from the last stanza, which
reveals the child, in a charming reversal of divine omnis-
cience, as oblivious to cosmic happenings. One of the salient
traits of Khodasevich as symbolist-becoming-ironist is the
urge to diffuse large concepts such as myth and romance in
the personal and local.

For Khodasevich, as for many other Russian poets writing
after Pushkin, the everyday detail, the "verse prosaism," was
a Gordian knot to be cut. One of Pushkin's great gifts to
Russian poetry was the return of the flesh-and-blood image
to the poet's narrow field of vision. The delicate balance of
blank verse, elegiac mood, and intimate memory in "Again
I have visited" would have been unthinkable for Batyushkov
and Zhukovsky. Pushkin had discovered in the 1830s, at a
time in his own life when everyday reality was particularly

trying and at a time (following the Decembrist Uprising) in his generation's life when youthful idealism was particularly vulnerable, the weakness of plangent formulas and the hidden resource of what was simply at hand, before the poet's eyes. And indeed, the memory of his nurse's heavy footfall, her shuffling vigilance, speaks more powerfully, yet economically, of loss than any cataloguing of abstract attributes. Thus it is this apparently simple but in fact most complex lesson more than any other that Khodasevich had assimilated and begun to put to use by 1913. If 1911 was a turning point in his biography, one that made the passionate egotism of youth no longer possible, then 1913 was an *annus mirabilis* of another sort, for passing virtually unnoticed in the new modest idiom, the mood of "playful seriousness," and the eye for detail of several poems written that year were the precise tools of a master. What had happened to Derzhavin in 1775, as he worked on two early odes, had now happened to Khodasevich:

In the life of every poet (unless he is fated to be an epigone forever) there comes a moment when, half-consciously, half by feeling (but by a feeling that is infallible) he suddenly grasps within himself a system of images, thoughts, feelings, and sounds that are unified in a way they have never been unified within anyone before. His future poetry suddenly sends him a signal. He divines that poetry, not with his mind, but rather with his heart. The moment is ineffable and thrilling, like [the moment of] conception. If it hasn't been, one cannot pretend that it has: the poet either begins with this moment, or he does not begin at all. After this moment all the future is but the growth and bearing forth of the fruit (which process demands intelligence and patience and love).[60]

[60] Khodasevich, *Derzhavin* (Paris, 1931; rpt. Munich, 1975), p. 85.

4

THE WISE SOWER: 1914-1920

> Man is bathed in the abundance of vegetative life in forest
> and steppe, in mountain and valley. . . . And this
> primordial world is also the world of the Great Round and
> the Great Mother; she is the protectress, the good mother,
> who feeds man with fruits and tubers and grains, but also
> poisons him and lets him hunger and thirst in times of
> drought, when she withdraws from living things. . . . The
> individual passes and his death is as nothing in view of
> the unchanging abundance of renascent life. But this tragic
> aspect, this expression of the predominance of the Great
> Round over what is born of it and, psychologically
> speaking, of the unconscious over the consciousness, is
> only one side, the dark earthly side, of the cosmic egg. In
> addition to its earthly half, the Great Round has also a
> heavenly half; it embodies not only a transformation
> downward to mortality and the earth, but a transformation
> upward toward immortality and the luminous heavens.
> —Erich Neumann, *The Great Mother*

Khodasevich's major period begins with the poems he wrote
from 1914 to 1920 and included in *Grain's Way* (1920), his
third collection. The agricultural metaphor that appears in
the lead poem and gives the volume its title is by now no
longer decorative or iconographic; it informs and structures
Grain's Way (and has vital ramifications for *The Heavy Lyre*
and *European Night*, the collections to follow). Moreover, it
shows Khodasevich to be a fully conscious harvester of poetic seeds sown by other poets and other traditions—most
notably, Pushkin and Symbolism. Yet Pushkin and Symbolism, as the two great sources feeding the immature collections, were set to collide in the mature verse (less frequently, as it turns out, in *Grain's Way*, more and more
frequently in *The Heavy Lyre* and *European Night*). This

collision, as Weidlé has implied, is what makes some of Khodasevich's best work possible.[1] And this same collision produces a series of speakers who are among the most ironic in modern Russian poetry. "Irony," of course, has favored status in modern critical idiom, and there is no need, in this preface to Khodasevich's major period, to quarry out a rigorous typology of irony's use in lyric form. Still, as we prepare to discuss that period, it is worth taking a closer look at what is perhaps its most distinctive quality.

To begin with, irony for Khodasevich was not simply the rhetorical ruse—the "vicious dissimulation of one's political and social powers" for the purpose of escaping responsibility[2]—employed first by Demosthenes and Theophrastus. Rather it was something much larger and thoroughgoing, something that grew to be the only genuine way of dealing with a world that gave one personal freedom at the cost of stripping one of homeland and audience at the moment when, mature and confident, one was at the height of one's poetic powers. Khodasevich's use of irony is largely, as Wayne Booth would define it, "unstable."[3] It opposes the stable weapon used by satirists from Juvenal to Swift to Tolstoy, for it does not posit an implicit moral standard against which to judge the literal meaning of an ironic statement. Reading one of Khodasevich's later lyrics does not involve "seeing through" the speaker's straw statement: there is no "stepping up" from the ground level of factitious morality to the privileged height of genuine morality hidden behind the lines. As a rule, the stable ironist has a closed-world ideology; he knows, or seems to know, what is right. Tolstoy's rendering of Nicholas I's point of view in "Hadji Murad" is ironic to be sure, but it leaves no room for ambiguity:

[1] Veidle, "The Poetry of Khodasevich," p. 457.

[2] Norman Knox, The Word 'Irony' and its Context, 1500-1755 (Durham, N.C., 1961), p. 4.

[3] Wayne Booth, A Rhetoric of Irony (Chicago, 1974), pp. 1-27 and 233-277.

Having received all the New Year congratulations he passed on to church, where God, through His servants the priests, greeted and praised Nicholas just as worldly people did; and weary as he was of these greetings and praises Nicholas duly accepted them. All this was as it should be, because the welfare and happiness of the whole world depended on him, and wearied though he was he would still not refuse the universe his assistance.[4]

It is this sort of lack of ambiguity that Roland Barthes objects to in an ironist, since the real meaning of Tolstoy's statement, once reconstructed, puts an end to further discourse. "How can the ironist," argues Barthes, "criticize one point of view or attitude for being excessively limited without asserting the completeness and truth of his own view?"[5] What the speaker in Khodasevich deflates, however, is no mare's-nest, but something vital and dear to him, part of himself, and thus the result is a proliferation, rather than a reduction, of ambiguity. "What is set against appearance is not reality but the pure negativity of unarrested irony,"[6] as Jonathan Culler describes the hermeneutical difficulty inherent in this sort of instability. "Ironism," a view that sees no system of values as systematic any longer and that generates question after question without generating answers, comes to underlie the indirection and understatement of Khodasevich's later work. Eventually everything is to be doubted, including the poetic language in which Khodasevich expresses his doubts. Barbara Herrnstein Smith remarks of the modern poetic intelligence that "we know too much and are skeptical of all we know, feel, and say. All traditions are equally viable partly because all are equally suspect. Where conviction is seen as self-delusion, and all last words are lies, the only resolution may be in the affirmation of irresolution, and conclusiveness may be seen as

---

[4] Leo Tolstoy, "Hadji Murad," in *The Great Short Works of Leo Tolstoy*, trans. Louise and Aylmer Maude (New York, 1967), p. 623.

[5] Roland Barthes, *S/Z* (Paris, 1970), p. 212, quoted in Jonathan Culler, *Structuralist Poetics* (Ithaca, 1975), p. 157.

[6] Culler, *Structuralist Poetics*, p. 158.

not only less honest but *less stable* than inconclusiveness."[7]
To doubt the artistic use of language in an era of vanishing
values is to teeter on the edge of absurdity: a position we
associate in the West with the work of a writer such as
Beckett. Beyond that doubt lies only the silence, the ultimate
absence of artistic language, that overtook Khodasevich in
the last decade of his life.

Khodasevich's sense of irony began with the view he took
of his own language. By the writing of *Grain's Way*, the
sartorial dandyism of his youth had become the linguistic
urge to say the most with the least. "Stylistically speaking,"
says D. C. Muecke, "irony is dandyism, whose first aim, as
Max Beerbohm, ironist and dandy, tells us, is 'the production
of the supreme effect through the means least extrava-
gant.' "[8] "Sophisticated" rather than "enthusiastic,"[9] content to use the tradition at hand rather than insistent on
plunging into the future without it, Khodasevich was well
aware of the dangers awaiting an "archaist" in a world of
"innovators," and yet he believed that his language was neither so archaic, nor Mayakovsky's so traditionless, as was
commonly held.[10] Shortly after the publication of *Grain's
Way* he wrote in one of his notebooks:

Even those who understand and value my verse regret the archaic
nature of its language. That is short-sighted. All the same, my verse
will become the common domain only at that time when all our
present-day language has grown profoundly old-fashioned, and the
difference between Mayakovsky and me will be obvious only to
the subtlest of philologists. I fear that by then the Russian language

[7] Barbara Herrnstein Smith, *Poetic Closure* (Chicago, 1968), pp. 240-241.

[8] D. C. Muecke, *Irony* (London, 1970), p. 45.

[9] See the distinction made between "sophisticated" and "enthusiastic"
modern poets in Robert Roth, "The Sophistication of W. H. Auden: A Sketch
in Longinian Method," *Modern Philology* 48 (1950-1951), 193-204.

[10] See, for example, the discussion of "archaists" and "innovators" in
Iurii Tynianov, "Promezhutok" (The Interval), *Russkii sovremennik* (The
Russian Contemporary) 4 (1924), 208-221. "We [contemporary readers] deliberately underrate Khodasevich because we desire to see our own modern
verse; we have a right to that" (p. 214).

will have become, like Latin, "dead" also, and I will always be "for a few." And only that if they exhume me.[11]

Thus, aside from personal skirmishes, Khodasevich had manifest artistic reasons for opposing Mayakovsky.[12] Prosodically traditional, stylistically modest and understated, their tone intimate and chamberlike, their speakers ambivalent and multivoiced, the poems of *Grain's Way* and after are radically different from anything written by Mayakovsky.

The relationship between speaker and that situation or state of affairs he is speaking to is irony's mainspring, and after 1914 this relationship in Khodasevich's verse becomes increasingly complex. A certain dramatic rhythm emerges in many later poems. Here we find it in "Pereshagni, pereskochi" (Step over, jump over) (1922):

> Перешагни, перескочи,
> Перелети, пере—что хочешь—
> Но вырвись: камнем из пращи
> Звездой, сорвавшейся в ночи . . .
> Сам затерял—теперь ищи . . .
>
>   . . .
>
> Бог знает, что себе бормочешь
> Ища пенснэ или ключи.   (*SS*, p. 90)

> Step over, jump over,
> fly over, cross—however you like—
> but break loose: like a stone from a sling,
> like a star falling in the night . . .
> you lost it yourself—now look for it . . .
>
>   . . .
>
> God knows what you mumble to yourself
> looking for the pince-nez or the keys.

[11] Khodasevich, "Iz zapisnoi knizhki" (From the Notebook), *Glagol* (The Word), 2 (1978), 118.

[12] For Khodasevich's very negative view of Mayakovsky's poetry see Khodasevich: "Dekol 'tirovannaia loshad' " (The Horse Décolleté), *Voz* (1 September 1927); and "O Maiakovskom" (On Mayakovsky), *Stat'i*, pp. 221-231.

The speaker in the poem is both an observer, what might be called an *eiron*, and a victim, what might be called an *alazon*, whose situation the *eiron* is observing. The situation is dramatic; something is happening, so we might expect the irony to turn on the actions and reactions that are taking place, not on the exfoliation of a consistent lyrical mood (as in *Youth* and much of *The Happy Little House*). This sort of poem, which is not rare in Khodasevich, is rare in the Russian lyric tradition. One has to go all the way back to I. P. Klyushnikov and the 1830s to find a close analogue:

> Опять оно, опять былое!
> Какая глупость—черт возьми!
> От жирных праздников земли
> Тянуться в небо голубое,
> На шаг подняться—и потом
> Преважно шлепнуть в грязь лицом![13]

> Here it is again, here's the past again!
> What stupidity—the hell with it!—
> From the fat holidays of the earth
> to stretch into the blue sky,
> to take a step up, and then
> with such importance to plop face first in the mud!

Klyushnikov, called "Mephistopheles" by his circle of friends and, like Khodasevich, notorious for his bilious wit, suffered from what Belinsky described as "reflection" (*refleksiia*), a quality that both poets seemed to have possessed in abundance:

In the state of reflection, the person breaks down into two persons, one of which lives and the other of which observes and judges the one living. ... Just as soon as a feeling, intention, or action arises in the person, then immediately some sort of enemy hidden within him already begins to look over the embryonic form, to analyze it, to investigate whether such a thought is correct, true, whether such

---

[13] I. P. Kliushnikov, "Elegiia" (Elegy), in *Poety kruzhka N. V. Stankevicha* (Poets of the Circle of N. V. Stankevich), ed. S. I. Mashinskii (Moscow-Leningrad, 1964), p. 496.

a feeling is authentic, whether such an intention is legitimate, and what is the purpose, and to what can it lead.[14]

The romantic dualism (the "blue sky" versus the "face first in the mud") of Klyushnikov suggests obvious kinship with the romantic irony of the Germans—that discussed by Karl Solger and Friedrich Schlegel and that used artistically by Ludwig Tieck, E.T.A. Hoffman, Heinrich Heine (whose work Khodasevich knew well), and Thomas Mann. The artist who uses romantic irony uses it with the knowledge that art "can no longer be simply naive and unreflective"; that it must be "conscious of its own contradictory, ambivalent nature"; that it must present a "constant dialectical interplay of objectivity and subjectivity, freedom and necessity, the appearance of life and the reality of art."[15] Although the psychologism of the Romantic movement (the soul's urge for the "blue sky" coupled with its awareness of bodily captivity) found its greatest practitioner in Lermontov, a writer whose talent far outstripped that of Klyushnikov, romantic irony itself, as an element of poetic discourse, was largely untapped from the late 1830s until the mature lyrics of Khodasevich. When, for example, in "Gorit zvezda, drozhit efir" (A star shines, the air trembles) (1921), the speaker plays on the notion that the world is God's creation (a creation that is vulnerable because God, the supreme ironist, can take it away) and that the poem through which he (the speaker) speaks is the creation of another god (a creation that is also vulnerable because that deity, the poet, can take it away as well), Khodasevich is using the principles of romantic irony. He has become "the fully-conscious artist whose art is the ironical presentation of the ironic position of the fully-conscious artist."[16]

[14] V. G. Belinskii, *Polnoe sobranie sochinenii* (Complete Works) (Moscow, 1953-1959), IV, 253; quoted in Mashinskii, ed., *Poets of the Circle of N. V. Stankevich*, p. 52.

[15] Muecke, *Irony*, p. 78.

[16] Ibid., p. 20.

Historically speaking, however, Khodasevich's irony is not romantic, as is Klyushnikov's, but neoromantic. That is, his *dusha* (soul), perhaps the most prevalent theme in all his poetry, is only a distant relative of Lermontov's psychic exiles; much closer relatives might be found in Blok's Beautiful Lady and Bely's Woman Clothed in the Sun, those benign and pristine matrices of love that beckon from afar until the time when one tries to possess them, by marriage or seduction, in this world.[17] Khodasevich, born too late, by nature skeptical, never sought the incarnation of his *dusha*. By definition his *dusha* was free and noncontingent, the part of his psychic makeup that, "like a full moon," was "cold and serene";[18] yet at the same time it was housed in the "blue prison" of the body. This paradox, which the Symbolists resolved, or believed they could resolve, via ecstatic transfiguration, was for Khodasevich irresolvable and thus became in time the source of his multivoiced, "reflective" speakers.

But in the typical "Step over, jump over" we find more than romantic irony or the self-regarding artist who draws attention to what his language can and cannot do. We find as well in its short, epigrammatic form irony of a "metaphysical" or "general" variety, irony that does not rest until it has plumbed its own depths:

The basis for General Irony lies in those contradictions, apparently fundamental and irresolvable, that confront men when they speculate upon such topics as the origin and purpose of the universe, the certainty of death, the eventual extinction of all life, the impenetrability of the future, the conflicts between reason, emotion, and instinct, free will and determinism, the objective and the subjective, society and the individual, the absolute and the relative, the human and the scientific. *Most of these, it may be said, are reducible to one great incongruity, the appearance of self-valued*

[17] See "Iridion," *Stat'i*, p. 102, for the connection between Psyche and the Beautiful Lady.
[18] "Dusha," *SS*, p. 70.

110

and subjectively free but temporally finite egos in a universe that seems to be utterly alien, utterly purposeless, completely deterministic, and incomprehensively vast. The universe appears to consist of two systems, which simply do not gear together. The one functions, and can only function in terms of meanings, values, rational choices, and purposes; the other seems not to be comprehensible in these terms. . . . *One has also to add that General Irony is an irony of a rather special kind, in that the ironic observer is also among the victims along with the rest of mankind. As a result there is a tendency for General Irony to be presented as much from the point of view of the involved victim (who cannot help feeling that the universe really ought not to be quite so unfair in its dealings with men) as from the point of view of the detached observer.*[19]

Muecke's formulation, presented in the abstract terms of ironology, is a remarkably accurate gloss on the later poetry of Khodasevich. The *dusha* is the "self-valued and subjectively free but temporally finite ego" that cannot—particularly after *Grain's Way*—gear itself with an "utterly alien, utterly purposeless" universe. And the striking blend of the painfully comic (or the grotesque) found in "Step over, jump over" is the result of the speaker's position being both that "of the involved victim" and that "of the detached observer." Hence the speaker can only be objective to a point when presenting the pathos of his own situation. The reader experiences the play of voices as a rhetorical tug-of-war; caught for a moment in the imperative mood, the sheer will to break away, he feels himself, like the stone in the sling, propelled by some centrifugal force. The centripetal force, however, the gravitational pull of the banal (the pince-nez and the keys), is greater, and so the wry, epigrammatic force of the last two lines is redoubled (the elastic in the sling snapping back) by what has come before. Because the victory over hope and affirmation is in some way pyrrhic, the *eiron* is denied the serenity and exultation that go with being com-

---

[19] Muecke, *Irony*, pp. 68-69. (My emphasis.)

pletely detached from the personality of the victim he is observing.[20]

What should be becoming clear by now is that the speaker-victim, or *alazon*, of the major period is not simply credulous, ignorant, or self-important (his voice that of one infatuated with his own *ore rotundo*), although traditionally he is a character, such as Falstaff, who presents himself as more than he is. He is rather that aspect of the creative personality still moved by the ideals of youth, by the heroic aspects of Symbolism, by the urge (impossible to realize) for psychic integrity. While he continues to want to "step over, jump over" the limits of this world, he is, with increasing frequency, met at those limits by his ironic alter-ego, an expert on the here and now, and by the reminder of captivity. Conversely, the *eiron*'s "centripetal" urge for what is simple, prosaic, unpretentious, and "unpoetic" may come from the lessons of Pushkinian realism and from the "living down" of Symbolism. But as mentioned earlier, the grafting of the two voices, the mark of an artistic coming of age, is something Khodasevich arrived at independently.[21]

The speaker is therefore capable within an individual poem of being either the *alazon* or the *eiron*, or (more likely) both. As Khodasevich's work develops hereafter, the *eiron* generally becomes the more visible speaker, while the *alazon* begins to recede. (The departures from this tendency, such as the famous "Ballada," are very telling, however, and suggest privileged moments during which the victim suddenly turns victor.) By *European Night* the *alazon* offers a less than genuine counterbalance, and is routinely trundled out, like stage scenery, only to be quickly collapsed. Since the later poetry is largely governed by the choice of *eiron* as controlling voice, certain features of that voice emerge to predetermine matters of style and diction.

Wit is not the least of these features. The speaker is apt

[20] See D. C. Muecke, *The Compass of Irony* (London, 1969), p. 218.
[21] See note 6 to chapter 3 above.

to draw parallels between the abstract life of the soul and the domestic existence of the body that might appear far-fetched to the traditionalist:

Пробочка над крепким йодом!
Как ты скоро перетлела!
Так вот и душа незримо
Жжет и разъедает тело.   (SS, p. 87)

Cork on strong iodine!
How soon you have corroded through!
So too does the soul invisibly
burn and eat away the body.

The simile, which compares the body to a moldering cork and the soul, conventionally sacred and pristine, but now dangerously confined, to strong iodine, strikes the reader as a modern use of the metaphysical conceit, what Johnson first described opprobriously as "heterogeneous ideas yoked by violence together."[22] To find occasion for the eternal body-soul debate in a medicine chest seems appropriate for John Donne, the most famous of the Metaphysicals. The difference, of course, between one of Donne's elaborate conceits and this ironic simile is a matter of context, since Donne might compare his and his mistress' souls to twin compasses with the purpose of showing that love, a positive concept, will always keep the compass arms acting in concert, while Khodasevich's figure is designed to deflate its abstract tenor.

Another feature of the *eiron's* voice is that of the epigram.[23] The epigrammatic speaker weighs his words, suggesting much but saying little:

Палкой щупая дорогу,
Бродит наугад слепой,

[22] Samuel Johnson, *The Lives of the Poets* (Oxford, 1933), p. 14.
[23] Khodasevich's epigrammatic quality is mentioned in V. Pozner, *Panorama de la littérature russe contemporaine* (Paris, 1929), p. 242; and O. E. Mandel'shtam, "Buria i natisk" (Storm and Stress), *Sobranie sochinenii* (Collected Works), ed. G. P. Struve and B. A. Filippov (New York, 1966), II, 345-346.

Осторожно ставит ногу
И бормочет сам с собой.
А на бельмах у слепого
Целый мир отображен:
Дом, лужок, забор, корова,
Клочья неба голубого—
Все, чего не видит он.

(*SS*, p. 126)

Feeling the road with his cane,
the blind man guesses as he goes,
puts his foot down gingerly,
and mumbles to himself.
Yet on the eyes of the blind man
an entire world is reflected:
a house, meadow, fence, and cow,
snatches of blue sky—
the sum of what he cannot see.

Everything here is pruned to an absolute minimum. There are only two adjectives in the entire poem—a far cry from the atmospheric idiom of *Youth*. All meaning turns on the striking *contre-coup* of the last line. Khodasevich is often likely to display a gift for the untranslatable *nedogovorennost'*, for speaking precisely to a point and no further, and thus one of the strongest developments in his verse after 1914 is toward the condensation of the epigram.

Closely linked with the epigram, of which word play may be part, is the pun. The paronomastic speaker is moved by the urge to say two things with one word. Traditionally a very ironic trope, the pun relies on one's ability to subtract excess verbiage, to unify and simplify expression, even as meaning is multiplied. When Khodasevich's speaker says—

С той поры люблю я, Брента,
Одинокие скитанья,
Частого дождя кропанье
Да на согнутых плечах
Плащ из мокрого брезента.
С той поры люблю я, Брента,
Прозу в жизни и стихах.

(*SS*, p. 15)

> Since then, Brenta, I have loved
> solitary wanderings,
> the steady sprinkle of rain,
> and a cloak of wet canvas
> over my stooped shoulders.
> Since then, Brenta, I have loved
> prose in life and verse.

—he is playing on the romantic tradition associated with the river that traces back to *Childe Harold* (IV, 28) and *Eugene Onegin* (I, 49).[24] This tradition, by now a cliché, is brought down to a "prosaic" level with the word *brezent* (canvas), which rhymes with the river's name, punning on its exact sound like a portmanteau word. The comparison of a source of inspiration to a wet mackintosh can only succeed in deflating the former.

In *Grain's Way* Khodasevich refines a situational irony that would have been unthinkable in *Youth* or *The Happy Little House*. Several of the blank verse narratives, including "The Monkey" and "2-go noiabria" (The Second of November), function on one level "to present ironic situations or events to our sense of irony."[25] Khodasevich's genius seems to gravitate toward the dramatic or situational—a development all the more noteworthy if one considers the atmospheric, sinuous, antidramatic verse of *Youth*. The speaker in "The Monkey" encounters a "beggarly beast" that manages, through a quaint handshake, to restore meaning to the chaos of history. "Humanity" is found where one would least expect it and the lesson learned seems a mighty triumph. Then, separated from the text, comes the bald, journalistic conclusion: "V tot den' byla ob''iavlena voina" (On that day war was declared).[26] At least formally there is a narrative voice that should help us to interpret the statement, but in reality it is as if there is not. The absence of the speaker's

[24] See Aleksandr Pushkin, *Eugene Onegin*, trans. Vladimir Nabokov (Princeton, 1975), II, 185-186.
[25] Muecke, *The Compass of Irony*, p. 92.
[26] "The Monkey," *SS*, p. 52.

115

response begs for comment and the artful juxtaposition of the monkey's lesson with the actuality of war flexes in impossible silence.

Certainly the last (but not least) element to contribute to the *eiron*'s voice is that, appropriately, of closure. According to Herrnstein Smith, "Whether spatially or temporally perceived, a [poetic] structure appears 'closed' when it is experienced as integral: coherent, complete, stable."[27] Much of what Khodasevich writes after 1914 can be understood as coherent, complete, and stable, however, only if we appreciate it as ironic. Or to put the problem another way, the reader perceives the integrity in Khodasevich's verse only when he realizes that integrity in much modern poetry is closely related to anticlosure, or the tendency to leave major questions unanswered. Although a poetic experience is naturally "gratifying to the extent that those expectations that are aroused [by it] are also fulfilled,"[28] in a sense ironic poetry is gratifying because it fulfills the need to not be ultimately fulfilled. For example, by ending "Sunday Morning" with—

> Deer walk upon our mountains and the quail
> whistle about us their spontaneous cries;
> Sweet berries ripen in the wilderness;
> And, in the isolation of the sky,
> At evening, casual flocks of pigeons make
> Ambiguous undulations as they sink
> Downward to darkness, on extended wings.

—Wallace Stevens feels it necessary to first tease us with images of fructifying nature, then end with the image of "casual" pigeons that, undulating "ambiguously," descend into darkness. This is, it seems, the converse of the *torzhestvennyi pod"em* (solemn ascent) that Blok uses at the conclusion of *The Twelve*. Khodasevich's speaker also tends

[27] Smith, *Poetic Closure*, p. 2.
[28] Ibid., p. 3.

to "end" discourse not with a bang, but a whimper—the ironic *volte-face* at the end of "Step over, jump over" or the tantalizing question at the end of *Sorrento Photographs*.

THE YEARS 1914-1920, which witnessed the beginning of the First World War and the end of the Revolution, were the most physically trying years that Khodasevich was to live through. This seems a fact of considerable importance because it shows that, kept within the limits of human tolerance, the physical demands made on Khodasevich by everyday life were not a major factor in, perhaps indeed had very little to do with, his psychic health. That is not to say that the impossible living conditions in revolutionary Moscow did not greatly affect Khodasevich, as they certainly did nearly everyone else, for to be sure, it was largely those conditions, including the housing of Khodasevich, Nyura, and Nyura's son Garik in a leaky, unheated (5° Centigrade during the winter months), one-room basement flat on 7 Rostovsky Lane, that drove the family to Petersburg in November 1920. But the clearest index of Khodasevich's mood at this time is the poems he wrote then—they tell best how the poet's artistic self was able to grow (at times even thrive) in the face of adversity. Several of the most philosophically luminous and thematically far-ranging poems that Khodasevich ever wrote—"Noon," "The Encounter," "The Monkey," and "The House"—were composed during the last three years in Moscow. *Grain's Way* is Khodasevich's "ripest" Moscow collection, and its final poems, which seem positioned where they are to underscore the all-important agricultural metaphor and the "harvesting" of a wisdom that affirms historical and biographical process, reveal a poet in touch with his place of birth, in firm possession of a homeland and an artistic heritage. What these poems suggest has recently been corroborated by Khodasevich's correspondence with the poet Boris Sadovskoy: like Blok and Bely, Khodasevich accepted the Revolution, but on his own unorthodox terms.[29] If he later came to speak of the Bolshevik regime with bitterness, it was not because he was opposed on principle to revolutionary change but because the hopes placed on a coup "from below" were never realized. In a real sense, therefore, Khodasevich had to leave Moscow to survive. In Petersburg the living conditions were more tolerable and, perhaps no less important, the artistic freedom was greater. Yet Khodasevich's uprooting, begun in Petersburg and completed in various European cities, was to leave the sower of *Grain's Way* eventually disenfranchised.

Khodasevich and his family spent the summer of 1914 in Tomilino, a little town southeast of Moscow. The summer was, as presented a few years later in the opening lines of "The Monkey," an extended hot spell over which a thunderstorm was sooner or later to break:

> Была жара. Леса горели. Нудно
> Тянулось время. На соседней даче
> Кричал петух.   (*SS*, p. 50)

---

[29] Khodasevich wrote to the reactionary Sadovskoy in a letter dated 3 April 1919: "You are in agreement that it is necessary to reform life. Before our time that reforming process [*perestroika*], from Peter to Witte, proceeded from above. The Bolsheviks have stood history on its head: what was at the top turned out to be at the very bottom: the basement became the attic, and the reforming process once again proceeded from above: the dictatorship of the proletariat. If neither the dictatorship of the landowners nor the dictatorship of the workers appeals to you, then, excuse me, what would you like? Could it really be the dictatorship of the *bel-étage*? It causes me to vomit and spew forth bile. I understand the working man; I can somehow understand the nobleman, the idler by the grace of God; but I'll never be able to understand the bastard [industrialist] Ryabushinsky, the idler by the grace of his own brazenness. . . . I would understand you if you were dreaming about restoration. Now you understand me, who in the end is loyal to the Soviets. I won't join the Communists now because it is advantageous and thus base, but I won't guarantee that I won't join if it becomes risky." (Robert P. Hughes and John E. Malmstad, eds., "Towards an Edition of the Collected Works of Vladislav Xodasevič," *Slavica Hierosolymitana*, 5-6 [1981], 488.)

> It was hot. The forests were ablaze. Time
> wore on tediously. A cock crowed
> at the neighboring *dacha*.

Not the darkly beautiful "cock-crowing" night of Mandel-shtam's "Tristia," this seemed the breathless diurnal fore-boding before the news ushered in by the last line of the poem—"It was on that day that war was declared."

Perhaps it is not surprising that in the midst of this fore-boding Khodasevich was working on Pushkin, working his way deeper into that poet's tradition as events that he would view as the formal closing to that tradition were working their way closer to the surface.[30] His painstaking study of Pushkin's work was not a retreat to Axel's castle; it was, thought Khodasevich, the best way to place current chaos in some discursive order. In 1914 the idea first came to him to study the *samopovtoreniia*—"repetition of one's own" words, phrases, verses—that reappear throughout Pushkin's work (mainly the verse). This patient sleuthing led ten years later to *Poeticheskoe khoziaistvo Pushkina* (*Pushkin's Poetic Economy*), a book whose epigraph Khodasevich took from his beloved teacher, the great Pushkinist and literary historian Mikhail Gershenzon: "In difficult days I know of no greater joy than to read Pushkin and to make little dis-coveries about him."[31] Quite by chance the little discovery about Pushkin that Khodasevich was making that summer (on the verge of difficult days) was to become the link that forged the friendship with Gershenzon a year later: the ar-ticle on Pushkin's "Petersburg tales" (*The Bronze Horse-man*, "The Queen of Spades," *The Little House in Kolomna*) that he was finishing up for Muratov's *Sophia* was not des-tined to appear in the short-lived journal's pages, and when

[30] See Khodasevich, "The Shaken Tripod," pp. 107-121.
[31] See N. N. Berberova, ed., "Pis'ma M. O. Gershenzona k V. F. Khoda-sevichu" (The Letters of M. O. Gershenzon to V. F. Khodasevich), *Novyi zhurnal* (New Review), 60 (June 1960), 229.

he later sent it on, with some apprehension, to the renowned Gershenzon, the latter read the elegant analysis (its rigorous ferreting out of thematic and structural parallels was worthy of the Formalists, Khodasevich's subsequent archrivals) with genuine enthusiasm.

With the onset of war, Khodasevich had to face what seems in retrospect a series of annual tests of will. After an excursion in July 1915 to Finland and the Pushkin landmark Tsarskoe Selo, he returned to Moscow (Nyura had not made the trip) and found a new apartment for the three of them at 7 Rostovsky Lane. Back problems began that autumn when Khodasevich slipped and wrenched his spine at the poet Lyubov Stolitsa's name-day party. By spring 1916 he had come down with tuberculosis of the spine, the cure for which was to be corsetted in plaster, set in traction, and sent to the Crimea for three months to recuperate. It was at the same time (28 March), unfortunately, that Muni shot himself. After the loss of Muni (from which Khodasevich would never completely recover), the summer in Koktebel seems to have been the best medicine, however. Judging by a letter (18 July 1916) to his friend Boris Diatroptov, Khodasevich enjoyed the local color, put on playful airs, and—after first remaining aloof—made quite a circle of friends from among those at Maximilian Voloshin's *dacha*:

I am living well (a government secret [kept] from even my friends), and for now corset-less. Why is boring to say. I eat, drink, sleep. Outside of that nothing, save the pursuit of fame. I have never before been renowned to such a degree. My comings and goings are reported in the Simferopol newspaper (which serves Feodosia as well). Girls make up to me. Boys point at me. Wherever I go "versemaker" can be heard behind my back. I read at a poetry recital [*kontsert*] on the sixteenth. Today I'll send this letter from Feodosia, since at five a car is coming for me (I sent back the motorboat). I'm going to read at the Feodosia recital. It's being arranged here by the military and civilian authorities. And on the twenty-fourth the girl students are begging me to read for their benefit. I'm beginning to resemble Plevitskaya. It's not all for naught. I have made several acquaintances who could turn out to be very helpful if only the Feodosians aren't cunning deceivers.[32]

The letter goes on to catalogue irreverently and uproariously the various hosts, guests, and hangers-on at the artists' colony, including a preening, cigarette-cadging young Mandelshtam (who a few years later was to live down the hall from Khodasevich at the Petersburg House of Arts) and the "mystical epicure" Voloshin himself.

The trials ushered in by the October Revolution could be trivial as well as profound. The endless busywork, the waste of time and manpower occasioned by the inane *perpetuum mobile* of the new state's bureaucracy is the subject of wry humor in Khodasevich's memoirs and autobiographical

[32] J. E. Malmstad and G. S. Smith, eds., "Eight Letters of V. F. Khodasevich (1916-1925)," *Slavic and East European Review* 57 (January 1979), 74. N. V. Plevitskaya (Vinnikova) (1884-1941?), a stage performer of Russian folk songs who toured Russia from 1909 to 1917 and emigrated after the Revolution, was at the height of her popularity at the time Khodasevich wrote this letter. From 1 June to 7 August 1916 Khodasevich sent a total of twenty-seven letters and twenty postcards home to Anna Chulkova from Koktebel and the surrounding area; from 30 May to 24 June 1917, again vacationing in Koktebel, Khodasevich sent nine letters and eight postcards home to Chulkova. These letters are steeped in domestic concerns—the difficulties of obtaining, sending, and receiving money; the trials of wearing the corset and the fear that without it he would be drafted; the nourishing diet and the lazy routine of the beach resort—and show relatively little of Khodasevich the poet. In general, Khodasevich's correspondence tends to be of a personal rather than of a professional "literary" nature. As a poet, Khodasevich rarely included his views of art in letters that were intended to be "half public," earmarked for later generations of scholars. Still, these letters to Chulkova are interesting documents in themselves, providing both intimate looks at Khodasevich and passing (often hilariously sarcastic) sketches of Mandelshtam, Voloshin, Sergey Efron, Tsvetaeva, and others. As we can see from the letter to Diatroptov, Khodasevich was spending at least some of his time in Koktebel rather merrily. In the letters to Chulkova, however, presumably because he does not want his wife to think he is enjoying himself while she does drudgery in Moscow, Khodasevich insists repeatedly that he is bored with the people and the surroundings of Koktebel and is waiting impatiently for the end of his health cure. See "Unpublished letters of V. F. Khodasevich to Anna Ivanovna Khodasevich," item nos. 45 and 46, TsGALI.

sketches. From early 1918 until November 1920 Khodasevich tried his hand at a number of ill-fated positions. Unlike Tyutchev, with his delusions of grandeur about his role
as civil servant, Khodasevich was only pained and annoyed
by the mountains of futile paper work. He later recalled his
reason for undertaking clerical work:

Toward the end of 1917 I was possessed by an idea which I subsequently renounced but which now once again seems correct to
me. The original instinct did not deceive me: I was completely
convinced that literary activity under the Bolsheviks was impossible. Having decided to stop publishing and to write instead only
for myself, I conceived the idea of entering the Soviet service.[33]

His first position, that of secretary to the courts of arbitration, was comically short-lived. One day Khodasevich was
called in by his boss, V. P. Nogin—"an entirely respectable,
shaggy red-haired middle-aged man in spectacles."[34] Head of
the Commissariat of Labor, Nogin seemed suddenly to be
inspired by the idea that the Workers' State needed a code
of laws governing labor. He proposed that Khodasevich drop
his work at the courts of arbitration and use his way with
words to compile the new labor code. "It was difficult for
me not to smile. So it had turned out that the world proletariat, though for the time being in a 'transitional period,'
had still won in order that I, ultimately, might give it its
laws. 'Why all the struggle?' I thought."[35] The "unacknowl-
edged legislator's" departure from government service seemed
Khlestakovian:

Having for several days fussed over a heap of papers, resolutions,
decrees, and decrees, and directives, and having gathered from conversations
with Nogin that I had nowhere from which to expect explanations,
instructions, or missing materials, I sent in my resignation. It was
accepted. Then I simply stopped going to the Commissariat. The
decision "ripened" one morning. I got out of bed, drank some tea,

[33] "Zakonadatel' " (Legislator), *Stat'i*, p. 315.
[34] Ibid., p. 321.
[35] Ibid.

and suddenly realized that I couldn't go to the office. To such a degree was I unable to go that there was not even strength enough to stop by for my briefcase, which was left in my desk drawer. It was a splendid briefcase of light brown leather, with magnificent buckles.[36]

In late September 1918 Khodasevich was asked to read a course on Pushkin at the Moscow workshop of Proletkult (Proletarian Cultural and Educational Organization). Among others asked to lecture were the poet Nadezhda Pavlovich (a friend of Blok's and Khodasevich's) and Andrey Bely, who had agreed to give a course on rhythm. The proletarian students who enrolled were led by Gerasimov and Kazin, future members of the Smithy group. Within a few years Khodasevich would be pilloried in the Soviet press as "a permanent counterrevolutionary [lit: *chernosotenets*—member of the Black Hundreds] and herald of autocracy."[37] But in 1918 his status vis-à-vis the Soviet regime—both from his point of view and from the point of view of the regime—was not totally clear. Without doubt he was alarmed by the already perceptible drift in matters of literary conscience toward tendentiousness, denouncement, repression. He had not, however, burned his bridges. Though skeptical of the possibility of "proletarian" art, he was not cynical about the students themselves; quite the contrary, he was rather touched and impressed by their enthusiasm and dedication: "I can attest a number of wonderful qualities [characterizing] the Russian working man's audience—first and foremost, its genuine quest for knowledge and its intellectual honesty."[38] But, unfortunately, the attendance at Khodasevich's and Bely's lectures was so high and the attendance at the partyline colleagues' lectures was so low that the leadership at Proletkult felt compelled to wage administrative war against

[36] Ibid., pp. 321-322.
[37] See Khodasevich, "Pro domo sua," *Dni* (Days), no. 854 (15 November 1925).
[38] "Proletkul't," *Stat'i*, p. 326.

the "counterrevolutionary" forces of the "bourgeois specialists."[39] To the utter confusion of Khodasevich and his students, the course format was capriciously altered from lecture style to seminar style, then back to lecture style again. Constant shuffling of students gave Khodasevich an impossible mix of levels with which to work. When it appeared that the proletarian students were beginning to learn something from Pushkin's poetic technique (the original desideratum), Khodasevich was instructed to speak on Pushkin's biography. The final blow came that spring (1919) when lectures were cancelled altogether and the students were ordered to the front.

Khodasevich also tried work at Teo, the Theatrical Department of the People's Commissariat of Education (Narkompros). It was at Teo that a number of Moscow writers, including Balmont, Bryusov, Baltrushaytis, Vyacheslav Ivanov, Pasternak, and Khodasevich, eked out a living during the Revolution. Teo was run by Olga Kameneva, the sister of Trotsky and the wife of the powerful Lev Kamenev, one of Lenin's closest associates. By Khodasevich's account she seems to have been a conniving woman of limited intellect, "an impersonal being, half dentist and half midwife."[40] At this time she was vying with Gorky's second wife, M. F. Andreeva, for the position of "first lady" of Soviet culture. Having no artistic sensibility, she substituted vacuous form for substance, peripatetic committee work for real decision making. Her "leadership" set the tone for work at Teo:

People primarily sat in meetings but it is likely that no two meetings had the same staffing. For this reason, no question was posed precisely and no matter of business was pursued to its conclusion. By the way, nobody had any idea what to do. People spoke primarily "for the agenda" and were permanently "getting organized," though to what end it was unknown.[41]

[39] Ibid.
[40] "Belyi koridor" (The White Corridor), Stat'i, p. 347.
[41] Ibid.

124

The repertory section in which Khodasevich sat was chaired by Yurgis Baltrushaytis. It was charged with selecting plays to be performed that season and with deciding which new plays were worthy of publication (ironically, most of Moscow's presses had stopped printing and there was a shortage of paper). The section members' urge to preserve some semblance of a classical repertory was continually stalemated by the Communists' urge to introduce a "revolutionary" repertory. Citing their proletarian origins, invoking the name of Lenin, a motley multitude of self-taught or simply self-proclaimed playwrights came to argue their cases before the section. In 1918 such half-baked dramatists were least of all concerned with a play's artistic merits—one submission, for example, was a marathon tragedy in twenty-eight acts. Through it all what Khodasevich chafed at most was "the consciousness of lying": "By our very presence at Teo and by our conversations about art with Kameneva we were already lying and pretending."[42]

In his article about the "White Corridor," the Kremlin inner sanctum where the Kamenevs, the Lunacharskys, and Demyan Bedny lived, Khodasevich describes in withering satire the Bolsheviks' cozy nest of warmth and satiety in the dark expanse of chilled and starving Moscow. He visited the White Corridor three times: twice during his tenure at Teo; once after he had left his position there. All three visits could only be called failures or disappointments. During the first, Gershenzon, Baltrushaytis, Bely, Pasternak, Georgy Chulkov, and Khodasevich gained an audience with Anatoly Lunacharsky in hopes of improving the lot of beleaguered Moscow writers, but what they heard was self-importance, blandishment, lukewarm liberalism, and assurance that "the people's government wishes [you] every success, but asks [you] not to forget that when a forest is cut, the chips fly."[43] During the second, the repertory section at Teo, having ar-

[42] Ibid., p. 348.
[43] Ibid., p. 351.

rived at the Kamenevs' for a supererogatory meeting to discuss "two Irish plays," were forced to listen to Lunacharsky
read the new dramas of Bolshevik favorite and alcoholic hack
Ivan Rukavishnikov. And during the third, Khodasevich came
alone to Kamenev to ask for help in finding a new apartment
only to have first his request glibly shunted aside and then
(after Kamenev's departure) his brief respite from the cold
interrupted by Kameneva's leading questions about the political reliability of friends. The grotesque irony caught in
Khodasevich's feuilleton is that Lunacharsky and Kameneva, though all-powerful, still needed the approval of cultural figures whose work the new state (and they—even if
moderating forces—by association with that state) had already begun to denounce. These revolutionaries were pris-
oners of prerevolutionary tastes in art. Even Lenin could not
fail to gush about Beethoven's *Appassionata*: "I could listen
to it every day. Amazing, superhuman music. I always think
with pride, naively perhaps, what miracles man can work.
. . . But I can't listen to music often, it affects my nerves,
makes me want to say silly compliments, stroke people on
the head for living in this filthy hell and creating such
beauty."[44] The Kamenevs' book shelves were lined with rare
editions of Decadent and Symbolist works, and it was obvious that Kameneva had aspirations of being a sort of Bolshevik Anna Schérer—the witty hostess of a salon on the
White Corridor. Rukavishnikov's plays were a disastrous
mélange of Balmont, Leonid Andreev, and Maeterlinck. And
Lunacharsky apparently spent hours rehearsing his dramatic
reading of Rukavishnikov. "Lunacharsky is long since dead,"
said Khodasevich years later, "and now it's somehow awkward to recall his long, sonorous, languid meowing in rou-
lades. But at the time it was unbearably funny to watch the
Minister of Public Education meowing with such artistic

[44] M. Gor'kii, *Sobranie sochinenii* (Collected Works) (Moscow, 1949-1955),
XVII, 39-40. Quoted in Boris Thompson, *Lot's Wife and the Venus of Milo*
(Cambridge, England, 1978), p. 63.

abandon. And the main thing was it was impossible to get free of the funny thought that he had, perhaps together with the author, rehearsed the meowing."[45]

Khodasevich's last two positions in Moscow were held simultaneously: he was the head of the Moscow office of "Vsemirnaia literatura" (World Literature), Gorky's Petersburg-based publishing house (from late 1918 through the summer of 1920), and the head of the "Moskovskaia Knizhnaia Palata" (Moscow Book Chamber) (from late 1919 through the spring of 1920). Like the jobs before them, these were the sort of tedious stopgaps that saved the artistic community from starvation (though not by much). Khodasevich has little to say about the work at World Literature; Gorky hoped that mass printings of world literature classics translated into Russian would catch on, but the low rate of payment for translations, coupled with the sharp rise in the rate of inflation, made it difficult for Khodasevich to secure new translations. The dark role of de facto censor attributed to Bryusov, who preceded Khodasevich as head of what became the Moscow Book Chamber, had luckily been legislated out of the position by the time Khodasevich took over. Now the task at the Book Chamber was simply to register all new publications and see that requisite copies were sent to various repositories.

However haltingly, these jobs carried Khodasevich through the early months of 1920. But the delicate status quo took a turn for the worse that spring. Khodasevich came down with furunculosis. Rivulets of melting snow seeped through the windows of the apartment as Nyura repeatedly treated and dressed the hundred and twenty-one open sores on her husband's body. Recovery was slow and tormentingly painful. Gershenzon arranged for Khodasevich to spend the summer in a Moscow sanatorium "for exhausted workers of mental labor."[46] (It was during Khodasevich's stay there that Ger-

---

[45] "The White Corridor," p. 360.
[46] "Zdravnitsa" (The Sanatorium), *Stat'i*, p. 378.

shenzon and Vyacheslav Ivanov, roommates living nearby, wrote their famous *Correspondence from Two Corners*.)[47] In the fall, still suffering from sores that had not healed completely and from recurring pain in his spine, Khodasevich (age thirty-four) was declared fit for military duty. The case was reconsidered, and Khodasevich released from duty, only through the good offices of Gorky, who personally took Khodasevich's letter (addressee: Lenin) to the Kremlin. Convinced by Gorky that the situation in Petersburg was considerably better, Khodasevich, at the end of his rope, agreed to make the move.[48] On the eve of his departure all of his and Nyura's belongings were stolen from their apartment.

One wonders how Khodasevich, against the background of such mounting difficulties, wrote poetry, particularly the poetry of *Grain's Way*. But these years held major triumphs as well. Perhaps the greatest personal triumph was Khodasevich's friendship with Gershenzon. That the first meeting with the "simple, serious, yet serene" Gershenzon took place in fall 1915,[49] with *Grain's Way* just begun, and had as its pretext the article on Pushkin's Petersburg tales seems a richly fitting footnote to the development of Khodasevich's artistic views after 1914. Just as years earlier Khodasevich had been initiated into the abstract essences of Symbolism through Bryusov's public lecture at the Circle of Art and

[47] See ibid., pp. 378-379.

[48] As Khodasevich wrote the Pushkinist P. E. Shchyogolev on 3 October 1920: "Circumstances of various sorts, both day-to-day and psychological, are driving me from Moscow. Gorky is promising me all manner of worldly blessings in Petersburg. That's fine, but blessings from heaven he won't be able to offer, and without them it's difficult. . . . What do you think, could there be found work for me in Petersburg that is historico-literary, of the most academic, the most painstaking variety? That is precisely what I have been dreaming about seriously taking up for a long time now, and that is the only thing that can 'amidst worldly grief soothe' [a line from Pushkin's tragedy *Boris Godunov*] me" ("Pis'mo Khodasevicha V. F. Shchegolevu P. E." [Unpublished letter of V. F. Khodasevich to P. E. Shchegolev dated 3 October 1920], archive [*fond*] no. 28, item no. 418, Gorky Institute of World Literature [IMLI] [Moscow]).

[49] *Nekropol'*, p. 148.

Mikhail Gershenzon with his children in 1914, the year
before Khodasevich first met him.

Literature, so now, in the privacy of Gershenzon's study, he
was initiated into the Pushkinist's intimate, domestic cau-
serie on his favorite subject. Gershenzon's family occupied
the second floor of a house on 13 Nikolsky Lane; Gershenzon's study was located a floor higher in the attic. When
Khodasevich came to visit the charming Jewish sage, he
must have had a feeling not unlike that of one rising to
survey the philosopher Empedocles' perch on Etna.

Muni, Khodasevich's closest friend during the Symbolist
years, had been called up for duty in the early days of the
war, and Khodasevich saw him quite infrequently now. Yet
following the self-inflicted deaths of Symbolist friends Vik-

tor Gofman and Nadya Lvova, Muni's suicide in March 1916 was one of the most significant events in Khodasevich's life. It seemed to ritualize grimly what had been in preparation for several years—the end of Symbolism as the guiding ethos in Khodasevich's life and art. As we would expect, Khodasevich saw the death as a profound personal loss above all; there is no evidence to suggest that he connected the loss of his friend with the formal closing on his Symbolist years. Such a linkage would have been an abstract, insincere, self-dramatized response to real suffering. Instead his response was eloquently *sotto voce*: the writing of the beautiful "Look for Me" and the dedicating of *Grain's Way* to the memory of his friend.

And yet, although it would be a great mistake to make light of Muni's death, it seems almost prophetic that Khodasevich's friendship with Gershenzon was begun on the eve of that death. What Gershenzon came to represent for Khodasevich—wisdom, simplicity, inventiveness, tradition, honesty, selflessness, curiosity, serenity, liveliness, love of Pushkin—was the essence of psychic health, something altogether different from what Muni, with his penumbral reflections of other worlds and his psychic tensions bordering on hysteria, had represented. And though no simple identity exhausts the meaning of the poems in *Grain's Way*, the wisdom of that collection is in many ways the wisdom learned from Gershenzon and, not surprisingly, the wisdom learned by Gershenzon (who published *The Wisdom of Pushkin* in 1919) from Pushkin. To be sure, Khodasevich loved Muni no less than Gershenzon, and in terms of sheer psychic kinship he may have loved Muni more, but he loved Gershenzon with a love that anticipated needs, personal and artistic, at a particular moment in his life. Generally one to eschew hagiography, Khodasevich had higher praise for Gershenzon the man than for anyone else in *Necropolis*:

Those who lived through the most difficult years in Moscow—1916-18—will never forget what a good comrade Gershenzon was. . . . Not only in public but in private affairs Gershenzon knew how and liked to be a helping hand. . . . He knew how to guess another's misfortune, and he would rush—not simply with words but with deeds—to help. I can say regarding myself that had it not been for Gershenzon it would have been bad for me in 1916-18, when I was gravely ill. Gershenzon got work and money for me; Gershenzon, and nobody else, looked after my affairs when I left for the Crimea [Koktebel]. And as for spiritual support, it goes without saying [he did much]. But all this was done with amazing simplicity, without any posing or sentimentality. His concern and sensitivity were almost miraculous.[50]

Khodasevich loved everything about Gershenzon's uniquely winsome personality, from his nearsightedness and inability to orient himself on the street (he preferred to philosophize rather than to watch for traffic or landmarks), to his domestic economy in hard times (he devised a way to use cigarette paper twice), to his passion for historicity ("he 'felt' the dead as though they were living").[51] Like B. L. Modzalevsky, M. A. Tsyavlovsky, N. O. Lerner, S. A. Vengerov, P. E. Shchyogolev, and other Pushkinists of his generation, Gershenzon knew Pushkin, as the saying goes, better than Pushkin himself. The method used by Khodasevich in many later articles on Pushkin was honed on the "intuitive" scholarly rigor practiced by Gershenzon:

[50] Gershenzon's disinterested concern for Khodasevich can be seen in a letter he wrote to his friend recuperating in Koktebel: "I was very glad to learn that you are settled in well and are on the mend. I approve of your way of life; loaf about as long as your resolution holds out; don't hurry to take up the translation. And, therefore, as you will soon grow very bored without work, in order that you not be bored, but quite the opposite, get together with Max. Voloshin and his circle. He is a very fine and interesting man. . . . Forgive all the advice, it is dictated by sincere concern. . . . Well, stay healthy. Write again. Weigh yourself to see how much weight you've put on" ("Pis'mo Gershenzona M. O. Khodasevichu V. F." [Unpublished letter of M. O. Gershenzon to V. F. Khodasevich dated 16 June 1916], archive [fond] no. 537, item no. 61, TsGALI).

[51] Nekropol', p. 156.

CHAPTER 4

Gershenzon introduced into his historico-literary studies not only a creative, but even an intuitive principle. As it seems to me, the study of facts presented itself to him more as a means *for checking hunches* than as a means of obtaining material for [making] conclusions. More than once this method led to errors. His *The Wisdom of Pushkin* turned out largely to be "the wisdom of Gershenzon." But, in the first place, this was wisdom nonetheless, and, in the second place, that which Gershenzon guessed correctly could have been guessed only by him and only by his method. In a certain sense Gershenzon's errors are more valuable and profound than many truths. . . . But, to be sure, we also had dialogues such as the following:
I: "Mikhail Osipovich, it seems to me that you're mistaken. That's not right."
Gershenzon: "But I know that that's right."
I: "Yes but after all Pushkin himself. . . ."
Gershenzon: "And what of Pushkin himself? Perhaps I know more about him than he himself. I know what he wanted to say and what he wanted to hide, and what's more, I know what he was uttering when, Pythic-like, he himself did not understand."[52]

The Pushkinist Khodasevich's frequent brilliant discoveries and his less frequent, though no less brilliant errors (the hypothesis, for instance, that *Rusalka* [The Water Nymph] was Pushkin's artistic working-out of guilt that arose when a peasant girl on his estate drowned herself after he had seduced her) seem direct descendants of Gershenzon's "wisdom"—his flair for hunch-making coupled with his precise recall of, and buoyantly laboring affection for, everything having to do with Pushkin and his time. Khodasevich viewed the older man as his sternest judge; the true test of a new idea was whether it convinced Gershenzon.[53] Not by chance, then, the darkest moment in *Grain's Way* takes place in "The Second of November," one of the blank verse narratives, when the speaker, after visiting friends (in reality the Gershenzons[54]) and experiencing two epiphanies in the streets,

[52] Ibid., p. 155.
[53] See Berberova, ed., "Letters of Gershenzon to Khodasevich," pp. 230-231.
[54] See *Nekropol'*, pp. 141-143; and *SS*, p. 215.

132

returns home to find that Pushkin's *Mozart and Salieri* and *The Gypsies* hold nothing new, that the "little discoveries" by which one lives in hard times have been suddenly rendered absurd by the events of the day. Even Pushkin, suggests the poem's ending, that ubiquitous third interlocutor around whom friendly chats originate, has been momentarily silenced by the Revolution.

In addition to the important relationship with Gershenzon, Khodasevich met with other personal and professional successes during the war and revolutionary years. In the summer of 1916, while recovering at Koktebel, Khodasevich commemorated the one hundredth anniversary of Derzhavin's death by writing his first article on the poet, beginning a process that would culminate fifteen years later in a fine "artistic" biography of Derzhavin. He was fascinated by Derzhavin's heroic nature, his blending of high (odic) and low (realistic) styles, and his urge to be iconoclastic and to sing of Catherine's virtues "v zabavnom russkom sloge" (in the droll Russian language).[55] Several features of the later Derzhavin, including his domesticity and love of the earth, suggest clear links with the poet of *Grain's Way*: "Indeed, Derzhavin loved the earth profoundly and wisely, and on that earth he loved his happy and sturdy home."[56] The following year, now in Moscow, Khodasevich completed his article on *The Gavriliada*. And one gleam of hope in the murk of bureaucratic tedium was the "Knizhnaia Lavka Pisatelei" (the Writers' Book Mart), a book-selling venture contrived by Khodasevich and his friend Pavel Muratov in summer 1918. With a rotating staff of B. A. Griftsov, M. V. Lind, E. L. Yantarev, A. S. Yakovlev, M. A. Osorgin, Muratov, and Khodasevich, the book mart sold, on a commission basis, the books provided by friendly publishers. Though short-lived, the little store on Leontevsky Lane acquired a quasi-legendary status as a last outstation of the free market and as heroic

[55] Khodasevich, "Derzhavin," *Articles on Russian Poetry*, pp. 43-57.
[56] Ibid., p. 51.

proof of the writing community's resilience in the face of official indifference. But Khodasevich, himself a day-to-day participant in the life of the store, had a characteristically skeptical view of the romantic nimbus surrounding the venture: "I don't deny that the mart played some sort of cultural role [at the time], but of course 'its consciousness was determined by its existence,' and not vice versa, that is to say, put simply, the mart appeared because the writers had to live and had nowhere to publish."[57]

Finally, one activity Khodasevich undertook during the writing of *Grain's Way* deserves special mention, both because it combined personal ties (his friendship with Gershenzon) and creative skills and because, as evidence suggests, it played a leading role in the shaping of Khodasevich's third collection. To Western readers Pasternak is perhaps the foremost example of a Russian poet who turned his talent to translation when conditions made the publication of his own verse impossible. But it was not uncommon in these times of paper shortages and failing publishing houses for a poet to earn a few extra rubles, and to sharpen (albeit on someone else's text) his use of poetic language, by translating foreign classics. Since 1910 Khodasevich had been translating, in large popular editions, the Polish masters—Tetmajer (the Tatras tales), Reymont (*Chłopi*), Krasiński (*Irydion*). Then in 1916-1918 he expanded his talents as translator, collaborating extensively on various projects that were edited, jointly or individually, by Gorky and Bryusov: *The Poetry of Armenia from Ancient Times to Our Day* (1916), *A Collection of Armenian Literature* (1916), *A Collection of Latvian Literature* (1916), and *A Collection of Finnish Literature* (1917). Rather than labors of love, such projects may have been simply ways to ply a trade, simultaneous attempts, as the somewhat quixotic Gorky saw it, to educate the Russian reader and to feed the hard-pressed Russian writer. Khoda-

[57] Khodasevich, "Torgovlia" (Trade), *Stat'i*, p. 390.

sevich left little doubt, however, about his strong affection for the project he undertook in late summer 1917 and saw through to its publication the following summer.[58] This undertaking, carried out for the most part in Khodasevich's basement flat at 7 Rostovsky, was to have the title *Evreiskaia antologiia* (A Hebrew Anthology).

Gershenzon introduced Khodasevich to the Jewish writer and editor Lev Yaffe in summer 1917.[59] The two men soon struck up a close personal and professional relationship. In Khodasevich, Yaffe had found the man he needed—"a Russian poet who could work with [him] to edit an anthology of Russian translations of Hebrew poetry and to oversee the editing of the Russian texts."[60] Once under way, the work of editing and translating turned out to be long and arduous, but extremely rewarding. Often the very poets to be translated—Hayyim Bialik, Saul Tschernichowski, David Shimonowitz, Yaakov Fichman—would drop by to answer prickly points concerning the selection and translation of their texts. A few years hence, encouraged by the positive response to his translations, Khodasevich collected and republished those translations in *Iz evreiskikh poetov* (From the Hebrew Poets) (1922), and gave at that time his position on the vexed question of the target language's fidelity to the original. His belief in his own inventiveness and creativity, but his even greater respect for the language of the original seems to anticipate the method of Nabokov:

I should point out that, due to my ignorance of Biblical Hebrew, the translations offered here were not made from the originals, but from literal interlinear translations worked out by L. B. Yaffe. . . . It goes without saying that my constant concern was the accuracy

[58] See his prefatory remarks in Khodasevich, ed. and trans., *Iz evreiskikh poetov* (From the Hebrew Poets) (Petersburg-Berlin, 1922), p. 5.

[59] Bernhardt, "V. F. Khodasevich and Contemporary Hebrew Poetry," p. 23.

[60] L. B. Iaffe, "Vladislav Khodasevich," in *Tekufot* (Tel Aviv, 1948), p. 226; quoted in Bernhardt, "V. F. Khodasevich and Contemporary Hebrew Poetry," p. 23.

of the translations. However, while translating from the interlinear translations, I always used a Roman letter transcription of the Hebrew text. Thus, the distinctive phonetic characteristics of the originals—meter, stanzaic structure, rhythmic character, number of lines, and so on—were preserved. And where possible I tried to convey the distinctive characteristics of instrumentation [roughly: assonance and consonance] as well.[61]

Other poet-translators taking part in *A Hebrew Anthology* included Baltrushaytis, Bryusov, and Vyacheslav Ivanov. Gershenzon, who must have been hovering about the edges of the project, wrote an upbeat preface praising the lively, insouciant tone of the younger (post-Bialik) generation of Hebrew poets.

A Hebrew Anthology might have been only a happy diversion in the aimless flow of that revolutionary autumn and spring had it not been for important lessons learned by Khodasevich in translating Fichman, Shimonowitz, I. Katzenelson, Abraam Ben-Yitzhak, and, especially, Tschernichowski. Khodasevich had initially intended to entitle his third collection *Nozh* (The Knife). Apparently he lighted on the eventual title in December 1917 when he composed the lead (and title) poem, with its metaphor of sowing and reaping and its claim for some larger rhythm controlling the affairs of poets and states.[62] A clear response to the Revolution on whose heels it is written, the poem also bears a dateline well into the translation project. The life-affirming qualities of modern Hebrew verse extolled by Gershenzon are especially evident in Tschernichowski's "Pesn' Astarte i Belu" (Song to Astarte and Bel), a poem whose imagery (the path and the grain) and whose theme (wisdom) Khodasevich seems then to have taken up and adapted to the Russian condition:[63]

[61] Khodasevich, *From the Hebrew Poets*, pp. 5-6.

[62] My comments here on the relationship between Tschernichowski's "Song to Astarte and Bel" and Khodasevich's "Grain's Way" owe much to the excellent discussion found in Sylvester, "V. F. Xodasevič in Moscow and Petersburg," pp. 145-152.

[63] Tschernichowski, apparently returning the favor of Khodasevich's at-

Человек, восторг встречай,
Светлый путь ему равняй!
Горсть пшеницы золотой
Брошу я в тебя рукой.
В зернах—тайна, в зернах—сок,
В соке—вечной жизни ток.
Тайна в дух твой западет;
Огнь в крови твоей зажжет . . .
Вспрянь, желай и будь силен:
В этом—мудрость и закон.[64]

Man, receive the joy,
make a bright path for it!
I will cast into you
a handful of golden wheat.
A secret is in the grains, sap is in the grains,
the current of eternal life is in the sap.
The secret will sink into your spirit;
it will kindle a fire in your blood . . .
Take heart, feel desire and be strong:
there is wisdom and law in that.

Even more to the point, however, Khodasevich did not merely borrow the imagery and themes of Tschernichowski's poem. He made them his own, cultivated them with his own poetic tools, "grafted" them (as he would have put it) to the unique stock of *Grain's Way*. It was not simply, considering the circumstances, that the graft took hold; it was that it resulted in sudden, almost miraculous growth. That winter and spring (1918), with the future more than ever uncertain, the present chaotic, and the past receding at breakneck speed, Khodasevich was floundering at his job at the courts of arbitration when he burst forth with a series of poems—"Look for Me," "To Anyuta," "The Loaves," "Without Words," "Noon," and "The Encounter"—more full of radiant wit and *joie de vivre* than anything written before

---

tention, then translated "Grain's Way" into Hebrew in *Haowed* (Warsaw), 13-14 (1923).

[64] Chernikhovskii, "Song to Astarte and Bel," in Khodasevich, *From the Hebrew Poets*, p. 48.

or after. And when early in the summer he began "The Monkey," in which a thirsty Darius and a thirsty simian are made equal in the face of history, Khodasevich appears to have again acknowledged Tschernichowski as a rich point of departure. The affection for Jewish local color, the humorous, yet still profound juxtaposition of the great with the small, the stylistic balancing of the archaic and the modern are qualities that Khodasevich came to admire deeply and, *mutatis mutandis*, use often. What he later said about Tschernichowski's long idyll *Svad'ba El'ki* (Elka's Wedding) (which he translated in emigration) might be said equally well about "The Monkey" and "The House," poems whose meaning is central to *Grain's Way*:

The meaning of such idylls is not descriptive but philosophical. Constantly drawing the reader to allusions about Homer, Tschernichowski seems to want to underscore [the idea] that only outward appearances change, but the essence of man's life is always the same, and the difference between Nausicaa and [the Jewish girl] Elka is not, after all, so great.[65]

KHODASEVICH opens *Grain's Way* and his major period with a pun on his own name:[66]

---

[65] Khodasevich, "O Chernikhovskom" (On Tschernichowski), *Evreiskaia tribuna* (Hebrew Tribune), no. 13 (189), dated mid-1924.

[66] In the original 1920 edition of *Grain's Way* the title poem does not open the collection but appears well into it—after "Look for Me" and "Zoloto" (Gold), the spring poems about death, and before "The Second of November." Khodasevich apparently thought the poem functioned more successfully as frontispiece. Several poems that were included in the opening pages of the 1920 edition—including "Aviatoru" (To the Aviator), "Uedinenie" (Solitude), "Rybak" (The Fisherman), and "Vospominanie" (Recollection)— were excluded from the 1927 edition of collected verse: perhaps Khodasevich felt these poems resembled too closely work done in an earlier manner. Interestingly, however, the poems that were later excluded, with their early positioning in the collection and their themes of doubt and anxiety, give additional evidence that the diurnal and seasonal metaphor taken from "Grain's Way" was intended by Khodasevich to structure the entire collection. Of the number of reviews of *Grain's Way* that appeared

Проходит сеятель по ровным бороздам
Отец его и дед по тем же шли путям.   (SS, p. 11)

The sower passes along the even furrows.
His father and grandfather went along these same paths.

It becomes apparent from what follows, however, that the poet sees this as much more than a clever bit of advertising. Khodasevich begins his poetic sowing in the first syllables of the first line of the title poem: "Grain's Way," written in 1917, serves in 1920 as the collection's frontispiece and as a frame for the events of the Revolution. As was suggested earlier, the agricultural metaphor is quite deliberate; it colors the entire collection, gives it a general rhythm and individual poems their placement, and concludes only with the last poem, "The Loaves," in which a guardian angel swears to the poet that the only truths are "zemlia, liubov', i trud" (earth, love, and work) (SS, p. 60). From first to last Khodasevich seems to say that the seed placed in soil has a purpose—it is to become the loaf that nourishes. Although the events of the Revolution constitute their own sort of grim reaper, they have not in "Grain's Way" removed the furrows (versus, as Khodasevich, with his classical education, would have known, means both "furrow" and "verse"), the tradition, of the father and grandfather, the poet's forebears. Doubtless chief among these ancestors for Khodasevich is Pushkin, whose lines of verse remain in the face of history intact, "even." Thus Khodasevich's poetic word, the grain itself, has even in this unlikely season the promise not only of death but of growth and fruition:

---

in the Soviet press, see especially G. Ivanov, "O novykh stikhakh" (On New Verse), *Dom Iskusstv* (The House of Arts), 2 (1921), 96; and G. Adamovich, "Vladislav Khodasevich: Putem zerna" (Vladislav Khodasevich: *Grain's Way*), *Tsekh poetov* (The Poets' Guild), 3 (1922), 60-62. "Grain's Way," with its message of wisdom and patience, may also be meant to play off the futile image of sowing in Pushkin's "Svobody seiatel' pustynnyi . . ." (Freedom's barren sower . . .) (1823). My thanks to Professor Sergei Davydov of Bryn Mawr for alerting me to the pun in the first line of "Grain's Way."

Autograph of "Putem zerna" (Grain's Way), the title
poem of Khodasevich's third collection of verse, dated
December 23, 1917.

Сверкает золотом в его руке зерно,
Но в землю черную оно упасть должно.

И там, где червь слепой прокладывает ход,
Оно в заветный срок умрет и прорастет. (SS, p. 11)

In his hand the grain gleams like gold,
but it must fall into the black earth.

And there, where the blind worm breaks its path,
it will die and germinate at its appointed time.

To be sure, there are poems of darkness and death in *Grain's Way* and several examples of the cruel sort of irony for which Khodasevich is famous. Sluchevskian descriptions of violence, terrible in their distancing and restraint, are already beginning to make their appearance in Khodasevich's verse. Still, the human fact, while more than once tragic in this collection, is not yet absurd. By the last poems, as the Edmund of *King Lear* would say, "the wheel is come full circle," and man and nature, their season finished (perhaps the leading theme in *Grain's Way* is "vsiakomu ovoshchu svoe vremia" [there is a time for everything]), make way for the next generation. For this reason Khodasevich is able to synchronize his poetic and biographical fate with the fate of his country in the last three stanzas of the title poem:

Так и душа моя идет путем зерна:
Сойдя во мрак, умрет—и оживет она.

И ты, моя страна, и ты, ее народ,
Умрешь и оживешь, пройдя сквозь этот год,—

Затем, что мудрость нам единая дана:
Всему живущему идти путем зерна. (SS, p. 11)

So too does my soul go the way of grain:
once descended into darkness, it will die and come alive
      again.

And you, my country, and you, her people,
will die and come alive, having passed through this year.

Since a single wisdom is given us,
every living thing must go the way of grain.

141

Since the inner (psychic) and outer (biographically and historically conditioned) lives of the poet are in a provisional state of balance, the poem has no Klyushnikovian "reflection," but one uniform voice. At least for now there is movement (*prokhodit'*, *idti*) with purpose (*seiat'*), and as a result Khodasevich sees his poetic role as meaningful. Indeed, the title itself, "Putem zerna," might be read as the logical development of this relationship and of the pun that initiated it: *putem* is both the "path" and the "motion" (*khod*) required to take the path; *zerna* is the fruit of the "sowing" (*sev*).

"Grain's Way" telescopes time—the cycle of one year, one generation, one lifetime. Other short lyrics in the collection align themselves to a specific time of day, which can also be viewed as a time in the life of the poet and his country. (The longer poems in blank verse, which will be discussed in the next section, recapitulate this cyclical rhythm.) The general movement of the lyrics—from darkness to light to the edge of darkness again; from uncertainty about death to death itself to rebirth and reintegration into the cycle—appears to confirm Khodasevich's deliberate composition. Nearly all the poems written prior to the Revolution are included in the first half of the collection, while nearly all the poems written during the Revolution are included in the second half. But although the arrangement appears roughly chronological, a strict chronology is breached more than once in order that the larger structural rhythm be preserved. That Khodasevich indeed positioned subsequent poems with the cycle of "Grain's Way" in mind is further, and most convincingly, borne out by the choice to conclude the collection primarily with poems written or begun in the richly rewarding early months of 1918. Only through these poems, it seems, can the path taken by the grain be viewed as meaningful and complete.

Several of the poems immediately following "Grain's Way"—"Slezy Rakhili" (Rachel's Tears), "Ruchei" (The

Brook), "Sladko posle dozhdia" (Sweetly after the rain), "Mel'nitsa" (The Mill)—are vespertine or nocturnal in tone and setting. They suggest the note of doubt, anxiety, or pessimism on which the cycle opens. As the Biblical Rachel suffered for being barren, so now countless Russian Rachels weep unreplenishing tears because their sons and husbands, the fruits of their labors, have been stolen by war. The brook in the next poem gambols in the noonday sun until the second stanza when,

> Под вечер путник молодой
> Приходит, песню напевая;
> Свой посох на песок слагая
> Он воду черпает рукой
> И пьет—в струе, уже ночной,
> Своей судьбы не узнавая. (SS, p. 13)

> Towards evening a young traveler
> comes singing a song;
> laying his staff on the sand
> he scoops the water with his hand,
> and drinks, unable to make out
> his fate in the already nocturnal stream.

This plain little stanza was important to Khodasevich: it was the first of his work that he read to Gershenzon and the last of his work that he read to Muni before Muni's final departure from Moscow.[67] Moreover, "The Brook" originally opened the 1920 edition of *Grain's Way*. As Vyacheslav Ivanov remarked, much time (close to eight years) and experience had, like the mercurial stream of life, passed through the poet's cupped hands between the writing of the first and second stanzas.[68] The playful nature painting of the first stanza (here unquoted) has developed into the detached musing of the second. The poem offers a good illustration of Khodasevich's anticlosural technique. In the 1927 edition the doubt is made more personal and perhaps more threat-

[67] See Khodasevich's notes to his poems in *SS*, p. 213.
[68] Ibid.

ening by the isometric changes in the last line from "nich'ei sud'by ne prozrevaia" (perceiving no one's fate) to "svoei sud'by ne uznavaia" (not making out his fate).

"The Mill" is a sort of allegory of inertia. The mill wheel, which when in motion presents a vital link with the cycle of "Grain's Way," has fallen idle. Various images of desuetude suggest that at this point in the collection the grain's progression from seed to bread has been arrested:

> Мельница забытая
> В стороне глухой.
> К ней обоз не тянется,
> И дорога к мельнице
> Заросла травой.   (SS, p. 16)

> A forgotten mill [stands]
> in an out-of-the-way place.
> No string of carts draws up to it,
> And the road leading there
> is overgrown with grass.

As the speaker passes a gently humorous eye over the scene, his language mimics that of the old miller, the only force, human or mechanical, to still exert its being on this evening still life. The miller descends the stairs of the mill into the sights and sounds of what-used-to-be or might-still-have-been, pauses for a moment to shake his finger at the distant smoke of a modern world, and returns up the stairs. The gesture of defiance is humorous and empty: unlike that of a Evgeny rising up against the terrible "progressive" spirit of Peter, it brings down no tragic consequences on the "little man's" head. Reminiscent of Firs in *The Cherry Orchard*, the old man is left to be master not merely of emptiness, but of emptiness that was once fullness. One of poetry's functions, as Aristotle says in the *Poetics*, is to dwell on possibilities—here a preindustrial "way of grain"—that history in its inexorability has forgone.[69] In the last two stanzas

---

[69] One of Muni's favorite expressions of world-weariness and wasted possibility was "to pour water on the mill of reality" (*Nekropol'*, p. 111).

Khodasevich again reverts to anticlosure. The old world's power, even its grammatical agency, is removed through passive constructions, and is left in the end (despite the implied verb "to be") effectively verbless:

> Потрудились камушки
> Для хлебов да каш.
> Сколько было ссыпано—
> Столько было смолото,
> А теперь шабашь.
>
> А теперь у мельника—
> Лес да тишина,
> Да под вечер трубочка,
> Да хмельная чарочка,
> Да в окне луна. (*SS*, p. 17)

> The stones have done their work
> for the loaves of bread and cereal.
> A great deal was poured in,
> and an equal amount ground,
> but now it's quitting time.
>
> And now the miller has [only]
> the forest and the quiet,
> and his pipe toward evening,
> and his cup of spirits,
> and the moon in the window.

The atmosphere of doubt, anxiety, and gathering night in the early poems of *Grain's Way* seems to reach a climax in "Obo vsem v odnikh stikhakh ne skazhesh'" (You can't speak of everything in verse alone), a poem in which the speaker compares life to an intricately knitted scarf that some dark guest arrives to unravel. (This alarming inversion of a domestic activity will be countered by the warm and playful image of sewing in "Without Words," one of the last poems in the volume.) The group of poems that follows— "So slabykh vek" (From weak eyelids), "V zabotakh kazhdogo dnia" (In the cares of each day), "Pro sebia; I, II" (About Myself; I, II), "Sny" (Dreams), "O, if only in that hour," "Milye devushki" (Sweet girls), "Shveia" (The Seamstress),

CHAPTER 4

"Na khodu" (On the Move)—clusters around the theme of the soul and the soul's correlative activities, sleeping and dreaming. The progression from vespertine setting to nocturnal pastime is a logical one: sleeping leads to dreaming, and dreaming, as an expression of subconscious will, leads to a freeing of the soul from bodily captivity. In the image of oneiric flight we see psychic desire in its pure form; even during the day, mired in the painful commonplaces of the waking world, the *dusha* makes its urges felt. But at this early stage the soul is still in conflict with the phenomenal world and conscious reality. Moments of release are imperfect because they are short-lived: the return each morning to the "blue prison" brings frustration and unhappiness rather than catharsis. In the absence of some ultimate release (and death is already beginning to present itself as such a release in several of the later poems in this group), the ravages of this ongoing conflict will continue to leave the poet weary and troubled. Thus, these poems, whose settings detail the constant traffic between day and night, waking and dreaming, consciousness and subconsciousness, are a disturbing expression of psychomachia and a direct posing of the central question of *Grain's Way*: how is the unearthly orbiting of the *dusha* to be synchronized with the earthly cycle of grain?

The question receives perhaps its clearest distillation in "Dreams":

Так! наконец-то мы в своих владеньях!
Одежду—на пол, тело—на кровать.
Ступай, душа, в безбрежных сновиденьях
    Томиться и страдать!

Дорогой снов, мучительных и смутных
Бреди, бреди, несовершенный дух.
О, как еще ты в проблесках минутных
    И слеп, и глух!

Еще томясь в моем бессильном теле,
Сквозь грубый слой земного бытия

THE WISE SOWER: 1914-1920

Учись дышать и жить в ином пределе,
    Где ты—не я;

Где отрешен от помысла земного,
Свободен ты . . . Когда ж в тоске проснусь,
Соединимся мы с тобою снова
    В нерадостный союз.

День изо дня, в миг пробужденья трудный,
Припоминаю я <u>твой</u> вещий сон,
Смотрю в окно и вижу серый, скудный,
    <u>Мой</u> небосклон,

Все тот же двор, и мглистый, и суровый,
И голубей, танцующих на нем . . .
Лишь явно мне, что некий отсвет новый
    Лежит на всем.   (*SS*, pp. 24-25)

So! At last we're in each other's possession!
Clothes [thrown] to the floor, body [thrown] on the bed.
Embark, my soul, to languish and suffer
    in boundless dreams!

Muddle on, and on, imperfect spirit,
by the road of dreams, tormenting and dim.
O, how in momentary flashes you are still
    blind and deaf!

Still languishing in my powerless body,
learn through the coarse layer of earthly reality
to breathe and live in another realm
    where I am not, but you are.

Where, released from earthly thought,
you are free . . . But when in anguish I awake
we'll join together once again
    in unhappy union.

Day after day, at the difficult moment of waking,
I recall *your* prophetic dream,
I look through the window and see *my*
    gray, meager horizon,

the same old courtyard, hazy and bleak,
and pigeons dancing on it . . .
It's obvious only to me that some new reflection
    lies over it all.

The soul is a *nesovershennyi dukh* (imperfect spirit) because it moves in the interspace between mortal body and perfect divine spirit; the oneiric orbit is tormenting because it leads back to the waking world and because it cannot pull free of personal desires. The ingenious "I"-"thou" dialectic in the poem grows out of the soul's centrifugal urge to be a completely separate impersonal "thou"; but as long as the personal "I" lives, the ineluctable gravitational force exerted from its center makes flight out of this miniature solar system impossible. Thus each morning the "I" and the "thou" join in an unhappy union. The "I" is left only with the bittersweet satisfaction that its conscious world contains scattered evidence of the soul's wanderings, and the "thou" is left only with the bittersweet anticipation of the next night's dreams.

Death becomes the only way out of this labyrinth, the only way to propel the soul into perfect spirithood. As Khodasevich says in a poem a little later, once free of the body, the soul can "savor a deep [or fetal: *utrobnyi*] sleep in the earth" (*SS*, p. 39), a sleep without mortal desires, and thus refreshed, can begin a new life and reembark on the grain's path. After prefiguring his own end in "O, if only in that hour," "Sweet girls," and "The Seamstress," Khodasevich begins, in the middle of *Grain's Way* and, as it turned out, in the middle of life's journey (he was thirty-one in October 1917 and would live to be fifty-three), his Dantesque descent into the *mrak* (darkness) of death promised in the title poem. But the act of dying is not given nocturnal attribution in the next series of lyrics—"Utro" (Morning), "V Petrovskom parke" (In Petrovsky Park), "Smolenskii rynok" (Smolensky Market), "Po bul'varam" (Along the Boulevards), "U moria" (By the Sea), "Variatsiia" (Variation), "Gold," and "Look for Me." With one exception, the treatment of death or dying in these poems is set in the morning or early day.[70] The suggestion,

[70] "Along the Boulevards" (*SS*, p. 33) is the only one of these poems clearly set at night. "Gold" (*SS*, p. 39), while not specifying a morning setting,

148

in keeping with Khodasevich's design, is that the poet has passed beyond the initial note of vespertine uncertainty and beyond the psychomachia and nightly wanderings of the soul that followed and now, in the morning, has come face to face with death. Moreover, the theme of death has not only a matinal but a seasonal coloration: the autumnal detailing in "Morning" and "In Petrovsky Park" becomes hiemal in "Smolensky Market" and "Along the Boulevards," then estival in "By the Sea" and "Variation," and finally vernal in "Gold" and "Look for Me."[71] Subtly, with the superimposing of a seasonal model, Khodasevich is laying the groundwork for a progression from hopeless to hopeful death. The reversal of the spring-summer sequence can therefore be seen as motivated by the urge to give the last lyrics about death spring—and Eastertime—associations.

In "In Petrovsky Park" we discover a hanged man's violent gestures that have been frozen by the immobility of death. Against the early morning background the details of suicide seem etched in unemotional black and white:

Висел он, не качаясь,
На узком ремешке.
Свалившаяся шляпа
Чернела на песке.
В ладонь впивались ногти
На стиснутой руке.

---

depicts the gold coin that shines among remains of the deceased like a "little sun."

[71] Khodasevich tended to give these poems about death the coloring of the season in which they were composed: "Morning" (SS, p. 30) and "In Petrovsky Park" (SS, p. 31) were written in November 1916 (although the events of "In Petrovsky Park" were actually witnessed in the spring of 1914); "Smolensky Market" (SS, p. 32) was written in December 1916 and "Along the Boulevards" (SS, p. 33) was written from late March to early April 1918; "By the Sea" (SS, p. 34) was begun in July and completed in December 1917; and "Variation" (SS, p. 38) was written in August 1919. The two important exceptions—spring poems that were written in the deep of winter—are "Gold" and "Look for Me" (SS, p. 40): they were written a year apart in January 1917 and January 1918.

А солнце восходило,
Стремя к полудню бег,
И перед этим солнцем,
Не опуская век,
Был высоко приподнят
На воздух человек.

И зорко, зорко, зорко
Смотрел он на восток.
Внизу столпились люди
В притихнувший кружок.
И был почти невидим
Тот узкий ремешок.   (SS, p. 31)

He hung, not swinging,
on a thin cord.
His fallen hat
lay black on the sand.
The nails of his clenched hand
stuck into his palm.

And the sun was rising,
urging its flight toward noon,
and in front of that sun,
not lowering his eyelids,
the man was raised high
into the air.

And sharply, sharply, sharply
he looked into the East.
Down below people crowded
into a hushed circle.
And that thin cord
was almost invisible.

The description is based on an actual suicide victim that
Khodasevich witnessed while returning home at daybreak
from a restaurant in Petrovsky Park in the spring of 1914.[72]
In a cruel reversal of traditional Easter symbolism, the sun
(Christ, warmth, renewal) is rising out of the East before the
vigilant gaze of a dead man. The irony of "zorko, zorko,
zorko" (sharply, sharply, sharply) is grotesque and unavoid-

[72] SS, p. 214.

able, particularly as it is juxtaposed with the picture of a crowd struck dumb by circumstances (reminiscent of the ironic endings of *Boris Godunov* and *The Inspector General*). The force of the last two lines is intensified by the speaker's detachment: not breaking the rhythm of indifferent description (the repetition of the conjunction *i* suggests a logical continuation of thought), he acknowledges the presence of the cord almost as a postscript and records its appearance, which seems harmless enough, as if he were a census taker. We do not know why the man killed himself, and that is part of the poem's irony. Any explanation would serve to place the violence in a discursive order, remove it to a safe distance. But here any hoped for resolution is frustrated, creating a poem that is the emotional equivalent of a continually clenched jaw. The dramatizing irony of "In Petrovsky Park" is the "sort of irony [that] turned back on itself is the natural vehicle for the writer who wishes to jar our civilization into the realization of its own frustration and spiritual chaos."[73]

"Smolensky Market" might be described as a prison of sound. Its use of a diabolically entrapping structure is not unlike that perfected by Baudelaire in "Harmonie du soir":

> Смоленский рынок
> Перехожу.
> Полет снежинок
> Слежу, слежу.
> При свете дня
> Желтеют свечи;
> Все те же встречи
> Гнетут меня.
> Все к той же чаше
> Припал—и пью. . . .
> Соседки наши
> Несут кутью.
> У церкви—синий
> Раскрытый гроб,

[73] David Worcester, *The Art of Satire* (Cambridge, Mass., 1940), p. 108.

151

Ложится иней
На мертвый лоб . . .
О, лет снежинок
Остановись!
Преобразись,
Смоленский рынок!　　　　　　　　　　　　　　(*SS*, p. 32)

I am crossing
Smolensky Market.
I am following
the flight of snowflakes.
The candles shine yellow
in the light of the day.
The same old meetings
are weighing me down.
I have fallen before, and am drinking from,
the same old cup . . .
The women from next door
are carrying pudding for a wake.
A blue coffin sits
wide open by the church;
hoarfrost gathers on
the dead brow . . .
O, flight of snowflakes
cease!
Transfigure yourself,
Smolensky Market!

The anguish that Khodasevich manages to compress in this short piece is remarkable. Not surprisingly, "Smolensky Market" was, with its clipped verses and its ingenious use of phonetic and rhythmic interplay, one of Marina Tsvetaeva's favorite poems.[74] The various images associated with death in the poem have trapped the speaker in a present tense and an indicative mood that are terrifying: as the verb forms suggest, there is no communication, no higher ground covered in the act of walking, between the "I" of the speaker and those details, presented in the third person, which he passes. As the speaker crosses the marketplace and as the

---

[74] *SS*, p. 214.

"thud-thud" of his footfall echoes in relentless dimeter, we discover that the last four lines are a partial mirroring (but in reverse, as if to say that the speaker is now emerging from the marketplace) of the first four. By shifting to the imperative mood (the first suggestion of a "you" in the poem), the speaker tries to halt the aimless flux of the present and bridge the tragic gap between himself and those things he has seen on his way. Thus the physical act of traversing (with the verb in the first person and the Russian prefix—*pere*—calling for a bodily crossing over) in the second line becomes a plea for transfiguration (with the verbal form now imperative and the Church Slavic prefix—*pre*—calling for a spiritual crossing over) in the penultimate line.

But in *Grain's Way* death as an ending is destined to become death as a beginning. The speaker in "Gold" looks forward to death as a return to the earth; he hopes one day to sprout up as spring grass. The poem's title is taken from a passage of Krasiński's *Irydion*, which Khodasevich cites, in his Russian translation, as an epigraph. It refers to the traditional gold coin placed on the mouth of the deceased. What will always shine among the poet's remains is this piece of gold, this "solntse maloe" (little sun) (*SS*, p. 39). And then one day some stranger (a future poet) will stumble upon the gold coin and cherish it. Khodasevich's point appears to be that a small part of him, a psychic core, will never die; it will survive in his verse and continue to be found by later explorers. As Krasiński's gold was Khodasevich's find, so Khodasevich's gold will be a find for someone else.[75]

"Look for Me" is one of Khodasevich's finest lyrics, a spring creation full of sunlight and word play:

> Ищи меня в сквозном весеннем свете.
> Я весь—как взмах неощутимых крыл,

---

[75] Khodasevich repeats here the same image of gleaming gold that is used in connection with the emblematic grain of the title poem.

Я звук, я вздох, я зайчик на паркете,
Я легче зайчика: он—вот, он есть, я был.

Но, вечный друг, меж нами нет разлуки!
Услышь, я здесь. Касаются меня
Твои живые, трепетные руки,
Простертые в текучий пламень дня.

Помедли так. Закрой, как бы случайно,
Глаза. Еще одно усилье для меня—
И на концах дрожащих пальцев, тайно,
Быть может вспыхну кисточкой огня.   (*SS*, p. 40)

Look for me in the transparent spring light.
I am all as the flutter of imperceptible wings,
I am a sound, a sigh, a sunbeam on parquet,
I'm lighter than a sunbeam: here it comes, here it is, there
    I was.

But, eternal friend, there is no parting us!
Hark, I am here. I feel the touch of
your vibrant, trembling hands
extended into the lambent flame of day.

Tarry thus. Close, as if by chance,
your eyes. I'll make just one more effort,
and on your straining fingertips perhaps
I'll burst, mysteriously, into a tassel of fire.

This poem is crucial to *Grain's Way*, for it is Khodasevich's response to the death of Muni, a death without some fitting answer to which the volume's metaphor of psychic growth appears empty. Khodasevich is not yet—neither in "Look for Me" nor in *Grain's Way*—"one of the few genuinely pessimistic Russian poets."[76] The speaker in the poem is Muni, calling out to his friend from that other dimension which he saw only as a reflection while still alive but which has become his home after death. Rather than some dark or ponderous elegiac ice floe, Khodasevich chooses an allegro mood without once jeopardizing the seriousness of his subject. One eulogistic model Khodasevich may have had in

[76] Gleb Struve, "The Double Life of Russian Literature," *Books Abroad* 28, no. 4 (1954), p. 405.

mind is Batyushkov in "Ten' druga" (The Shade of a Friend),
who calls out to the apparition of his dead friend (I. A. Petin),

> О! молви слово мне! Пускай знакомый звук
> Еще мой жадный слух ласкает,
> Пускай рука моя, о незабвенный друг!
> Твою с любовию сжимает . . .[77]

> O! give me a word! Let the familiar sound
> caress once more my greedy ear,
> Let my hand, o unforgettable friend!
> squeeze yours once more with love . . .

But the traditional pathos of the pastoral elegy, that note of
loss and tragic separation struck in various laments from
those of Bion and Moschus to those of Spenser, Milton, Shelley, and Batyushkov, is reversed in Khodasevich's brief domestic lyric. Muni is speaking to his dearest friend, reestab-
lishing contact. The first stanza's flashing images and
alliterative play of *s* and *z* suggest those visual and phonetic
sleights-of-hand in which Muni, now pure spirit, can be
glimpsed. Like the Mallarmé of "Les Fenêtres," Khodasevich
never tires of burnished surfaces—windows, parquetry, mir-
rors, anything that reflects. Such surfaces catch the irony of
existence by joining on one plane what is present—the reflecting surface—with what is absent—the object reflected
in the surface. But the speaker says that "perhaps" (one of
Khodasevich's most tantalizing and poignant instances of
near certainty) he can penetrate that surface, alter the laws
of modality, and reenter that mortal dimension where his
friend still lives. The "tassel of fire" (which may be a pun
on "Kissin," Muni's real name) that bursts like a divine spark
onto the friend's fingertips in the last line is a privileged
moment in Khodasevich. Indeed, it turns the poem into an
Easter song and a triumph over solipsism. That flash of re-
latedness counters the cold, deadly morning of "In Petrovsky
Park" and "Smolensky Market."

[77] K. Batiushkov, "The Shade of a Friend," *Polnoe sobranie sochinenii*
(Complete Works) (Moscow-Leningrad, 1964), p. 171.

Following "Look for Me," the last lyrics of *Grain's Way* reveal speakers who are reintegrated into the mortal rhythms of the title poem. With settings suggesting ripeness and harvest time, "Stanzas" and "I veselo, i tiazhelo" (It's both happy and hard) might be described as late afternoon, or early autumn, poems. Leading back to the evening poems that opened *Grain's Way*, these poems show speakers who are no longer threatened by the uncertainty of old age and death. In "Stanzas," after presenting the approach of old age in stark detail, the speaker takes comfort in the image of his silently germinating soul:

> Но душу полнит сладкой полнотой
> Зерна немое прорастанье.　　　　　　　　　(*SS*, p. 56)

> But my soul is filled with sweet fullness
> by the grain's silent germinating.

And in "It's both happy and hard" death, which Wallace Stevens calls the mother of beauty, is now seen as the necessary frame for every picture of birth and life. Comparing his body to an apple tree that in autumn is overburdened with fruit, and addressing youth, which is proud and seemingly immortal, the speaker closes with a lovely image of getting in touch with the earth:

> И не постигнуть юным, вам,
> Всей нежности неодолимой,
> С какою хочется ветвям
> Коснуться вновь земли родимой.　　　　　　(*SS*, p. 58)

> And you, young ones, cannot grasp
> all the invincible tenderness
> with which the branches desire
> to touch once more their native earth.

These two poems, particularly if we consider the anticlosural techniques of "The Brook" and "The Mill," offer a nice balance, a sense of belonging to an organic pattern that resolves life's opposites—body and spirit, youth and age, passion and wisdom—in life's flux.

Along with poems of reintegration *Grain's Way* ends with two examples of bright irony. The cosmos of "To Anyuta" and "Without Words" is a benign and happy one. Where there was anxiety about a demonic unraveling of life's *habitude* in "You can't speak of everything in verse alone," now there is security in God's hands. The speaker in "Without Words" tells how his mistress (another incarnation of Anna Chulkova) has silently presented him with a well-stitched seam sewn along white cambric. Then, building on this homely conceit, he goes on to compare his life to a series of stitches woven along the light fabric of existence by the nimble hand of God. In the end he turns the fabric over and sees how the stitchwork on one side—the pattern of his life—and the stitchwork on the other—the pattern of his death—are interwoven, and how a stitch sewn by God in one direction presupposes a stitch sewn in the reverse direction.

Holding another reference to Khodasevich's wife, the title of "To Anyuta," like its subject, is diminutive.[78] The poem itself is a religious credo as different from Derzhavin's "God" as the spirit of the New Testament is from the *lex talionis* of the Old:

> На спичечной коробке—
> Смотри-ка—славный вид:
> Кораблик трехмачтовый
> Не двигаясь бежит.
>
> Не разглядишь, а верно—
> Команда есть на нем,
> И в тесном трюме, в бочках,
> Изюм, корица, ром.

[78] See Khodasevich, *Derzhavin*, p. 18: "Derzhavin decided that in the future he would not chase after Pindar but would sing simply, in a manner such as this: 'Chego zhe mne zhelat'? Pishu ia i tseluiu / Aniutu doroguiu' [Whatever could I wish for? I write and I kiss / dear Anyuta]." The endearing "Anyuta" appears in many of Khodasevich's letters to Anna Chulkova. See "Unpublished letters of V. F. Khodasevich to Anna Ivanovna Khodasevich," item nos. 44, 45, 46, 47, 48, 51, and 52, TsGALI.

И есть на нем, конечно,
Отважный капитан,
Который видел много
Непостижимых стран.

И верно—есть матросик,
Что мастер песни петь
И любит ночью звездной
На небеса глядеть . . .

И я, в руке Господней,
Здесь, на Его земле,—
Точь в точь как тот матросик
На этом корабле.

Вот и сейчас, быть может,
В каюте кормовой
В окошечко глядит он
И видит—нас с тобой.   (*SS*, p. 57)

A nice picture—take a
look there—is on a match-box:
a little three-masted ship
is, without moving, sailing by.

You can't make out, but probably
there is a crew on it,
and raisins, cinnamon, and rum
in barrels in the crowded hold.

And of course it's also got
a valiant captain
who has seen many
uncharted lands.

And probably it has a little sailor
who is a master at singing songs
and who loves of a starlit night
to gaze at the heavens . . .

And I, in the Lord's hand,
here, on His earth,
am exactly like that little sailor
on that little ship.

And right now, perhaps,
in the aft cabin,

> he is looking out the window
> and seeing you and me.

In Derzhavin's time a widespread custom existed of writing couplets on candy wrappers.[79] For reducing the odic form to more human dimensions and for depicting the empress of Russia and her august retinue with wit and humor, Derzhavin received from his Felitsa a lovely gold snuffbox. Though Khodasevich does not model this lyric on Derzhavin's ode about God (quite the opposite), it is intriguing to imagine that he is playing off the tradition of the candy wrappers and the snuffbox. The snuffbox, filled with diamonds and gold coins, was the sign that Derzhavin's risky venture (the light depiction of the great and powerful) had succeeded; perhaps the modest matchbox is Khodasevich's version of the sign— his evidence that God, the greatest and most powerful, can smile at the flippant treatment of his grandeur and look kindly on the poet's voyage through life. In any case, the poem's sense of microcosm and of scaling down ideas of profundity and ubiquity generally associated with God is a charming ironic touch. Each element of "To Anyuta" has its proper place in the elfin diorama. Suggestive of the Trinity, the three-masted ship is, in a lovely image that is almost early Mandelshtamian, moving in place—a *contradictio in adjecto*.[80] And the lively inventory that follows, from the contents of the hold to the Lord-like valiant captain to the poetlike singing sailor, is all whimsical and gently deflating. Finally, the last stanza turns the poem inside out, giving in effect the tiny, overscrutinized, clearly manipulated sailor the ultimate word. The ironic *tour de force* ends with its Lilliputian hero looking up and out at Gulliver and his mistress just as the poet looks through the window of his poem at God above.

[79] See Khodasevich, *Derzhavin*, p. 28.

[80] See Clarence Brown, "On Reading Mandel'štam," in Mandel'shtam, *Collected Works*, I, i-xxvii.

THE SIX narratives in blank verse that constitute the nerve center of *Grain's Way* are among Khodasevich's finest creations. Without them the volume would have, despite its impressive skeining of lyrics, an anthological character. But with them, and with the ballast provided by their deep, meditative character, *Grain's Way* is able to make a larger statement about the meaning of history. And in the midst of war and revolution, it was the question of this meaning that Khodasevich must have felt needed answering. Importantly, the first of these narratives begins shortly after the nightmarish dawn of "In Petrovsky Park." As becomes evident, the six poems present in microcosm the book's macrocosmic movement from death and psychic dislocation to life and reintegration. Thus, in keeping with the diurnal and seasonal models structuring the shorter lyrics, "The Episode" and "The Second of November" are darkly matinal, the first set in winter and the second in late autumn; they tell of the death of the poet and the death of his country, respectively. "Noon" and "The Encounter" are insouciantly mid-day, warm and summery; they celebrate life at its fullest. And "The Monkey" and "The House" reflect gradual change from afternoon to evening, warmth to coolness; they show life making peace with its own decline and with the eternal return of history's wheel.

Longer than the traditional lyric and shorter than the traditional *poema* (though Baratynsky wrote a *poema* of only a few pages), progressing through narrative time rather than expanding on some timeless present moment, as does the lyric, and written in a blank verse that conveys remarkably well the meditative character and the weightiness of their far-ranging subjects, these little masterpieces escape precise definition. Khodasevich of course was not the first to set down the musings of a peripatetic speaker in blank verse: Pushkin's great "Again I have visited," to name just one

potential model, is a poem of which he surely was aware.[81]
But "Again I have visited" is primarily a lyrical piece, whereas
these poems by Khodasevich are as dramatic as they are
lyrical. For their use of dramatic principles in combination
with one "lyrical" speaker they might be compared to
Browning's dramatic monologues—with, however, the important disclaimer that Browning's group of multivoiced failed
questers are both him and not him, while Khodasevich's
speakers never appear to be anything other than transparent
images of the ironic Khodasevich himself. Wladimir Weidlé
was the first to notice that Khodasevich's *dramatic* use of
the blank verse form has perhaps another analogue in Pushkin:

Only in *Grain's Way*, having immersed himself totally in Pushkin,
does Khodasevich become himself. The poems written in blank
verse, the best in the collection, at first trace almost word for word
[*pochti kal'kiruiut*] Pushkin's works in blank verse. The most perfect (and latest), such as "The Monkey" or—included in *The Heavy
Lyre*—"The Music," are less derivative, yet in "The House" there
are still words which, if not uttered by Salieri, ought to have been.[82]

It is tantalizing to consider how literally Weidlé took the
comparison to the *Little Tragedies*.[83] But a closer look at the
poems suggests that there is little likelihood that Khodasevich was seeking a narrow parallelism or was playing off
or with the subjects of Pushkin's dramatic sketches. The
very seriousness of Khodasevich's poems, their themes of

[81] Khodasevich's speakers in these narratives in blank verse experience
epiphanies in a variety of locales and generally while on foot—either while
walking the streets (as in "The Second of November," "The Encounter,"
"The House") or while taking the air on the grounds around a *dacha* (as in
"The Monkey"). Only in "The Episode" and "Noon" do speakers sit
throughout the poem.

[82] Veidle, "The Poetry of Khodasevich," p. 456.

[83] For Khodasevich's views on the language of the *Little Tragedies*, see
Khodasevich: "Pushkinskii spektakl' " (The Performance of Pushkin), *Voz*,
no. 743 (15 June 1927); and "People and Books," *Voz*, no. 3732 (22 August
1935).

death and history, seems to militate against their taking on a primarily parodistic function. Still, the allusion to the *Little Tragedies* may not be so farfetched; in fact, as if to corroborate Weidlé's hypothesis, the notion of a Pushkinian cosmos dismantled by the events of 1917 is one of the leading themes of these poems. As someone sensitive to every nuance of Pushkin's work, Khodasevich must have been aware that there are indeed certain points of contiguity between his narratives in blank verse and the *Little Tragedies*. To begin with, there is the blank verse itself. That each poet took up blank verse to present a series of dramatic situations and then never, at least in the same compressed form and with the same dramatic function, took it up again should tell us something about that form and that function.[84] In Pushkin's case it may be that the logic of dialogue was inconsistent with the spirit of rhyme: the traditional lyrical "I" is inclined to "strum the strings" of only his own thoughts and feelings. In Khodasevich's case, however, other reasons must be found, since his cycle contains much narration and thinking aloud, but almost no dialogue. Thus the external dramatic situation in Pushkin is internalized in Khodasevich; perhaps it is something in the nature of the situation described that undoes the logic of rhyme? Furthermore, each cycle presents a series of dramatic situations to the attention of the reader, who is left very little by way of authorial voice to unravel the ironies of those situations.[85] Characterization in the *Little Tragedies* is so elusive because we have no narrative or authorial voice, only the voices of the characters themselves. What is striking in Khodasevich is that the narrative voice that is present is, in several instances, so distanced and ironic as to seem to be absent. Finally, Pushkin

[84] "Muzyka" (The Music), the opening poem of *The Heavy Lyre*, is the only other narrative in blank verse that Khodasevich wrote and collected in a volume appearing after *Grain's Way*.

[85] On dramatizing irony, see Muecke, *The Compass of Irony*, pp. 92-94.

is mentioned more than once in Khodasevich's poems: his death mask appears significantly in "The Episode"; a wry reference to *Mozart and Salieri* and *The Gypsies* concludes "The Second of November"; and the setting of "The House" is reminiscent of that of "Again I have visited," and a passage from the same poem suggests strong ties with the hymn to death in *A Feast During the Plague*. Khodasevich was certainly not implying that his works were recastings of the *Little Tragedies*. But what is tragic in his cycle of poems— despite their upward movement and the upward movement of *Grain's Way* in general—is that Pushkin, the spirit of a once healthy Russian culture, is hovering here as a guest at his own undoing.

"The Episode" presents the accidental bifurcation of the poet's self, the nearly Zen-like perception of one self, physically limited, by another, outside and noncontingent—a sort of free-floating eyeball. Khodasevich recalls the actual episode that served as his source:

I read [the poem] at a soirée at the Tsetlins to the 'loud' raptures of Vyacheslav Ivanov (with the raising of hands). Then on account of these verses the Anthroposophists started to pester me. In their opinion [the poem's epiphany] is called the separation of the ether body. This [event] had happened to me at the end of 1917, in the morning or during the day, in my study. . . . [It was] a day as full of tension as any in my life. (*SS*, pp. 214-215)

It is revealing, and not unendearing, that Khodasevich treats Ivanov's effusions and the Anthroposophists' proselytizing with mocking humor. The event was surely a unique revelation. Yeats calls such moments "visions," Joyce "epiphanies," Proust the *entre deux* of pure time. But for Khodasevich the moment is simply an "episode."

The tone of the poem is set in the opening lines:

> . . . Это было
> В одно из утр, унылых, зимних, вьюжных,
> В одно из утр пятнадцатого года.   (*SS*, p. 35)

> ... It was
> on one of those mornings, depressing, wintry, stormy,
> on one of those mornings of the year 1915.

Rather than an overture to a mystical moment, this sounds, with the *in medias res* of the ellipsis and the "It was on one of those mornings," like newspaper reportage. Everything in the speaker's surroundings is fixed with painful physicality—the shelf of books, the yellow wallpaper, the death mask of Pushkin. Perhaps significantly, this poem takes place inside, and the apartment, like the speaker's body, is a kind of prison. There is no purposeful verb of motion, as in "Grain's Way," for the speaker sits, alone and will-less, in his room. The sounds of children playing outside that will revitalize the speaker of "Noon" are here muddled and obstructed by the condition of accidie and the onset of the process of bifurcation.

Khodasevich's ruling concern in presenting the epiphany-like bifurcation seems to be: the more mystical the context, the greater the need to maintain balance by introducing less-than-grand images from the phenomenal world. The limbolike state between unification and bifurcation is compared rather flatly to the shouts and movements of sailors on deck that a diver hears from underwater. And, continuing with the metaphor of sea change, the speaker sees himself as someone in a small boat embarking from shore (that is, the real world) with a quick shove of an oar. From the vantage of the free-floating rowboat, the speaker goes on to describe his other self, still trapped on shore, with utter detachment:

> Самого себя
> Увидел я в тот миг, как этот берег:
> Увидел вдруг со стороны, как если б
> Смотреть немного сверху, слева. Я сидел,
> Закинув ногу на ногу, глубоко
> Уйдя в диван, с потухшей папиросой
> Меж пальцами, совсем худой и бледный.   (*SS*, p. 36)

In that moment
I saw myself as that shore:
I saw [myself] suddenly from the side, as though
to look a little from above, from the left. I sat,
with my legs crossed, [my body] sunk
deep into the couch, a burned out cigarette
between my fingers, [looking] completely thin and pale.

The sensation of the disembarked, disembodied self is one
of tranquility and lightness. Looking on, this second self sees
in the beleaguered shell of its alter-ego an expression of death
that smooths its face and removes its bitter smile. The death
mask of Pushkin witnessed earlier has now become the
speaker's death mask. This is the precise moment in *Grain's
Way* when Khodasevich might be said to experience his own
physical death:

И человек, сидящий на диване,
Казался мне простым, давнишним другом,
Измученным годами путешествий.
Как будто бы ко мне зашел он в гости,
И замолчав среди беседы мирной,
Вдруг откачнулся, и вздохнул, и умер.   (*SS*, pp. 36-37)

And the man sitting on the couch
seemed to me a simple, old-old friend,
beleaguered by years of journeying.
It was as if he had dropped in to visit
and, falling quiet in the middle of a friendly talk,
had suddenly slumped back, and sighed, and died.

Then, as quickly and strangely as it began, the moment
passes. The liberated "I" returns to the envelope of the captive "I" in a metamorphosis that the speaker undergoes only
unwillingly, as a snake forced to reenter its already molted
skin. Back in the world of things, once again a prisoner of a
body that is in turn imprisoned in a house, the speaker can
only remember what has happened as a synesthetic *plennyi
otzvuk* (captive echo). The sea change has been reduced to
the distant roar made by raising a conch shell to one's ear.

165

"The Second of November" is the most desperate and gloomy of Khodasevich's poems in blank verse. The themes of time, history, and revolution are telescoped in a simple date and throughout the poem strain at the surface of its prosaic title. Written between 20 May and 1 June 1918, and taking up the matter-of-fact tone of "The Episode," the poem opens with some more reportage:

> Семь дней и семь ночей Москва металась
> В огне, в бреду.   (SS, p. 41)

> Seven days and seven nights Moscow tossed about
> in fire, in delirium.

This, though, considering what follows, is a parody of Genesis and the seven days of creation—that is, a recollection of hell-in-the-making or the time it takes to dismantle what God has created. The distanced and dispassionate speaker does not describe violence in progress, but its result. No third Rome, Moscow turns in her bedclothes like a delirious patient. The speaker shifts forthwith to an irony that is corrosive, almost truculent:

> Но грубый лекарь щедро
> Пускал ей кровь—и обессилев, к утру
> Восьмого дня она очнулась. Люди
> Повыползли из каменных подвалов
> На улицы. Так, переждав ненастье,
> На задний двор, к широкой луже, крысы
> Опасливой выходят вереницей
> И прочь бегут, когда вблизи на камень
> Последняя спадает с крыши капля . . .
> К полудню стали собираться кучки.   (SS, p. 41)

> But a churlish doctor freely
> let her blood—and, wasted, toward the morning
> of the eighth day she came to. People
> crept out from stone cellars
> onto the streets. Likewise, having waited out foul weather,
> do rats in cautious file come out into
> a back yard towards a large puddle
> and scatter when a last drop falls

166

> from a roof onto a nearby stone . . .
> By noon small groups began to gather.

In this scene the controlling force is not God, a sort of master surgeon, but some churlish, blood-letting physician: *lekar'* is either anachronistic or pejorative, and etymologically he is one who applies leeches to heal. Moscow's citizens, correspondingly, are reduced to the level of frightened rats. Here is the sort of irony that Northrop Frye defines as "the sense of looking down on a scene of bondage, frustration, or absurdity."[86] Having lost all dignity or nobility, people are sooner associated with the animal world.

In a deft fitting of form to content Khodasevich suggests this splintered world with intentionally graceless enjambments and cacophonous mixtures of dental ("t," "d") and velar ("k," "g") stops:

> Длинные хвосты[87] тянулись
> У лавок. Проволок обрывки висли
> Над улицами. Битое стекло
> Хрустело под ногами.   (SS, p. 41)

> Long lines stretched out
> near the shops. Pieces of wire hung
> above the streets. Broken glass
> crunched underfoot.

This is no time for singing; the Orpheus of the lyric form has, as it were, slowed his poetry down to prose. People have become chary of their movements, and the well-turned phrase, like the ideal euphony of a "poetic" utterance, is in this context unnecessary effort.

After visiting friends (an allusion to the Gershenzons)—

> К моим друзьям в тот день пошел и я.
> Узнал, что живы, целы, дети дома,—
> Чего ж еще хотеть?   (SS, p. 42)

---

[86] Northrop Frye, *Anatomy of Criticism* (Princeton, 1957), p. 34.

[87] Khodasevich seems to be playing on the Russian *khvost*, which in this context suggests both the "lines" of people and the "tails" of the rats mentioned in the poem's opening.

167

That day I too went to visit friends.
I found them alive, whole, their children at home—
indeed, what more could one wish?

—the speaker wends his way homeward. En route he experiences two epiphanies, the first of which involves a carpenter who is putting the finishing touches on a coffin he has just constructed. The irony of events is presented to our attention without explanation:

> Мой приятель
> Заканчивал работу: красный гроб.
> Я постучал в окно. Он обернулся.
> И шляпу сняв, я поклонился низко
> Петру Иванычу, его работе, гробу,
> И всей земле, и небу, что в стекле
> Лазурью отражалось. И столяр
> Мне тоже покивал, пожал плечами
> И указал на гроб. И я ушел.[88]   (*SS*, pp. 42-43)

> My friend
> was finishing up work: a red coffin.
> I knocked at the window. He turned around.
> And taking off my hat, I bowed low
> to Petr Ivanych, his work, the coffin,
> and all the earth, and sky, reflected
> azure-like in the glass. And the carpenter
> gave me a nod too, shrugged his shoulders
> and pointed at the coffin. And I left.

By combining, as in "Look for Me," what the speaker sees through the glass and what he sees reflected in it Khodasevich captures the sprung logic of a world where azure skies and red deal coffins meet in the artist's eye. The force of the repeated conjunction *i* is to suggest that logic here is even-stepping and all items in this world, living or dead, animate or inanimate, are on equal terms. Hence there is nothing to hang onto, nothing save the slight crescendo of emotion

[88] "The carpenter was a stranger, but in fact existed. During my childhood Petr Ivanych was the name of the carpenter in my father's photography studio" (*SS*, p. 215).

contained in the list of those items the speaker bows to. But one is nonetheless curious: is the bow ironic, a ridiculous formality amid anarchy? Or does the speaker respect the carpenter's dedication and his mastery of detail in the face of overwhelming chaos? Is it possible to find support and order for one's life by building houses for the dead? By applying the mode of dramatizing irony, Khodasevich leaves the answers to the reader.

The second epiphany regards a "chubby four year old" (*let chetyrekh butuz*) who has left his friends and is sitting on a rock and smiling silently. He has been watching the others as they set free a pair of doves from a wicker basket:

> Но вот—
> Протяжно заскрипев, открылась дверца,
> И пара голубей, плеща крылами,
> Взвилась и закружилась: выше, выше,
> Над тихою Плющихой, над рекой . . .
> То падая, то подымаясь, птицы
> Ныряли, точно белые ладьи
> В дали морской. (*SS*, p. 43)

> But here,
> After long drawn-out creaking, the lid opened,
> and a pair of doves, rustling their wings,
> climbed describing circles: higher, higher,
> above the placid Plyushchikha, above the river. . .
> now falling, now rising, the birds
> were plunging like white barques
> in a distant sea.

The pair of doves, whose flight from captivity is beautifully imaged by the white barques broaching to an open sea, tells us of freedom, peace, and, of course, the Holy Spirit. Again, it is a situation of "dovetailing" irreconcilables: what is the bird of peace doing in the midst of war? What meaning can children's laughter have in a world plundered by cheerless adults?

Looking into the youngster's eyes, the speaker realizes that the boy is smiling to himself, to the thought of something

incomprehensible growing within him. And then, with the
same feeling of drama just witnessed at the carpenter's window straining again between the lines, the speaker says:

> . . . Среди Москвы,
> Страдающей, растерзанной и падшей,—
> Как идол маленький, сидел он равнодушный,
> С бессмысленной, священною улыбкой.
> И мальчику я поклонился тоже.   (SS, pp. 43-44)

> . . . In the middle of Moscow,
> suffering, lacerated, and fallen,
> like a tiny idol, he sat there unperturbed,
> with a senseless, sacred smile.
> And I bowed to the boy also.

The child's graven image is Buddha-like, his happiness inscrutable, as it could only be in this context. While his growth
is preconscious and prelapsarian, and while he, like the carpenter, does not demand meaning, the speaker is all too
conscious that the world, the context for the smile, is post-
lapsarian. The nonverbal bow recalls Christ's answer, a kiss,
to the Grand Inquisitor; still, the bestower casts doubt on
his own gesture of approval.

The little odyssey ends with the speaker's return home to
the prisonlike apartment of "The Episode." The inevitable
feeling of psychological upheaval is treated, as we might
expect, ironically. Knowing Khodasevich's deep love for
Pushkin and his commitment to art, we find a speaker un-
moved by either *Mozart and Salieri* or *The Gypsies*. To the
average mortal the last lines of "The Second of November"
might be diaristic, holding no surprises. Yet described rather
flatly, there could be no greater violence than this done to
the creative personality:

> Дома
> Я выпил чаю, разобрал бумаги,
> Что на столе скопились за неделю,
> И сел работать. Но, впервые в жизни,

Ни "Моцарт и Сальери", ни "Цыганы"
В тот день моей не утолили жажды.   (*SS*, p. 44)

At home
I drank some tea, sorted out the papers
that had collected on my desk over the week,
and sat down to work. But for the first time in my life
neither *Mozart and Salieri* nor *The Gypsies*
could slake my thirst that day.

Though written before "The Second of November" (from
19 April to 1 May 1918), "Noon" was placed immediately
after that poem in the various editions of *Grain's Way*—
more evidence that the collection's heliotropic movement
was intentional on Khodasevich's part. Full of sunshine and
pastel coloring, "Noon" is, along with "Brenta" and "The
Encounter," a Venetian poem. The amiable lyricism of the
first few lines (Khodasevich's instructions to himself as he
drafted the poem were "[keep it] light and wise") suggests
an immediate contrast with the grotesque opening of "The
Second of November":

Как на бульваре тихо, ясно, сонно!
Подхвачен ветром, побежал песок
И на траву плеснул сыпучим гребнем . . .
Теперь мне любо приходить сюда
И долго так сидеть, полузабывшись.   (*SS*, p. 45)

How quiet, clear, and sleepy it is on the boulevard!
Caught up by the wind, some sand has taken off
and splashed on the grass in a friable crest . . .
Now it's pleasant for me to come here
and sit, half-dozing, like this.

In place of scurrying anthropomorphized rats is a scene opening onto lazy, beatific quiet; rather than moving through
"suffering, lacerated, and fallen" Moscow (Khodasevich's verb
for disorientation is often *brodit'*—"to wander"), the speaker
sits on a park bench and muses contentedly. Even the real
world is reassuring: there is no trace of barbed wire or broken

glass; the sand forms charming designs as it blows and splashes like wavelets in the wind.

In "The Episode" and "The Second of November" children are either the source of sounds coming dimly from another world or inscrutable idols. They are not so in "Noon," however, where their laughter and games delight the speaker:

> Мне нравится, почти не глядя, слушать
> То смех, то плач детей, то по дорожке
> За обручем их бег отчетливый. Прекрасно!
> Вот шум, такой же вечный и правдивый
> Как шум дождя, прибоя или ветра. (*SS*, p. 45)

> I like to listen, almost without looking,
>> now to the laughter, now to the crying of children, now to the clarion
> [sound of their] running down the path after a hoop. How wonderful!
> It's a sound as eternal and veritable
> as the sound of the rain, the surf, or the wind.

It would be difficult to make too much of the image of the hoop. After the chaotic hiatus of "The Second of November," the hoop that the children chase suggests some immemorial, cyclical rhythm—that of "Grain's Way." Khodasevich in fact, as he says in *Necropolis*, associates the image of the hoop with a life force that ever renews itself and, interestingly, with the childhood of Andrey Bely: "Golden curls fell to the boy's shoulders, and his eyes were blue. With a golden stick he rolled a golden hoop along a golden path. Thus eternity, 'the playful child,' rolls the golden circle of the sun."[89]

Lest we get carried away in this lyrical mood, Khodasevich hastens, much like the Yeatsian speaker of "Among School Children," to present his own image with self-effacing details and light irony:

> Никто меня не знает. Здесь я просто
> Прохожий, обыватель, "господин"

[89] *Nekropol'*, p. 63.

В коричневом пальто и круглой шляпе,
Ничем не замечательный.   (*SS*, p. 45)

No one knows me. Here I'm simply
a passer-by, a resident, a "sir"
in a brown coat and round hat
[who is] in no way remarkable.

But the detachment of this passage is already quite different
from that of the otherworldly eyeball of "The Episode" or
that of the pitiless, probing gaze of "The Second of November." Now instead, in the "simply," the "sir" (by 1918 already becoming a vestigial amenity to be set off by quotes),
and the "in no way remarkable," we find the humor of a
sage and smiling *eiron*.

Like "The Second of November," "Noon" turns on the
speaker's observation of one child. Yet the boy of this poem
does not strike the speaker as an error of the times but as a
reminder of the past harmoniously interwoven with the present. In an application of what the Formalists would call
ostranenie (making strange), Khodasevich handles this exchange of the remembered past and the still unfolding present by using, as it were, different lenses and camera angles.
As the speaker sits and ponders the presence of the toddler
who, with pail and shovel in hand, plays at his feet, a reversal
in perspective takes place. The little child first magnifies by
contrast the speaker's size, making the adult feel like Gulliver in the land of the Lilliputians, then gently chips away
at the speaker's size and importance by triggering a recollection of a giant stone lion in Venice (what, humorously,
the man must look like now to his tiny neighbor) at the base
of which years earlier (in 1911) the adult once sat, when he
was Gulliver in the land of the Brobdingnagians. The juxtaposition of the diminutive with the grand, of the comic
with the tragic, of the future that is an open book with the
past whose pages have been read, generates the kind of *fris-
son* that seems unique to Khodasevich:

173

Над этой жизнью малой,
Над головой в картузике зеленом,
Я возвышаюсь, как тяжелый камень,
Многовековый, переживший много
Людей и царств, предательств и геройств.
А мальчик деловито наполняет
Ведерышко песком и, опрокинув, сыплет
Мне на ноги, на башмаки . . . Прекрасно!　　(*SS*, p. 46)

Above this little life,
above this head in a green cap,
I tower as a heavy stone,
centuries-old, that has survived many
people and kingdoms, acts of treachery and heroism.
But the boy dutifully fills
his pail with sand and, turning it over, covers
my feet, my shoes . . . How wonderful!

Then, moved by the softening, *sfumato*-like overlay of viewpoints, the speaker engages in one of the rare lyrical free flights in Khodasevich. Anticipating the speaker in *Sorrento Photographs*, he superimposes the past on the present, the Venice of 1911 on revolutionary Moscow, to produce a moment of Proustian pure time. We begin to feel (almost against better judgment) that the propellent lyricism will succeed in disengaging the speaker, that it will indeed lift him from the park bench and return him to an astral state of lost innocence. But such vertiginous heights of feeling are short-lived for Khodasevich. Quietly, in a delicate Chekhovian manner, Khodasevich ends the poem by bringing himself and us back to safer ground with the words of a young woman who has been reading nearby:

. . . И еле внятно
Мне слышен голос барышни: "Простите,
Который час?"　　(*SS*, p. 47)

. . . And almost indistinctly
I hear the voice of the young lady: "Pardon me,
what time is it?"

Free to ask anything, she asks about the present time.

"The Encounter" might be seen as Khodasevich's tongue-in-cheek reply to the Symbolists' various hypostatizations of Sophia, the principle of the Eternal Feminine. Vladimir Solovyov, the chief model for the second generation of Symbolists, named the visitations of Sophia by the formal *svidanie* (meeting); perhaps Khodasevich, in lighting on the less formal *vstrecha* (encounter), wanted to imply that his meeting in the flesh with an ideal feminine beauty could occur by happenstance rather than by divine plan. Written in May 1918, "The Encounter" has as its source Khodasevich's brief encounter with an English girl at the Campo Santa Margherita in Venice in the summer of 1911.[90] It is one of the relatively few poems that Khodasevich wrote on request (he submitted it for an "Italian" issue of *Vlast' naroda* [The People's Power] that his friend Mikhail Osorgin was preparing).

Neither pure Marian spirit nor chthonian *Erdgeist*, Khodasevich's ideal of feminine beauty and grace can be ideal only because, vulnerable and delicate like the flower petals that are its image, it once partook of a particular Venetian time and space:

> В час утренний у Santa Margherita
> Я повстречал ее. Она стояла
> На мостике, спиной к перилам. Пальцы
> На сером камне, точно лепестки,
> Легко лежали. Сжатые колени
> Под белым платьем проступали слабо ...   (*SS*, p. 48)

> It was in a morning hour at Santa Margherita
> that I ran into her. She stood
> on a little bridge, with her back to the railing. Her fingers,
> as though petals, lay lightly
> on the gray stone. Her knees, drawn tightly together,
> stood out slightly beneath the white dress ...

[90] *SS*, p. 215.

175

The painterly concern for detail and the innocent sexuality of these lines might belong, in another medium, to Veronese, whose Venetian works of art, thought Khodasevich, were the essence of the High Renaissance. Or they might belong to the Pushkin of *The Gavriliada*, whose Mary, despite the web of seduction carried on around her and with her, "proceeds [through the poem] pure and unsullied," for "so great was the degree of Pushkin's devout reverence before the sacred object of beauty that . . . through sin itself Mary radiates innocence."[91] True, this virginal English girl is certainly not the Mary of Pushkin's work. Still, what links her to Pushkin's ideal heroines (Tatyana, the provincial maidens of *The Tales of Belkin*) is the sense that her sexuality is alive but not yet self-conscious. The knees pressing against the white dress and the euphonious liquid *l* of "*l*epestki *l*egko lezha*l*i . . . ko*l*eni . . . be*l*ym p*l*at'em prostupa*l*i s*l*abo" convey this awakening sexuality by joining image to sound.

As the speaker begins to drift away from simple description and to pose questions about the girl's biography, his ironic alter-ego suddenly surfaces to express disapproval:

> Она ждала. Кого? В шестнадцать лет
> Кто грезится прекрасной англичанке
> В Венеции? Не знаю—и не должно
> Мне знать того. Не для пустых догадок
> Ту девушку припомнил я сегодня.   (*SS*, p. 48)

> She was waiting. For whom? Whom does a
> beautiful English girl at sixteen dream of
> in Venice? I don't know, and it's not
> for me to know. Not for empty guesses
> did I recall that girl today.

There is an unwillingness to go beyond the surface of tangible details, to romanticize the encounter beyond that moment, to give it an ulterior purpose. Therefore, as in "Look for Me," the speaker returns to the fleeting externals—the brim of her Panama hat and the slope of her shoulders—and

---

[91] Khodasevich, "On *The Gavriliada*," p. 105.

to the reflecting surfaces—her gaze—from which a poetic imagination can generate its own profundities.

If "The Encounter" is about the charming happenstance of one day in Venice, it is also about the process of making poetry from such happenstance. Poetry is not, suggests Khodasevich, the fully exposed reality underlying such an encounter but the potential reality of words—precisely those questions left unanswered by the girl's swift passage into and out of the poet's ken—that the encounter makes possible. It is better perhaps that the girl is foreign. Khodasevich has no wish to possess her, to draw any closer to her world. Pornography and art, as Khodasevich himself would argue, are mutually exclusive: the former is an empirical stripping away of all convention, an ultimate "realism" and absence of mystery, whereas the latter is a deliberate process of veiling (the white dress slightly binding young knees).[92] Hence what the speaker sees in the girl's eyes—

Синий

И чистый взор лился оттуда, словно
Те воды свежие, что пробегают
По каменному ложу горной речки,
Певучие и быстрые . . . Тогда-то
Увидел я тот взор невыразимый,
Который нам, поэтам, суждено
Увидеть раз и после помнить вечно.   (SS, pp. 48-49)

A blue
and pure gaze flowed from there [under the hat] like
those fresh waters that run
along the stony bed of a mountain stream,
singing and rapid . . . It was then
I glimpsed that inexpressible gaze
that we poets are fated
to see once and thereafter remember forever.

—and what he then calls *vliublennost'* (being in love) is just a first taste. The *vechnyi khmel'* (eternal intoxication) that

---

[92] See Khodasevich, "O pornografii" (On Pornography), *Voz*, no. 2445 (11 February 1932).

produces a poem such as this years later is something quite distinct from actual passion or traditional notions of inspiration. It is an act of imaginative empathy that, by universalizing the particular, gives the poetic experience its constant savor.[93]

"The Monkey" and "The House" are the last two narrative poems in *Grain's Way*. With the exception perhaps of *Sorrento Photographs*, these poems are riper (one wants to use the word more "epic") than anything else Khodasevich wrote. If the irony of discrete historical events gave rise to a bitter speaker in "The Second of November," the irony of a historical process that can be seen now as continuous and somehow familiar give rise in "The Monkey" and "The House" to speakers who are wise and philosophical. Applying the same mode of dramatizing irony used in "The Second of November," Khodasevich has altered its context and consequently altered its meaning.

"The Monkey" was begun in early June 1918 shortly after the writing of "The Second of November" and completed more than six months later in mid-February 1919. The narrative tells of a simple incident that happened to Khodasevich in 1914 while he was vacationing in the town of Tomilino. There, in the hot afternoon sun, the poet met a thirsty Serb at the gates of his *dacha*. Along with the wanderer was a monkey, which the speaker's prehensile memory brings to life with simple details:

Выше, на заборе,
Сидела обезьяна в красной юбке

[93] An important source for Khodasevich's ideas on inspiration may have been Pushkin's *Eugene Onegin* (I, 57-59). In Nabokov's translation (I, 120-121) we find: "It used to happen that dear objects / I'd dream of, and my soul / preserved their sacred image; / the Muse revived them later: / thus I, carefree, would sing / a maiden of the mountains, my ideal, / as well as captives of the Salgir's banks." And: "Love passed, the Muse appeared, / and the dark mind cleared up. / Once free, I seek again the concord / of magic sounds, feelings, and thoughts." See as well Khodasevich, "The Appearance of the Muse," *On Pushkin*, pp. 8-38.

И пыльные листы сирени
Жевала жадно. Кожаный ошейник,
Оттянутый назад тяжелой цепью,
Давил ей горло. *(SS,* p. 50)

> Higher up, on the fence,
> a monkey was sitting in a red skirt
> and chewing greedily dusty leaves
> of lilac. A leather collar,
> pulled back by a heavy chain,
> was squeezing at its throat.

Man in this passage has obviously mastered beast: the collar is fastened tightly to the chain. All appears transparent enough—nothing to capture the eye of a philosopher of history.

Having in effect lulled the reader to sleep with prosaic description, Khodasevich turns to the irony hidden in an interchange that suddenly takes place between monkey and "master." Before drinking the proffered water, the Serb lays the dish on a bench, whereupon the monkey grabs it, drains it on all fours, and flings it from its place. Who now is master and who beast? Observing the monkey in the act of drinking, the speaker comments:

Так, должно быть,
Стоял когда-то Дарий, припадая
К дорожной луже, в день, когда бежал он
Пред мощною фалангой Александра. *(SS,* p. 51)

> Thus, probably,
> did Darius once crouch, falling down
> at a wayside puddle, on the day when he fled
> before Alexander's mighty phalanx.

Gershenzon, for one, objected to these lines with their literal comparison of a Persian king to a wretched simian.[94] But on another level, the one on which Khodasevich probably intended an understanding of the poem to be based, the irony is not a bitter act of negation. The monkey *is* noble; not

[94] *SS,* p. 215.

only mastered by man, he is man's master, teaching us how history turns back on itself and how man survives to see it all unfold again.

After drinking down the water, the monkey rises from all fours and offers the poet his hand:

И—этот миг забуду ли когда?—
Мне черную, мозолистую руку,
Еще прохладную от влаги, протянула . . .
Я руки жал красавицам, поэтам,
Вождям народа—ни одна рука
Такого благородства очертаний
Не заключала! Ни одна рука
Моей руки так братски не коснулась!
И видит Бог, никто в мои глаза
Не заглянул так мудро и глубоко,
Воистину—до дна души моей.   (*SS*, p. 51)

And—shall I ever forget that moment?—
the monkey extended to me a black,
calloused hand, still cool from the moisture . . .
I have shaken the hands of beauties, poets,
leaders of the people—not one hand
contained the outline of
such nobility! Not one hand
had for mine so brotherly a touch!
And God knows, no one has peered
into my eyes so wisely and deeply,
truly—to the bottom of my soul.

Here we find the wisdom to counterbalance the madness and chaos of "The Second of November," and here too the nobility and understanding that the speaker could not make out in the indifferent faces of Petr Ivanych and the "little idol." And the striking image of the black, calloused hand, with its combination of strength and weakness, is one of Khodasevich's finest. Thus the monkey's silent gesture of gratitude and faith seems to answer the disquieting bow of the earlier poem.

The speaker is renewed and given back that sense of historical patterning he had lost: "The sweetest legends of deep antiquity / were revived in my heart by that beggarly beast" (Glubokoi drevnosti sladchaishie predan'ia / Tot nishchii zver' mne v serdtse ozhivil) (*SS*, p. 51). The Serb and his animal then depart, only the monkey, significantly, has turned the tables and is sitting atop its master's shoulders like a Maharajah on his elephant. The ending that follows is full of irony:

В тот день была объявлена война.   (*SS*, p. 52)

On that day war was declared.

Separated from the preceding section, this detached statement of historical fact is greatly affected by the entire context of "The Monkey." It is obviously placed where it is to jolt the reader, to make him come to grips with the irony of history. The question immediately arises whether this fact undoes the monkey's lesson or whether the lesson is indeed the only key to understanding history. Where there was no clear choice to be made in "The Second of November," perhaps one can be made now based on the *context* of the speaker's newly found wisdom.

"The House," written and rewritten many times by Khodasevich between 1919 and 1920, is even more than "The Monkey" a poem dedicated to finding the meaning of history. Mellow and contemplative, a poem of gathering evening, it does not depend so much on dramatizing irony as do its companion pieces, "The Second of November" and "The Monkey." The "action" details the speaker's wanderings through the skeleton of an old house and his attempts to resurrect the life that once took place in it. Rather than confine the speaker as in "The Episode," this house effects the opposite, leaving him open, in one of Khodasevich's charming phrases, to "time's spaciousness" (*prostor vremeni*).

The method of description used in "The House" is somewhat different from that met with in earlier poems. In poems such as "Noon," "The Encounter," and "The Monkey," the

speaker began by building on images that were at ground
level, close to his face. Here he seems to give some breathing
room to his philosophical disquisition. Starting from above
with images of the sky and the youthful outline of trees, he
moves down to a naturalistic description of what the inhabitants of the house might have been like, where they
might have quarreled and made up, hidden their soiled money,
borne children, and died quietly. At this point Khodasevich
begins to dilate again, making his way outward, not unlike
a student of anatomy, from the bones of the house and its
inhabitants to the vital organs, flesh and blood, and grand
body that they might have inherited at the right moment
from history:

> —все теперь
> Прохожему открыто.—О, блажен,
> Чья вольная нога ступает бодро
> На этот прах, чей посох равнодушный
> В покинутые стены ударяет!
> Чертоги ли великого Рамсеса,
> Поденщика ль безвестного лачуга—
> Для странника равны они: все той-же
> Он песенкою времени утешен . . .   (SS, pp. 53-54)

> Now everything
> is open to the passer-by. O, blessed is he
> whose free foot steps briskly
> on these ashes, whose indifferent staff
> strikes at the abandoned walls!
> Whether the chambers of great Ramses,
> or the shack of an unknown day-laborer—
> to the wanderer they are all one: he is
> still comforted by the same song of time . . .

Once again, as in "The Monkey," the comparison of the
chambers of Ramses to the shack of a day-laborer or of a
magnificent peristyle to the holes in old doors is doubtless
ironic. Yet the end result is to make us all equal in the face
of history. Like the monkey, we are both master and slave.

The house's stairway leads to a mezzanine that reminds the speaker of an ancient tribune. The staircase seems a potential route to the stars. And from this coign of vantage the speaker watches with complete detachment the pitched battle between man and history going on below. Yeats says in "Lapis Lazuli" that from the Chinamen's distant aerie tragedy is gay and joy is tragic. What Khodasevich says now is quite similar:

> Сердце человечье
> Играет, как проснувшийся младенец,
> Когда война, иль мор, или мятеж
> Вдруг налетят и землю сотрясают;
> Тут разверзаются, как небо, времена—
> И человек душой неутолимой
> Бросается в желанную пучину.[95]   (SS, p. 54)

> The heart of man
> frolics like a just-wakened infant
> when war or famine or revolt
> suddenly falls upon and shakes the earth;
> here the ages, like heaven, open wide—
> And man with his insatiable soul
> hurls himself into the desired abyss.

Man's thirst for life is even greater than the thirst for meaning that could not be slaked by Pushkin's art in "The Second of November." Time is man's medium, his amniotic fluid, and it needs no reason to exist. The movement of man in time is as ineffable and natural to him as the movement of other creatures in their legendary elements is to them:

> Как птица в воздухе, как рыба в океане,
> Как скользкий червь в сырых пластах земли,
> Как саламандра в пламени,—так человек
> Во времени.   (SS, pp. 54-55)

---

[95] Cf. this passage and the famous hymn to death in Pushkin's *A Feast During the Plague*. Khodasevich had used this same work by Pushkin as a point of departure in "Golos Dzhenni" (The Voice of Jenny), one of the poems in *The Happy Little House*.

Like the bird in the air, like the fish in the ocean,
like the slimy worm in the damp layers of the earth,
like the salamander in the flame—so is man
in time.

The poem slowly builds to its climax. Somewhere an axis
turns, but man is not meant to draw closer to his goal. The
process of living leads back to itself, its logic being circular
without being empty. And knowing this, the speaker's heart
beats in place, fluttering from its crow's-nest, awed by its
bird's-eye view of life's timeless passage:

И трепещет сердце,
Как легкий флаг на мачте корабельной,
Между воспоминаньем и надеждой—
Сей памятью о будущем . . .[96]   (*SS*, p. 55)

And the heart flutters,
like a light flag on a ship's mast,
between recollection and hope—
this memory of the future . . .

With this lovely image, Khodasevich begins his ironic descent, already customary, back to earth. His reverie is interrupted by an old woman come to gather up the house's
remains.

But the realism of the closing scene—the old woman's
humped back, her wrinkled hand, the shingles, and the tow—
is different from that which opened the poem. There has
gathered over the details a sort of patina. And reconciled at
last the speaker says:

Молча подхожу
И помогаю ей, и мы в согласьи добром
Работаем для времени. Темнеет,
Из-за стены встает зеленый месяц,
И слабый свет его, как струйка, льется
По кафелям обрушившейся печи.   (*SS*, p. 55)

[96] Viktor Shklovsky takes these lines (perhaps a secret compliment to
Khodasevich because he ascribes them to Batyushkov?) as an epigraph to
Vstrechi (Encounters) (Moscow, 1944), his book of memoirs.

> Silently I approach
> and help her, and we in kindly consort
> work for time. Darkness gathers,
> a green moon rises from behind a wall,
> and its faint light, like a streamlet, pours
> over the tiles of a tumbledown stove.

It is the irony of this sort of situation, the telescoping of past, present, and future at the site of an old stove, once the hearth and the "heart" of the house, that colors some of Khodasevich's finest poetry. Here is a kind of poignancy, like the tow creeping through the tiles, that grows almost despite the efforts of an ironic voice between the lines. "Working for time" in a house that is both history's grave and imagination's cradle, Khodasevich has reaped the unlikely harvest of *Grain's Way*.

__5__

THE LYRE GETS HEAVY: 1920-1922

Make me thy lyre, even as the forest is:
What if my leaves are falling like its own!
The tumult of thy mighty harmonies

Will take from both a deep, autumnal tone,
Sweet though in sadness. Be thou, Spirit fierce,
My spirit! Be thou me, impetuous one!
—Shelley, "Ode to the West Wind"

Between 1914 and 1927 Khodasevich wrote almost all of the
poetry on which he felt his reputation stood. In 1927 in Paris
(by then his permanent residence in exile) he published the
only edition of his collected verse to appear during his lifetime: this thin little book of less than two hundred pages
consisted of *Grain's Way* and *The Heavy Lyre*, earlier collections now republished with slight variations in format,
and *European Night*, poems collected during five years of
emigration. Never prolific, always exacting, Khodasevich already seemed to sense that whatever place on the Russian
Parnassus was to be his had been staked out by the hundred
odd poems collected in this book. For by the late 1920s,
despite the fact that Merezhkovsky hailed him as the Arion
of Russian poetry and a number of influential critics (Aikhenvald, Bely, Mochulsky, Nabokov, Weidlé) recognized
his poetry as among the most significant being written at
the time, Khodasevich had begun to write very little verse
indeed. When once asked by his friend Korney Chukovsky
why he had stopped writing verse after the Revolution, Blok
replied, "All the sounds have ceased. Can it be you don't
hear there are no more sounds?"[1] Khodasevich would not, I

[1] Kornei Chukovskii, *Sovremenniki* (Contemporaries) (Moscow, 1962),
pp. 487-488.

think, have compared himself to Blok, nor would he have identified the poetic silence of his last years with the great Symbolist's mystical deafness. Yet it might be said that by 1927 (if not in fact sooner) Khodasevich's *dusha*, his favorite source of otherworldly music, had begun to turn a deaf ear on him.

That Khodasevich's poetic output over these years was modest is not in itself an important fact; it merely points up his understanding of the relationship between poet and muse as something organic, unsponsored, necessary in its way, but never controlled by will. Moments of creativity or "secret hearing" came when it was time for them to come; they were not, à la Bryusov, oxen to be whipped onward by the poet's indefatigable lashings. This being said, it becomes a fact of some importance that Khodasevich wrote over half of the poems collected in his *Sobranie stikhov* (Collected Verse) between April 1921 (after he, Nyura, and Garik had moved to Petersburg and he had finally shaken a relapse of furunculosis) and September 1923 (after he had spent some fifteen months in emigration). This period of two and a half years saw the writing of nearly all of *The Heavy Lyre*, what may be Khodasevich's finest collection,[2] and more than half of *European Night*. It was, in short, the most productive time in Khodasevich's otherwise unprolific career as a poet.

What was indigenous to the Petersburg of 1920-1922 that seemed to set Khodasevich's internal metronome to ticking? First, Petersburg's fame as geographical, historical, and cultural interface was of course not lost on Khodasevich. This perhaps most mythical of all Russian cities—its Petrine hubris; its diabolical mists, grandly rectilinear architecture, sordid market places; its baffling split between serene intellect and brain fever; its imperial past and apocalyptic future written about in some of the finest work of Pushkin,

---

[2] Both Vladimir Nabokov and Nina Berberova consider it so. See Nabokov, *Speak, Memory*, p. 285; and Berberova, "Vladislav Khodasevich—a Russian Poet," *Russian Review* 2 (April 1952), p. 81.

Gogol, Dostoevsky, and, more recently, Bely—had reached
a transitional (some would say ultimate) stage in its development. Much of the memoir literature devoted to this period, including that of Olga Forsh, Vsevolod Rozhdestven-
sky, Anna Elkan, and Khodasevich himself, focuses, with a
predictable "forward-" or "backward-looking" orientation,
on this transitional character.[3] In a deliberate use of the
metaphor Khodasevich recalls Petersburg as a corpse that
has been laid out for its wake. The city's loveliness and
serenity are all the more poignant and memorable because
the onset of decomposition is not far off:

... In this period [1920-1922] Petersburg itself became as uncom-
monly beautiful as it had not been for a long time, perhaps even
ever.... [Anyone] possessing feeling, intelligence, and understanding could not help but see to what extent misfortune was becoming
to Petersburg.

Moscow, deprived of its commercial and administrative bustle,
would have been, most likely, pathetic. Petersburg became majestic. It was as if, together with its signs, all excess coloration fell
away. Buildings, even the most ordinary, took on that proportion
and severity which previously only palaces possessed. Petersburg
became unpeopled [obezliudel] (by that time there numbered in it
only about seven hundred thousand inhabitants), trams stopped
moving through the streets, only rarely did hooves clatter or an
automobile blow its horn—it happened that immobility was more
becoming to Petersburg than motion. Of course, nothing was added
to the city, it acquired nothing new, but it lost all that was un-
becoming. There are people who grow more attractive in their
coffins: such was the case, it seems, with Pushkin. Undoubtedly,
this was the case with Petersburg.

This [sort of] beauty is temporary, momentary. The terrible ug-
liness of decomposition follows after it. But in the contemplation
of such beauty there is an inexpressible painful delight. Before our

[3] Anna El'kan, "Dom iskusstv" (The House of Arts), *Mosty* (Bridges), 5
(1960), 289-298; Ol'ga Forsh, *Sumasshedshii korabl'* (The Insane Ship)
(Washington, 1964); Vsevolod Rozhdestvenskii, *Stranitsy zhizni* (Pages from
Life) (Moscow, 1974), pp. 261-281; and Khodasevich, "Dom iskusstv" (The
House of Arts), in *Stat'i*, pp. 399-412.

eyes the decay had already begun to touch Petersburg: here some beams had collapsed; here some plaster had crumbled; here a wall was shaky; here an arm on a statue had broken off. But even this barely apparent decay was still beautiful, and the grass, which here and there had forced its way through cracks in the sidewalk, did not yet disfigure, but only beautified, the wonderful city, as ivy beautifies classical ruins.[4]

It is this purgatorial state, striking in its haunting beauty and deathlike immobility, that provides the context for *The Heavy Lyre*. And this transitional state of a "transitional" city seems the ideal setting for a collection deeply rooted in, and yet at the same time uprooted from, the Symbolist tradition. What became clear to Khodasevich, as the details of literary and political *byt* (everyday life) began to crowd in, was that artistically speaking there was no longer a path to take or a soil to cultivate, as there had been in *Grain's Way*. As the almost domestic intimacy with which Khodasevich, Gershenzon, and their generation had known Pushkin made way for monolithic hero-worship, and vital traditions were caught in the momentary beauty of death masks (placing both Pushkin and Petersburg in coffins is, one suspects, not unintentional on Khodasevich's part), there was nowhere to go but inward.[5] Finally, Symbolism itself, a movement in which Khodasevich had been born too late to take a leading part but which he nonetheless understood implicitly and which his memoirs, aptly entitled *Necropolis*, bring eloquently to life (or "life-in-death"), is now dead. As Khodasevich remarked later, "*That* Petersburg ended in 1922. The Soviet government *suffocated* it with NEP, censorship, exile, and moral disintegration."[6] Petropolis, the city of Peter (and

---

[4] *Stat'i*, pp. 399-400. Note the connection between the grass growing up through the cracks in the sidewalk and the last lines of "Puskai minuvshego ne zhal' " (Let the past not be pitied), in *SS*, p. 74.

[5] See Khodasevich, "The Shaken Tripod," p. 120.

[6] Khodasevich, "People and Books," *Voz*, no. 3725 (15 August 1935). (My emphasis.)

of Pushkin, Blok, and in a sense Russian poetry and culture) had become Necropolis, the city of the dead.

When Khodasevich, encouraged by the ever solicitous Gorky, moved his wife and stepson to Petersburg in mid-November 1920, however, he could not have known he was entering a necropolis. His perception of Petersburg and Russian culture at the brink grew out of his experiences during the nineteen months prior to emigration and only took final form in the years of exile, though it should be said that as early as February 1921, in his famous Pushkin speech, "Koleblemyi trenozhnik" (The Shaken Tripod), he had strong premonitions of what was at hand.[7] Still, such premonitions came gradually at first, for what Khodasevich found upon arriving and settling in at "Dom iskusstv" (House of Arts) was a "literary, theatrical, and artistic [life that] had burst to the surface with unprecedented vividness. The Bolsheviks were already trying to take control of this life, but had not yet managed to, and so it was living out its last days of freedom with genuine creative élan."[8]

Before moving into the House of Arts, Khodasevich, Nyura, and Garik took temporary lodging at 13 Sadovaya Street. Although as a lifelong Muscovite he must have experienced some initial pangs of homesickness (Gershenzon told him that soon he would forget his "lover" and remember only Moscow, his "lawful wife"[9]), Khodasevich, at least to judge by the postcard sent to his friend Boris Diatroptov in late November, seems to have been buoyantly playful in the new surroundings. Perhaps he was simply pleased to have the difficult final months in Moscow behind him:

The entire city is aroused by our arrival. The streets are full of couriers, and more couriers. The weather is great; we have not an apartment, but a palace: 119 rooms, 768 sazhens of firewood. The

[7] See Khodasevich, "The Shaken Tripod," pp. 114-121.

[8] Stat'i, pp. 400-401.

[9] Berberova, ed., "Letters of M. O. Gershenzon to V. F. Khodasevich," p. 223.

Petrograd City Council sent me a golden wreath. . . . I have 24 lovers from local high society. We eat only bananas and wash them down with sherry. Nyura complains that the diamond diadem she wears is heavy for her. [But that's] a trifle, she'll get used to it.[10]

By entering the now legendary House of Arts (which was no easy task, since the election process was a complex and selective one: each prospective member needed five recommendations, and was only then elected by secret ballot—but one suspects that in Khodasevich's case Gorky's strong support may have had its way of ensuring the candidate's success[11]), Khodasevich was entering what more than one nostalgic memoirist has described as the heart of Petersburg's postrevolutionary creative life. "Disk," as the House of Arts was called by its inhabitants, was lodged in a venerable building that bordered on three streets: the Moyka, Nevsky Prospekt, and Morskaya Street. At one time Catherine's winter palace, the building had, prior to the Revolution, housed an "English" store, a bank, and the opulent apartments of its owner, the prominent food merchant Eliseev.[12] Disk itself was allocated, among other space, the Eliseev family apartments, which spread out over three floors, their rooms of various sizes and bizarre shapes providing domicile for a number of writers, musicians, and artists. Like so much else at the time, the House of Arts owed its existence largely to Gorky, who came to the aid of a group that, under Korney Chukovsky's leadership, had since July 1919 been petitioning (though unsuccessfully) the authorities for working and living space for writers involved in translation projects at World Literature and in the various literary studios and seminars organized and run in the early months of that year by Gumilyov, Chukovsky, Lozinsky, and Zamya-

[10] Malmstad and Smith, eds., "Eight Letters of V. F. Khodasevich," p. 76.
[11] See Barry Scherr, "Notes on Literary Life in Petrograd, 1918-1922: A Tale of Three Houses," *Slavic Review* 36, no. 2 (1977), p. 261.
[12] *Stat'i*, pp. 401-402.

tin.[13] But only when Gorky gave the immense authority of his name to Chukovsky's efforts was Disk able to open in December 1919, roughly a year prior to Khodasevich's arrival in Petersburg.

Hence Disk was already buzzing with artistic activity of all sorts when Khodasevich made his appearance,[14] and this infectious devotion to the life of the mind at a time when material life was utterly barren must have had its salutary effect on the poet's burst of creativity. Various forms of artistic pursuit seemed to reinforce each other here in a state of almost ideal symbiotic ferment. One could study poetry writing under Gumilyov (the "Resounding Shell" now met in a parlor at Disk), verse translation under M. L. Lozinsky (a "true wizard" of the translating art, as Khodasevich calls him[15]), graphic art and design under Mstislav Dobuzhinsky (vice-president of Disk and head of its art section), and modern prose techniques under Zamyatin. Other classes were taught or lectures delivered by Eikhenbaum, Zhirmunsky, Chukovsky, Gorky, Tynyanov, Shklovsky, Tomashevsky, and Vasily Kamensky.[16] The constant flow of new life reached perhaps its high-water mark with the formation of the Serapion Brothers, whom Khodasevich was very fond of: Fedin, Kaverin, Vsevolod Ivanov, Nikitin, Lev Lunts—the soul of the group, though destined to die prematurely—and others would regularly crowd into the smoke-filled room of the otherwise sleep-loving Mikhail Slonimsky.[17] Factionalism at Disk tended to be not bitter, but intellectually invigorating. Akim Volynsky, the elder statesman of Symbolism, would, while sitting on the stove in the kitchen, unleash

[13] See Scherr, "A Tale of Three Houses," pp. 259-260.

[14] For a lively description of Khodasevich's appearance at the House of Arts, see Shklovsky, *A Sentimental Journey*, pp. 236-237.

[15] *Stat'i*, p. 408.

[16] See Scherr, "A Tale of Three Houses," p. 262.

[17] See *Stat'i*, pp. 404-405. Khodasevich expresses his fondness for the Serapions in "O sebe" (About Myself), *Novaia russkaia kniga* (New Russian Book), 2 (July 1922), pp. 36-37.

nightly his impressionistic word hordes on the sharp-witted young Formalist Viktor Shklovsky.[18] Lunts and Evgeny Shvarts merrily countered an older generation's potential self-importance and nostalgia about Symbolist *temps perdu* by staging charades and hilarious minidramas.

This, then, was the rich life that Khodasevich took part in at Disk, and although at least one member has described him during this period as somewhat standoffish,[19] Nina Berberova, another well-known habituée, remembers him as still quite young (Khodasevich was thirty-four when he arrived at the House of Arts) and alive to the world of that time.[20] Both of course may be right, for it is true that Khodasevich was not by nature gregarious, but it is equally true, as we shall see a little later, that his last months in Petersburg were especially colored and animated by his growing love for Berberova. There can be little doubt, however, about Khodasevich's prominent role in the life of Disk and "Dom literatorov" (Writers' House: a much larger organization that opened on Basseynaya Street a year earlier than Disk and was made up exclusively of writers, a number of whom opposed Gorky and had leanings toward the *ancien régime*), since he was, along with Akhmatova and Zamyatin, on the governing boards of both.[21]

The Khodaseviches were allotted two rooms in Disk. One of the rooms went to Garik, and the other, which was situated in a corner of the building and formed a perfect semicircle, to Khodasevich and Nyura.[22] Khodasevich was to write much of *The Heavy Lyre* while sitting by the windowsill of this room. The room's whimsical shape and its

[18] See Forsh, *The Insane Ship*, pp. 86-88.
[19] See El'kan, "The House of Arts," pp. 294-295. Elkan, an admirer of Georgy Adamovich, says that at Disk Khodasevich was not well liked for his wit and impatience and was nicknamed *Golova Adama* (Adam's Head).
[20] *Kursiv*, p. 157.
[21] See Scherr, "A Tale of Three Houses," pp. 262-263.
[22] Descriptions of Khodasevich's room are found in Malmstad and Smith, eds., "Eight Letters of V. F. Khodasevich," p. 77; and *Stat'i*, p. 408.

The facade of the Petersburg *Dom iskusstv* (House of Arts) where Khodasevich wrote much of *Tiazhelaia lira* (The Heavy Lyre). The windows of Khodasevich's apartment are on the top floor, the first and second from the left. Today the upper stories of this building house a movie theater.

expansive view of Nevsky Prospekt and the Moyka Embankment seem, in Khodasevich's own words, to have been especially conducive to the mutually contrastive exploration of outer and inner space so characteristic of his fourth collection:

Anyone entering my room says, "What a marvelous view you have!" And that's the truth: the view is nice. Directly under my window (which is on the corner) is the bridge over the Moyka, while to the right stretch out tall poplars (through which the water shows glass-like), and straight ahead, in the distance, Nevsky can be seen right up to the State Publishing House, crowned with a squat cupola and glass dome—as if it were an empty head. . . . Nevsky is spacious, clear, flat, dry, and almost always empty.[23]

Among the neighbors on Khodasevich's corridor were the artist E. V. Shchekotikhina, soon to leave Disk for marriage abroad with Ivan Bilibin; Lozinsky; Mandelshtam, whom Khodasevich recalls at this time as "a strange and charming creature, in which pliancy cohabited with stubbornness, intelligence with silliness, remarkable abilities with the inability to pass even one university examination, laziness with diligence, . . . [and] harelike cowardice with almost heroic courage";[24] the artist Vladimir Milashevsky;[25] the poet Nadezhda Pavlovich, a good friend of Khodasevich and the first to tell him of Blok's imminent death;[26] and Olga Forsh, who shows herself, in the bravura passages of *The Insane Ship*, to be "a passionate epicure of all manner of ideas that were forever boiling, seething, and bubbling up in her."[27]

Khodasevich experienced some initial difficulties, including the relapse of furunculosis and a delay in the transfer of his writer's ration—Bryusov's negative evaluation of his former protégé's political leanings had, as it turned out, tem-

[23] From "Okno na Nevskii" (Window on Nevsky), a fragment published in *Liricheskii krug. Stranitsy poezii i kritiki* (Lyric Circle. Pages of Poetry and Criticism), 1 (Moscow, 1922) pp. 79-84. The fragment was written by Khodasevich some time before his emigration to Western Europe in June 1922. A copy in Khodasevich's hand was given to his acquaintance I. I. Bernshtein, to whose family I wish to express my special thanks for their allowing me to study the Khodasevich papers in their possession.

[24] *Stat'i*, pp. 408-409.

[25] See Vladimir Milashevskii: "V dome na Moike" (In the House on the Moyka), *Zvezda* (Star), 12 (1970), pp. 187-201; and for a fleeting picture of Khodasevich shortly after his arrival, see *Vchera, pozavchera* (Yesterday, the Day Before Yesterday) (Leningrad, 1972), pp. 184-185.

[26] See *Nekropol'*, p. 139.

[27] *Stat'i*, p. 409. Khodasevich also used a ship metaphor (a compliment to his old friend Forsh?) to conclude his description of Disk (p. 412).

porarily achieved the desired result.²⁸ But soon Khodasevich had fallen in step with the pace of life at Disk and was receiving his weekly ration at "Dom uchenykh" (Scholars' House), yet another organization that had opened in January 1920 with the aim of providing scholars with a diet adequate to do their work (among other "Wednesday-ers" in Khodasevich's group were Tynyanov, Tomashevsky, Shklovsky, Gumilyov, and Vladimir Pyast).²⁹ With the onset of spring and particularly summer the creative flurry of the period of *The Heavy Lyre* was well under way.³⁰ Khodasevich seemed intent as always on continuing his practice of avoiding poetic schools and "isms":³¹ though he read to the younger generation at the apartment of Ida Nappelbaum (a member of Gumilyov's studio), and even had followers from among them, such as the ebullient Nikolay (Kolya) Chukovsky,³² he himself by this time was following no one. He quit Gumilyov's "second" "Tsekh poetov" (Poets' Guild) in early 1921 when he discovered that this guild would be made up exclusively of Acmeist "Gumilyovians" (*gumiliata*) led by Georgy Ivanov, Georgy Adamovich, and Nikolay Otsup.³³ The first, "partyless" Guild, by contrast, had at various times invited such different poets as Blok, Gorodetsky, Georgy Chulkov, Nikolay Klyuev, Yury Verkhovsky, Vladimir Narbut, Mandelshtam, Akhmatova, and Gumilyov to participate. Considering Khodasevich's independent spirit and his deep admiration for Blok and Bely, the two great representatives of

²⁸ See Berberova, ed., "Letters of M. O. Gershenzon to V. F. Khodasevich," p. 222; Malmstad and Smith, eds., "Eight Letters of V. F. Khodasevich," pp. 77-78; and *Nekropol'*, p. 58.
²⁹ See Scherr, "A Tale of Three Houses," p. 265.
³⁰ As Khodasevich says in *SS*, p. 216, he felt that the period of *The Heavy Lyre* began on 4 April 1921 with the writing of "Psikheia! Bednaia moia!" (Psyche! My poor one!). According to the dates of composition given for the poems of *The Heavy Lyre* in *SS*, pp. 216-219, June and July 1921 were the most poetically productive months of Khodasevich's life.
³¹ See *Kursiv*, p. 151.
³² See Khodasevich, "People and Books" (15 August 1935).
³³ See *Nekropol'*, pp. 127-136.

high Symbolism, it should come as no surprise that he eschewed any compromising affiliation with Acmeism, which to his mind was one more soulless avatar of Bryusovism.[34]

In addition to Nina Berberova, whom Khodasevich would meet only at the end of 1921, Khodasevich's closest friends during this period were Gorky and Bely. Gorky's views on art were in many ways antithetical to those of Khodasevich; thus their relationship would never be one based on literary affinity—and this despite the fact that they would soon be editing *Beseda* (Colloquium) together. To put it somewhat crudely, Gorky was a prose writer with a dream of transforming the world around him, while Khodasevich was an intensely private poet in search of his own other worlds. But it was with the move to Petersburg that the domestic, almost familylike nature of their friendship was established. Khodasevich's niece Valentina (Mikhail's daughter), the portraitist and set designer, was living with her husband in an apartment adjoining Gorky's on Kronverksky Prospekt: this one circumstance, perhaps more than any other, "defined . . . not the businesslike or the literary, but the totally private, everyday" character of the two men's relationship.[35] Clearly charmed by the bustling Gorky household and by the wittily "improvising" *raconteur* himself,[36] Khodasevich, as it often happened, would pass the night at his friend's in order to avoid the long trek back to Disk. Little did he know that from the time of his emigration in June 1922 until the time the friends split nearly three years later, he and Gorky would be spending a great deal of time together under one roof.[37]

If the relationship with Gorky was more personal than

[34] For Khodasevich's negative feelings about the phenomenon of Acmeism, see Khodasevich: "Infancy," p. 101; *Nekropol'*, pp. 118-119, 127; and "O Gumileve" (On Gumilyov), *Voz*, no. 4044 (19 September 1936).

[35] *Nekropol'*, p. 231.

[36] Ibid., p. 253. Gorky in fact did not improvise at all but, feigning spontaneity, told the same stories over and over again.

[37] See ibid., pp. 234-235.

literary, the relationship with Bely was closely tied with the fateful year 1921 and with the meaning that year had for the past and future of Russian culture in general and Russian poetry in particular. Like Khodasevich, Bely had recently fled Moscow for the freer atmosphere of Petersburg and that spring was in the process of writing *Pervoe svidanie* (The First Encounter), according to many his greatest work in verse. Khodasevich had the distinct pleasure of being the first to hear this work: Bely, who was living in a hotel on Gogol Street, would drop in on his friend from time to time and on one occasion brought his just-completed masterpiece. It was also during this period that Bely was at work on his first article on Khodasevich's verse. Together with a more expansive study written during Bely's Berlin period, this article—included, interestingly, in the last issue of *Zapiski mechtatelei* (The Notes of Dreamers) that Blok coedited—had much to do with establishing Khodasevich's reputation as a major poet.[38] As though in keeping with the unique spirit of the times, Khodasevich and Bely, surrounded only by the milky eeriness of the White Nights, would walk the streets together, pay quiet homage to Falconet's magisterial statue of the Bronze Horseman, visit the house on the Moyka where Pushkin died.[39]

On a larger front 1921 was marked by the Kronstadt Uprising in March, which shook Petersburg (or Petrograd, as it was generally called by then) to its foundations and indicated to everyone the lengths to which the Bolsheviks would go to maintain order.[40] To artistic Petersburg, however, 1921 was year of three tragic deaths. Blok died a mysterious death

---

[38] See ibid., p. 86; and the notes to "Iskushenie" (Temptation) and "Buria" (Tempest), in *SS*, pp. 216-217. The article was A. Belyi, "Rembrandtova pravda v poezii nashikh dnei" (Rembrandt's Truth in the Poetry of Our Days), *Zapiski mechtatelei* (Notes of Dreamers), 5 (1922), pp. 136-139.

[39] Ibid.

[40] For the importance that Khodasevich himself attached to the Kronstadt Uprising, see Khodasevich: "People and Books" (15 August 1935); and "Gor'kii," *SZ* 70 (1940), 138-139.

in August; Gumilyov was suddenly arrested and executed that same month; and Anastasia Chebotaryovskaya, Sologub's wife and one of the original chairmen of "Soiuz deiatelei khudozhestvennoi literatury" (Union of Belletrists), drowned herself in the fall. The deaths seemed to be saying the same thing to different generations. Blok, whose life from early on seemed fatally linked with Bely's, and who was, to Khodasevich and many others, unquestionably the finest lyric poet of the Silver Age,[41] was dying slowly, visibly, before helpless friends and admirers because his inner world had ceased to resonate. The execution of Gumilyov, aside from any purely political motivation for it (the poet had been a White officer and was now reputed to be a member of the counterrevolutionary Petrograd Minuteman Organization), may have been an example to the young, whom he led. And Chebotaryovskaya killed herself in a fit of depression after she and Sologub had decided to emigrate to the West and the authorities continued to vacillate on the question of their passports.[42] Quite sensitive to what was in the air, Khodasevich knew all three persons (oddly enough, considering their differences, he was perhaps on most cordial terms with Gumilyov[43]) and understood implicitly the meaning their deaths held for this brief period of artistic ferment and freedom. No doubt it was these epoch-framing deaths coupled

[41] Khodasevich states his preference for Blok over all other lyric poets of the twentieth century in Khodasevich, "Blok i teatr" (Blok and the Theater), *Voz*, no. 2620 (4 August 1932).

[42] When Anatoly Lunacharsky discovered that the Politbyuro had decided to issue passports to Sologub and his wife, but not to Blok, he "sent the Politbyuro a nearly hysterical letter in which for no reason at all he sank Sologub. His line of reasoning was approximately the following: 'Comrades, what are you doing? I asked for both Blok and Sologub, but you are letting out only Sologub, while Blok, a poet of the Revolution, our pride—there was even an article about him in the *Times*—[you are not].' . . . The Politbyuro turned its decision inside out: Blok was given a foreign passport, which he was no longer able to use, and Sologub was held back." (*Nekropol'*, pp. 176-177.)

[43] By chance, Khodasevich was the last to see Gumilyov as a free man. See *Nekropol'*, pp. 138-139.

with the intense life at Disk that gave Petersburg, for Kho-dasevich, its "life-in-death" countenance.

While it is true the sudden deaths of Gumilyov and Che-botaryovskaya were unspeakably cruel, they must have struck Khodasevich, with his Symbolist orientation, as dark coda-like notes that could be heard to answer the last solo per-formance of, in Akhmatova's wonderfully apt phrase, "the epoch's tragic tenor."[44] Blok's death was special, somehow prophetic—an ending that deepened and made still more mysterious the now legendary blend of his life and art. Kho-dasevich was present at the Writers' House for the Pushkin festivities on 13 February 1921 when Blok took the podium to speak of the poet's sacred role and of the danger posed to that role by a world of bureaucrats:

Pushkin was not killed at all by the bullet of D'Anthès. He was killed by the absence of air. It was his culture dying with him. . . . *Peace of mind* and *freedom*. They are essential to a poet for the release of his harmony. But they [the bureaucrats] take away peace of mind and freedom as well. Not external, but creative peace of mind. Not childish liberty [*volia*], not the freedom [*svoboda*] to act liberally, but creative liberty—a mysterious freedom. And the poet dies because he no longer has anything to breathe. Life has lost its meaning.[45]

Blok was too great a romantic personality to be speaking only of Pushkin; he of course was alluding to *his* culture, and to himself. Since Kraevsky it had seemed natural to speak of Pushkin as the "sun" of Russian poetry (and Russian culture).[46] That sun had recently (in March and November of 1920) been "buried" in two of Mandelshtam's lyrics—

---

[44] A. Akhmatova, *Stikhotvoreniia i poemy* (Lyrics and Narrative Poems) (Leningrad, 1976), p. 259.

[45] A. Blok, "O naznachenii poeta" (On the Poet's Role), *Sobranie sochinenii v vos'mi tomakh* (Collected Works in Eight Volumes), eds. V. N. Orlov, A. A. Surkov, K. I. Chukovskii (Moscow-Leningrad, 1960-1963), VI, 167.

[46] V. Veresaev, *Pushkin v zhizni* (Pushkin in Life) (Moscow, 1936; rpt., The Hague, 1969), II, 442.

"Sisters—Heaviness and Tenderness" and "We will gather in Petersburg again." And Khodasevich had said (on the same evening of the thirteenth) that "[Pisarevism] was the first eclipse of Pushkin's sun. As it seems to me, a second eclipse is not far off."[47]

Now the stage seemed set not only for a second solar eclipse in Russian poetry but for a "lunar" eclipse as well. Just as the sun of a Golden Age had been extinguished, in Blok's mystical view, by the absence of air, so now Blok himself, who might be called the moon of a Silver Age, was somehow slowly being snuffed out. It was perhaps fitting, therefore, that Bely, with his great sense of epochal drama and his intimate ties with the Blok legend, should be the first to see this connection and to announce that his friend had "choked to death" in the atmosphere of 1921. Khodasevich explains, "The words relating to Blok's 'choking to death' . . . were subsequently repeated many times by many people. Judging by the fact that that expression appeared in a letter to me just a day after Blok's death [August 7] and that it wasn't in Bely's nature to repeat what had already been uttered by others, I am sure that the expression belongs precisely to him first."[48] Indeed, Khodasevich, as Bely's letter indicates, was privy to Bely's immediate reaction to Blok's death and to the sense of gathering crisis that pursued Bely into Western Europe and ultimate rejection that autumn by Rudolf Steiner and the community of anthroposophists at Dornach:

What is there to say? For me it's simply clear: that was the phase [he was going through]; he choked on the very difficult air of life; others were saying aloud, "It's stuffy." He simply fell silent, and . . . choked to death.

For me this death is the fatal tolling of the clock: I sense that a part of my very self has gone with him. You know that we weren't

[47] Khodasevich, "The Shaken Tripod," p. 114.

[48] Khodasevich, ed., "Tri pis'ma Andreia Belogo" (Three Letters of Andrey Bely), SZ 55 (1934), p. 257.

seeing each other and hardly speaking, but Blok's "existence" simply on a physical plane was for me like [having] an organ of sight or hearing. I sense that now. One can live as someone blind too. The blind either *die* or *are illuminated* from within: that's just how his death struck me: *awake* or *die; begin* or *end*.[49]

But if Khodasevich experienced Blok's passing through his friendship with Bely, he experienced it in genuine personal terms too. Like the Auden of "In Memory of W. B. Yeats," Khodasevich had by 1921 acceded to a post-Symbolist poetic tradition that had grown up largely in reaction to the private mythologies and full-throated lyricism of an older generation. Yet like Auden as well, he could not fail to come to grips with the leading figure of that generation and with that figure's quixotic attempts to merge poetry and biography. "It seems," as Khodasevich remarked in an article written for the tenth anniversary of Blok's death, "that the ideal of Symbolism—the merging of the poet and the man—was realized in the person of Blok after all. One might say (and these wouldn't simply be 'words') that Blok's entire physical being was permeated with poetry: With the end of the poet the physical being had also to end."[50] On the evening of 26 February—the last of those devoted to the Pushkin festivities—Khodasevich and Blok sat in an empty room at Petersburg University and waited their turn to speak. What emerged from the conversation was a memory that Khodasevich would cherish forever and a privileged look at the great, and greatly spent, Symbolist:

We sat at a cold, oilskin-covered table for an hour and a half. We began with talk of Pushkin, then passed on to the early period of Symbolism. Blok spoke with a loving smile about that time, about the mystical infatuations of those days, about Andrey Bely and Sergey Solovyov. People recall their childhoods in such a way. Blok admitted that he no longer understood many of the poems he had

---

[49] Ibid., p. 258. Bely's italics allude to lines from Goethe's poem "Selige Sehnsucht."

[50] Khodasevich, "Ni sny, ni iav' " (Neither Dreams nor Reality), *Voz*, no. 2256 (6 August 1931).

written then: "I have forgotten what many of those words meant. And you know they seemed sacred. But now I read those verses as if they were someone else's, and I don't always understand what it was exactly that the author wished to say."

On that evening . . . he was more melancholy than ever before. He spoke a good deal about himself, as though with himself, as though he were looking—with great restraint, at times with half-hints, vaguely, confusedly—deeply into himself, but behind the words one sensed a stern, sharp truthfulness. It seemed that he saw the world and himself in tragic nakedness and simplicity. For me truthfulness and simplicity have always remained linked with the memory of Blok.[51]

Within months of this conversation Blok would be dead. And if Bely caught the mystical terror of Blok's death with his allusion to suffocation, then Khodasevich caught the utter inexorability of that death with a restrained epigrammatic force that is a special quality of his prose:

As strange as it seems, Blok was dying for several months, before the eyes of all; doctors treated him; and no one named, or could name, his illness. It began with a pain in his leg. After that they spoke of a weak heart. . . . But what after all did he really die from? No one knows. He died somehow "in general," because he was sick through and through, because he could live no longer. He died of death.[52]

With the death of Blok and the execution of Gumilyov the ominous sense that some end was at hand suddenly became real and palpable. Artistic Petersburg had lost two primary sources of creative energy and could no longer be assured of its right to fully cultivate new sources. After spending the month of August at "Belskoe uste,"[53] Disk's estate in Pskov Province, during which time he ate with great relish the

[51]*Nekropol'*, p. 126.

[52] Ibid., p. 136.

[53] For Khodasevich's impressions of his August sojourn in the country, see Malmstad and Smith, eds., "Eight Letters of V. F. Khodasevich," pp. 78-81; and Khodasevich: "About Myself"; "Poezdka v Porkhov" (Trip to Porkhov), *Voz*, nos. 3627 and 3634 (9 and 16 May 1935); and "Vo Pskove" (In Pskov), *Voz*, no. 3795 (24 October 1935). See as well "Unpublished letters of V. F. Khodasevich to Anna Ivanovna Khodasevich," item no. 48 (letters from 5 September to 11 October 1921), TsGALI.

abundant fruit that grew there and in general relaxed and regained his strength in the pleasant country surroundings, Khodasevich returned to Petersburg to find that Bely, in the aftermath of Blok's death nearly hysterical with persecution mania, and Gorky, now beset by a feud with the mighty Grigory Zinovev, were leaving Russia.[54] Khodasevich had to decide whether he could continue to live and write under the present conditions or whether he too would be forced to choose temporary (or more terrible—though as yet a lesser possibility—permanent) exile in Western Europe.

The onset of cold weather and the winter months of 1921-1922 seemed to bring a temporary suspension of movement to the West. But everything broke loose, as Nina Berberova recalls, with the spring thaw of 1922:

The end appeared in the air at first like some kind of metaphor, collective and abstract, which became clearer from day to day. It was said that soon everything would close up—that is, private publishing houses—and that "all" would be turned over to Gosizdat [the State Publishing House]. It was said that in Moscow censorship was even more severe than with us, and that in Petersburg it would soon be the same. . . . With frosts and blizzards all had held together somehow, but presently everything started flowing, ran in streams, there was nothing to hold on to, all was running somewhere.[55]

It was during the winter months prior to this springtide that Khodasevich and Berberova, then a striking twenty year old and recently a visitor to Gumilyov's studio, grew to be friends and then lovers. Though Khodasevich would continue to be on amicable terms with Nyura and would continue to worry about her after his emigration, he was drifting apart from her.[56] Khodasevich first met Berberova in late November

[54] See Khodasevich, "Gorky," pp. 139-141.
[55] *Italics*, pp. 144-145; *Kursiv*, p. 165.
[56] In "About Myself" Khodasevich remarks cryptically that "beginning in February [1922] certain events in my private life unsettled my working routine and then led me here to Berlin." The assumption made by some that Khodasevich secretly took up with Berberova and "abandoned" Nyura in Petersburg is not borne out by surviving letters. The marriage between

1921 at one of the poetry readings constantly being organized at the apartment of Ida Nappelbaum.[57] Young, winsome, eager to learn, herself passionately committed to "poetry forever,"[58] Berberova seems to have infected the skeptical and often introverted Khodasevich with her *joie de vivre* and thirst for discovery. By the time they were celebrating the new year together their relationship had become serious;[59] by April Khodasevich had reached the conclusion that emigration (his for reasons of "health," hers for reason of "further education") was the only way they could save each other, for by then any future other than one of "being together" had become an impossibility:

Khodasevich made the decision to leave Russia, but he certainly did not foresee that he was leaving forever. He made his choice, only a few years later he made a second one: not to return. I followed him. If we had not met and not taken the decision then to "be together" and "survive," he undoubtedly would have remained in

Khodasevich and Nyura had begun to falter some time before 1922, and during the time Khodasevich was growing close to Berberova, Nyura was in fact seeing someone else (the young critic I. I. Bernshtein). But Khodasevich's deep concern that Nyura be provided for is evident both in his letters to her from abroad (see "Unpublished letters of V. F. Khodasevich to Anna Ivanovna Khodasevich," item nos. 51 and 52 [letters from 7 January to 5 December 1924 and 23 February to 18 November 1925], TsGALI) and in his (undated) letter to Akim Volynsky ("Pis'mo Khodasevicha V. F. Volynskomu A. L." [Unpublished letter of V. F. Khodasevich to A. L. Volynsky], archive [fond] no. 95, item no. 875, TsGALI): "I am going abroad and am writing you in haste. I am aware of your kind feelings for Anna Ivanovna and myself and of your kindness in general. It is for this reason that I'm asking you to help me keep both my scholar's ration and my room at the House of Arts in my wife's name. I know that you will respond to this request and do all that's possible. . . . You are aware of the events of my life over the last months and you will understand me without [further] words, for which I have neither strength nor time at the moment."

[57] *Kursiv*, p. 150.

[58] As Khodasevich had written in his calendar in 1903, Berberova now (at the end of 1921) wrote in hers "stikhi navsegda" (poetry forever). (Unpublished papers of Vladislav Khodasevich. Courtesy of the family of M. M. Karpovich.)

[59] See note to the poem "Bel'skoe ust'e," in *SS*, p. 218; and *Kursiv*, pp. 157-161.

Russia: there is no possibility, not even the slightest, that he would have gone abroad alone. . . . I would have remained of course in Petersburg. Having made his choice for himself and me, he arranged it so that we came out together and survived—that is, survived the terror of the thirties, in which almost certainly I would have perished. My choice was *him* and my decision was to follow him. One can say now that we saved each other.[60]

Thus Khodasevich's decision to emigrate ripened under the influence of his love for Berberova. It was motivated, one notes, at least as much by personal reasons as by professional or artistic ones. But a bittersweet—bitter for Khodasevich himself, sweet for his readers—*quid pro quo* would take place over the years: though the relationship with Berberova would eventually cool and she would leave him ten years later, a large part of his literary estate would survive Nazi bombings and occupation thanks to her efforts. When on 22 June 1922 Khodasevich and Berberova boarded the train in Petersburg and set off for Berlin (via Riga), they had little idea of what was ahead of them. They did not know that the geographical, almost umbilical presence which Russians refer to as *rodina* (motherland) had been by this act permanently relegated to memory, to the category of absence. Khodasevich had wanted to keep their departure a secret (presumably from Nyura), and so they had no opportunity to take proper leave of friends and relatives. Armed with the only future he had—Berberova and his beloved eight-volume Pushkin—Khodasevich was leaving a world where his lyre had been heavy, but still playable, and entering a world of European night, and eventual poetic silence.

IT IS PERHAPS no exaggeration to say that Khodasevich was a poet who seemed to experience time almost physically. The present moment, as it was inevitably borne from the future into the past by the personal and historical currents that filled the air, had for Khodasevich what in more ordinary

---

[60] *Italics*, p. 146; *Kursiv*, p. 166.

206

circumstances might be termed atmospheric pressure. Since time is still a benign force in *Grain's Way*, and since, as we learn in "The House," it has a certain spaciousness (*prostor vremeni*) in which imagination, partaking of the future, and memory, partaking of the past, are free to roam and intermingle, the present emerges not as something difficult to breathe, but as something oxygenated. Especially in the poems in blank verse, the present moment, even when colored by the havoc of the Revolution, can be combined with a past moment to release a burst of clarity and heightened consciousness comparable to Proust's "pure time." History, importantly, is not yet working against the poet; the gestures of a monkey recapitulate those of a fleeing Darius and suggest that there is a larger manifold holding everything in place. Khodasevich's guardedly optimistic view of the present in a collection written during years of hardship was of course largely determined by his conviction that the time he was living through was not an ending but a continuum and that the future, with whatever cultural tradition it chose to forge for itself, could not break the chain leading back, and perforce giving legitimacy, to the past. Khodasevich was never, as some have argued, a "reactionary" in literature and a relic of the past.[61] He did not simply, in his views on art, fear the future and retreat to the past. Rather what he feared and roundly condemned was a present generation (led by his

---

[61] "Any literature has the property that it preserves its existence only by being in a state of constant internal movement. . . . The spirit of literature is the spirit of eternal explosion and eternal renewal. In such conditions the preservation of literary tradition is nothing other than seeing to it that those very explosions take place in a rhythmically correct fashion, expediently, and that they do not destroy the mechanism. Thus, literary conservatism has nothing in common with literary reaction. The goal of the former is not in the least the cessation of those little explosions or revolutions by which literature moves forward, but exactly the opposite—the preservation of those conditions in which such explosions can take place ceaselessly, expediently, without hindrance. The literary conservative is an eternal instigator: the keeper of the fire, not the one to put it out." (*Stat'i*, p. 262.)

arch enemy Mayakovsky) that saw its future as a triumphant revolutionary break with the past. The question of the poet's relation to the present and (equally significant) the present's relation to the poet was never academic: Khodasevich's perception of that interrelation as harmonious in *Grain's Way* was genuinely sanguine; the dashing of that hope in subsequent years had to be genuinely painful.

As was suggested in the preceding section, the circumstances surrounding the writing of *The Heavy Lyre* were dramatically different from those surrounding the writing of *Grain's Way*. Now the setting is primarily Petersburg, Khodasevich's last home before a pillar-to-post existence in Western Europe. That Khodasevich saw Petersburg as a beautiful corpse and experienced the last months in Russia as a present in which *his* Pushkin no longer had a place and Blok died "gasping for air" certainly influenced the making of *The Heavy Lyre*. Khodasevich was living through a series of endings—privately, he was breaking with Anna Chulkova and falling in love with Nina Berberova; artistically, he was witnessing the eclipse of those traditions that had fed his poetry; historically, he was paying farewell to the city of Peter, soon to be the city of Lenin. All these endings make their way into *The Heavy Lyre*. The atmosphere is more heavy, the irony more trenchant, the grotesquerie more pronounced, the "zigzag of poetic truth," as Bely calls Khodasevich's play with light and shadow,[62] more troubling and spasmodic. Khodasevich has, with one exception, turned away from the generously dilating form and philosophy of the poems in blank verse and turned inward to a short, intimate lyric form stressing the moment at the expense of narration through time. Structurally, *The Heavy Lyre* reads a good deal differently from *Grain's Way*. The earlier collection's overarching metaphor, with its implicit link between the psychic life of the poet and the psychic life of his country, is now plainly

[62] Belyi, "Rembrandt's Truth in the Poetry of Our Days," p. 138.

out of joint. It is replaced by the image of a lyric tradition grown almost too ponderous for the modern poet, yet one that can still be lifted and played at the *dusha*'s bidding. Add to the various endings involved in the making of *The Heavy Lyre* the fact that Khodasevich is parting with his *dusha*, the cherished source of otherworldly music (for by *European Night* this theme virtually disappears), and we as readers begin to grasp how poignantly "ultimate" is this collection for Khodasevich and for the modern poetic tradition in Russia.

As early as 1923 Andrey Bely, by then an avid metrist, made the claim that Khodasevich's use of iambic tetrameter in *The Heavy Lyre* was closest to that of Tyutchev (with Pushkin second).[63] More recently G. S. Smith has scrutinized the stanza rhythm and stress load of a number of poems in *The Heavy Lyre* and has noted elsewhere that in his mature period Khodasevich used iambic tetrameter more (almost seventy-five percent of the time) than any other major or minor émigré poet.[64] The main point to be drawn from such rigorous studies is certainly defensible: Khodasevich did not gravitate toward iambic pentameter (which was to become by the late 1930s the favorite homogenous meter in Russian poetry[65]), but stuck with the leading meter of the nineteenth-century classical tradition; nor did he experiment to any significant degree with free or mixed meters, as did poets such as Mayakovsky and Tsvetaeva. In a word, Khodasevich may have hewn to his metrical line as a way of countering what he felt to be the metrical adventurism of Mayakov-

[63] A. Belyi, "Tiazhelaia lira i russkaia lirika" (*The Heavy Lyre* and Russian Lyric Poetry), *SZ* 15 (1923), 384-388.

[64] G. S. Smith: "Stanza Rhythm and Stress Load in the Iambic Tetrameter of V. F. Xodasevič," *Slavic and East European Journal* 24 (Spring 1980), 25-36; and "The Versification of Russian Émigré Poetry, 1920-1940," *Slavic and East European Review* 56 (January 1978), 40-41.

[65] See James Bailey, "The Evolution and Structure of the Russian Iambic Pentameter from 1880 to 1922," *International Journal of Slavic Linguistics and Poetics* 16 (1973), 119-146; and Smith, "Russian Émigré Poetry," p. 40.

sky.[66] But Khodasevich's much discussed traditionalism is always deceptive, and to argue, as the almost breathlessly computing Bely does, that Khodasevich's first cousins are Tyutchev, Pushkin, and Baratynsky is to omit at least half of the problem. Metrically, it is true, Khodasevich is not iconoclastic. But many of the words that Khodasevich weaves into a poem's ictic fabric and that the metrist scans and identifies (in a typical disposition) as Tyutchevian or Pushkinian are not words that Tyutchev or Pushkin would have used. Conscious stylistic deformation and dark, unstable, at times grotesque and absurd irony were not the stock-in-trade of Tyutchev and Pushkin.[67] "Ballada," perhaps Khodasevich's most famous lyric and the last poem in *The Heavy Lyre*, begins with a stunned speaker gazing almost catatonically at a ceiling likened to a plaster sky and at a light in that ceiling likened to a sixty-watt sun—it is safe to say that no lyric written by Tyutchev or Pushkin commences with the assumption of so devastatingly barren a cosmos.[68] Such

[66] See Smith, "Russian Émigré Poetry," p. 45.

[67] Pushkin's use of the verse prosaism, for instance, was not intended to deflate or "debunk" the style of "harmonious precision" (i.e., the grand style) of Zhukovsky and Batyushkov. See Ginzburg, *On Lyric Poetry*, pp. 212-222.

[68] To corroborate this semantic disparity we might experiment by taking the opening stanzas of metrically similar lyrics by Tyutchev and Khodasevich. Though the poems are not precise rhythmic doublets, they are written in iambic tetrameter with an aBaB rhyme scheme, are more or less "typical" of the mature Tyutchev and the mature Khodasevich, and have similar themes. Tyutchev's "O veshchaia dusha moia!" (O my prophetic soul!) (in *Polnoe sobranie sochinenii* [Complete Poetic Works] [Leningrad, 1957], p. 202) begins: "О вещая душа моя! / О сердце, полное тревоги, / О, как ты бьешься на пороге / Как бы двойного бытия! ..." ("O my prophetic soul! / O heart, full of anxiety; / O how you thrash about on the threshold / Of what seems a double existence! ...").

And Khodasevich's "Iz dnevnika" (From the Diary) (*SS*, p. 88) begins, "Мне каждый звук терзает слух, / И каждый луч глазам несносен. / Прорезываться начал дух, / Как зуб из-под припухших десен." ("Every sound tears at my ears, / and to my eyes every ray of light is unbearable. / The spirit has begun to cut its way through / like a tooth from under swollen gums").

210

ever-questioning irony and destructive use of detail were
possible in Russian poetry only after, say, Annensky and
Sluchevsky (who called the artist a "Doubting Thomas"[69]),
poets with whom the later Khodasevich easily shares as much
as he does with Pushkin, Tyutchev, and Baratynsky. Thus,
if the metrical form of Khodasevich's verse suggests to some
a classical amphora, perhaps it is worth remembering that
that vessel may contain semantic vitriol. Or, to use Khodasevich's metaphor for his artistic travails in *The Heavy
Lyre*, what he achieved in his last months in Russia was a
graft of "the classical rose [of nineteenth century tradition]
to the Soviet wilding [of shattered, soon to be traditionless,
postrevolutionary life]."[70]

The Heavy Lyre opens with "Muzyka" (The Music), the
last blank verse narrative that Khodasevich included in his
collected verse.[71] Composed on 15 June 1920 while Khodasevich was still living in Moscow and built around the theme
of psychic music that will run through the collection until
its ultimate treatment in "Ballada," the poem offers a nice
transition from the setting and narrative form characteristic
of *Grain's Way* to the chief thematic concern of *The Heavy
Lyre*. As the poem begins, the speaker emerges into a courtyard covered with snow. It is the morning after a heavy
snowfall; the air is brisk and limpid; everything has a fore-
shortened look about it due to the new snow and the clear
expanse of sky:

> Всю ночь мела метель, но утро ясно.
> Еще воскресная по телу бродит лень,
> У Благовещенья на Бережках обедня
> Еще не отошла. Я выхожу во двор.
> Как мало все: и домик, и дымок,

---

[69] Quoted in Khodasevich, "O sovetskoi literature" (On Soviet Literature),
Voz, no. 4132 (20 May 1938).

[70] Khodasevich, "Petersburg," *SS*, p. 123.

[71] See the verse fragment about Venice (dateline c. 1925-1927), which
Khodasevich did not include in the 1927 edition of his collected verse but
which Berberova included in the 1961 edition (pp. 191-192).

Завившийся над крышей! Сребророзов
Морозный пар. Столпы его восходят
Из-за домов под самый купол неба,
Как будто крылья ангелов гигантских.   (SS, p. 63)

A snowstorm blew all night, but the morning was clear.
A Sunday laziness still strayed over my body;
At "The Annunciation on the Banks" mass
was still being said.[72] I go out into the courtyard.
How small everything is: the little house and little wisp of
     smoke
curling above the roof! Silvery-roseate
is the frosty steam. Its columns mount
from behind the houses right up to the dome of the sky,
as though they were the pinions of giant angels.

The details that seem to fit so effortlessly into this painterly
scene are quite deliberate. About to be visited by his own
poetic annunciation, the speaker makes out wings in the
columns of smoke, which throughout *The Heavy Lyre* sym-
bolize passage to an empyreal realm beyond the senses. And
angels, to whom the wings belong, are of course the messengers from that realm. But here the "kak budto" (as though)
keeps the grand vision a playfully distanced artifice.

The speaker, now getting attuned to what is in the air,
has come to chop wood—a prosaically necessary chore for
anyone wintering in Moscow. In the courtyard he meets his
stocky neighbor Sergey Ivanych.[73] The bright irony of "The
Music" derives from the humorous juxtaposition of the tiny
neighbor with the broad sky, of his workman's hands (*ruki*)
and the "tuk! tuk! tuk!" (bang! bang! bang!) of his ax with
the elusive sounds (*zvuki*) of the symphony going on above
the scene and audible only to the speaker.

---

[72] Annunciation on the Banks (Blagoveshchen'e na Berezhkakh) was the
church located at the end of Rostovsky Lane—the lane on which Khodasevich lived his last years in Moscow.
[73] Sergey Ivanych Voronkov was Khodasevich's upstairs neighbor on Rostovsky (note to "The Music," in *SS*, p. 216).

И маленьким таким вдруг оказался
Дородный мой сосед, Сергей Иваныч.
Он в полушубке, в валенках. Дрова
Вокруг него раскиданы по снегу.
Обеими руками, напрягаясь,
Тяжелый свой колун над головою
Заносит он, но—тук! тук! тук!—не громко
Звучат удары: небо, снег и холод
Звук поглощают . . .

(SS, p. 63)

And suddenly my stocky neighbor Sergey Ivanych
seems so very small.
He's in a sheepskin coat and felt boots. Firewood
is scattered around him in the snow.
Straining with both arms,
he lifts his heavy hatchet
above his head, but—bang! bang! bang!—go
the muffled blows: the sky, snow, and cold
swallow the sound . . .

Khodasevich is leading us into the music of his heavy lyre by leading us through the only music that the phenomenal world can make. Sergey Ivanych's hatchet—*tiazelyi* (heavy) like the lyre that is passed to the speaker in the last poem of the collection—is his musical instrument. And its hollow *tuk* serves to counterpoint the lyre's miraculous notes.

But the speaker, also forced to make music à la Sergey Ivanych, is less than adept at it. Soon he tires of wood-chopping and asks his neighbor:

"Постойте-ка минутку,
Как будто музыка?" Сергей Иваныч
Перестает работать, голову слегка
Приподымает, ничего не слышит,
Но слушает старательно . . . "Должно быть,
Вам показалось", говорит он. "Что вы,
Да вы прислушайтесь. Так ясно слышно!"
Он слушает опять: "Ну, может быть—
Военного хоронят? Только что-то
Мне не слыхать." Но я не унимаюсь:
"Помилуйте, теперь совсем уж ясно.

И музыка идет как-будто сверху.
Виолончель . . . и арфы, может быть . . .
Вот хорошо играют! Не стучите".—
И бедный мой Сергей Иваныч снова
Перестает колоть. Он ничего не слышит,
Но мне мешать не хочет и досады
Старается не выказать. Забавно:
Стоит он посреди двора, боясь нарушить
Неслышную   симфонию.   (*SS*, p. 64)

      "Wait a moment,
isn't that music?" Sergey Ivanych
stops his work, slightly raises
his head, hears nothing,
but listens diligently . . . "It must be
your imagination," he says. "Come now,
just listen closely. It's so clearly audible."
He listens again: "Well, perhaps
a soldier is being buried. Only for some reason
I can't make it out." But I don't let up:
"Pardon me, but now it's really quite clear.
This music is coming as though from up above.
There's a 'cello . . . and harps, perhaps . . .
How well they're playing! Don't bang."
And so my poor Sergey Ivanych again
stops his chopping. He can't hear a thing,
but does not wish to bother me, and tries
not to show his irritation. How amusing:
he's standing in the middle of the courtyard afraid to
    disturb
an inaudible symphony.

The irony of the witty exchange turns on the difference
between listening (from the verb *slushat'*), which everyone
is free to do, and hearing (from the phonetically and semantically related verb *slyshat'*), which is not an act of will
but a gift of grace. The repeated "kak budto"—now in the
dialogue itself, and presumably placed where it is to alert
and orient "my poor" deaf Sergey Ivanych—is part of the
speaker's shadow play, for there is no longer any convention
or artifice ("it's as if . . .") separating him from his music,

while no amount of artifice can bear that music to the ears
of Sergey Ivanych. Finally taking pity on the thoroughly
confused neighbor, the speaker declares the symphony concluded, and the two men resume the homely music of the
ax. But the poem ends almost aposiopetically—with an elliptical shift away from the "tuk! tuk! tuk!" with the significant absence of any mediating "kak budto," and with
the feathery presence of angels promising more of their music:

> . . . Но небо
> Такое же высокое, и так же
> В нем ангелы пернатые сияют.   (*SS*, p. 64)

> . . . But the sky
> is just as high, and just the same
> do feathered angels shine in it.

The next two poems seem both elegiac and invocative,
and may be, along with "The Music," the limen through
which we enter the inner space of the *dusha*. Personally and
artistically, they suggest those points of departure—Symbolism and Pushkin—that have made Khodasevich's poetry
possible. But because the persons and historical traditions
that Khodasevich associates with them are dead, the poems
also sound a certain valedictory note characteristic of *The
Heavy Lyre*. "Ledi dolgo ruki myla" (The lady has been long
washing her hands) is a poem about Muni, who has been
dead now for six years:[74]

> Леди долго руки мыла,
> Леди крепко руки терла.
> Эта леди не забыла
> Окровавленного горла.

> Леди, леди! Вы как птица
> Бьетесь на бессонном ложе.
> Триста лет уж вам не спится—
> Мне лет шесть не спится тоже.   (*SS*, p. 65)

[74] Note to "The lady has been long washing her hands," in *SS*, p. 216.

215

The lady has been long washing her hands;
the lady has been vigorously rubbing her hands.
This lady has not forgotten
the bloody throat.

Lady, lady! Like a bird you
thrash about on your sleepless bed.
Three hundred years you haven't slept—
I've not slept for six years myself.

This tragedy in miniature is not merely another poem about insomnia in the manner of Pushkin or Tyutchev. Much time has passed, yet the guilt that Khodasevich bears for not being present to help his best friend in a moment of desperation is no less intense. During the Symbolist years, as their private lives unfolded on the fringes of literary bohemia and their daily experiences grew to resemble magic-lantern projections of noumenal worlds onto phenomenal ones, Khodasevich and Muni had lived in almost preternatural closeness. With Muni's suicide, this closeness was, on the plane of biography, severed, and so it was that Khodasevich's primary link with the "bio-aesthetic" experience of Symbolism was severed also. To the traditional image of a sleepless, hand-rubbing Lady Macbeth, Khodasevich adds an image of fierce immediacy—the cage that surrounds the thrashing bird (wings in this context are futile) is implied rather than depicted. It is so, I think, because it is as invisible, yet as real, as guilt itself.

"Ne mater'iu, no tul'skoiu krest'iankoi" (Not by my mother, but by a peasant woman from Tula) is a poem axial to Khodasevich's major period. It tells of origins, of the bittersweet right to sing; it blends autobiography with the ancient myth of poetic inspiration; it generates that sense of *trompe l'oeil* so characteristic of Khodasevich by which grand abstractions suddenly come alive in the presence of homely details, even as those details "rise to the occasion" of that grandeur; and it shows that where two parental figures—Pushkin and a

peasant nurse—left their mark Khodasevich found the very
omphalos of his poetic universe:

Не матерью, но тульскою крестьянкой
Еленой Кузиной я выкормлен. Она
Свивальники мне грела над лежанкой,
Крестила на ночь от дурного сна.

Она не знала сказок и не пела,
Зато всегда хранила для меня
В заветном сундуке, обитом жестью белой,
То пряник вяземский, то мятного коня.

Она меня молитвам не учила,
Но отдала мне безраздельно все:
И материнство горькое свое,
И просто все, что дорого ей было.

Лишь раз, когда упал я из окна,
Но встал живой (как помню этот день я!)
Грошевую свечу за чудное спасенье
У Иверской поставила она.

И вот, Россия, "громкая держава,"
Ее сосцы губами теребя,
Я высосал мучительное право
Тебя любить и проклинать тебя,

В том честном подвиге, в том счастьи песнопений,
Которому служу я в каждый миг,
Учитель мой—твой чудотворный гений,
И поприще—волшебный твой язык.

И пред твоими слабыми сынами
Еще порой гордиться я могу,
Что сей язык, завещанный веками,
Любовней и ревнивей берегу . . .

Года бегут. Грядущего не надо,
Минувшее в душе пережжено.
Но тайная жива еще отрада,
Что есть и мне прибежище одно:

Там, где на сердце, съеденном червями,
Любовь ко мне нетленно затая,
Спит рядом с царскими, ходынскими гостями
Елена Кузина, кормилица моя.   (SS, pp. 66-67)

Not by my mother, but by the Tula peasant woman
Yelena Kuzina was I reared. She would
warm my swaddling-clothes above the stove-bench,
ward off bad dreams at bedtime with the sign of the cross.

She knew no fairy tales and did not sing,
and yet she always kept for me
in a cherished trunk covered in white tin-plate
either a Vyazemsky gingerbread[75] or a mint gingerbread
    horse.

She did not teach me prayers,
but gave me absolutely everything she had:
both her bitter motherhood
and simply all that was dear to her.

Only once, when I fell from a window,
but rose alive (how I remember that day!),
she placed a penny candle
for the wondrous saving at the icon of the Iberian
    Virgin.[76]

And so Russia, you "renowned power,"
by pulling at her teats with my lips,
I sucked out the agonizing right
to love and curse you;

in that honorable feat, in that happiness of poetic song,
which I serve each moment,
my teacher has been your wonder-working genius
and my walk of life your magical tongue.

And still at times I can be proud
before your weak sons
that this language, bequeathed through the ages,
I guard more lovingly, more jealously . . .

The years rush by. I need no future,
the past is burned up in my soul,
yet still alive is the secret joy
that I too have one refuge:

[75] A Vyazemsky gingerbread is one baked in the form of a little brick,
often with a fruit filling, and originally sold in the town of Vyazma.

[76] Chapel of the Iberian Virgin (Chasovnia Iverskoi bozh'ei materi), which
held the icon that gave it its name, was located near the edge of Red Square.

> There in a heart eaten by worms,
> cherishing a love for me that is imperishable,
> sleeping next to tsarist, Khodynka guests
> is Yelena Kuzina, my nurse.[77]

This poem has a history almost as miraculous as its subject. Khodasevich had penned the first four stanzas, with their largely domestic, autobiographical thrust, back in 1917. But he had not been able to finish. Something was missing.[78] Then suddenly, on 2 March 1922, the last five stanzas erupted in one morning and afternoon spurt. Shortly afterward Khodasevich went to the Haymarket to buy some galoshes, but when they turned out to be a size too large, he stuffed the draft of the just completed poem in the toe of the new galoshes (in this instance there was no question of what was poetically prior—*dulce* or *utile*!) and continued on his way to Nina Berberova's. Once at Berberova's he recited the poem from memory (the draft was still in the galoshes). Those present were so struck by its high seriousness and splendor that no one ventured to read any of his own poetry after that. In one of those vagaries of fate that Khodasevich as ironist obviously appreciated, the draft turned up a year later—

[77] "Khodynka" refers to the site of calamitous festivities in 1896 when, during the coronation of Nicholas II, presents were distributed to huge crowds of people and more than a thousand were crushed to death in the pandemonium that ensued. Khodasevich noted that a similar disaster occurred during the famous fête put on by Prince Potyomkin in honor of the Empress Catherine in 1791. See Khodasevich, "Dve Khodynki" (Two Khodynkas), in "Melochi" (Trifles), *Voz*, no. 2963 (13 July 1933).

[78] Khodasevich's original fifth stanza (composed on 12 February 1917), with its transparent patriotism, its lack of complexity, and its silence about the pain of the poet's personal and artistic "coming forth," clearly left him unsatisfied: "Так! Из ее сосков, бескрайная Россия, / Я высосал любовь к твоим сынам. / Твои поля [alt: леса]—и мне родные, / Твоей земле свой прах я передам." ("So! From her teats, boundless Russia, / I sucked a love for your sons. / Your fields [alt: forests] are kindred to me; / to your earth I'll give up my ashes."). ("Tetrad' stikhotvorenii 1917-1918. Chernovye nabroski" [Verse Notebook of V. F. Khodasevich for 1917-1918. Rough Drafts], archive [*fond*] no. 537, item no. 22, TsGALI.)

still in the galoshes, but now exiled to Berlin.[79] What bridge, the reader asks, had Khodasevich laid between the fourth and fifth stanzas? How was the writing of the poem suddenly resumed and completed?

Although we can never know the precise chain of events that led to the completion of the poem, it is my guess that Khodasevich's sudden success was linked to a discovery he had made in his Pushkin studies—a discovery that was later incorporated into two of his articles on the poet.[80] This discovery involved what Khodasevich found to be the intimate, organic relationship between Pushkin's nurse Arina Rodionovna and the appearance of his Muse. That Khodasevich sensed a personal echo in this discovery is not in itself surprising, though the reader should realize by now that an older Khodasevich would never simply "borrow" the personal-cum-mythical framework from Pushkin; instead, that framework had to be experienced as something genuine by Khodasevich and "grafted" to his unique circumstances and poetic personality. What is noteworthy, however, is that this translation of the personal into the poetic took place during the later period of the writing of *The Heavy Lyre* (by March 1922 thoughts of emigration must have begun to cross Khodasevich's mind), at a time marked by introspection, retrospection, and general stock-taking, and could only then be given expression. Perhaps it had something to do with Khodasevich's hard-earned confidence. He was now a major poetic voice; his place in the history of Russian poetry, con-

<hr/>

[79] See note to "Not by my mother, but by a peasant woman from Tula," in *SS*, p. 216; and *Kursiv*, p. 162.

[80] Khodasevich: "Arina Rodionovna" and "The Appearance of the Muse," *On Pushkin*, pp. 9-38. The second article was conceived and written much earlier, although it did not appear in the disastrously abbreviated *Poeticheskoe khoziaistvo Pushkina* (Pushkin's Poetic Economy) published in Leningrad in 1924. In an unpublished letter of 22 June 1925 to Anna Chulkova (see note 56 above) Khodasevich mentions the piece about Pushkin's Muse and asks his wife to look into the possibility of having the Pushkinist M. A. Tsyavlovsky publish it.

firmed by those such as Bely, was unshakeable, even if the future of that poetry and of the reading public's taste promised additional tremors. Hence the poem emerges as a genealogy (in several senses) and a summing up. But before turning to the important shift that takes place in stanza five, we might look at the autobiographical detail that gives that shift its authenticity.

Thanks chiefly to an iambic verse length—alternating pentameter and hexameter—rare for Khodasevich after *Grain's Way*, we know immediately that we are in the midst of something weighty and serious. The acts and circumstances that the child first noticed and may have taken for granted as belonging to his world are now recalled vividly, "retarded," as it were, metrically, by the poet who fully understands their significance. Stanzas one through four tell us that Elena Kuzina was Khodasevich's Russian mother, for she loved him as a mother and was his first contact with Russianness—a contact his blood mother, a Jewish convert to Roman Catholicism and Polish culture, could not provide. Elena Kuzina's motherhood was bitter because in order to have enough milk to nurse the weak Vladya, she gave up her own son (the "all" that was dear to her) to a foundling hospital where he died.[81] So in a real sense, Khodasevich, born to a Polish father and Jewish mother, owed his life to the sacrifice of Elena Alexandrovna's Russian son. Just as the memories of Sophia Yakovlevna, Khodasevich's own mother, are closely tied with Mickiewicz (Poland's national poet) and Roman Catholicism, his memories of Elena Alexandrovna, his "adopted" mother, cluster around Pushkin and Russian Orthodoxy. Once, while sitting on the windowsill in his nanny's room, Vladya had become engrossed in the happenings in the courtyard below, had leaned out the window, lost his balance, and gone hurtling headfirst down the roof—only to stop short of a potentially fatal fall when his

---

[81] See Khodasevich: "Infancy," p. 102; and note to "Not by my mother, but by a peasant woman from Tula," *SS*, p. 216.

heel miraculously caught the gutter. Thus, in stanza four, the connection between the wondrous saving and the candle placed at the icon of the wonder-working Iberian Virgin (one of the most famous icons in Russia):

After [the fall] [I hear] nanny's scream and [see] raised above me nanny's huge leg in a white stocking with a red ribbon below the knee. She takes me into her arms and we return through the window into the room. No one's at home. Nanny dresses me and we set off in a cab right for the Chapel of the Iberian Virgin. Nanny lights a candle, prays for a long time, kisses all the icons, and forces me to kiss them.[82]

Even in these first tightly focused, very personal stanzas, as though sensing an inchoate affinity but not yet sure how to develop it, Khodasevich invites a comparison of the two nurses, Arina Rodionovna and Elena Alexandrovna. In "Son" (Sleep), an early verse fragment, Pushkin recalls that Arina Rodionovna would come at night to ward off spirits and make the sign of the cross over him.[83] And while Arina Rodionovna did not sacrifice her own child for Pushkin, Khodasevich believed she would have: "Pushkin's nurse would not have spared even her own daughter for him: . . . she loved him as she would her own offspring."[84] But the chief difference between the nurses is seen in the second stanza. Pushkin was genuinely inspired by his nanny's fairy tales. Those tales greatly enriched the stock of his poetic language and were perhaps his closest bond (in an otherwise ambiguous relationship) with the *narod* (people).[85] To Khodasevich, however, that door to a popular imagination and language-rich tradition was closed. He would have to win his poetic spurs some other way.

Khodasevich theorized that the key to Pushkin's under-

[82] Khodasevich, "Infancy," p. 114.

[83] Khodasevich quotes this fragment in his article, "Arina Rodionovna." See note 80 above.

[84] Ibid.

[85] See the discussion of Pushkin's use of language in his fairy tales in Khodasevich, "Notes on Verse," *PN*, no. 1573 (11 June 1925).

standing of poetic inspiration could be found in the unfin-
ished "Napersnitsa volshebnoi stariny" (Confidante of magical antiquity) (1822). Pushkin, thought Khodasevich,
remained unsatisfied with the poem because the first twelve
lines, with their explicit depiction of Arina Rodionovna leaving a charmed poet's pipe (*svirel'*) with the baby, shift too
abruptly to a conventional depiction of a lovely young Muse
in the last ten lines. The four-line transition—child becomes
man, old nurse becomes young goddess—is too transparent,
and hence clumsy. It links the concretely personal with the
conventionally mythical in a way that violated poetic canons
still respected by Pushkin. Yet the poem is an important
one to Pushkin's *oeuvre*, for in it we see the precise moment
(even if that moment made Pushkin uncomfortable) at which
autobiography becomes myth. When, for example, Pushkin
says on another occasion that—

> С утра до вечера в немой тени дубов
> Прилежно я внимал урокам девы тайной,
> И, радуя меня наградою случайной,
> Откинув локоны от милого чела,
> Сама из рук моих свирель она брала.
> Тростник был оживлен божественным дыханьем
> И сердце наполнял святым очарованьем.[86]

> From morning to evening in the silent shade of oaks
> I followed diligently the lessons of the secret maiden,
> and, pleasing me with a chance reward,
> tossing back the tresses off her sweet brow,
> she herself would take the pipe from my hands.
> The reed was given life by divine breath,
> and it filled my heart with sacred delight.

—he has managed to erase the concrete evidence of his nurse
from the conventional picture, but the nurse as an implied
presence and as a first source of poetic inspiration is nonetheless there. "From early on," concludes Khodasevich, "Arina

---

[86] Pushkin, "Muza" (The Muse), *Complete Works*, II, 164. Quoted in
Khodasevich, "Arina Rodionovna."

Rodionovna was for Pushkin a person of a half-real, half-mythical order, a being eternally young, like the Muse, and eternally aged, like his nurse. . . . She was the embodiment of the Russian Muse."[87]

This revelation, I believe, is what permitted Khodasevich to complete the work. There are additional references to Pushkin in the second half of the poem that alert us to his collusion—Aleko's words from *The Gypsies* about Rome's "renowned [lit: 'loud'] power" and the allusion to poetry as a *podvig* (feat) that may trace to "To the Poet," a poem that also served as the point of departure for Khodasevich's speech "The Shaken Tripod."[88] But these are more sign posts than points of destination. In the fifth stanza Khodasevich makes his shift from autobiography to myth. He does not make the explicit jump from nurse to goddess—*that* transformation had already been seen to by Pushkin. Living in a different poetic time and space, one with its own unique injunctions, Khodasevich has to manage the mythopoesis otherwise. The actual milk with which Elena Kuzina nursed the infant becomes in the last five stanzas the psychic milk, the Russian language, that still nourishes Khodasevich, but in another way. In fact the poet, no longer an infant, has taken on the attributes of a solicitous and loving parent. And the miracle that saved Khodasevich from the fall (his *dusha*, by the way, often seems to be falling), and that the nurse lights a candle for at the icon of the *wonder-working* Virgin, is transformed into the miracle of poetic speech, with its *chudotvornyi genii* (wonder-working genius).[89] Of course, the source of inspiration, the embodiment of Khodasevich's Muse, remains the nurse, but the identification is left unsaid, below the surface.

[87] Khodasevich, "Arina Rodionovna."

[88] The allusions to *The Gypsies* and "To the Poet" are mentioned in Sylvester, "V. F. Xodasevič in Moscow and Petersburg," p. 39.

[89] The link between the "miracle-working" icon and the "miracle-working genius" of the Russian language is made in Sylvester, "V. F. Xodasevič in Moscow and Petersburg," p. 38.

The reader must cast his own bridge between the physical act of giving milk and the metaphorical act of blowing on the shepherd's reed or handing the poet his lyre.

After the opening invocative pieces, Khodasevich begins what might be called his psychic diary. The following group of poems—"Tak byvaet pochemu-to" (So it happens for some reason), "K Psikhee" (To Psyche), "Dusha" (The Soul), "Psikheia! Bednaia moia!" (Psyche! My poor one!), "Isku-shenie" (The Temptation), "Puskai minuvshego ne zhal' " (Let the past not be pitied), "Buria" (The Tempest), "Liubliu liudei, liubliu prirodu" (I love people, I love nature), "Gos-tiu" (To My Guest), and "Kogda b ia dolgo zhil na svete" (When I've lived a long time on earth)—were written for the most part in the spring and summer of 1921. They focus on the status of the *dusha* as it passes from a sphere of icy detachment to one in which the lacerated and disputatious heart tries to make its urges felt. By definition there is never any way that the heart and soul can communicate, but the dialectic becomes fiercer as the heart and the waking world rise to the poetic surface. Thus the first four poems operate entirely within the realm of the *dusha* (with the last of them, "Psyche! My poor one!" already showing signs of the intrusion of other feelings); from "Let the past not be pitied" through "To My Guest" we are in a tightly restrictive waking world, one in which the speaker is wise and weary, slightly misanthropic, no longer moved by literal or figurative tempests;[90] "The Temptation" is transitional—a dialogue form in which the crude, colloquial, heavily ironic speech of the heart is offset in the last stanza by the unapproachable wis-

[90] "With bad weather, the tempest, and the hurricane Pushkin compares everything that lies outside the field of influence of a separate personality. A wicked government, popular uprising, high mortality, war, state neces-sity, the force of the mass over the person, all that fetters individual free-dom, all that is beyond the walls of one's home—all that [he calls] bad weather." (Khodasevich, *Poeticheskoe khoziaistvo Pushkina* [Pushkin's Po-etic Economy] [Leningrad, 1924], p. 59.)

dom of the soul; and "When I've lived a long time on earth," the last of the group, is recapitulative.

Perhaps the closest Khodasevich ever came to expressing in words the total ulteriority and "otherness" of his *dusha* is the poem of the same name, the first one he wrote in Petersburg:

> Душа моя—как полная луна:
> Холодная и ясная она.
>
> На высоте горит себе, горит—
> Но слез моих она не осушит:
>
> И от беды моей не больно ей,
> И ей невнятен стон моих страстей;
>
> А сколько здесь мне довелось страдать—
> Душе сияющей не стоит знать.[91]   (*SS*, p. 70)

> My soul is like a full moon:
> she is cold and serene.
>
> On high she burns her way, she burns,
> but my tears she will not dry:
>
> and she does not feel the pain of my misfortune,
> and does not hear the moan of my passions;
>
> and as much as it is my lot here to suffer,
> it would not do for my shining soul to know.

Khodasevich, it seems, is isolating the character of the *dusha* through vocalic instrumentation (*instrumentovka*). It is well known that of all the vowels in Russian *a* is the most optimally compact and is often associated, as in the verse of Blok, with feelings of vastness, completeness, balance.[92] Bely, for one, remarked in *Symbolism* that "*a* is the most open

---

[91] Khodasevich defends as Pushkinian his quaint use here of the dative form of the pronoun *sebia* (oneself) in Khodasevich, *Pushkin's Poetic Economy*, p. 22.

[92] See Kiril Taranovski, "The Sound Texture of Russian Verse in the Light of Phonemic Distinctive Features," *International Journal of Slavic Linguistics and Poetics* 9 (1965), 117.

sound, expressing wholeness."[93] But the opposition of the soul's stability and the passions' instability is not apparently carried through the poem by a "compact" (*e, o, a*)/"diffuse" (*i, y, u*) vocalic opposition. Instead, the dominant *a-o* combination of stressed vowels in the first and fourth stanzas opposes the dominant *i-e* combination in the second and third stanzas to give a "grave"/"acute" ("dark"/"bright" in Taranovski's terminology) alternation of distinctive features. To "semanticize" the alternation, one might read the poem like this: the soul is surrounded only by its serenity (the *a-o* quality) in the first stanza; the passionate and fallen world (the *i-e* quality) of the heart tries to, but cannot, breach that serene otherness in the next two stanzas; and the soul's victory, and heart's failure, is betokened in the last stanza by a return to the distanced calm (the *a-o* quality) of the first stanza. Therefore, Khodasevich manages to express indirectly, in the vocalic drama of this tiny poem, the entire metaphysic of absence that is the key to the *dusha*.

During the summer and fall of 1921—that period when Blok died, Gumilyov was executed, Chebotaryovskaya committed suicide, and Bely and Gorky left for Western Europe—Khodasevich wrote a series of lyrics in which the serene world of the *dusha* recedes, the cramped and stuffy, sometimes violent world of the heart comes to the fore, and the feelings of tension and desperation caused by the shift become unbearable. Once the conscious, waking world (which, in a reversal of the semantics of *Grain's Way*, Khodasevich now likens to a world of bad dreams) establishes its tyranny in "Den' " (Day), "Iz okna" (From the Window), "V zasedanii" (In Session), and "Ni rozovogo sada" (Not a rose-colored garden), the soul and spirit (*dukh*) try to break out of their bodily prison in "Probochka" (The Cork), "Iz dnevnika" (From the Diary), and "Lastochki" (The Swallows). The chief semantic mark of these latter poems, and of "Zhi-

---

[93] A. Belyi, *Simvolizm* (Symbolism) (Moscow, 1910), p. 411, quoted in Taranovski, "The Sound Texture of Russian Verse," p. 117.

zel' " (Giselle)—which precedes "Day"—and of "Pereshagni" (Step Over)—which follows "The Swallows"—is the
verbal prefixes *pere-* and *pro-*. It appears that these two prefixes, suggesting, respectively, motion over and through
something, provide Khodasevich with a powerful way of im-
aging his speaker's psychic and spiritual efforts to break free.

In "Day" we find a speaker who has undergone diametric
change since "The Soul." Smothering in the close air of his
room, looking out a window that frames a hell of the quotidian (cf. "From the Window," the following poem), the
speaker comments,

> Горячий ветер, злой и лживый.
> Дыханье пыльной духоты.
> К чему душа, твои порывы?
> Куда еще стремишься ты?
>
> Здесь хорошо. Вкушает лира
> Свой усыпительный покой
> Во влажном сладострастьи мира,
> В ленивой прелести земной.
>
> Здесь хорошо. Грозы раскаты
> Над ясной улицей ворчат,
> Идут под музыку солдаты,
> И бесы юркие кишат:
>
> Там разноцветные афиши
> Спешат расклеить по стенам,
> Там скатываются по крыше
> И падают к людским ногам.
>
> Тот ловит мух, другой танцует,
> А этот, с мордочкой тупой,
> Бесстыжим всадником гарцует
> На бедрах ведьмы молодой ...
>
> И верно, долго не прервется
> Блистательная кутерьма,
> И с грохотом не распадется
> Темно-лазурная тюрьма.
>
> И солнце не устанет парить,
> И поп, деньку такому рад,

Не догадается ударить
Над этим городом в набат.   (*SS*, pp. 80-81)

Hot air, nasty and false;
The breath of dusty closeness.
Why, soul, your fits?
Where can you still be rushing to?

It's nice here. The lyre tastes
its sleep-inducing peace
in the world's humid sensuality,
in the earth's lazy charm.

It's nice here. Peals of the storm
grumble above the bright street;
soldiers pass to the sound of music;
and darting demons swarm:

There they race to paste
multi-colored affiches on the walls;
there they roll down a roof
and fall to people's feet.

That one catches flies, another dances,
and this one, with a stupid mug,
prances like a shameless horseman
on the thighs of a young witch . . .

And it's true, this brilliant bustle
won't break off for a long time,
and the dark-azure prison
won't collapse with a crash.

And the sun won't tire of sweltering,
and the priest, pleased at such a day,
won't guess to sound
the tocsin over this city.

This is no grand, Luciferian sort of hell, but one of petty
demons. With the image of demons running wild in the sun
and heat, Khodasevich seems to be reversing the situation
of Pushkin's famous "Besy" (The Demons), in which the
speaker is harassed by swarming demons in a snowstorm.
The frustration and heavy irony ("It's nice here") of the first
stanzas erupt into a grotesque daydream that climaxes in

the fifth stanza with what may be a mocking allusion (painful of course to Khodasevich) to the Bronze Horseman. This world, from which there is no exit in sight, is the sole province of the *eiron*. And thus masking his true feelings with furious levity and resigning himself to irresolution, the speaker concludes by invoking the image of Fet's blue prison and by singling out a man of faith to preside in ignorance over the farce.

Repeated attempts to escape from the prison of "Day" led Khodasevich to write "The Swallows," a lyric of exquisite anguish:

> Имей глаза—сквозь день увидишь ночь,
> Не озаренную тем воспаленным диском.
> Две ласточки напрасно рвутся прочь,
> Перед окном шныряя с тонким писком.
>
> Вон ту прозрачную, но прочную плеву
> Не прободать крылом остроугольным,
> Не выпорхнуть туда, за синеву,
> Ни птичьим крылышком, ни сердцем подневольным.
>
> Пока вся кровь не выступит из пор,
> Пока не выплачешь земные очи—
> Не станешь духом. Жди, смотря в упор,
> Как брызжет свет, не застилая ночи.   (*SS*, p. 89)

> If you have eyes, through day you'll see night,
> not the one lit up by that inflamed disk.
> In vain two swallows are bursting to get out,
> darting at the window with a faint chirp.
>
> One cannot puncture with a sharp-angled wing
> that transparent, but sturdy membrane over there;
> nor can one, with a bird's tiny wing or
> a captive heart, flit there.
>
> Till all the blood has come out of your pores,
> Till you have cried out your earthly eyes,
> You won't become spirit. Wait, looking point blank,
> as the light splashes without covering the night.

The hirundine image has a rich tradition in Russian poetry, and Khodasevich expects the reader to see his lines against that tradition. The famous poems by Derzhavin, Fet, and Maykov are ones that were close to Khodasevich: he had ended his early article on Derzhavin with the opening lines of the latter's swallow poem; he had been present at Bryusov's early lecture when Fet's lines about the swallow's flight were used to encourage the audience "to scoop up a drop of otherworldly essence"; and he had as a child recited to the aging Maykov the lyric that is that poet's expression of the impossible desire for wings. But Khodasevich breaks with this tradition in a manner that is especially poignant. His predecessors' swallows are, first, concrete birds, taken from nature and bodied forth in the act of flight, and, second, symbols of the soul's immortality (Derzhavin) or of the poet's inspired "I" (Fet) or simply of the spirit of free movement (Maykov). (Only Maykov's poem, in which the speaker is denied the freedom of the bird, approaches the somberness of Khodasevich's poem.) Khodasevich's swallows, on the other hand, are *metaphysical*—the entire poem takes place inside the speaker; there is no correlative in nature—and their image is one of frantic captivity. We find two of them because they are the poet's eyes: rather than traditional pathways to the soul, they have become the opposite—the ocular routes by which the soul wants desperately to make its way to freedom. The importunate repetition of *pro-* (*proch', prozrachnuiu, prochnuiu, probodat'*) and of its various phonetic echoes (na*pra*sno, vy*por*khnut', *por*, u*por*) suggests the swallows' wings that, flapping to no avail, cannot break through the glass. Only when those eyes, those metaphysical windows, have been cried out will the psychic swallows be set free. The poem is one of the most terrifyingly beautiful that Khodasevich ever wrote.

In the final months of 1921, Khodasevich wrote several poems—"Vakkh" (Bacchus), "Lida," "Bel'skoe ust'e," and "Ballada"—in which the speaker assumes a mythical mask (Bacchus, Satan, Orpheus) or watches, as in "Lida," as his subject assumes one. Each of these poems in its own way has to do with the act of creation that Khodasevich is celebrating, albeit painfully, through much of *The Heavy Lyre*. By this stage in Khodasevich's development the myths are nowise decorative but have been worked into—and in a sense, worked out from—Khodasevich's idiosyncrasies as man and poet. And as in so many of the other poems being written at this point, these poems do not mythologize, make statements that are larger-than-life, without the sobering ballast of irony and concrete detail. The staff-carrying speaker of "Bacchus" enters the scene as the poem opens and departs as it closes. What he brings is the magic vine of his art, which he enjoins his followers to cultivate (literally *privit'*—"to graft"). When the time comes, the plant produces a *zhivotvoriashchii sok* (life-giving juice) that, once drunk, transforms reality and intoxicates all save the vintager-creator Bacchus himself with its secret knowledge. In "Lida" the speaker is the only one who does not seek the favors of his maenadic subject; his reward for the artist's abstinence is a vision at dawn of Lida rising out of the local context and giving her hand to Satan.[94] And the concrete summer setting of "Bel'skoe ust'e" becomes the Garden of Eden, and Khodasevich's vacationing speaker another avatar of Satan:

> А я росистые поляны
> Топчу тяжелым башмаком,
> Я петербургские туманы
> Таю любовно под плащем,
>
> И к девушкам, румяным розам,
> Склоняясь томною главой,
> Дышу на них туберкулезом,
> И вдохновеньем, и Невой,
>
> И мыслю: что ж, таков от века,
> От самых роковых времен,

---

[94] Nina Berberova has told me that the original source for Lida was a girl "of easy virtue" who helped a number of the Serapions to lose their virginity. See as well Malmstad and Smith, eds., "Eight Letters of V. F. Khodasevich (1916-1925)," p. 81.

Для ангела и человека
Непререкаемый закон.

И тот, прекрасный неудачник
С печатью знанья на челе
Был тоже—просто первый дачник
На расцветающей земле.

Сойдя с возвышенного Града
В долину мирных райских роз,
И он дыхание распада
На крыльях дымчатых принес.   (SS, pp. 96-97)

And I trample down
the dewy glades with my heavy shoe;
I conceal lovingly beneath my cloak
the mists of Petersburg;

and leaning my languid head
to the maidens, flushed and roseate,
I breathe on them tuberculosis,
and inspiration, and the Neva;

And think: well, from time [immemorial],
from the most fatal of times,
the incontrovertible law has been the same
for angel and man.

And that one, the beautiful misfit
with the stamp of knowledge on his brow,
was also just the first vacationer
on the flowering earth.

Descending from the City on High
to the valley of Eden's peaceful roses,
he too brought the breath of decay
on his smoky wings.

The artist is like Satan because he brings knowledge of good and evil to the home of innocence, because he blows on the flora and fauna of this provincial paradise the breath of Petersburg, of mortality, of the fall. In a moment of self-recognition, Khodasevich likens his musty cloak smelling of necropolis to the smoky wings of the Devil. The "ironization" of the myth of the fall, seen most clearly in the penultimate stanza, with its ingenious stand-off of styles and its rhyming of *prekrasnyi neudachnik* (beautiful misfit) and *prosto pervyi dachnik* (just the first vacationer), thwarts our expectations and invigorates the ancient tradition of that myth.

The theme of Luciferian, or "light-bearing," wings finds its darkest treatment in "Avtomobil' " (The Automobile), a poem written in December 1921. Khodasevich seems to have placed the poem where he did—that is, prior to the radiant surge of lyrics that concludes *The Heavy Lyre*—because he saw it as some ultimate (yet, happily for this book, still provisional) stage of psychic disintegration.

> Бредем в молчании суровом.
> Сырая ночь, пустая мгла.
> И вдруг—с каким певучим зовом
> Автомобиль из-за угла.
>
> Он черным лаком отливает
> Сияя гранями стекла,
> Он в сумрак ночи простирает
> Два белых ангельских крыла
>
> И стали здания похожи
> На праздничные стены зал,
> И близко возле нас прохожий
> Сквозь эти крылья пробежал.
>
> А свет мелькнул и замаячил,
> Колебля дождевую пыль . . .
> Но слушай: мне являться начал
> Другой, другой автомобиль . . .
>
> Он пробегает в ясном свете,
> Он пробегает белым днем,
> И два крыла на нем, как эти,
> Но крылья черные на нем.
>
> И все, что только попадает
> Под черный сноп его лучей,
> Невозратимо исчезает
> Из утлой памяти моей.

Я забываю, я теряю
Психею светлую мою,
Слепые руки простираю,
И ничего не узнаю:

Здесь мир стоял, простой и целый,
Но с той поры, как ездит <u>тот</u>,
В душе и в мире есть пробелы,
Как бы от пролитых кислот.   (*SS*, pp. 100-101)

We stroll in a silence that's severe.
The night is damp, the darkness empty.
And suddenly, with what a songlike call
there's an automobile from behind the corner.

Shining with facets of glass,
it is shot with a black luster;
it extends into the night's dusk
two white angelic wings.

And buildings have begun to resemble
the festive walls of large rooms,
and nearby us a passer-by
has run through these wings.

And the light has flickered, hovered vaguely,
stirring up a rainy spray,
but listen: I've begun to glimpse
another, another automobile . . .

It runs by in radiant clarity,
it runs by in broad daylight,
and it has two wings, like these others,
but its wings are black.

And everything that simply falls
under the black shaft of its rays
disappears irretrievably
from my poor memory.

I forget and I lose
my radiant Psyche;
I reach out my blind hands,
but cannot recognize a thing:

Here a world stood, simple and intact,
but ever since that other is on the road,

235

in my soul and world are gaps
as though from spilled acid.

From the imagery of this poem Khodasevich need make just a short step to the grotesque, impenetrable murk of *European Night*. Here we find the soon to be familiar world of machines and gadgets—trams, motorcycles, gramophones, radios, and electric saws—that cause the speakers of Khodasevich's last collection such anguish. Unlike Marinetti, and more like Henry Adams with his fear of the dynamo's "multiverse," Khodasevich uses the figure of the automobile to suggest the diabolical incursion of uncontrolled man-made motion into the fragile realm of the *dusha*. Some of his favorite tropes are now turned inside out: the play with reflecting surfaces that anticipated penetration to inner space in "Look for Me" and the appearance of angelic wings that announced an otherworldly symphony in "The Music." In a way such images have "programmed" us to expect a benign revelation, and hence the first half of the poem may be said to operate under a familiar system of lyrical assumptions. Indeed, the automobile whose headlights are transformed into wings appears to fill the speaker's nocturnal wanderings with its strange enlightenment. Its miraculous passage might be an act of grace, another annunciation. But the second half of the poem, which is a sort of photographic negative of the first half, blots out the sensation of enlightenment and returns the speaker to a state more perilous than the initial darkness. The last stanza, with its yoking of spilled acid and psychic damage in an unlikely and bitterly "unpoetic" simile, is especially adumbrative of the endings of many of the poems in *European Night*.

The Heavy Lyre ends with a handful of lyrics composed mainly in the spring and summer of 1922. These poems, several of them charming pieces grown out of the new love for Nina Berberova that ripened that spring, reveal the mood of quiet affirmation with which Khodasevich entered his last weeks in Petersburg and his first weeks in emigration. They are, one might say, Khodasevich's last lingering goodbye to the bright, resonant world of the *dusha*. This is the last time that Khodasevich creates a speaker who wants to believe and to sing, as in "Vecher" (Evening); or one who comes to watch fishermen cast off for the evening catch and stays to see the transfiguration of distant sails into angelic wings, as in "Gliazhu na grubye remesla" (I look at coarse trades); or one who feels the heartbeat of fetal life in what is old and thread-bare, as in "Ni zhit', ni pet' pochti ne stoit" (It is almost not worth it to live and sing); or—perhaps most telling—one who is present for the magic moment when the *dusha*, leaping up for joy, wings its way toward the lambent sphere of its primordial home, as in "Elegiia" (Elegy). Thus, the closing notes played by Khodasevich's heavy lyre are triumphant. But the last note itself, the one that gives the collection its title, belongs to "Ballada."

"BALLADA" may be the finest lyric that Khodasevich wrote, a poem that Vladimir Nabokov once described as attaining "the limits of poetic skill."[95] Even alone, when first appearing, it had no small part in the making of Khodasevich's reputation.[96] It is also the final poem in *The Heavy Lyre*, and, like "Grain's Way," another title poem, we may assume it is intended in some sense as that collection's frame. But just as "Grain's Way" saw time as benign or at least benignly indifferent, and therefore was "forward-looking," appropriately placed as frontispiece, so "Ballada" may be in some ways the opposite—"backward-looking" and ultimate. Correspondingly, if historical and personal time have become purposeless, destructive without being regenerative, then they

[95] V. Sirin [Nabokov], "Vladislav Khodasevich" [a review of *The Collected Verse*], *Rul'* (The Rudder), no. 2142 (14 December 1927).

[96] The importance of "Ballada" for the subsequent growth of Khodasevich's reputation is mentioned in *Kursiv*, p. 151; and V. Veidle, "Khodasevich izdali-vblizi" (Khodasevich from Far and Near), *Novyi zhurnal* (New Review), 66 (1961), 135.

cannot be joined in but must be overcome in some other
way.

> Сижу, освещаемый сверху,
> Я в комнате круглой моей.
> Смотрю в штукатурное небо
> На солнце в шестнадцать свечей.
>
> Кругом—освещенные тоже,
> И стулья, и стол, и кровать.
> Сижу—и в смущеньи не знаю,
> Куда бы мне руки девать.
>
> Морозные белые пальмы
> На стеклах беззвучно цветут.
> Часы с металлическим шумом
> В жилетном кармане идут.
>
> О, косная, нищая скудость
> Безвыходной жизни моей!
> Кому мне поведать, как жалко
> Себя и всех этих вещей?
>
> И я начинаю качаться,
> Колени обнявши свои,
> И вдруг начинаю стихами
> С собой говорить в забытьи.
>
> Бессвязные, страстные речи!
> Нельзя в них понять ничего,
> Но звуки правдивее смысла,
> И слово сильнее всего.
>
> И музыка, музыка, музыка
> Вплетается в пенье мое,
> И узкое, узкое, узкое
> Пронзает меня лезвие.
>
> Я сам над собой вырастаю,
> Над мертвым встаю бытием,
> Стопами в подземное пламя,
> В текучие звезды челом.
>
> И вижу большими глазами—
> Глазами, быть может, змеи—
> Как пению дикому внемлют
> Несчастные вещи мои.

И в плавный, вращательный танец
Вся комната мерно идет,
И кто-то тяжелую лиру
Мне в руки сквозь ветер дает.

И нет штукатурного неба
И солнца в шестнадцать свечей:
На гладкие черные скалы
Стопы опирает—Орфей.   (*SS*, pp. 118-120)

I sit, illumined from above,
in my round room.
I look into a plaster sky
at a sixty-watt sun.

Around me, illumined also,
are chairs, and a table, and a bed.
I sit, and in confusion have no idea
what to do with my hands.

Frozen white palms
bloom noiselessly on the windowpanes.
My watch with a metallic sound
runs in my vest pocket.

O, stale, beggared paltriness
of my hopelessly closed life!
Whom can I tell how much I pity
myself and all these things?

And, embracing my knees,
I begin to rock,
and all at once I begin in a daze
to talk with myself in verse.

Unconnected, passionate speeches!
You can't understand them at all,
but sounds are truer than sense
and the word is strongest of all.

And music, music, music
threads its way into my singing
and sharp, sharp, sharp
is the blade that pierces me.

I begin to outgrow myself,
to rise above my dead being,

with steps into the subterranean flame,
with brow into the fleeting stars.

And I see with great eyes—
the eyes, perhaps, of a snake—
how to my wild song [now] harken
my wretched things.

And in a flowing, revolving dance
my entire room moves rhythmically,
and someone hands me
a heavy lyre through the wind.

And the plaster sky
and the sixty-watt sun are no more:
onto the smooth, black boulders
it is Orpheus planting his feet.[97]

[97] It is interesting to compare my literal translation against Nabokov's "free" translation, which appeared under the title "Orpheus" (in Karlinsky and Appel, eds., *The Bitter Air of Exile*, pp. 69-70):

"Brightly lit from above I am sitting / in my circular room; this is I— / looking up at a sky made of stucco, / at a sixty-watt sun in that sky. //

"All around me, and also lit brightly, / all around me my furniture stands, /chair and table and bed—and I wonder / sitting there what to do with my hands. //

"Frost-engendered white feathery palmtrees / on the window-panes silently bloom; / loud and quick clicks the watch in my pocket / as I sit in my circular room. //

"Oh, the leaden, the beggarly bareness / of a life where no issue I see! / Whom on earth could I tell how I pity / my own self and the things around me? //

"And then clasping my knees I start slowly / to sway backwards and forwards, and soon / I am speaking in verse, I am crooning / to myself as I sway in a swoon. //

"What a vague, what a passionate murmur / lacking any intelligent plan; / but a sound may be truer than reason / and a word may be stronger than man. //

"And then melody, melody, melody / blends my accents and joins in their quest / and a delicate, delicate, delicate / pointed blade seems to enter my breast. //

"High above my own spirit I tower, / high above mortal matter I grow: / subterranean flames lick my ankles, / past my brow the cool galaxies flow. //

"With big eyes—as my singing grows wilder— / with the eyes of a serpent maybe, / I keep watching the helpless expression / of the poor things that listen to me. //

Khodasevich began the poem on 9 December and completed it two weeks later on 22 December 1921. The stark realistic details belong to the familiar surroundings of apartment 30a in Disk.[98] At precisely the moment "Ballada" was completed Korney Chukovsky paid Khodasevich a visit and thus turned out to be the first to hear the poet read his poem.[99] The first public reading of "Ballada"—to a Petersburg "grow[n] attractive in its coffin"[100]—took place that evening at the apartment of Ida Nappelbaum.

"Ballada" is written in regular amphibrachs, a meter that Khodasevich uses only one other time in his collected verse.[101] Unlike binary verse, in which the majority of Khodasevich's poems are written and which allows the poet more freedom to individualize rhythm within a fixed meter, the rhythmic pattern in ternary verse is as a rule much closer to, even coterminous with, the metrical scheme.[102] Why Khodasevich opts for this rhythmic regularity should become clear

---

"And the room and the furniture slowly, / slowly start in a circle to sail, / and a great heavy lyre is from nowhere / handed me by a ghost through the gale. //

"And the sixty-watt sun has now vanished, / and away the false heavens are blown: / on the smoothness of glossy black boulders / this is Orpheus standing alone."

[98] Khodasevich's room was in fact not circular (as in the poem), but semicircular. See *Stat'i*, p. 408. Khodasevich recalls that while writing the poem, he was particularly reminded of a billiard table that Van Gogh painted. This is most likely a reference to "Night Cafe in Arles" (1888), in which the Dutch painter presents, with a great sense of *Angst*, a "sixty-watt sun" and a "plaster sky" overhanging a billiard table.

[99] Note to "Ballada," in *SS*, p. 219.

[100] *Stat'i*, p. 400. Khodasevich, according to Berberova and Weidlé, was an excellent reader of poetry.

[101] See Khodasevich, "Akrobat" (The Acrobat), *SS*, p. 18.

[102] B. Unbegaun, *Russian Versification* (Oxford, 1956), p. 46. Eikhenbaum, in *The Melodics of Russian Lyrical Verse* (p. 23), says that the iamb can be defined as "the closest to conversational speech [*samyi razgovornyi*] of all meters" and that "it is not by chance that in the history of our lyrical poetry periods of a developing melodious [*napevnyi*] style correspond to the flourishing of ternary meters, the rhythmical diversity of which is very restricted by comparison to that of the iamb. Pushkin is the master of iambic tetrameter, Fet the master of the anapest and dactyl."

as we look closer at the structure of the poem. At first glance, at least, the amphibrachs' smooth, tidal rhythm seems especially suited to the poem's chantlike quality, its emphasis on music, and its final allusion to Orpheus, the legendary pre-Homeric poet, master of the lyre, and votary of Dionysus. Furthermore, though the amphibrachic meter is found relatively infrequently in Russian poetry, it does predominate in the ballad form (e.g., Zhukovsky's "Teon and Eskhin" and his adaptation of "Der Erlkönig"), which may explain the poem's title and the perfect amphibrach ("Bǎllǎdǎ") contained in it.[103] The stanzaic pattern (AbCb) is also regular, with rhyming occurring only between the catalectic feet ending each second and fourth line.

But the absolute identity of rhythmic pattern and metrical scheme is not always (indeed, not usually) poetically fruitful, as the profusion of ideally realized wooden iambs in the early odes of Lomonosov proves. Fet, for instance, was unusually successful with ternary meters largely because he introduced syntactical and compositional devices that gave those meters unexpected vitality even as he tapped the sources of their predictable "melodiousness" (*napevnost'*).[104] Speaking simply on a mechanical level, to Khodasevich there falls the task of somehow modulating through various means what by nature may be too regular. One means available to the poet, and one which seems potentially significant for "Ballada," is instrumentation—"the artistic disposition of a verse's vowels and consonants" that was seen to function in a poem such as "The Soul."[105] In fact, Khodasevich begins in the first stanza by marking his language with phonetic recurrence and parallelism. Two strong alliterations, those based on *s* and *k*, are complemented by the stressed vowel *u* (the frequency of which in unmarked speech is quite limited).[106]

---

[103] Unbegaun, *Russian Versification*, pp. 48-49.
[104] See Eikhenbaum, *The Melodics of Russian Lyrical Verse*, pp. 119-195.
[105] Zhirmunskii, *Theory of Literature, Poetics, Stylistics*, p. 170.
[106] "The vowel *u* is the least frequent stressed vocalic phoneme in the

And this phonetic patterning is further reinforced in the next three stanzas: the poet continues to use *s* and *k* alliteratively and to depend more heavily on the stressed *u* than on any other vowel. The acoustic "programming" seems to converge in the fourth stanza with the poet's exclamation of hopelessness: all the tension can be seen to fall on the abstract noun *skudost'* (paltriness), which brings together for the first time all three phonetic elements (*s* + *k* + *ú*) in one semantic unit.[107]

In stanzas five and six the *s* and *k* alliterations continue to manifest themselves, though perhaps not quite so persistently. The stressed *u*, however, all but disappears. Only in the seventh stanza does it resurface in combination with *s* and *k* to dominate that stanza's vocalic quality—six out of twelve of the stressed vowels are *ú*. Here the thrice-repeated *muzyka* (containing two of the three marked phonetic elements, with the *z* being a voiced equivalent of *s*) and *uzkoe* (containing all three, with the *z* now devoiced) suggest, along with *skudost'*, important phonetic turning points in the poem. Here too, for the only time in the poem, words with a dactylic ending momentarily take over: "múzўkă, múzўkă, múzўkă"; "úzkŏĕ, úzkŏĕ, úzkŏĕ."[108]

Following stanza seven, the *s* + *k* + *ú* complex seems to lose strength: the *s* alliteration shows up briefly in the eighth and eleventh stanzas, the *k* alliteration disappears altogether (until the final stanza), and the stressed *ú* appears only four (out of a total of forty-eight) times in the last four stanzas.

Russian language; it accounts for less than 10% of all stressed vowels (9% in speech . . . and 7% in literary prose . . .)" (Taranovski, "The Sound Texture of Russian Verse," p. 120).

[107] The autograph of "Ballada" shows that Khodasevich toyed with *skuka* (boredom), *skudnoe* (paltry), and *skudost'* (paltriness) in line one of stanza four. Thus he seems to have been intent on working the *s* + *k* + *ú* combination into the line. My thanks to Professor Robert P. Hughes of Berkeley for kindly providing me with this information along with his notes to the autograph.

[108] The dactyls are mentioned in Nabokov, "Vladislav Khodasevich" (see note 95 above).

Thus the last four stanzas may be said to function independently of the phonetic device that up to this point has played an important role. There is more phonetic variety in them, and less acoustic programming. If we allow that the first stanza functions on one level as a prologue to introduce the $s + k + ú$ complex and the eleventh stanza functions as an epilogue in a "ringlike" (*kol'tsevaia*) structure to recapitulate and "negate" that complex ("I *net* shtukaturnogo

```
s + ú-----------s ---------------s      #1      s------------------s ----------------      #6
-----k---------k + ú-------------        s k ú   ---------------------------------------  s k ú
s + ú---------k + ú-------------         | | |   --------------kú-----------s + s          | | |
-----s-------------s------------- s      7 3 4   -------------s-----s--------------- s      7 1 1

----------------s ------------------     #2      --ú + k-------ú + k ------ú + k            #7
---------s + ú--------s ---------k        s k ú   s -----------------------------------      s k ú
s + ú-------------s-------------          | | |   --------------ú[s]k-ú[s]k-ú[s]k           | | |
k -------------------úk----------          5 4 3   ---------------------------------------   4 6 6

---------------------------------------  #3      ----s-----------s ---------------s         #8
---s + k-----ú----------------ú           s k ú   ---------------s + ú -------------         s k ú
s----s-----------------------ú            | | |   s -----------------------------------      | | |
-------k------------------------ú          3 2 4   ------------kú --------------------         5 1 2

------k------------------ skú + s          #4      ---------------------------------------   #9
---------------------------------------    s k ú   ---------------------------------------   s k ú
k + ú--------k + k -----------k            | | |   --------------------k-------------         | | |
s---------s -----------------------        4 6 2   s -------------------------------------    1 1 0

---------------------------------------k  #5      ---------------------------------------   #10
k------------------------------- s        s k ú   s ------------ k-------------------        s k ú
-------------ú[k] --------------- s        | | |   -------------- k--------------            | | |
s --------------------------------------   3 3 1   ---------------úk----s + [s]------          3 3 1

                                                  -------k + ú----------------              #11
Note: Brackets indicate phonetic               -----s-------------s------------- s           s k ú
spelling; italics indicate sound in            -------k------------------------ sk           | | |
word initial position.                         s --------------------------------------       5 3 1
```

+	+	skudost'	+	muzyka uzkoe	+	0	+	−

		I	II	III	
s	7	12	14	9	5
k	3	12	10	5	3
ú	4	9	8	3	1

244

neba . . ."), then the poem's composition can be described as a perfect triad: three parts (of three quatrains each) plus a prologue and epilogue. A graphic representation of the frequency of the three marked phonetic elements and of the poem's composition would look like the accompanying diagram.

How is the phonetic structure of "Ballada" expressive of its meaning? The phonetic elements that converge in the *skudost'* of the fourth stanza are located on a semantic level in those words designed to present the "paltriness" of the poet's shrunken cosmos. Rather than the purposeful movement of "Grain's Way," we find here a speaker who sits ("*sizhú, osveshchaemyi sverkhu*") and stares ("*smotriú v shtukatúrnoe nebo*") into the sky of his private universe. His room is circular ("v *komnate krúgloi moei*"), its design and narrow compass a metaphorical extension of the poet's solipsistic self. Lighting is provided by an artificial sun ("*solntse v shestnadtsat' svechei*"), perhaps a wry allusion to Pushkin, the "sun" of Russian poetry whose eclipse Khodasevich had predicted a few months earlier in "The Shaken Tripod." From the landscape of "Grain's Way," the poet seems in some ultimate way to be moving inward—into his round prison of a room, into his position (presumably) at the center of the room, into, at last, himself. The first four stanzas, therefore, suggest themselves as a separate, enclosed semantic unit; it is in them that both the sound and sense of limitation, banality, "paltriness"—the persistent phonetic "rehearsing" of *skudost'* combined with its meaning—lead to a sort of impasse whose ultimate naming in the fourth stanza is an ending as well as a recognition of failure. One by one the items in the speaker's phenomenal world (*komnata," "solntse," "stúl'ia," "stol," krovat'," "rúki," "stekla," "karman"*) are drawn into this phonetic/semantic force field, each ironically adding to the sense of decrement. Palm trees, an image of tropical warmth, are forced into an oxymoron-like bloom as splayed figures on a winter windowpane. And time, reduced from philosophical category to the annoying sound of a pocket watch, adopts the verb of motion of "Grain's Way," but without direction or goal. Thus the movement (*idti*—to go) and purpose (*tsvesti*—to bloom, a result of *seiat'*—to sow) of the earlier poem are blocked, and the reversal of the poet's cherished role may explain why the "hopelessly closed life" follows—physically, grammatically, and semantically—so closely on the heels of *skudost'*: "O, kosnaia, nishchaia skudost' / *Bezvykhodnoi* zhizni moei!"

In a moment of desperation the poet embraces himself and his own lost lyricism. There is no change, aside from the rocking, in his external position: palingenesis, his birth into another time and space, must come, if at all, through some internal change wrought over his external state. His body rocks (the *k* sound: "*k*achat'sia *k*oleni") and words (the *s* sound: "*s*lovo *s*il'nee vsego") are suddenly (the *ú* + *k* sounds: "vdrú[k]") given birth in the amphibrachs' cradling rhythm (the *ú* + *k* sounds again: "zvúki"). Sound for the first time is becoming greater than sense. Here the *zvúki* seem to be the poet's new hands, sounding very much like the old ones, which were as dead as the other items in his room. It is with these new hands that he will play the heavy lyre soon to be passed to him. The metamorphosis takes place in the seventh stanza and is signaled by the reconvergence of the three sounds (imperfect in *muzyka*, perfect in *uzkoe*) and the appearance of the dactyls. Importantly, what makes the change possible are the phonetic and semantic characteristics of the "music," or *mousikē*, and art over which the Muses preside. It is verbal music composed precisely of those elements of sound and sense, now in a way "turned inside out," that make poetry in other circumstances impossible.

The speaker is now able to grow out of his plaster sarcophagus, and himself. As we learn in another poem in *The Heavy Lyre*, perhaps the blade that pierces him is the one from whose incision will grow new wings.[109] The last four stanzas, with their image of an open-ended, revolving dance, stand in contrast with the image of a closed, motionless circle of the first stanzas. Turning on the final pun of *stopa*,[110] they reveal a poet whose life and surroundings have been filled with new movement (N.B. the verb *idti*) and who sees and hears both the physical footsteps and metrical feet of Orpheus. The latter's soul has undergone many reincarnations to reach the twentieth-century ironist. Like Orpheus and Dionysus Zagreus, whose ritualistic deaths penetrated the mysteries of good and evil, the poet must forfeit his physical existence in order to be reborn into his music.[111] And Orpheus' lyre is heavy because it has been lifted from the dross of a modern world. Yet reputed to charm wild beasts—here the no less deadly inhabitants of apartment 30a ("I vizhu bol'shimi glazami . . . Kak peniiu dikomu vnemliut / Neschastnye veshchi moi.")—and given into hands transformed by sound, it plays in the last lines a *torzhestvennyi pod"em* (solemn ascent) quite unique in Khodasevich. Like the Chinamen (one of whom plays a "musical instrument") of Yeats's "Lapis Lazuli," looking down from their aerie on "all the tragic scene," the poet's Orphic image turns to look back for a moment as it ascends out of a now disappearing quotidian hell.

To sum up, then, the structure of "Ballada" is tripartite. Each section constitutes a stage in the poet's palingenesis: the first four stanzas suggest his imprisonment in the phenomenal world; the next three stanzas describe the spell he

---

[109] "Ne veriu v krasotu zemnuiu" (I don't believe in earthly beauty), *SS*, p. 110.

[110] *Stopa* is only a visual pun here, since the plurals for physical steps (*stopý*) and metrical feet (*stópy*) have different stresses.

[111] Orphism derives from the legend that the Titans, at the bidding of the jealous Hera, devoured all of Zagreus save his heart, which Athene took to Zeus. Supreme among the gods and giver of fertility, Zeus swallowed the heart, from which a new Zagreus was later born. See *Oxford Companion to Classical Literature*, ed. Sir Paul Harvey (Oxford, 1974), pp. 298-299.

casts over this world through the agency of his art; and the last four stanzas show him purged, renewed, capable of singing beyond the absurd universe of his room. This is another way of saying that first *skudost'* alone prevails, then there is a balance struck between the pain of *uzkoe* (tightly linked with *skudost'*) and the pleasure of *muzyka* being born, and finally it is *muzyka* that prevails—the phonetic character of *skudost'* has been "semanticized" out of the poem and can only be suggested metaphorically by the lyre's "heaviness." That each respective section begins with a mention of "ia" and a verb in the first person singular ("Sizhu, osveshchaemyi sverkhu, / *Ia*"; "I *ia* nachinaiu kachat'sia"; "*Ia* sam nad soboi vyrastaiu") seems significant, for it suggests the various stages of the Orphic image *in statu nascendi*: the poet's "I" both moves syntactically to the front of the section and semantically to a position above or beyond the *skudost'*. But the poem's "psychic" accent, as it were, as in the amphibrachic foot itself, falls on the second section.

"Ballada" might be read, at least for Khodasevich, as an end to several things: the end of the Pushkin-Petersburg connection in Russian poetry; the end of lyricism in a state with no sense of resonant past; the end of the poet's Orphic role in such a state. What is remarkable, I think, is the ability, if for only a privileged moment, to steal new life from these endings, from the teeth of the wild beasts of apartment 30a. Such ability is not typical of the mature Khodasevich, and its appearance could not come at a more poignant time. With an almost Blokian intuition of tragic finality, and with the Symbolist's view of another world seen through the demeaning details of this one, Khodasevich rises to the occasion, shifts from the minor key of his elegant chamber music to the major key of Blok's full-throated lyricism.[112] Such a sense of momentary balance and cathartic

---

[112] " 'Ballada' . . . is not so characteristic of Khodasevich: poetry in the

release would not, at least in the same form, come again.[113] By the time Khodasevich writes his second "Ballada,"[114] clearly a cruel mockery of the first, the possibility of a former lyricism is defiantly rejected. An image of dismemberment (a one-armed husband) is absurdly juxtaposed with an image of fertility (a pregnant wife) in the presence of an art form, the cinema, which Khodasevich regarded as philistine and culturally corrupt.[115] The world of his last poems, to anticipate a little, is one in which the magic moment of Symbolism, capable of overcoming the present, indeed all temporal categories, is replaced by discrete, absurdly unrelated moments of lost time. It is a world that might be defined less by "irony" as a rhetorical device, what Barthes describes as "nothing but the question posed to language by language,"[116] than by "ironism" as an ontological state: for what eventually comes to underlie the semantic ambiguity is not a willing sense of play but a condition of being stripped of ultimate values (Pushkin, Petersburg, Russian poetry). Out of this state arises the bilious protest of the second "Ballada," when the poet, handed the same lyre of the earlier poem, cannot play it the same way. The absurdity is too great, and the speaker responds by taking a scourge (instead of the lyre) and whipping the angels, once happy messengers from his Orphic realm, for all he is worth. The second "Ballada" is

usual, or, say, Blokian sense is less concealed in it" (Veidle, "Khodasevich from Far and Near," p. 135).

[113] *Sorrento Photographs* is one of the few poems, perhaps the only poem, in *European Night*, Khodasevich's last collection, in which there is a provisional balance struck between the lighter irony of *Grain's Way* and the black irony of the last poems. A unique poem in any case, and one of Khodasevich's finest creations, it is not typical of *European Night*.

[114] *SS*, pp. 164-166.

[115] See Khodasevich, "On the Cinematograph."

[116] Roland Barthes, *Critique et vérité* (Paris, 1966), pp. 74-75, quoted in Donald Fanger, *The Creation of Nikolai Gogol* (Cambridge, Mass., 1979), p. 121.

one of the last poems in *European Night,* Khodasevich's last collection.[117] The impasse alluded to in the first "Ballada" is now complete. And it is at this point that Khodasevich, an émigré in more ways than one, lapses into the almost total poetic silence of the last ten years of his life.

[117] *European Night* was not published as a separate collection but appeared under one cover with *Grain's Way* and *The Heavy Lyre* in the 1927 edition of the collected verse.

6

SEEDS OF WRATH AND IMPOTENCE:

1922-1927

> Then Judah said to Onan, "Go into your brother's wife,
> and perform the duty of a brother-in-law to her, and raise
> up offspring for your brother." But Onan knew that the
> offspring would not be his; so when he went in to his
> brother's wife he spilled the semen on the ground, lest he
> should give offspring to his brother. And what he did was
> displeasing in the sight of the Lord, and he slew him also.
> —Genesis

History has shown with ferocious consistency that to be a
Russian poet is a perilous enterprise. "In a certain sense the
history of Russian literature might be called the history of
the destruction of Russian writers," said Khodasevich at the
outset of his later (1932) article "Krovavaia pishcha" (Bloody
Food).[1] At the end of the same article, after recounting the
multitude of Russian writers who had been systematically
persecuted, silenced, or murdered, or who had taken their
own lives (Khodasevich had known personally eleven), Khodasevich summed up the mysterious ritual by which the
Russian people tear to pieces what should be, and perhaps
somehow still is, most sacred and precious to them:

Of course we know of Dante's exile, Camões' poverty, André Ché-
nier's scaffold, and much more, but, nonetheless, nowhere outside
of Russia have people gone to such lengths, by whatever means
possible, to destroy their writers. And yet, this is not a cause for
our shame, but may even be a cause for our pride. That is because
no other literature (I am speaking generally) has been as prophetic
as Russian literature. . . . It is the business of prophets to prophesy

---

[1] Khodasevich, "Bloody Food," *Stat'i*, p. 285. The title of the article comes
from Pushkin's poem "Uznik" (The Prisoner).

251

and the business of the people to strike them with stones. . . . It seems that in the suffering of their prophets the people expiate their own suffering. The slaughter of the prophet becomes a sacrificial act, an immolation. It places a most indissoluble, bloody bond between the prophet and the people. . . . What is sacrificed is always what is best, more pure, most precious. The destruction of poets, by its own nature secret, is mysterious, *ritualistic*. It will cease in Russian literature when the source of prophecy runs dry. But that will never be. . . .[2]

Even in 1932, when Khodasevich's own source of creativity had run dry and he had turned almost exclusively to the tasks of biographer, critic, and literary historian, he was arguing, hoping against hope, that those convictions that had fed Russian literature from early on and that many of Russia's finest writers had paid dearly for were still operating, however imperceptibly and subcutaneously, and would eventually dispel the mood of abulia and weariness that was weighing down émigré literature and the mood of false optimism that was making Soviet literature equally one-sided, but in the opposite direction. As Khodasevich said a year later, "Russian literature is severed in two."[3] Perhaps there was no one who understood better than Khodasevich the absurd game of "heads or tails" that each artist with a conscience had to play—on one side was freedom without homeland and audience; on the other was homeland and audience without freedom.

In terms of sheer life and death drama and of the ritualistic bloody repast of which Khodasevich spoke, there is of course little that can compare with the psychic asphyxiation of Blok, the suicides of Esenin, Mayakovsky, Tsvetaeva, and the murders of Gumilyov, Klyuev, Mandelshtam.[4] To the Western reader it may seem, prima facie, strange even to

[2] Ibid., pp. 289-291.

[3] Khodasevich, "Literatura v izgnanii" (Literature in Exile), *Stat'i*, p. 257.

[4] See Roman Jakobson, "On the Generation that Squandered Its Poets," in *Major Soviet Writers: Essays in Criticism*, ed. Edward J. Brown (New York, 1973), pp. 7-32.

link the fate of Khodasevich, who died of natural causes seventeen years after he emigrated and who over that period had the freedom to say and write what he wanted, with that of Blok or Esenin or Mandelshtam. Khodasevich did not suddenly, dramatically, lose the will to live; he did not lay hands to himself (though he had occasion to consider it); he was not hounded into near madness by the secret police. Still, notwithstanding the indisputable horror of these other deaths and murders, the ensuing poetic silence of Khodasevich (or perhaps the *silencing* of him, for that same law of ritual sacrifice may have been operating here as well) was, in its own way, equally tragic.

We can only guess at the drama that took place inside Khodasevich. When he left Russia in the summer of 1922, he was acknowledged to be one of the major Russian poets of this century. Over the next several years articles and reviews by Bely, Aikhenvald, Mochulsky, Nabokov, Bem, Struve, and Merezhkovsky continued to define and flesh out that reputation. Speaking from within Russia, where the attack on émigré literature was already under way, Mandelshtam complained in 1924 that Khodasevich was one of those modern poets toward whom contemporaries had shown "monstrous ingratitude."[5] But speaking from outside Russia, Gorky raved that "Khodasevich writes utterly amazing verse" and that "Khodasevich, to my mind, is modern-day Russia's best poet."[6] Then, for reasons that were not immediately apparent but were implicitly linked with his status as an exile, Khodasevich began to stop writing poetry. What he said about Esenin in May 1926, at the time when his poetic productivity had started to fall off noticeably, could be applied with equal force to himself:

[5] O. Mandel'shtam, "Vypad" (Attack), in *Sobranie sochinenii v trekh tomakh* (Collected Works in Three Volumes), ed. G. P. Struve and B. A. Filippov (Washington, 1971), II, 228.

[6] M. Gor'kii, *Literaturnoe nasledstvo, tom semidesiatyi: Gor'kii i sovetskie pisateli* (Literary Inheritance, Vol. 70: Gorky and Soviet Writers), ed. I. I. Anisimov (Moscow, 1963), pp. 285, 563.

What is especially noteworthy is that the purely poetic tendencies in Esenin change simultaneously and in a parallel fashion with changes in his views. His psychic drama is immediately reflected in the devices of his writing. Esenin's style proves to be a true barometer of his psychic life. Its arrow fluctuates not over the haphazard influences of literary trends but under the pressure of internal necessity.[7]

The psychic drama that led to the otherworldly music of *The Heavy Lyre* was now leading, with relentless internal necessity, through the dark poems of *European Night* to silence. Khodasevich, in a word, was not capable of *writing* his way out of the mood of *European Night*. As Gleb Struve correctly saw as early as 1928, he had written his way into a "spiritual and poetic cul de sac."[8]

Khodasevich's status as émigré writer was never something he bore lightly, and by the late 1920s he realized that he was living in a world of rapidly vanishing options. At first he would not, and later he could not, return to the Soviet Union. Unlike many (mostly younger) Russian émigré belletrists and critics who eventually overcame the narrowness and sometimes stubborn nostalgia of various émigré enclaves and found audiences and places for themselves in the West—Jakobson, Mark Slonim, Nabokov, Berberova, Struve—Khodasevich had little truck with those of other cultures and viewpoints who might have shared his interests. Earlier poems such as "Grain's Way" and "Not by my mother, but by a peasant woman from Tula" indicate the extent to which Khodasevich saw his poetic role as consanguineously bound with Russia and modern Russian poetry. It was not his desire, or perhaps even in his power, to deny that role and plunge, Prospero-like, into the sea of Western European letters. One wonders why he did not "return his ticket," take the option chosen by Tsvetaeva, the other great and hope-

---

[7] Khodasevich, "Parisian album," *Days*, no. 1019 (30 May 1926).

[8] G. Struve, "Tikhii ad" (Quiet Hell), *Za svobodu* (For Freedom), no. 59 (11 March 1928).

lessly isolated poet of the emigration. Khodasevich valued life, but he did not fear death. If anything, death for him had always been a sort of liberation. Yet what kept Khodasevich alive perhaps more than anything else and, considering the ominous mood of the thirties, what made his last years so poignant was his service to Russian literature.

One reason we can speak of Khodasevich's fate as tragic even against the background of Mandelshtam in a Stalinist labor camp or Tsvetaeva in Elabuga is that Khodasevich had the especially agonizing experience of living through his own eclipse as an artist. It is arguable that no other modern Russian poet of comparable stature has suffered more from literary politics, from the legacy of his own silence, and from what Simon Karlinsky calls "Western self-censorship"—"the conviction, inherited from the thirties, that a Russian writer who resides outside the Soviet Union cannot be of any interest to a Western reader."[9] As though confirming whatever doubts Khodasevich had about the future, the eclipse has remained largely in effect to the present day. Despite the efforts of Berberova, Nabokov, Weidlé, and others, there have appeared since the late 1920s just a handful of scholarly articles devoted to his poetry. Thus the bitter pun that Khodasevich made in an article written in 1936 seems to exemplify his personal tragedy as well as the tragedy of Russian émigré literature: what was thwarting the creation of new art was not the *sotsial'nyi zakaz* (societal demand) that prevailed in the Soviet Union but the equally oncrous *sotsial'nyi otkaz* (societal rejection), the loss of readership and the declining interest in the arts, that prevailed in emigration.[10] By the 1930s the victories to be won—the fine biography of Derzhavin, the expanded book on Pushkin, the publication of *Necropolis*—were, for Khodasevich the poet,

[9] Simon Karlinsky, "Foreword," *The Bitter Air of Exile*, ed. Karlinsky and Appel, p. 7.

[10] Khodasevich, "Pered kontsom" (Before the End), *Voz*, no. 4040 (22 August 1936).

in a way pyrrhic. Filling a silence that must have been deafening after twenty-five years of poetic creativity, they may have seemed bought at too great a price. By late 1938, several months before his death, Khodasevich, taking the cue from Wladimir Weidlé, was speaking of "the death of art."[11]

Khodasevich and Berberova arrived in Berlin on 30 June 1922 and took lodging at the pension "Nürnbergerplatz." Almost immediately, as a letter of 9 July to Boris Diatroptov indicates, Khodasevich began to have strong negative feelings about the émigré community around him:

O, dear Boris, I swear to you that here you would sing the "Internationale" for days on end. I feel that if not today then tomorrow I'll start experiencing flights of Communism. You can't imagine these swine: loafers by conviction, by principle, surrounded by three hundred pound wives and an unbelievable number of four hundred pound daughters tormented by boredom, glad rags, and the futile chase for bridegrooms. . . . These people think of one thing—to "string up" the Bolsheviks. They won't agree to anything less. If you leave sentiments aside, I, sinful man that I am, would line them all up against the wall. The only consolation is that all this, after stinking up all Europe, will rot and die off here.[12]

The letter clearly casts doubt on the simplified Soviet version of Khodasevich as incorrigible counterrevolutionary. Though in the years ahead he would publish much of his work in the right-wing émigré press (there was little other choice) and would eventually speak out openly against literary politics in the Soviet Union, there was no love lost between Khodasevich and those against whom the Soviets mounted their revolution. This is the same White emigration in Berlin that Nabokov satirizes in *Mary* and *The Gift*. Their mortal sin is *poshlost'* (philistinism or bourgeois vulgarity), and, speaking as one who still plans on returning

[11] Khodasevich, "Umiranie iskusstva" (The Dying of Art), *Voz*, no. 4158 (18 November 1938).
[12] Malmstad and Smith, eds., "Eight Letters of V. F. Khodasevich," pp. 82-83.

home, Khodasevich sees Russia as healthier for their absence.

Unsure about when (and soon whether) he would be returning to Russia, Khodasevich set out quickly to establish contact with other fellow writers sojourning in or nearby Berlin. On 3 July he saw Bely, who dropped by before leaving for Zossen (he would be returning to Berlin that fall); on 4 July Shklovsky; on 5 July Tsvetaeva; and on 6 July he took some letters, which could not be entrusted to the Soviet mail and had to be hand-carried across the border, to Gorky, who was staying at Heringsdorf, a watering spot on the Baltic Sea. Over the summer and fall, he met frequently at the Café Landgraf (the Berlin version of Disk) and the Prager Diele with Pasternak, Ehrenburg, Tsvetaeva, Shklovsky, Zaytsev, Muratov, and Bely. There were a number of poetry readings and at-homes. The divisions between émigrés and non-émigrés, between those in Western Europe to stay and those there to visit, were in many cases not yet clear. Bely and Gorky, to be Khodasevich's closest friends during the first years of emigration, also shared the state of limbo between a committed "here" and a committed "there." Russian Berlin did not begin to thin out, remaining alive with numerous factions, until the fall of 1923, at which time Bely, Gershenzon (in Germany for a health cure), Shklovsky, Aleksey Tolstoy, and Pasternak had returned or were returning to Russia, and Khodasevich and Berberova left for other parts of Europe. Indeed, the gypsylike existence that Khodasevich and Berberova led during this initial period was their way of putting off the ultimate decision of permanent residence: as Khodasevich wrote Diatroptov, from the date of their arrival until mid-November 1925, they had lived in forty-two different rooms in Berlin, Prague, Marienbad, Rome, Turin, Paris, London, Belfast, Naples, Sorrento, and other European cities.[13] Although it later became apparent that

[13] See *Kursiv*, pp. 251-252.

Khodasevich's name was on the list of more than 160 members of the intelligentsia (among them Berdyaev, Frank, Lossky, Stepun, Sergey Bulgakov, and Aikhenvald) who were exiled by the Soviet government in the fall of 1922—with Soviet passports that had no return dates—and that his chances for returning were therefore almost nonexistent, he tried to fend off what for him was the most fatal of truths.

Khodasevich's relations with Bely and Gorky over the initial period of his emigration form a fascinating chapter in modern Russian letters. The sections of *Necropolis* devoted to Bely and Gorky contain passages of insight and analytic intelligence perhaps unequalled in Khodasevich's prose. Khodasevich isolated and glossed, with a unique blend of irony (objectivity) and sympathy (subjectivity), the strengths *and* weaknesses that made these writers seminal (though in opposite ways) for the modern period. He did not simply remember his friends, add to the mass of hagiographic memoir literature (especially about Gorky) that touches up and smooths over significant "flaws," but he tried through the mnemonic process to solve the enigma of their personalities. The final verdict on Gorky is one of the most revealing statements ever made about the writer, and goes far to restore ambiguity and vitality to what has become, at least in the Soviet Union, a monolithic, cut-to-order biography of the "stormy petrel of the Revolution."

According to Khodasevich's calendar, he met with Bely a hundred and nine times from July 1922 to September 1923.[14] Bely relied on Khodasevich as perhaps on no one else during this period of his great spiritual crisis. After years of deprivation in Moscow and after the shattering news of Blok's death in Petersburg, he had come to Europe to tell Rudolf Steiner and the anthroposophical community at Dornach of the sufferings of the Russian people. But Steiner, Bely's last hope as bedrock father figure, and Asya Turgeneva, his last

[14] Ibid., p. 177.

hope as feminine ideal, unceremoniously renounced him: the one deflected Bely, who had flown up to him at a meeting in Berlin, with a witheringly casual "Na, wie geht's"[15] and the other threw him over for the second-rate poet Alexandr Kusikov. By this point in his life Bely had worked his way through a massive amount of art and autobiography to get to the bottom of his urges as son and lover—only to ultimately, hopelessly, find himself parentless.[16] Though Khodasevich had little faith in occult systems and took a dim view of anthroposophy (especially after the snub by Steiner), he respected his friend's genius, understood that his Weltanschauung was flying apart at every turn, and served, along with Berberova, as the audience for his nightly *cris de coeur*. Totally gray-headed, the blue of his eyes washed out almost to a white, Bely wore a frozen smirk on his face and often aped the froglike movements of his hero Nikolay Ableukhov.[17] It was in this last year of his Berlin period that Bely began to drink heavily and to dance his bizarre, revolting *pas de deux* with uncomprehending barmaids.

Russian Berlin observed Bely's mad improvisations with not a little malicious humor. Few understood the meaning of his dancing. But Bely, thought Khodasevich, was not simply drunk; his barroom pyrotechnics were his way of answering the insults of Dornach, mocking the present and its nonrecognition of his genius, turning over, like cinders that refused to go out, the past, and "symbolically trampling underfoot the best in himself."[18] Thus the dancing seemed the image of Bely's personal symbolism turned inside out—instead of Logos, the principle of masculine creativity, there were Bely's drunken overtures; instead of Sophia, the principle of the Eternal Feminine (*Das Ewig Weibliche*), there

[15] *Nekropol'*, p. 88.
[16] See Khodasevich, "Ableukhovy-Letaevy-Korobkiny" (The Ableukhovs-Letaevs-Korobkins), *Stat'i*, pp. 187-218.
[17] See *Kursiv*, p. 182.
[18] *Nekropol'*, p. 89.

were the mocking or perplexed expressions of barmaids; and instead of ideal syzygial motion, the state (envisioned by Vladimir Solovyov, Blok, and Bely) wherein Logos and Sophia act in concert and word becomes flesh, there were the absurd gyrations of "Herr Professor" and "Mariechen."[19] Bely's nature had always been deeply dual. Much of his artistic life had been a struggle to contain and unify the antinomies within himself. And as long as he had had anagogic keys (Solovyov's sophiology, Steiner's anthroposophy) to keep the antinomies in some homeostatic balance, his nervous brilliance had worked tirelessly for him and for his generation. Now, however, like so many devils, the antinomies—Logos and Sophia, male and female, spirit and matter, East and West—and the antinomies within the antinomies—the male as father and the male as son, the female as mother and the female as lover—had gotten the best of him. His reaction was to play a sort of Pyotr Verkhovensky, to let his devils run wild in a carnival atmosphere. Khodasevich, both well-versed in Symbolist myth-making and free and skeptical of it, realized what was taking place within Bely and transformed his friend's "symbolic trampling of the best in himself" into the black irony of *European Night*. "An Mariechen," the cruelest poem that Khodasevich ever wrote, describes the deflowering and murder of the young barmaid who served as Bely's last incarnation of Sophia.

Among the dancing and the wild perorations were flashes of the old Bely. He still had his amazing energy and his capacity for work. During this time, on long visits with Khodasevich and Berberova in Saarow (a resort area two hours from Berlin where the couple moved in November 1922), Bely recast and expanded his memoirs of Blok into *Nachalo veka* (The Beginning of the Century). The title was suggested to him by Nina Berberova. Khodasevich's role in the conception of this version of Bely's memoirs—the first of *The*

[19] Ibid., p. 90.

Beginning of the Century, the fourth of the original work on Blok—is an intriguing footnote to that strange series of works that began as an apologia for a friend and ended as a paranoid self-apologia:

Considering the psychological (or, better, neurotic) condition of Bely, I insistently put forward the idea that, having expanded the initial framework, Bely would be better served by turning his purely memoiristic work into a memoiristic-historical one, that is, [it would be better if Bely], while conducting his narration from the first person, did not fall in any way into autobiogaphy, but strived that the protagonist of his future book be *Symbolism rather than Andrey Bely.* I calculated that if Bely would try not to lose sight of such a task and if he would hold to it even nominally, then the book would take on a wider meaning, and the pronouncements about separate persons would become more objective. I was under no delusions about Bely's being able to conquer completely his momentary bursts and passionate opinions, but I hoped that I could manage to attain some results. It seemed that at least in part my efforts were about to be crowned with success. In the spring of 1923, the first volume of *The Beginning of the Century* was completed. As an objective indication that Bely had heeded my urgings there was an extensive introductory chapter in which the author, having made one of my poems a sort of leitmotif, announced that Symbolism was the axis of his life in general and of the given work in particular.[20]

Unfortunately, this version of *The Beginning of the Century*, which might have been the finest of all Bely's memoirs, was never published. Already set by the printers and ready to go to press, it was abandoned in the fall of 1923 when Bely broke with Khodasevich and fled back to Russia. In the later versions of *The Beginning of the Century* and *Between Two Revolutions* that appeared in the Soviet Union, any historical objectivity gave way to the whims of autobiography and the once guiding figure of Khodasevich was correspondingly caricatured and vilified.

The final split with Bely came on 8 September 1923, some

[20] Khodasevich, "Nachalo veka" (The Beginning of the Century), *Voz*, no. 3319 (5 July 1934).

weeks before his return to Russia. Later Khodasevich felt guilty about it, for he understood that if logic and loyalty were on his side, a perhaps greater need for some higher understanding was on Bely's. A number of old friends, including Khodasevich, Berberova, Bely, Muratov, Zaytsev, Remizov, and Berdyaev, had turned out for a farewell dinner in a Russian restaurant on Berlin's Gentienerstrasse. Bely, glowering and smirking, seemed on pins and needles. When he finally rose and furiously demanded that all drink to his health because he was "going to his crucifixion,"[21] Khodasevich balked and quietly but firmly replied "Only not for me. . . . I don't want you to be crucified."[22] Bely broke relations with Khodasevich on the spot, announcing to those gathered that "all his life [Khodasevich] has poisoned [my] best moments, cut short [my] most noble acts, with his skepticism."[23]

Khodasevich did not want to hurt Bely, but he had learned from Gershenzon before the latter's return to Russia that Bely, in his efforts to finagle a visa at the Soviet consulate in Berlin, had slandered and denounced his friends in emigration. In anyone else, such hypocrisy would have been deplorable. Bely, however, was no longer answerable for his actions; his duality and duplicity were not premeditated but "sincere"; and he was capable, in his state of paranoia, of seeing as correct, and even righteous, both his denouncing of friends and his willingness to mount the cross for them. Thus, Khodasevich's error was to demand loyalty and consistency of action from one who was hopelessly split. And, while he never forgave himself this error, Khodasevich tried to right it in the closing remarks of his memoir of Bely.[24]

Khodasevich's relationship with Gorky was perhaps not as intense as that with Bely, and it certainly had no ties with

---

[21] *Nekropol'*, p. 95.
[22] *Italics*, p. 166; *Kursiv*, p. 187.
[23] *Nekropol'*, p. 95.
[24] See ibid., pp. 93-99.

historical Symbolism, but it was equally revealing and may have played an instrumental role in Khodasevich's decision to burn all bridges leading back to the Soviet Union. Both men admired each other greatly, though for different reasons. The fact that their relationship broke down, that immediately after the break (not formal, as with Bely) Khodasevich returned to Paris, and to the émigré press, permanently and Gorky continued his path toward reconciliation with the Soviets, suggests *in nuce* the failure of Soviet and émigré literature to find a common ground. The rift between Gorky and Khodasevich was not personal; the letters and reminiscences show no sign of harsh words being passed between them. Rather it was professional, a matter of artistic conscience. It began, developed, and finally grew unbridgeable over *Beseda* (Colloquium), the journal that they coedited.

It should be said at the outset that Khodasevich had mixed feelings about Gorky: if the two writers were to cross swords professionally, then personally Khodasevich was much indebted to Gorky for the kindness and hospitality shown him and Berberova over the years of transition to émigré life. There is no doubt that without Gorky and his bustling world of belletristic activity Khodasevich would have suffered the initial shock of emigration more keenly. Both men had anxieties about the future of Soviet and émigré literature and about their positions vis-à-vis each camp and both discussed these anxieties openly and, for a while at least, seemed to shoulder them together. Yet even as their professional positions began to drift apart, their domestic relations showed little sign of strain.

From July 1922 to 18 April 1925, the date on which Khodasevich left Sorrento and parted with Gorky for the last time, there were three periods when the friends either lived under the same roof or in close proximity and saw each other almost daily: from November 1922 to June 1923, when they lived in Saarow; from November 1923 to March 1924, when they lived in Prague and Marienbad; and from October 1924 to April 1925, when they lived in Sorrento.[25] Thus it turned out that Berberova and Khodasevich would visit the large cities of Europe in the summer months and spend the off-season winter months in secluded watering spots with Gorky. When Gorky and Khodasevich were not living together, they were maintaining a lively correspondence.[26]

In September 1922 Gorky moved from Heringsdorf to Saarow. Later that fall he persuaded Berberova and Khodasevich to join him there, which they did, arriving in early November. The couple took up residence at the Bahnhof Hotel. Availing themselves of Gorky's generosity and fitting into the "transient-hotel character" of his ever-present entourage, Khodasevich and Berberova quietly passed their first winter abroad.[27] There was much friendly card-playing and strolling around the lake shore. On Christmas Eve a merry throng (Gorky, Khodasevich, Berberova, Shklovsky, Gorky's son Maxim, Maxim's wife Timosha, Khodasevich's niece Valentina, Gorky's second wife M. F. Andreeva, the artist Ivan Rakitsky, the sculptor N. A. Andreev, the publisher Z. I. Grzhebin, the actor K. I. Miklashevsky, and several others) gathered at the family Christmas tree for a photograph. Miklashevsky took the picture, but Gorky, feeling such festivity somehow "shameful," had the negative destroyed.[28]

On 11 June 1923 Khodasevich and Berberova left Saarow and returned to Berlin. Save for a two-week trip in August to Prerow (where they enjoyed the Baltic shore with the Muratovs, the Zaytsevs, and the Berdyaevs) and a brief outing to Freiberg, there they remained, staying at the Krampe boardinghouse, until the fall, when Russian Berlin began to

[25] See N. Berberova, "Tri goda zhizni M. Gor'kogo" (Three Years in the Life of Maxim Gorky), *Mosty* (Bridges), 8 (1961), 262-277.

[26] See Khodasevich, ed., "Pis'ma Maksima Gor'kogo k V. F. Khodasevi-chu" (Letters of Maxim Gorky to V. F. Khodasevich), *Novyi zhurnal* (New Review), 29-31 (1952), 205-214, 189-202, 190-205.

[27] *Italics*, p. 178; *Kursiv*, p. 203.

[28] *Italics*, p. 196; *Kursiv*, p. 224.

empty out. In November they moved on to Prague, but soon found life at the Hotel Beránek boring—and this despite a number of interesting meetings with Marina Tsvetaeva and Roman Jakobson. They could not feel at home in the old guard ambiance of Russian Prague; the cliquishness of the Chirikovs and the Nemirovich-Danchenkos seemed to exclude them.[29] So when Gorky arrived, they decided (in December) to make the change to Marienbad and the Hotel Maxhof. Gorky was often being pestered by the foreign press, and the privacy and quiet offered by this Czech watering spot suited everyone better. Here another pleasant Christmas was celebrated: they found a tree, exchanged presents, played charades, and listened to the gramophone.[30] The only unpleasantness that winter involved the pulling of all Khodasevich's remaining teeth, a painful and quite enervating process.

The following spring (1924) Gorky received a visa for Italy and departed Marienbad for Sorrento. That March began a seven-month period of extensive travel for Khodasevich and Berberova: by 9 October, when they arrived at Gorky's in Sorrento, they had visited, among other European cities, Venice, Rome, Turin, Paris, London, Belfast, and Naples. These peregrinations seemed to have a depressing effect on Khodasevich. He wrote to Anna Chulkova from Rome on 25 March 1924: "In general, I know nothing about my life beyond tomorrow, and that is oh so wearisome."[31] Life in emigration, he had discovered, was taking on a definite, irrefragable shape. Venice was no longer the city of his youth, the one that had introduced him to the art of Veronese and had resonated with his love for Zhenya Muratova. Its stone palaces had "so aged," thought Khodasevich, "that they might

---

[29] See *Kursiv*, p. 237.
[30] See ibid., p. 211.
[31] "Unpublished letter of V. F. Khodasevich to Anna Ivanovna Khodasevich," item no. 51 (dated 25 March 1924), TsGALI.

crumble any moment."[32] The rainy weather and the monotonous architecture made Belfast, where Khodasevich and Berberova spent sixty days that summer, dour and unappealing.[33] And Paris threw Khodasevich into a turmoil of anxiety and indecision. Berberova recalls the first stay in Paris before the final winter with Gorky in Sorrento:

Khodasevich's indecision about remaining here, about planting both feet on ground that was considered firm, became even greater. Fear at making decisions tortured him. Earnings seemed ephemeral, an adequate job not in view. I remember the last days and nights before our departure for Italy. At that time, Khodasevich already knew that his name was on the list of those writers and scholars who were exiled from Russia in 1922 . . . and he understood that not only was no return possible but that he would soon find it impossible to be printed by the Gosizdat [State Publishing House]. That he was on the list merely stressed something in his mind, eliminated the possibility of returning home and drew the first blueprint of the future. A breath of cold came from it. . . . I remember one sleepless night—it was perhaps the last night before our departure for Sorrento (this journey was a delay of the inevitable). Khodasevich, exhausted by insomnia, could not find himself a spot: *"Here*, I cannot, cannot, I cannot live and write, *there* I cannot, cannot live and write."[34]

[32] *Italics*, p. 210; *Kursiv*, p. 244.

[33] Khodasevich quipped to Chulkova in a letter dated 15 September 1924 that Ireland is "an excellent place to exile someone" ("Unpublished letter of V. F. Khodasevich to Anna Ivanovna Khodasevich," item no. 51, TsGALI). See as well Khodasevich, "Bel'fast," *PN*, no. 1560 (16 May 1925).

[34] *Italics*, p. 217; *Kursiv*, pp. 251-252. We catch a glimpse of Khodasevich's black mood during his first stay in Paris in a letter written to Chulkova on 24 April 1924: "An entire week went in the exhausting search for an apartment. Paris is absolutely packed. We were forced to live in the nursery at the home of the publisher of *The Heavy Lyre* [Zinovy Grzhebin]. Finally, some sort of residence was found—tiny and expensive, with no elevator, on the fourth floor by Parisian standards, on the sixth by ours. In addition there was the heat, the stuffiness, the dirt, the rushing about on business— I am very tired. Paris (forgive me) does not make me happy. It's just passable, and that's all. Anyhow, 'my eyes are not inclined to look'; I am thinking and worrying about other things." (Unpublished letter from V. F. Khodasevich to A. I. Khodasevich," item no. 51, TsGALI.)

It must have been with a certain uneasy joy, therefore, that Khodasevich and Berberova set off for the reunion with Gorky: after the winter retreat to Sorrento, permanent domicile in Paris, the tawdry hell of the last poems of *European Night*, loomed up ahead. Khodasevich and Berberova arrived to find Gorky and his family living in a rambling villa (Villa Massa) that had to be vacated by December. As the moving day approached, Khodasevich and Maxim (Gorky's son) went on a foray to turn up another villa—preferably, with a warmer southern exposure. The only villa still available in the vicinity was "Il Sorito," which they were obliged to rent. Despite the villa's lack of furniture, its draughtiness, and its location on a sliver of land that, prone to landslide, overlooked a sheer precipice, all turned out to be quite happy there. From their balcony on the second floor, Khodasevich and Berberova could see Vesuvius, Ischia, and the Bay of Naples.[35] Soon the domestic routine that had ruled in the apartment on Kronversksky and in Saarow and Marienbad set in here as well. Gorky, who always adhered to a strict schedule, was deeply engrossed in *The Artamonov Business*, the first part of which he completed that fall and read to those at Il Sorito. Berberova and Maxim kept busy with the editing of *Sorrentinskaia pravda* (Sorrento Pravda), a monthly humor magazine. As was his wont, Khodasevich wrote late into the night and lounged about in the mornings. The idea for a new narrative poem (*poema*) was coming to him. The work was to grow from the interplay of two central images, that of a double-exposed snapshot and that of a motorcycle ride, and it was to comment, in a manner both whimsical and profound, on the distance between prerevolutionary life in Russia and postrevolutionary life in exile. Important narrative and thematic points of departure for the poem were suggested to Khodasevich by some of his activity in and around Sorrento, especially his day trip to Pompeii and his

[35] See *Nekropol'*, p. 242; *Kursiv*, p. 218.

rides on Maxim's motorcycle through the hills near Amalfi, Ravello, and Graniano. Thus, on 5 March, the first seventeen lines of *Sorrento Photographs*, perhaps Khodasevich's most intriguing work, were written. Several weeks later Berberova and Khodasevich left Il Sorito and returned to Paris.

The brief life and slow death of the journal *Beseda* spanned the period of Khodasevich and Gorky's relations in emigration. A look at the history of this ill-fated journal shows how close, at least in theory, Soviet and Russian émigré literature once were to finding a common forum and then how far they drifted from the original desideratum in the space of three years. As Khodasevich relates, the original idea, conceived in the fall of 1922, belonged to Viktor Shklovsky:

Before 1922 there existed in Russia only war-time censorship. [But] in 1922 a censorship was introduced that was general, extremely bullying and—like any of that type—completely idiotic. Moreover, private journals and publishing houses ceased to exist and those that were state-owned began to demand ever more openly propaganda items. So Shklovsky came up with the idea of publishing a journal in which writers living in the Soviet Union could go over the head of the censorship and the state-owned editorial offices to publish their work, provided of course that such work, while not written at government bidding, did not contain attacks against the government. Now [in 1938] such a notion would seem farfetched. But at that time it was totally feasible. . . . Getting hold of funds also proved no difficulty because the Soviet government zealously spread the rumor that it intended to allow into Russia foreign publications not containing agitation against the regime and printed according to the new orthography. . . . Shklovsky intrigued Gorky and me with his idea. We worked out a plan for the journal. The editorial staff of the literary section was composed of Gorky, Andrey Bely, and me. The scientific section, introduced on Gorky's insistence, was given over to Professors Braun and Adler. On my suggestion, the future journal was named *Beseda*, in memory of Derzhavin.[36]

[36] Khodasevich, "Beseda" (Colloquium), *Voz*, no. 4114 (14 January 1938). See also Khodasevich: "Gor'kii," pp. 131-155; and "Letters of Maxim Gorky to V. F. Khodasevich."

Khodasevich and Gorky, then, saw *Beseda* as an experiment in cultural cross-fertilization. Young Soviet writers—especially the Serapions—who felt themselves hidebound by Soviet editorial policy could find an outlet for their work at the same time that leading non-Russian writers (Gorky was counting on the participation of those such as Shaw, Wells, Rolland, and Zweig) could develop a new audience in Russia. In an unprecedented fashion, Western ideas were to make their way into Russia and Russian ideas were to make their way into the West. The plan was noble, if not a little quixotic. And it was inconceivable without the mighty aegis of Gorky.

Believing the overtures made by the Soviet government and counting on the name of Gorky to keep the Soviets to their word, S. G. Sumsky-Kaplun and D. Yu. Dalin, who owned the Berlin publishing house "Epokha" (Epoch), agreed to publish *Beseda*. No one seemed to realize, Gorky perhaps least of all, that as a result of the feud with Zinovev, Gorky's authority at home had been seriously eroded. As the first issues of the journal appeared, the Soviets bought a few token copies, but with the promise that as soon as official confirmation was given, they would buy up copies in the thousands. By the fall of 1923 Gorky was trying more direct measures to prod the Soviets into action: first he wrote letters to Moscow, then he asked the vacationing Alexey Rykov, one of Lenin's chief lieutenants, if he could help matters along; and finally, when all else failed, he openly refused to collaborate in any Soviet publications until *Beseda* was allowed into Russia. But nothing seemed to help. By now the manuscripts of young Soviet writers were trickling in in smaller numbers: Moscow had clearly begun to apply pressure and was attempting, as Khodasevich now realized, to sabotage the project. Even the Western writers whom Gorky had asked for submissions were for some reason sending nothing. As a last resort, in the spring of 1924 Gorky wrote N. K. Krupskaya a letter in which he demanded in the strongest terms possible that the matter of *Beseda* be decided. The "ultimatum" seemed to work. In May, Mura Budberg, Gorky's secretary, informed Khodasevich that *Beseda* was to be let in, and on 26 June, Sumsky-Kaplun told him that the Soviets had agreed to purchase a thousand copies of each issue. Then this too turned out to be a ruse, for by the end of September only eighty of the promised five thousand copies had been bought, and *Beseda* was teetering on the edge of financial ruin. The journal struggled through one more issue (March 1925) and closed. Gorky had, as Sumsky-Kaplun put it, "simply been led by the nose."[37]

Khodasevich could have forgiven Gorky his faith in the Soviets, but the matter was not so simple. Not only was Gorky fooled by the straw promises coming from Moscow; more serious, and to Khodasevich totally unforgivable, he *allowed himself* to be fooled. Gorky could not part with his biography as "stormy petrel." It was not that he sought the outer forms of fame or recognition. On the contrary, he was, believed Khodasevich, a man of unfeigned modesty and a writer who could be exacting toward his own work. Yet he needed the "elevating deceit" (*vozvyshaiushchii obman*) of Marxism, the idea that man can take control of his environment and raise himself out of "the lower depths."[38] He was to become the patron saint of socialist realism precisely because his work combines verisimilitude in the detailing of a scene and (a *contradictio in adjecto*, as Sinyavsky has pointed out) characterization that is, in its own "down-and-out" key, romantic and ennobling. Down to card sharps and jugglers, Gorky preferred those who carried off a crafty distortion of reality. And so, in a manner that Khodasevich could not countenance, his friend had opted for the deceit of the Soviets' promise to buy *Beseda* over the truth of their actual plan to bankrupt the venture. No matter how nakedly

[37] Khodasevich, "Beseda."
[38] See *Nekropol'*, pp. 259-297.

apparent Moscow's intentions, Gorky still managed to dress them in the king's clothes.

As *Beseda* began to die a slow death (Gorky had a difficult time parting with the idea even after the journal was closed), Khodasevich, as was his nature, grew more skeptical. Yet one would be wrong, I suspect, to assign him the role of *agroikos* in this little drama. Khodasevich understood that what was hanging in the balance in the clash between his essentially ironic nature and Gorky's essentially idealistic nature was more vital than personal feelings. On the one side was a truth that could not ignore what was happening to Russian literature, and on the other was a lie that shunted aside such facts. By breaking his vow not to publish in the Soviet press, by listening to Soviet suggestions that *Beseda* be published there (if it were published there, then its original raison d'être would be lost), by gradually capitulating to the entreaties to return home, Gorky was removing one of the last bargaining chips left to those émigré writers who, neither "Red" nor "White," wanted a Russian literature that was free from interference and that was read and appreciated. Khodasevich could not remain silent about Gorky's weakness: the stormy petrel needed the myth that had grown up around him as much as did the Soviets. To his last (published posthumously) thoughts on Gorky, therefore, he affixed the harsh beam of judgment:

A great admirer of dream and elevating deceit (which because of the primitiveness of his thinking he could never distinguish from the most ordinary, often vulgar lie), Gorky at some point acquired for himself his own "ideal"—in part genuine, in part imagined—image as poet of the Revolution and the proletariat. And although the Revolution itself turned out to be something other than what he had created with his imagination, the thought of possibly losing this image, of "spoiling his biography," was unbearable to him. Money, cars, houses—all that was necessary to those surrounding him. He needed something else. In the end he sold out—not for money, but for the possibility of preserving for himself and for others the chief illusion of his life. Rebelling and persisting in his obstinacy, he knew that he would not hold out and would rush back to the Soviet Union because, no matter what sort of revolution had taken place there, it alone could provide him the glory of a great proletarian writer and leader during his lifetime and a niche in the Kremlin wall for his urn and ashes after death. In return for all that the Revolution demanded from him, as it demands from everyone, not honest service, but servility and flattery. The position he was placed in was such that from a writer and a friend of writers he turned into their jailer. And he agreed to that. One could make a long list of what else he agreed to. In short, he turned into the complete opposite of that elevating deceit for the preservation of which he had made his peace with the Soviet government. I won't venture to say whether he acknowledged the full tragedy of this. Probably, he both did and didn't: to the extent that he acknowledged [this contradiction] he tried to hide it from himself and from others with the help of new illusions and new elevating deceits, [those very illusions and deceits] that he loved so much and that in the end destroyed him.[39]

The return to Paris on 22 April 1925 must have been anything but joyful. With his journeying over, Khodasevich was returning to his permanent place of exile and to a world characterized by decrement. For a poet so steeped in his own Russianness Paris would never be the City of Light. Though he still corresponded with friends in Russia and tried to have his new poems circulated there among those who might appreciate them, as a geographical entity Russia was now behind Khodasevich as never before.[40] Soon one of his last roles as *littérateur*, that of eulogist for Russian poetry, would make greater demands on his creative energy. Viktor Gofman (d. 1911), Nadya Lvova (d. 1913), and Muni (d. 1916),

---

[39] Khodasevich, "Gorky," p. 156.

[40] The letters that Khodasevich wrote to Anna Chulkova during 1924-1925 indicate that he was still looking vigorously for an audience in Russia for his poems. He hoped that Chulkova could find publishers for his work and that, in return, she could receive his honoraria as a means of support. See "Unpublished letters from V. F. Khodasevich to A. I. Khodasevich," item nos. 51 and 52, TsGALI. Khodasevich also circulated his new poems among friends that had stayed behind in Russia: see Serafima Polianina, ed., "Pis'ma V. Khodasevicha M. Fromanu" (Letters of V. Khodasevich to M. Froman), *Chast' rechi* (Part of Speech), 1 (1980), 292-297.

with whom he had personally shared the Symbolist years, and Blok (d. 1921), Gumilyov (d. 1921), and Bryusov (d. 1924), who had led the modernist movement in poetry, were gone. Relations with Bely and Gorky were severed. And over the next several years, Khodasevich would write necrologies and memorial articles for those friends and acquaintances who had made contributions to Russian poetry and culture: Gershenzon, Boris Sadovskoy (who had in fact not died, though Khodasevich believed that he had), Esenin, Baroness Iskul von-Gillenband, Nina Petrovskaya, Sologub, Aikhenvald. The "yellow envelope," as he called it, that is, the file he kept on fellow writers and cultural figures who had died, was beginning to bulge with its contents of loss.

What was behind him was not compensated for by what was before him. Living in demeaning poverty, Khodasevich and Berberova began to scratch out a hand-to-mouth existence. Unsavory hotels and apartment houses, including the Pretty Hotel on the rue Amélie and a flat on the rue Lamblardie, were the only residences they could afford. Work came sporadically. Khodasevich had a hard time adapting to the constraints placed on him by editors. It was said that those in control feared his irony and lack of forbearance. (In these years Khodasevich was dropping the pseudonym "Fyodor Maslov" under which he had attacked instances of Soviet stupidity and repression and was sallying out into polemical duels more under his own name.) Coming both from the Soviet and émigré quarters were insults inconceivable to the poet of *Grain's Way* and *The Heavy Lyre*: while he was being called a "permanent counterrevolutionary"[41] and "a whiner of mysticism and restoration"[42] in the Soviet journals *The Life of Art* and *On Literary Guard*, Pavel Milyukov, the editor of *The Latest News*, was telling him that the newspaper "did not need him at all."[43] Khodasevich was

[41] Quoted in Khodasevich, "Pro doma sua."
[42] Quoted in *Italics*, p. 220; *Kursiv*, p. 255.
[43] *Italics*, p. 219; *Kursiv*, p. 254.

growing desperate. Physically tormented by insomnia and the reappearance of furunculosis and mentally stricken by a sort of abulia, he was coming perilously close to thoughts of suicide.[44] Berberova, who had been forced to resort to all manner of piecemeal work (stringing beads, cross-stitching, inscribing Christmas cards, working as an extra in movies) to help support them, was afraid to leave him alone. Only when Khodasevich found a permanent position as head of the literary section at *The Renaissance* in 1927 and their financial position became more tolerable did his black mood begin somewhat to abate. The immediate crisis gradually passed. That year Khodasevich published his *Collected Verse*, in which *European Night* was included as the last section. Having inured himself as best he could to the loss of Russia, friends, and the Psyche that had inspired his art, Khodasevich was entering the last stage of his career.

In *Grain's Way* Khodasevich had been intrigued by the image of a wise sower moving along even furrows and dispensing his grain. The seed itself had been the poetic word, the even furrow the poetic line, and the darkness that initially covered the seed the years of war and revolution. If the present generation lost sight of the seed, the sower knew that the seed would still bear fruit for a future generation. Then in *The Heavy Lyre* the continuous spiritual-biological rhythm of the grain was interrupted. The speaker as wise sower gave way to the speaker as psychic amanuensis—a recorder of discrete privileged moments when the *dusha* appeared in an atmosphere of freedom and ulteriority, amid images of angelic wings and strangely wonderful music. The poet did not control the appearance of the *dusha*, and that is why we might call such moments of visitation privileged, mysterious, unbidden. These moments did not belong to the earthly order of time whose rhythm Khodasevich praises in *Grain's*

[44] See Vishniak, *Contemporary Annals: Memoirs of the Editor*, p. 205; and *Kursiv*, p. 258.

Way. And as it turns out, the magic moments were also in a sense ultimate, for by *European Night*, Khodasevich's last collection, they have all but disappeared.[45]

It might be said that *European Night* is the most "unlyrical" collection of lyrics in the Russian language, if by "lyrical" we mean the *ta mele*, the "poems to be sung," of which the Greeks spoke.[46] As Northrop Frye has pointed out, one of the chief tendencies of the modern lyric form in the Western European tradition is to cut away at the pure base of *melos*—the sound associations of rhyme, assonance, alliteration, and so on—with powerful doses of *opsis*—the visual associations of the riddle, the ideogram, the intellectually precise image, the "curiously wrought" object, and so forth.[47] Khodasevich has often been described as a "thinking" or metaphysical poet, one who in his passion for self-reflection is closer to Baratynsky than to Pushkin.[48] In this respect his career may be viewed as a steady progression from the polarity of *melos* to the polarity of *opsis*, from the Fet-like melodic devices of *Youth* (recall that book's heavy use of anaphora and of the coordinating conjunction *i*, with its weakened logical emphasis) to those devices of restrained wit (the ironic rhyme, the concrete domestic image, the pun) that characterize later collections. (Russian poetry, by the way, for reasons perhaps inherent in the Russian language, has drifted away from the polarity of *melos* at a slower rate than, say, English poetry. Even in periods of what Eikhenbaum calls a rising "conversational style"—that of the later Pushkin, or that of Akhmatova—only the most heavily marked melodic devices have disappeared. And to the present day—as opposed to an Anglo-American tradition that

---

[45] The exception is *Sorrento Photographs*, Khodasevich's *poema*, which is discussed later in this chapter.

[46] Save for *Sorrento Photographs* and *Dzhon Bottom* (John Bottom), Khodasevich's grotesque mock ballad, *European Night* is made up entirely of lyrics.

[47] Frye, *Anatomy of Criticism*, pp. 270-281.

[48] See, e.g., Struve, "Quiet Hell."

has gradually, under the immense influence of William Carlos Williams, seen the sharp visual image gain ascendance at the expense of traditional melodic devices—there have been relatively few poets in the Russian poetic tradition that have found it necessary to dispense entirely with metrical structure and rhyme. The point to be made is that what for Khodasevich and the tradition he was writing in was a marked drift toward *opsis*, or a more "intellectual" poetry, might be for Pound, H. D., and the English imagists something still traditionally melodic.) Importantly, however, there are still poems in *Grain's Way* and *The Heavy Lyre*—"Ballada" seems the most striking example—in which the drift toward *opsis* was momentarily arrested. Melody and reflection, subconscious "inspiration" and conscious observation, were in a unique dialectical struggle. If a victory were to be awarded to one side, it would have to be to the sacred "babble" of melody and inspiration.

But the poems of *European Night* are, on many levels, a deliberate, often violent rejection of the *melos* of lyric poetry. Phonetically, they reject what is euphonious; semantically, what is the traditional or "grand" lexicon of poetic speech; thematically, what is related to psychic breakthrough or "inspiration." There are occasions in which the syntactic grace and balance of an earlier poem such as "The Soul" are now shattered by swarming verbs and adjectives.[49] Moreover, the images in this collection are more optically precise than ever before: as Nabokov ingeniously put it in his review of the *Collected Verse*, there has gathered over the later poems a sort of "optical-pharmaceutical-chemical-anatomical deposit."[50] Caught in a world that is totally conscious and "loathsomely material,"[51] the speakers of *European Night* observe their fallen state and take perverse pleas-

---

[49] See Veidle, "The Poetry of Khodasevich," p. 461.
[50] Sirin [Nabokov], "Vladislav Khodasevich."
[51] Veidle, "The Poetry of Khodasevich," pp. 460-463.

ure in "singing the unsingable."[52] Wladimir Weidlé has suggested that Khodasevich has now entered an "alien" (*chuzhoi*) realm, one that has little or nothing in common with the realms of *Grain's Way* and *The Heavy Lyre*, and the implication is that this alien element is not only linked with the Western European locale of the poems, but with their nature as poetic form.[53] When he wrote of the "other" that was his *dusha*, Khodasevich was speaking of what was more essentially "his" (even though he could not possess it) than his body or his physical surroundings. But the element of otherness in *European Night* is entirely foreign and inimical to the poet. As we shall be seeing, the word-seeds that once fell into the "black earth" of a still vital Russian poetic tradition are cast, in Khodasevich's last collection, onto the alien pavement of European cities. Unable to take root, they harvest only the consciousness of the poet's failed role and, most painful for Khodasevich, the inevitable absence of poetic speech.

European Night opens as *The Heavy Lyre* closed—with the poet looking back. Written on 12 December 1926 in Chaville, "Petersburg" tells, in graphic images now customary for Khodasevich, of the poet's place in the artistic life of his last Russian home:

> Напастям жалким и однообразным
> Там предавались до потери сил.
> Один лишь я полуживым соблазном
> Средь озабоченных ходил.
>
> Смотрели на меня—и забывали
> Клокочущие чайники свои;
> На печках валенки сгорали;
> Все слушали стихи мои.
>
> А мне тогда в тьме гробовой, российской,
> Являлась вестница в цветах,

[52] Sirin [Nabokov], "Vladislav Khodasevich."
[53] Veidle, "The Poetry of Khodasevich," pp. 460-463.

И лад открылся музикийский
Мне в сногсшибательных ветрах.

И я безумел от видений,
Когда чрез ледяной канал,
Скользя с обломанных ступеней,
Треску зловонную таскал,

И каждый стих гоня сквозь прозу,
Вывихивая каждую строку,
Привил-таки классическую розу
К советскому дичку.   (*SS,* p. 123)

There they indulged themselves to the limit
in calamities monotonous and pitiful.
Only I, like a half-alive temptation,
moved about amid the distraught.

They looked at me, and they forgot
their boiling teakettles;
their felt boots were burning on their stoves;
Everyone was listening to my poems.

And then in that sepulchral Russian murk
a beflowered messenger appeared to me,
and in the hurly-burly of the winds
a harmony of the Muses was revealed.

And I went mad with such visions
when crossing over an icy canal
and slipping off broken steps,
I carried some stinking cod;

and driving every verse through prose
and every line pulling out of joint,
I still managed to graft the classical rose
to the Soviet wilding.

As I suggested in preceding chapters, the opening poems of
Grain's Way and *The Heavy Lyre* serve as frontispieces;
emblematic, they establish a mood for what follows. But
unlike "Grain's Way," in which the speaker anticipates the
death and life of the grain with examples of the future tense,
and "The Music," in which the speaker overhears music
from another sphere in an otherwise prosaic present tense,

"Petersburg" is written wholly in the past tense. By late 1926 there is little to look forward to. The poet is now taking a retrospective glance at the graft of "classical" and "modern" that produced some of his finest verse. Of course, the urge to dislocate by prosaism what is lyrically plangent and the startling combination of visionary poet and stinking cod seem typically Khodasevichian. What is new, in terms of this opening volley, is the past tense and perfective aspect of the key verb *privil-taki* (still I did graft). Once successful, the artistic grafting of the classical rose and Soviet wilding is no longer taking place.

An intriguing formal development in *European Night* is phonetic. In a manner much broader than seen heretofore Khodasevich uses the formal qualities of sound in a controlled attempt to present spiritual impasse. Whereas a poem's rhythmic-phonetic bloodstream, as it were, was apt to flow more or less evenly in *Grain's Way* and *The Heavy Lyre*, it is now apt to develop "aneurisms" (motivated on another level by the speaker's growing frustration), spots where the smooth circulation of iambs is deliberately retarded or impeded:

Весенний лепет не разнежит
Сурово стиснутых стихов.
Я полюбил железный скрежет
Какофонических миров.

В зиянии разверстых гласных
Дышу легко и вольно я.
Мне чудится в толпе согласных—
Льдин взгромо́жденных толчея.

Мне мил—из оловянной тучи
Удар изломанной стрелы,
Люблю певучий и визгучий
Лязг электрической пилы.

И в этой жизни мне дороже
Всех гармонических красот—
Дрожь, побежавшая по коже,
Иль ужаса холодный пот,

Иль сон, где, некогда единый—
Взрываясь, разлетаюсь я,
Как грязь разбрызганная шиной
По чуждым сферам бытия.

(SS, p. 125)

The spring babble will not soften
sternly clenched lines of verse.
I've fallen in love with the iron gnashing
of cacophonous worlds.

In the gaping of wide-open vowels
I breathe easily and freely.
I imagine in a crowd of consonants
the crushing of ice floes piled high.

Sweet to me from a cloud of tin
is the blow of a broken arrow,
I love the singing and the screeching
clatter of the electric saw.

And in this life dearer to me than
all harmonious beauties
is the shiver running along my skin
or the cold sweat of terror,

or the dream where, at one time whole,
I, exploding, fly apart
like mud splashed by a tire
along the alien spheres of being.

As Wladimir Weidlé has remarked, this untitled poem is a sort of *ars poetica* for the later Khodasevich.[54] It was written in late March 1923, polished in 1927, and was apparently intended to be read in tandem with "Zhiv Bog" (God is Alive), the poem preceding it, as an answer to the "trans-sense language" (*zaumnyi iazyk*) of Kruchyonykh and Khlebnikov.[55] Khodasevich felt that the attempts of Kruchyonykh to develop a poem's phonetic potential at the expense of any semantic component, to suggest, in the terminology of the

---

[54] Wladimir Weidlé, "A Double-Edged *Ars Poetica*," *Russian Literature Triquarterly* 2 (Winter 1972), 339-347.

[55] Marina Tsvetaeva mistook "God is Alive" to be an attack on Pasternak and herself. See Simon Karlinsky, *Marina Cvetaeva: Her Life and Art* (Berkeley, 1966), p. 72n.

time, that a poem's "form" is all the "meaning" it possesses, were futile and absurd.[56] Yet he would also argue, as he does here, that the phonetic character of a poem is nowise secondary, that neither "sound" nor "sense" is prior or posterior in terms of aesthetic causality, but each motivates the other, and that the Radical critics of the 1860s and the Formalists of this century made the same error, only the second group had turned "inside out" (from the priority of "content" to the priority of "form") the error of the first group. Thus "Vesennii lepet ne raznezhit" (The spring babble will not soften) may be seen as Khodasevich's programmatic way of making vivid the mutual dependence of sound and sense in poetic structure. And, indeed, rarely in Khodasevich does one find such a "graphic example of sound imitating and expressing sense."[57] The numerous phonetic tropes in the poem work to heighten what is tense or grinding and to undermine what is euphonious: the playful e-based assonance of the first line (the phonetic image of "spring babble") is quickly corseted by the $s + t$ consonantal alliteration of the second line (the phonetic image of "sternly clenched lines of verse"); in the same stanza the onomatopoetic interplay of voiced sibilants zh and z and voiceless stop k suggests the buzzing and clashing of "cacophonous worlds"; in the next stanza the loss of two stresses in the last line ("l'dĭn vzgrŏmŏzhdénnўkh tŏlchĕiá") and the bottleneck of consonants in the difficult-to-pronounce vzgromozhden-nykh tell of the phonetic clogging of iambic movement that is conveyed on the semantic level by the image of "ice floes piled high"; in the third stanza the grating sound of an electric saw is heard in the repetition of the affricate ch; and in the fourth stanza the skeining of hushing sibilants zh and sh phonetically depicts a shiver crossing the skin. All this

[56] See Khodasevich: "O formalizme i formalistakh" (On Formalism and Formalists), *Voz*, no. 646 (10 March 1927); and "O Maiakovskom" (On Mayakovsky), *Stat'i*, pp. 221-222.
[57] Weidlé, "A Double-Edged *Ars Poetica*," p. 340.

is perhaps a little heavy-handed for Khodasevich, a poet not normally known for the extensive use of consonantal instrumentation. The presence of such a poem in the opening pages of *European Night* implies that by 1923 Khodasevich felt that the balance of power in modern Russian poetry was shifting in the direction of Futurism and it was time to make an unequivocal (and, therefore, artistically not totally successful[58]) statement about the dangers of such a shift.[59]

With the absence of the *dusha* as a real force in *European Night* comes a marked stylistic shift "downward" in the range of traditional poetic speech. In *The Heavy Lyre* a visit by the *dusha* often brought with it a lexicon that was cold and distanced ("The Soul," "Psyche! My poor one!") or grand and larger-than-life ("Elegy"), whereas the presence of the dunning heart brought with it a lexicon that was heavily ironic, specific, and often colloquial ("The Temptation," "Day"). Much of the semantic richness and ambiguity of *The Heavy Lyre* grew out of the medley of voices established between different speakers or even in the same speaker: the soul's *sotto voce* reply to the angry monologue of the heart in "The Temptation." Hence one voice, which sought psychic breakthrough and might be associated with the "lyric" style and diction of Pushkin, Baratynsky, Tyutchev and the nineteenth-century poetic tradition, and another voice, which recognized that such breakthrough was no longer possible and might be associated with the "heaviness" of phenomenal reality after 1917, were in a constant tug-of-war until "Ballada," when the lyre was lifted despite its weight and one voice achieved a provisional triumph over the other. But now, as we see in "Net, ne naidu" (No, I won't find), a poem begun in late March and finished in early June 1923, the voice of the *eiron* has completely taken the upper hand:

---

[58] Khodasevich was displeased with "The spring babble will not soften." See his note to the poem in *SS*, p. 219.

[59] Weidlé, "A Double-Edged *Ars Poetica*," p. 342.

Нет, не найду сегодня пищи я
Для утешительной мечты:
Одни шарманщики, да нищие,
Да дождь—все с той же высоты.

Тускнеет в лужах электричество,
Нисходит предвечерний мрак
На идиотское количество
Серощетинистых собак.

Та—ткнется мордою нечистою
И повернувшись отбежит,
Другая лапою когтистою
Скребет обшмыганный гранит.

Те—жилятся, присев на корточки,
Повесив на бок языки,—
А их из самой верхней форточки
Зовут хозяйские свистки.

Все высвистано, прособачено.
Вот так и шлепай по грязи,
Пока не вздрогнет сердце, схвачено
Внезапным треском жалюзи.   (SS, p. 141)

No, today I won't find food
for comforting dream:
There are only organ grinders, and beggars,
and rain falling from the same old height.

The electricity flashes dully in the puddles,
the pre-evening gloom descends
on an idiotic number
of bristly-gray dogs.

That one will poke about with its dirty snout
and, turning around, then run away,
another will scratch with its sharp-clawed
paw the well-worn granite.

Those, squatting down and hanging
their tongues to the side, are straining [to defecate],
while from the highest window vent they
are being called home by their masters' whistles.

All is whistled out, be-dogged through and through.
So just like this shuffle through the mud

> until your heart winces in the grasp
> of a sudden slamming of the jalousie.

While out of context *sharmanshchik* (organ grinder), *ni-shchii* (beggar), *luzha* (puddle), *sobaka* (dog), *lapa* (paw), *granit* (granite), *iazyk* (tongue), *fortochka* (window vent), *zhaliuzi* (jalousie) are simply common nouns, in context they function to trap the speaker in a world of objects as perhaps never before. Only the *uteshitel'naia mechta* (comforting dream) of the second line—expressed in a negative construction—suggests some former state of ulteriority and grace. In addition, the numerous colloquialisms (*tknut'sia*—"to poke about"; *obshmygannyi*—"worn down or rubbed up and down"; *zhilit'sia*—"to strain"; *shlepat'*—"to shuffle") indicate a more pronounced shift away from the "elevated" or pristine semantics of the *dusha*. Finally, the speaker reaches such an impasse that even colloquial speech proves an inadequate vehicle for conveying his impotent rage: in the last stanza he finds it necessary to coin his own word to describe the unbearable *status quo*—the world has become "be-dogged through and through" (*prosobacheno*).

In *European Night* Khodasevich comes close on a number of occasions to an intentional parody of poetic speech. Poems that "make strange" the lyric form on which he was raised (or as he, being an organicist, would have preferred to express it, that find the precise form appropriate for his inner estrangement) might best be viewed as new variations on an aging tradition rather than as efforts to break with that tradition and start anew. In this regard, of course, Khodasevich is akin to the "sophisticated" Pushkin, who was apt to invigorate a cliché-ridden tradition through parody, and opposed to the "enthusiastic" Mayakovsky, who was apt to turn his back on tradition altogether.[60] The element of parody in *European Night* is particularly evident at the level of rhyme, where the phonetic and semantic functions of poetic

[60] See note 9, chapter 4, above.

speech often overlap. Already in *Grain's Way* and *The Heavy Lyre* we noted Khodasevich's penchant for the deflating or self-ironizing rhyme: the pairing of *brezenta* (the genitive form for "tarpaulin") with *Brenta*, the famous river, in "Brenta," and the pairing of *neudachnik* (misfit) with *dachnik* (vacationer) in "Bel'skoe ust'e." But in *European Night*, where self-ironizing devices are more prominent, Khodasevich suggests that the "elevating" rhyme (one of the chief ingredients of *melos* in poetry) that inspired earlier generations is, in the present circumstances, absurd. Of the last poems in the collection there are several, including "Okna vo dvor" (Windows to the Courtyard), "Bednye rifmy" (Poor Rhymes), "Skvoz' nenastnyi zimnii denek" (Through the foul winter day), and the second "Ballada," that derive great force from the presence of absurd or grotesque rhyme.[61] Perhaps it is not by chance that these poems, all completed in Paris between May 1924 and January 1927, are as dark as any ever written by Khodasevich, and show him on the verge of total despair and silence. The *tour de force* among them is the one written last—"Through the foul winter day":

Сквозь ненастный зимний денек
—У него сундук, у нее мешок—

По паркету парижских луж
Ковыляют жена и муж.

Я за ними долго шагал,
И пришли они на вокзал.
Жена молчала, и муж молчал.

И о чем говорить, мой друг?
У нее мешок, у него сундук . . .
С каблуком топотал каблук.   (*SS*, p. 163)

Through the foul winter day—
he's got a trunk and she a bag—

---

[61] In "Windows to the Courtyard" (*SS*, pp. 160-161) Khodasevich rhymes *trup* (corpse) with *sup* (soup) and *ladon'* (palm) with *ogon'* ([hell] fire).

in the parquetry of Parisian puddles
the wife and husband hobble along.

I walked after them for a long while,
and they came to the station.
The wife kept quiet, and the husband kept quiet.

What's there to say, my friend?
She's got a bag, and he a trunk . . .
heel was clattering with heel.

The devices that Khodasevich uses here to echo the sound of meaningless motion, the "clip-clop" of homeless heels on alien sidewalks, are subtle, especially if we consider the utter simplicity of his word choice.[62] Among such devices are the shuffling of anapests and iambs and the profusion of stop consonants (k, b, t, p), with their phonetic implication of clacking heels, in the last line. But perhaps even more ingenious is the slightly sing-song, almost excessive use of adjoining rhyme. Though the masculine rhymes themselves are not absurd (as they are, for example, in "Windows to the Courtyard"), their disposition in adjoining doublets and triplets suggests the presence of self-parody. The poem's dark meaning is deliberately "upstaged" by rhymes that teeter on the edge of what is dittylike, idiotically regular. Therefore, "Through the foul winter day" manages a tightrope walk between seriousness and parody, and its form may be the poet's way of saying that the convention of rhyme, in the émigré's state of psychological upheaval, has turned back to laugh at itself through tears. Our reaction, it seems, to this strange yoking of the comic and the pathetic is the uneasy smile that lies at the heart of the grotesque.[63]

Another revealing index of Khodasevich's shift to the mode of unstable irony is his use of imagery in *European Night*. As I mentioned in chapter 4, from the statement of the stable

[62] See Weidlé, "A Double-Edged *Ars Poetica*," pp. 346-347.
[63] For a discussion of the grotesque in Khodasevich, see Philippe Radley, "Khodasevich—poet groteska" (Khodasevich: A Poet of the Grotesque), *Vozdushnye puti* (Aerial Ways), 4 (1965), 256-262.

ironist the reader is usually able to "process" the in-context irony and posit another system of values (often directly opposing the one advanced by the statement's literal meaning) that the ironist has hidden behind the lines. In the statement of the unstable ironist, however, no such system of values can be extrapolated. One of the masters of unstable irony is, of course, Kafka: logic for a character such as Joseph K. is nothing more than a screw with stripped threads; each effort to argue or defend oneself is a revolution that leaves one at the same loose, unhinged beginning. The imagery of *European Night* is, in this regard, closely aligned to the Kafkaesque model. To tell of the loss of higher values, including that of individuality itself (Joseph K., by the way, is deprived of a surname and its link with parents and origins), Khodasevich, like Kafka, resorts to pictures of violence and disfiguration that may be presented in a manner disarmingly flat or understated. The speaker in "Berlinskoe" (Berlinian) looks into the windows (the reflecting surface that formerly propelled Khodasevich into other worlds) of a tram just in time to see his decapitated head float by; a one-armed man arouses in the speaker in "Ballada" not feelings of pity, but wry humor;[64] drafted for service in the war, the tailor of *Dzhon Bottom* (John Bottom) loses his renowned right arm and his life in lines that are lilting and nursery-rhymish.[65] Rather than *The Trial*, the animal imagery in *European Night* suggests perhaps another Kafkaesque analogue—"The Metamorphosis":

Уродики, уродища, уроды
Весь день озерные мутили воды.

[64] "If Khodasevich intended to arouse pity, sympathy, and the like in the reader, then he failed. One may be carried away with his images, his music, or his virtuosity, yet in regard to his fate-battered personas one experiences absolutely no human feelings." (Sirin [Nabokov], "Vladislav Khodasevich.")

[65] See Zinaida Gippius' understanding of the loss of identity in *John Bottom* in Gippius, *Letters to Berberova and Khodasevich*, pp. 45-47.

Теперь над озером ненастье, мрак,
В траве—лягушачий зеленый квак.

Огни на дачах гаснут понемногу,
Клубки червей полезли на дорогу,

А вдалеке, где все затерла мгла,
Тупая грамофонная игла

Шатается по рытвинам царапин,
И из трубы еще рычит Шаляпин.

На мокрый мир нисходит угомон ...
Лишь кое-где, топча сырой газон,

Блудливые невесты с женихами
Слипаются, накрытые зонтами,

А к ним под юбки лазит с фонарем
Полуслепой, широкоротый гном.   (SS, p. 142)

Little-, giant-, and medium-sized freaks
were muddying the lake water all day long.

But now over the lake there is foul weather, gloom,
and in the grass the frog's green croaking.

Little by little the lights of the *dachas* go out,
tangled clumps of worms climb onto the road,

and in the distance, where the murk has rubbed out
                         everything,
a dull gramophone needle

skips along scratched grooves,
and Shalyapin still growls from the speaker.

Peace descends to the wet world . . .
and only here and there, trampling down the damp grass,

lecherous brides and their grooms
stick together under the cover of umbrellas,

while crawling under their skirts with a lantern
is a half-blind, broad-mouthed gnome.

Composed in June 1923 in Saarow and finished up in August 1924 in Ireland, "Dachnoe" (Vacationing) gives ample evidence of the additional sharpness and grotesquerie taken on by the images of *European Night*. Whereas in *The Heavy*

Lyre the *dusha* might be compared to a full moon, now, in this soulless atmosphere, everything descends to ground level. Man has been transformed into a lower form of life. Both the clusters of worms and the vacationing couples are stuck together by the same force of brute sexuality. Those higher qualities of intellect that separate man from beast have been stripped from this world. As Khodasevich felt it necessary at the semantic level in "No, I won't find" to go beyond common lexical usage and coin a new word to convey his frustration, here in the last couplet he feels it necessary at the level of the image to go beyond the elements of the actual landscape and mix the real with the surreal in the picture of the obscene gnome.

What should be becoming clear by now is that the various aspects of the poetic manifold in *European Night* lead back, with a relentless consistency, to the overarching theme of loss, alienation, exile. In a collection dominated by the unforgiving eye of Khodasevich, the theme finds its cruelest treatment in "An Mariechen," a poem written on 20-21 July 1923 in Berlin:

Зачем ты за пивною стойкой?
Пристала ли тебе она?
Здесь нужно быть девицей бойкой,—
Ты нездорова и бледна.

С какой-то розою огромной
У нецелованных грудей,—
А смертный венчик, самый скромный,
Украсил бы тебя милей.

Ведь так прекрасно, так нетленно
Скончаться рано, до греха.
Родители же непременно
Тебе отыщут жениха.

Так называемый хороший,
И в правду—честный человек
Перегрузит тяжелой ношей
Твой слабый, твой короткий век.

Уж лучше бы—я еле смею
Подумать про себя о том—
Попасться бы тебе злодею
В пустынной роще, вечерком.

Уж лучше в несколько мгновений
И стыд узнать, и смерть принять,
И двух истлений, двух растлений
Не разделять, не разлучать.

Лежать бы в платьице измятом
Одной, в березняке густом,
И нож под левым, лиловатым,
Еще девическим соском.   (*SS*, pp. 138-39)

Why are you at the bar of a beer hall?
Does it really suit you?
Here one must be a brazen lass,
but you are pale and sickly.

You wear at your unkissed breasts
some sort of huge rose,
but the most modest paper crown of the deceased
would adorn you more fetchingly.

After all, it's so wonderful, so pristine
to die early, before one sins.
Without doubt your parents
will seek out a groom for you.

This so-called good
and—indeed—honorable man
will weigh down with his heavy burden
your weak and short life.

Surely it would be better—I hardly dare
to think of it to myself—
if a villain fell upon you
in a deserted grove some evening.

Surely it would be better in several moments
to learn of shame, to accept death,
and not to have to divide and separate
two seductions, two corruptions.

You would lie in a crumpled dress
alone in a birch wood

with a knife under your left, violet-colored,
still maidenly nipple.

The source for Mariechen was a girl whom Khodasevich often observed tending bar at a *Bierstube* located in Berlin at the intersection of Lutherstrasse and Augsburgerstrasse: the modest daughter of the proprietor (for some reason, she reminded Khodasevich of Nadya Lvova, his friend from the Symbolist years who had committed suicide), she was easily frightened by the half-mad Bely, who forced her to take part in his wild dancing. It was in this beer hall, between drinking, dancing, and card playing, that Bely and Khodasevich would have conversations "about the ultimate" (*o poslednem*).[66] Mariechen can be seen as the last pathetic incarnation of Sophia, the Symbolist myth of divine wisdom in feminine form that had been a prime mover of much of the early thinking and work of Blok and Bely. But by 1923 all the innocent hopes originally placed on a Sophia-become-flesh have been dashed. This ironic hypostatization of Sophia is foreign, plain, unmysterious. Her handsome *tsarevich* (the young Blok, the young Bely) has been reduced to some hopelessly down-to-earth young Berliner. In fact, the only quality that Mariechen does share with her mythical counterpart is innocence. Yet in the fallen world of *European Night* such innocence is absurd and inappropriate. The raping and killing of Mariechen imagined in the poem is an expression of utter disenchantment, and seems Khodasevich's "objective correlative" for the conversations with Bely "about the ultimate" and for "the symbolic trampling of the best in himself" that Bely acted out in his dancing. In any case, "An Mariechen" is one of the most chilling lyrics in modern Russian poetry; its ironic distancing—and especially the exquisite detail of the last stanza—is reminiscent of Manet's dead toreador.

If "An Mariechen" is Khodasevich's ultimate expression

---

[66] Note to "An Mariechen," in *SS*, p. 220. See also *Nekropol'*, p. 90.

of the fall of innocence, "Pod zemlei" (Underground), written
also in Berlin on 23 September 1923, is his most terrifying
and powerful expression of the condition of exile:

Где пахнет черною карболкой
И провонявшею землей,
Стоит, склоняя профиль колкий
Пред изразцовою стеной.

Не отойдет, не обернется,
Лишь весь качается слегка,
Да как-то судорожно бьется
Потертый локоть сюртука.

Заходят школьники, солдаты,
Рабочий в блузе голубой,—
Он все стоит, к стене прижатый
Своею дикою мечтой.

Здесь создает и разрушает
Он сладострастные миры,
А из соседней конуры
За ним старуха наблюдает.

Потом в открывшуюся дверь
Видны подушки, стулья, стклянки.
Вошла—и слышатся теперь
Обрывки злобной перебранки.
Потом вонючая метла
Безумца гонит из угла.
И вот, из полутьмы глубокой,
Старик сутулый, но высокий,
В таком почтенном сюртуке,
В когда-то модном котелке,
Идет по лестнице широкой,
Как тень Аида—в белый свет,
В берлинский день, в блестящий бред.
А солнце ясно, небо сине,
А сверху синяя пустыня . . .
И злость, и скорбь моя кипит,
И трость моя в чужой гранит
Неумолкаемо стучит.   (*SS*, pp. 143-144)

There where it smells of black carbolic acid
and the reeking earth

he stands, bending his sharp profile
before a tile wall.

He does not step back, nor turn around,
just shakes all over slightly,
and the worn elbow of his jacket
is somehow working furiously.

School children, soldiers, a workman
in a blue shirt drop by—
still he stands, pressed to the wall
by his wild dream.

Here he creates and destroys
his voluptuous worlds,
and from the kennel next door
a gammer watches him.

Then through the opened door
one sees pillows, chairs, bottles.
She comes out, and now one hears
snatches of irritable squabbling.
Then a smelly broom
chases the madman from the corner.
And so, from out of the deep half-darkness
the old man, stoop-shouldered but tall,
in such a respectable frock-coat,
in a once stylish bowler hat,
walks—like a shade of Hades—up
the wide staircase into the white light,
the Berlin day, the shining delirium.
And the sun is bright, the sky blue,
and up above is a blue desert . . .
And my rage and grief seethe,
and my walking-stick incessantly taps
on the alien granite.

This poetic dramatization of the act of masturbation is grotesque in its own right; even on one quick reading, it shows
the degree of Khodasevich's repugnance at life in emigration.
More than the literal act of masturbation is involved here,
however. "Underground" is an extensive inversion of the
themes and imagery of "Grain's Way," the poem that perhaps more than any other is linked with the role of wise

sower once played by Khodasevich. Instead of the wise sower we find a version of the Biblical Onan; instead of the seeds that fall into Russian soil and its native poetic tradition, we find seeds that are cast onto "alien granite."[67] Onan was struck down by the Lord because he "spilled [his] semen on the ground, lest he should give offspring to his brother"— he had failed to fulfill *"the duty of the brother-in-law: . . . to raise up a male descendant for his deceased brother and thus perpetuate his name and inheritance."*[68] And now Khodasevich, aware of the tragic barrenness of Russian poetry in emigration, projects this modern image of Onan. As a poet, Khodasevich feels that he is being struck down by an angry Lord because his work has become seeds on foreign pavement; he too is unable to sire a new descendant for his dead brother, for the line of Russian poetry that remained behind in Russia. Therefore, the sowing process that produces fruit and has a purpose has become the act of sowing by itself, sexuality for its own sake. In keeping with many of the finales in *European Night*, the last lines of "Underground" capture Khodasevich's feelings with a picture of almost violent precision: like a divining rod searching futilely for something below the surface (the lost furrows of "Grain's Way"?), the walking stick that taps on the pavement seems an image of impotence and frustrated sexuality.

[67] There are several references to the cruel pavement of European cities in *European Night*. The most striking example of a poem in which the speaker is oppressed by the loss of *pochva* (soil) and by the presence of stoniness is "Vse kamennoe" (All is stony) (*SS*, p. 145). The murderous rage that Khodasevich expresses in many of these poems caused him to compare himself to an eczematous Cain in the cycle "U moria" (By the Sea) (*SS*, pp. 128-134). As we find in Genesis 4:10-14: "And the Lord said, 'What have you done? The voice of your brother's blood is crying to me from the ground. And now you are cursed from the ground, which has opened its mouth to receive your brother's blood from your hand. When you till the ground it shall no longer yield to you; you shall be a fugitive and a wanderer on earth.' " (*The New Oxford Annotated Bible*, eds. Herbert G. May and Bruce M. Metzger [New York, 1977], p. 6.)

[68] Genesis 38:8-10, and note in *The New Oxford Annotated Bible*, p. 48.

Each of Khodasevich's mature collections is intimately connected with his life during that period. Yet perhaps even more than *Grain's Way* and *The Heavy Lyre*, *European Night* offers convincing proof that poetry writing for Khodasevich was not an avocation but a way of life. When exile threatened that way of life with extinction, the reaction, found on nearly every page of *European Night*, was rage, revolt, frustration. In his last collection Khodasevich's speakers imagine scenes of murder, rape, disfiguration, grotesquerie, and raw sexuality, because his art, that which made him human and the world around him bearable, was being taken from him. The absence of art implied the absence of that transfiguring medium that made phenomenal reality other than bestial. And so at the level of sound, word, image, and theme Khodasevich's art can be seen to be moving toward the threshold of absence, of silence. By "Zvezdy" (The Stars), the last poem in *European Night*, the still expanding cosmos of *The Heavy Lyre* has shrunk to the stage of a *café chantant* and to a constellation of nude dancing girls. What began under the open sky of "Grain's Way," underwent a transfiguration to the universe of apartment 30a of "Ballada," ends with the fake scenery, the obscene celestial bodies, and the parody of God's creation of "The Stars":

> Глядят солдаты и портные
> На рассусаленный сумбур,
> Играют сгустки жировые
> На бедрах Étoile d'amour,
> Несутся звезды в пляске, в тряске,
> Звучит оркестр, поет дурак,
> Летят алмазные подвязки
> Из мрака в свет, из света в мрак.
> И заходя в дыру все ту же,
> И восходя на небосклон,—
> Так вот в какой постыдной луже
> Твой День Четвертый отражен! ...
> Не легкий труд, о Боже правый,
> Всю жизнь воссоздавать мечтой

Твой мир, горящий звездной славой
И первозданною красой.   (SS, p. 178)

Soldiers and tailors look
at the chaos of tinsel,
clots of fat play
on the thighs of the *Étoile d'amour*,
the stars run by dancing, shaking,
the orchestra blares, the ass sings,
diamond-studded garters fly
from dark to light, from light to dark.
And passing still into the same hole,
and rising up to the horizon,
this is the sort of shameful puddle
in which Your Fourth Day is reflected! . . .
It is no easy task, O righteous Lord,
to recreate all life long by dream
Your world, blazing with celestial glory
and pristine beauty.

THOUGH found in his last and darkest collection, Khoda-sevich's most elaborate verse narrative bears the sunny title *Sorrentinskie fotografii* (Sorrento Photographs). Its sage and sometimes enigmatic speaker, its personal as well as national themes, and its Petersburg setting (among others) suggest that this ironic *poema* has its headwaters—more remote than a direct comparison can justify—in Pushkin and *The Bronze Horseman*. Indeed, while Khodasevich's earlier poems in blank verse have been described as replies to the *Little Tragedies*, in *Sorrento Photographs* we can only suspect that Pushkin was an abiding presence in the modern poet's mind.[69] Yet the liminal reference to Pushkin becomes more apparent when we notice that the perfectly modulated iambic tetrameter, the fluid, seemingly effortless enjambments, the ingenious rhymes, and the generally limpid style recall Pushkin's language perhaps more than anything else Khodasevich wrote.

Nevertheless, *Sorrento Photographs* could only belong to

[69] Veidle, "The Poetry of Khodasevich," p. 456.

a modern ironist. The central images, for one, are a double-exposed snapshot and a motorcycle. Manifestly, the concerns of a premodern age of poetry have now, some one hundred years later, been replaced by those of a modern one. The tone of Khodasevich's poem reflects in turn the elusive position of the modernist. With its emphasis on imagination and memory this work partakes of the playful, avowedly "artificial" world of artistic patterning and of the world of historical inexorability. The *poema*'s ironic tension arises from the superimposition of the former world on the latter. In a word, *Sorrento Photographs* is seriocomic, Khodasevich managing that balancing act which few, if any, Russian poets other than Pushkin have managed to do. This may be one reason why Robert Hughes calls the work "one of Khodasevich's most successful—if untypical—efforts,"[70] since he feels its tone is alien to the ubiquitous gloom of *European Night*. Yet, superimposing past on present, imagination on history, and the comic, morning mood of "To Anyuta" on the somber, evening mood of "An Mariechen," *Sorrento Photographs* stands at the center of Khodasevich's *oeuvre*.[71]

How, to begin with, did Khodasevich feel about Sorrento, the place where he spent his last winter with Gorky before returning to Paris? It seems that his feelings were mixed, ambiguous, like the tone of the *poema* itself. Khodasevich was certainly happy to be with Gorky, but he now saw a split with his old friend as inevitable; he was relieved to be free of Paris and of the "permanency" of exile he associated

[70] Robert P. Hughes, "Khodasevich: Irony and Dislocation: A Poet in Exile," *TriQuarterly* 28 (Spring 1973), 64.

[71] Irony is of course a salient feature in Khodasevich's three mature collections. But what is often a bright, matinal irony in the poems, such as "To Anyuta," of *Grain's Way*, develops gradually through *The Heavy Lyre*, a book whose poems generally show a more trenchant, angular variety of irony, into the desperate, bitter, and hence "nocturnal" irony of the poems, such as "An Mariechen," of the last collection. *Sorrento Photographs* is unique because, while located in *European Night*, it seems to briefly retrieve the mood of *Grain's Way*.

with that city, but he knew that a return was merely a matter of months; he was excited to be beginning what was to become his favorite work, but he was all too aware of the difficulties facing a Russian poet writing in Western Europe. Even Sorrento itself was an ambiguous blend of beauty (the Bay of Naples) and beast (Mount Vesuvius): from his balcony at Il Sorito Khodasevich could see the bay and the volcano at once, and this simultaneous awareness of attraction and danger seems to pervade *Sorrento Photographs*. What's more, Il Sorito, Khodasevich's perch above the bay and the breathtaking landscape, was located at the edge of a precipice, on land prone to landslide, and could be swept down the face of the cliff and into the sea at any time.

Vesuvius occupied a prominent spot in Khodasevich's memories of Sorrento. On 10 May 1925, less than a month after his departure from Gorky's, Khodasevich published in *Poslednie novosti* (The Latest News) "Pompeiskii uzhas" (Pompeian Horror), an essay describing his day trip to the city buried by the eruption of Vesuvius in A.D. 79. As he approached Pompeii, Khodasevich saw "Vesuvius, a *rust-colored* brown, towering up to the left. Its peak was surrounded by puffs of steam. Almost black around the crater, these puffs, brightening up and *dispersing*, trailed off to the southeast in the form of a whitish cloud."[72] A similar image of a "rust-colored" Vesuvius and "dispersing" clouds of smoke appears at the climax of *Sorrento Photographs*.

The immediate impression that the city of Pompeii made on Khodasevich strongly resembles the picture of postrevolutionary Petersburg found in his later memoirs:

We exit [the entrance area] and enter the "city." There is something astounding in the deathly silence and tidiness. Considering the number of extant streets, squares, and walls, this is anything but a heap of ruins. Indeed, it is a city, but one from whose face all that is temporary, incidental, momentary, and dirty has been wiped

[72] Khodasevich, "Pompeiskii uzhas" (Pompeian Horror), *PN*, no. 1547 (10 May 1925).

off: Pompeii is bathed, tidied up, "decked out," like someone deceased.[73]

Was there perhaps, in Khodasevich's view, something other than mere physical resemblance tying this image of a "decked out" Pompeii to that of a Petersburg "grown attractive in its coffin"?[74]

Proceeding further, Khodasevich began to see horror through the beauty. He could not witness the ruins with the objectivity of a historian or the love for antiquity of a classicist. What he saw instead in the destruction of Pompeii was personal drama and symbolic retribution. More important, he made a direct link between this city of the dead and the necropolis he had left behind in Russia. History, it seems, was repeating itself before his eyes:

A cemetery is idyllic. Peace reigns there. Those who have completed their path on earth are taken by us to the cemetery, the city *of the deceased and of peace [gorod pokoinikov i pokoia].* What is the grave to us? *Parva domus, magna quies.* But here in these little [Pompeian] houses what is lacking is precisely [the sense of] great peace. In a cemetery there is reconciliation; here there is only horror. Everyone has died, but no one has made his peace with anything. Here are buried people who have been overtaken by death not only in the middle of their path on earth but, one might say, with a foot raised for the next step. Here everyone died in horror, frenzy, passion, rage. . . . They perished in uncomprehending horror and, according to the testimony of Pliny, many committed sacrilege—no doubt precisely because [at the time] they were sitting, drinking, eating, trading, cheating each other with their measuring and weighing, fighting, embracing. And suddenly you're about to die, not having finished drinking, eating, measuring, weighing, fighting, embracing . . .

> . . . Когда ж без сил любовники застыли
> И покорил их необорный сон,
> На город пали груды серой пыли,
> И город был под пеплом погребен.

---

[73] Ibid.
[74] *Stat'i*, p. 400. See chapter 5 above, pp. 187-190.

Века прошли; и, как из алчной пасти,
Мы вырвали былое у земли.
И двое тел, как знак бессмертной страсти,
Нетленными в объятиях нашли.

Поставьте выше памятник священный,
Живое изваянье вечных тел,
Чтоб память не угасла во вселенной
О страсти, перешедшей за предел!

When the lovers, worn out, grew cool
and inevitable sleep subdued them,
heaps of gray dust fell onto the city,
and the city was buried under the ash.

Centuries passed; and, as from a greedy maw,
we ripped out the past from the earth,
And two bodies, as a sign of immortal passion,
were found undecayed in an embrace.

Raise higher the sacred memorial,
the living sculpture of eternal bodies,
so that through the universe the memory shall burn
of passion that exceeds the limit.

God, what soulless decadence! "Raise [the memorial] higher!"
No, for God's sake, hide it, don't show it to anybody, bury it again![75]

The last stanzas from Bryusov's early (1902) poem "Pompeianka" (The Pompeian Woman) seem almost to cry out for an additional gloss. Bryusov, who died just seven months before Khodasevich wrote this article, was of course the leader of the Decadent movement in Russia. He was also Khodasevich's first teacher and early idol. Like so many others, Khodasevich had been quickly swept into the "bio-aesthetic" experience of Decadence. Now, in the spring of 1925, Bryusov and the movement he stood for were on Khodasevich's mind. The previous fall (1924) Khodasevich had written his memoir of Bryusov—excerpts from it appeared in the spring 1925 issue of *Sovremennye zapiski* (Contemporary Annals). Walking through Pompeii, Khodasevich was

---

[75] Khodasevich, "Pompeian Horror."

suddenly struck by the identification of the Decadent experience with the horror of death without atonement. In the years prior to the Revolution the Russian artistic community had been dancing on a volcano. The eruption of that volcano had allowed for no catharsis but had caught the intelligentsia, as it were, "with a foot raised for the next step." Like the Akhmatova of *Poema bez geroia* (Poem Without A Hero), Khodasevich was now at the stage where he could deal at a certain distance with that carnival atmosphere, understand at last its tragic residue. Decadence and Symbolism, as a collective ethos, had led to the last great flowering of Russian culture, yet the flowering was not without its excesses, and it was those excesses that were bringing the volcanic ash of retribution on everyone's head. If Khodasevich got his start with Bryusov and Decadence, and if the ambient madness of those years, the constant confusion of life and art, had contributed to the suicides of persons close to Khodasevich, then it might be said, based on the clear rejection of "soulless decadence" in this article, that *Sorrento Photographs* is Khodasevich's expression of personal and collective responsibility. The price for participation in the Decadent carnival was 1917, and in this regard the poem, even ambiguous about that which the poet has lost, is as much palinode as elegy for *temps perdu*.

Sorrento Photographs was written in three installments, Khodasevich tells us:

The first seventeen lines [were composed] in Saarow [Sorrento], at the beginning of 1925 (5 March). Then [I continued working] in Chaville, in February 1926. I finished it, hurriedly, in February [1926] in order to read it at the Tsetlins (I had promised). I wrote efficiently, every day, sometimes to this end going into Paris to the Cafe Lavenue. At times I wrote with great enthusiasm. As regards their sound, these are my favorite verses. "[Written] from within"—no, not exactly. Everything here is told just as it was.[76]

[76] Notes to *Sorrento Photographs*, in *SS*, p. 221. In the first line, "Saarow" is an obvious error in the 1961 edition and should read, as indicated, "Sor-

The praise that Khodasevich himself gives these verses is significant. He rarely praises his own poetry, and thus his definite preference for the sound of *Sorrento Photographs* suggests a new bench mark in his work.[77] It is curious that the *poema*, so balanced in its use of iambic tetrameter, was written at a time when Khodasevich was deliberately deflating the sound of poetry in other lyrics in *European Night*.

Sorrento Photographs is a very difficult work, integrating various surfaces on a large scale as several of Khodasevich's earlier lyrics had integrated them on a smaller one. The more recent memories surrounding the visit to Il Sorito constitute the work's narrative frame, and the literal and figurative vehicle of the narrative is young Maxim's motorcycle, which speeds through the Italian hills near Sorrento with the poet in its sidecar. As often happens in the ironist's world, he is allowed to go along for the ride, to observe the countryside from his privileged seat, and to fantasize freely, while the driving is left to someone else. But the stereoscopic theme of *Sorrento Photographs* does not stop here.[78] Instead, it pre-

---

rento." The Tsetlins are Mikhail Osipovich and Marya Samoylovna, who had a literary and political salon in Paris. Mikhail Tsetlin was a minor émigré poet and critic (see *Kursiv*, pp. 689-690).

[77] Though Khodasevich himself often records the praise of others in notes, he praises his own work only one other time, referring to "The Stars" as "very good verses" (*ochen' khoroshie stikhi*) (*SS*, p. 221).

[78] Khodasevich was clearly intrigued by the idea of the stereoscope. On several occasions, he used the metaphor of the stereoscope to praise the multi-tiered character of a work of art (see, e.g., "Slovo o polku Igoreve" [Song of Igor's Regiment], *Stat'i*, p. 22). This notion surfaces most explicitly, however, with language suggestive of *Sorrento Photographs* itself, in an unpublished fragment (dating probably to 1921 or early 1922) from one of Khodasevich's notebooks: "Works of artistic genius always possess multiple meanings. Thus in *War and Peace*, a meaning unfolds that is religious, historical, psychological, and otherwise, right up to the strategic [in military terms]. Depending on our criteria or our method of research, this or that meaning receives in our eyes a temporary predominance. *All this complex of meanings, as though one meaning were superimposed on the other, as though one were shining through the other, gives the work of genius that stereoscopic quality, that depth, that genuine fullness of life, that distinguishes the creations of a genius from those of a mediocre writer. The*

sents the memory of the poet's life in Moscow and Peters-burg *within* the memory of his life in emigration. Thus, throughout the *poema* the speaker, seeming to play with the knobs on a viewfinder, brings one surface into focus while removing the other surface to the background. Considering that one is dealing with poetry not prose, the result is a remarkable application of the principles of narrative irony and point of view, bringing to mind the "mirror gallery" technique (that is, the author observing the author observing) of André Gide's *Les Faux Monnayeurs*.

The first two stanzas of the poem set the tone for what follows, and therefore I shall quote them in full:

> Воспоминанье прихотливо
> И непослушливо, оно—
> Как узловатая олива:
> Никак, ничем не стеснено.
> Свои причудливые ветви
> Узлами диких соответствий
> Нерасторжимо заплетет—
> И так живет, и так растет.
>
> Порой фотограф-ротозей
> Забудет снимкам счет п пленкам
> И снимет парочку друзей,
> На Капри, с беленьким козленком—
> И тут же, пленки не сменив,
> Запечатлеет он залив
> За пароходною кормою
> И закопченую трубу
> С космою дымною на лбу.
> Так сделал нынешней зимою
> Один приятель мой. Пред ним
> Смешались воды, люди, дым
> На негативе помутнелом.
> Его знакомый легким телом
> Полупрозрачно заслонял
> Черты скалистых исполинов,

internal worth of a work of art can be measured by the degree of this 'semantic [*smyslovoi*] richness.' " (From the papers of Vladislav Khoda-sevich. Courtesy of the family of I. I. Bernshtein. My emphasis.)

А козлик, ноги в небо вскинув,
Везувий рожками бодал . . .
Хоть я и не люблю козляток
(Ни итальянских пикников)—
Двух совместившихся миров
Мне полюбился отпечаток:
В себе виденье затая,
Так протекает жизнь моя.   (*SS*, pp. 150-151)

Memory is capricious
as well as contrary—
like the knotty olive,
it cannot be hemmed in.
Inextricably it weaves
in knots of farfetched correspondences
its whimsical branches—
and so it lives, and so it grows.

At times a scatterbrained photographer
will lose count of shots and film
and snap a pair of friends
on Capri, beside a little white goat—
and on the spot, not changing film,
he will print over them the bay
beyond the steamer's stern
and the sooty stack
with a shock of smoke on its forehead.
This winter one of my friends
did just that. Before him
water, people, and smoke intermingled
on the turbid negative.
His friend in half-transparency
hid the features of rocky giants
with his light body, while
the little goat, its legs flung skyward,
was butting Vesuvius with its tiny horns . . .
Though I'm not in love with little goats
(or Italian picnics)—
the imprint of two worlds
telescoped caught my fancy:
concealing in itself a vision,
so does my life flow by.

Set at what seems a safe distance from the reality of revolution and exile, these lines generalize from a few comic particulars and constitute an amusing prologue to the sense of loss that will follow. In the opening line, Khodasevich introduces the theme of memory, which is the fulcrum of the entire work. The growth and organic intuition of the olive tree, simultaneously gnarled and beautiful, suggest the artistic process. To grow the tree must unite two elements, earth and air, just as the poem *in posse* unites memory, which is rooted in past experience, and imagination, which ramifies freely. A symbol of life and peace, the olive tree seems strangely out of place in the deadly landscape of *European Night*. And the branches, which intertwine like a series of coincidences, imply that the poet's life has been patterned by forces he admires but cannot understand.[79] There is more wonder and play in this eight-line frontispiece than in all of Khodasevich's last collection.

The second stanza presents what will become the overarching image of the double-exposed snapshot. The language is again playful ("scatterbrained photographer" [*fotografrotozei*], for example], simple, and more or less conversational. There is light humor as well in the aside "or Italian picnics" (*Ni ital'ianskikh piknikov*). Yet there is more here than meets the eye, and the movement of these apparently straightforward lines presents the same problem of focus as the scatterbrained friend's picture. First, Khodasevich is blurring various levels of reality—the world of things, of animals, of people—which he has done numerous times in his work. Next and more vital, through the agency of his memory he is perceiving two moments of time as if simultaneously, and consequently retrieving the present that exists in the past and the past that exists in the present, that is, the Proustian *entre deux* first associated with such verse

[79] Note that Khodasevich manages to tangle the branches (*"vetvi"*) in the knots of correspondences (*"sootvetstvii"*) and the living (*"zhivet"*) and growing (*"rastet"*) in the inextricable (*"nerastorzhimo"*) weaving.

narratives as "Noon" and "The Encounter."[80] Khodasevich seems to relate the past, or the province of tradition and memory, and the future, or the province of prophecy and imagination, as tinder to spark—there is no flame until both are brought together. And as he often opined, Soviet art was bound to fail as long as it ignored the tradition and collective memory of prerevolutionary culture.[81] Thus, imagination is not free to be wholly inventive or innovative and depends, in large part, on the "memory" of the poem's opening and on what the poet has actually lived through. As an ironist, Khodasevich maintains his distance, however, and he does not explore the kinetic energy of the actual present. Rather, he only hints at the potential for poetic fire as well as historical holocaust, here associated with the "smoky" surface of events and Mount Vesuvius, to which he will return in the poem's climax.

The speaker has two memories of Russia, triggered in turn by two different locations in or near Sorrento that he passes through on the motorcycle. The first memory, that of the funeral of Savelev, a Moscow floor polisher, is superimposed on the scenery of the Amalfi Pass, and the second memory, that of Petersburg, the Neva, and the angel on the Peter and Paul Cathedral, is reflected at dawn in the Bay of Naples with Mount Vesuvius in the background. Serving to foreshorten the "distant" viewpoint of these two memories is the "nearer," more recent, viewpoint of a third memory, sandwiched in between, describing a Roman Catholic

[80] T. S. Eliot explores the meaning of history and develops a similar concept of "pure time" in *Four Quartets*: "The historical sense involves a perception, not only of the past, but of its presence. . . . This historical sense, which is a sense of the timeless as well as of the temporal and of the timeless and temporal together, is what makes a writer traditional" (see "Tradition and the Individual Talent," in *Selected Essays*, p. 4).

[81] For Khodasevich's views on Soviet art and letters, see his "A Horse Décolleté"; "On Formalism and Formalists"; "On Soviet Literature"; "Pravo na konflikt" (The Right to Conflict), *Voz*, no. 4151 (30 September 1938); and "Proletarskie poety" (Proletarian Poets), *SZ* 26 (1925), 444-455.

procession that takes place in the streets of Sorrento on Good Friday. The two distant memories suggest themselves as Khodasevich's swan song to old Russia, the Russia with which the poet identified. Through these memories, the poet is possibly bidding farewell to the people, in the peaceful body of Savelev, and to Russian Orthodoxy and the imperial state, in the proud figure of the guardian angel high atop the Peter and Paul Cathedral. Hence, it would seem initially that Khodasevich has replaced Pushkin's Evgeny with his own Savelev and the Bronze Horseman with the angel on the Peter and Paul Cathedral. And the parallel is reinforced, if only superficially, by the fact that the "little man" has an unhappy fate and the angel (guarding Peter's tomb), like Peter's statue, changes poses. But here difference is more important than similarity, for history, both personal and national, has entered another era: Savelev does not die in the flood of history *during* the poem. When we meet him, he is already dead. Russia's guardian angel does not move the forces of history, but is moved by them.

Savelev's funeral is a simple, private affair. The speaker seems almost to be eavesdropping on his own recollection:

> Раскрыта дверь в полуподвал,
> И в сокрушении глубоком
> Четыре прачки, полубоком,
> Выносят из сеней во двор
> На полотенцах гроб досчатый,
> В гробу—Савельев, полотер. (*SS*, p. 152)

> A door is open wide into a basement flat,
> and, in acute grief,
> four washerwomen turn half-sideways
> to carry from the entry to the courtyard
> a deal coffin on towels;
> in the coffin [lies] Savelev, the floor polisher.[82]

[82] I have translated *polupodval* as "basement flat." Actually, it is a humble dwelling, perhaps one room, located partly below ground. From within, the inhabitants can see the feet of passers-by through the windows. The towels are probably not simple ones, but decorative ones reserved for this

Khodasevich has selected an artisan for this death scene. Dressed in a worn jacket and carrying on his breast the traditional icon, Savelev lies in his coffin with an air of benign indifference. By keeping the narration on a homely and personal level, the poet skirts a tragic interpretation. He does not allow us to know why Savelev died, since it is apparently not important. The speaker's gentle, nearly avuncular prodding of one of the keening washerwomen, perhaps the widow— "Now Olga, that's enough. Come out." (Nu, Ol'ga, polno. Vykhodi.)—likewise undercuts the implicit tragedy of the situation. Indeed, the image of Savelev and his coffin, swaying through the agaves of the mountainous region near Amalfi, is light and soothing to the eye :

И сквозь колючие агавы
Они выходят из ворот,
И полотера лоб курчавый
В лазурном воздухе плывет.   (SS, p. 152)

And through the prickly agaves
they come out of the gate,
and the floor-polisher's curly forehead
sails along in the azure air.

Finally joining the funeral procession in an olive grove, the speaker follows behind, tripping somewhat unceremoniously on the alien stones.

Before describing the second memory, which is closer to the actual present and hence strikes the reader as more immediate, Khodasevich turns the knob of his viewfinder. He bridges vast areas of time and space, the "before" and "after" of the Revolution, with the device of the motorcycle, which, turning this way and that, its headlights dancing on the rocky road, suggests the ironist's answer to a time machine. When the second memory does come into focus, it has a

occasion, and serve here in ritual allusion to the *vynos* (bearing-out) of Christ's *plashchanitsa* (shroud). *Polotentsa* (towels) and *plashchanitsa* have the same etymology: the former taking the more prosaic Russian form and the latter the more elevated Old Church Slavic form.

new orientation: instead of a funeral procession for one man, it is something large and public—a reenactment of Christ's Passion with a throng of believers. Proximity is juxtaposed to remoteness; a tradition that is alive in Italy and that relives Christ's death in order to celebrate his resurrection is set against a tradition over whose funeral Khodasevich will preside in the closing stanzas of the poem. The second memory expands gradually, and, as the speaker observes the streets of Sorrento in the nocturnal calm, there is little hint of what will follow:

> В страстную пятницу всегда
> На глаз приметно мир пустеет,
> Айдесский, древний ветер веет,
> И ущербляется луна.
> Сегодня в облаках она.
> Тускнеют улицы сырые.
> Одна ночная остерия
> Огнями желтыми горит.
> Ее взлохмаченный хозяин
> Облокотившись полуспит. (*SS*, p. 153)

> Always, on Good Friday,
> the world grows noticeably empty,
> an ancient, Hadean wind blows,
> and the moon wanes.
> Tonight the moon is in the clouds.
> The damp streets grow dim.
> Only an inn
> burns its yellow lights.
> Its tousled padrone
> half dozes on his elbows.

The padrone does not know his part in memory's play, yet he will, like Shakespeare's Bottom, humorously enter the action a little later. Now the singing of the procession grows more distinct and the crowd comes into view. Above their heads the people hold a sculptured likeness of the Virgin Mary. The "She" of these lines presses palm to palm and wears an immobile expression on her face. Akin to Mona

Lisa and perhaps reminiscent of Blok's Beautiful Lady and his feminine Jesus, the Virgin is distant and unapproachable. With the wisdom of one who understands human frailty and who speaks from the far side of fervent ideals, the poet asks rhetorically whether this inaccessibility is not what the people want:

> Но жалкою людскою дрожью
> Не дрогнут ясные черты.
> Не оттого ль к Ее подножью
> Летят молитвы и мечты,
> Любви кощунственные розы
> И от великой полноты—
> Сладчайшие людские слезы? (*SS*, p. 154)

> But Her serene features will not move
> with the people's pathetic trembling.
> Is this not why their prayers and dreams,
> the blasphemous roses of their love,
> and, out of [the heart's] great fullness,
> their sweetest tears
> fly to Her pedestal?

But Khodasevich the ironist turns away from the Blokian theurgy. Here the prosaic padrone surfaces, and the speaker, describing the gap between man and divinity in comic terms, wryly inserts:

> К порогу вышел своему
> Седой хозяин остерии.
> Он улыбается Марии.
> Мария! Улыбнись ему! (*SS*, p. 154)

> The gray-haired padrone
> has come out to the threshold.
> He smiles to Mary.
> Mary! Smile back!

Only an onlooker, the poet does not follow but watches the Virgin pass. Then in a radiant light and under a thunderous choir of voices, she enters a cathedral. As dawn breaks over Sorrento, the worshipers seem transfigured in the light. This mood, as one might expect, cannot be sustained for the *eiron*, however. The romantic crescendo and ellipsis—

> Яснее проступают лица,
> Как бы напудрены зарей.
> Над островерхою горой
> Переливается Денница . . .   (*SS*, p. 154)

> The faces stand out more clearly,
> as though made up by the dawn.
> Above the mountain's sheer peak
> the Morning Star spills its light . . .[83]

—are cut short by the image of the veering motorcycle, which introduces the third memory.

The poet's last memory is the most intriguing. On the one hand, he sets it in the background of Vesuvius, the legendary volcano that perennially consumes and renews itself:

> В тумане Прочида лежит,
> Везувий к северу дымит.
> Запятнан площадною славой,
> Он все торжествен и велик
> В своей хламиде темно-ржавой,
> Сто раз прожженной и дырявой.   (*SS*, p. 155)

> Procida lies in the mist,
> Vesuvius is smoking to the north.
> Sullied by the fame of the marketplace,
> the volcano is, in its dark rust-colored
> chlamys, a hundred times scorched and full
> of holes, still solemn and grand.

Like history's periodic convulsions, there is something constant in the volcano's destructive power. So Vesuvius stands

[83] *Dennitsa* (Morning Star), as Nina Berberova has suggested to me, may belong to a symbolic system combining the Virgin Mary and Lucifer. This would account for the curious transition from the Easter procession's promise of new life to the fall of Russia's guardian angel. The link between the Morning Star and Lucifer is made, for example, in V. Dal', *Tolkovyi slovar' zhivogo velikorusskogo iazyka* (Dictionary of the Living Great-Russian Language), 4th ed., vol. 1 (St. Petersburg-Moscow, 1912), p. 1,059. The *ostroverkhaia gora* prepares us for the poem's climactic image, the angel atop the *vos'migrannoe ostrie* (eight-faceted point).

out in the Italian countryside as a reminder of our great potential for self-annihilation. As Khodasevich said in the article on Pompeii, the streets of the doomed city seemed to lead back to "the huge mass of Vesuvius." The other figure in the background is Naples, which, in ironic opposition to the image of Petersburg soon to follow, stands up (*vstaet*) and out of the morning fog.

The speaker locates his memory of Petersburg *after* the fall, that is, following the volcanic eruption of 1917. Treated as *nature morte*, there are no battle scenes or cannon fire. The smoke of a once vital tradition, a tradition we might expect Khodasevich to associate with Falconet's magisterial statue and Pushkin's *poema*, has dispersed forever. But Khodasevich turns from the Russia epitomized by the equestrian figure of the tsar-conqueror. Pushkin selected the Bronze Horseman as symbol of imperial Russia at the zenith of its power; Khodasevich now selects the angel holding the cross as symbol of Russia in eclipse. More than any other monument in Petersburg, the angel presiding over the cathedral of the Peter and Paul Fortress exemplifies the dark, star-crossed side of the imperial capital. For two centuries the cathedral and the fortress had served as a royal burial vault and a prison. Therefore, returning to the poem's opening, but with much greater force, Khodasevich telescopes once again the past and the present—from the founding of Petersburg in 1703 at the walls of the fortress to the collapse of old Russia in the chill November of 1917—with the image of this "angel of death":

> Я вижу светлые просторы,
> Плывут сады, поляны, горы,
> А в них, сквозь них и между них—
> Опять, как на неверном снимке,
> Весь в очертаниях сквозных,
> Как был тогда, в студеной дымке,
> В ноябрьской утренней заре,
> На восьмигранном острие,

Золотокрылый ангел розов
И неподвижен—а над ним
Вороньи стаи, дым морозов,
Давно рассеявшийся дым.
И отражен кастелламарской
Зеленоватою волной,
Огромный страж России царской
Вниз опрокинут головой.
Так отражался он Невой,
Зловещий, огненный и мрачный,
Таким явился предо мной—
Ошибка пленки неудачной.   (*SS*, pp. 155-156)

I see bright expanses,
gardens, glades, and mountains sailing by,
yet in them, through them, and between them,
once more, as on the muddled photo,
all in transparent outline,
[I see] how then, in the freezing haze
of a November dawn,
atop its eight-faceted point,
the golden-winged angel was pink
and still, while above it
[moved] flocks of crows, and frosty smoke,
smoke long since dispersed.
And reflected in the greenish waves
of the Gulf of Castellammare,
the huge guardian of tsarist Russia
is toppled [there] headfirst.
Ominous, fiery, and brooding,
so had the Neva reflected him [then],
so had he appeared to me—
an error of the unlucky film.[84]

[84] Cf. N. N. Belekhov, gen. ed., *Pamiatniki arkhitektury Leningrada*
(Monuments of Leningrad's Architecture) (Leningrad, 1958), pp. 21, 24, 32.
These lines clearly refer to the angel on the Peter and Paul Cathedral—not,
for example, to another famous angel on the Alexandrine Column—because
the figure is gilded, thus "golden-winged," and it stands on the cathedral's
faceted spire (the Alexandrine Column, on the other hand, is round). It is
"huge" because it is the tallest (122.5 meters) landmark in central Petersburg, and it is "ominous, fiery, and brooding" because it looms over a place
known for its dark history and bears witness to the cataclysmic November
of 1917. I am grateful to Professor Jane Miller of Middlebury College and

Russia's guardian is reflected upside down in the Gulf of Castellammare. Stood on its head, the world as Khodasevich knew it can never be righted. Nevertheless, Khodasevich, a master of understatement, here reduces all the anguish and chaos to an optical illusion, a mistake on a photograph.[85]

Khodasevich ends his masterpiece on a whimsical note. Balancing the serious and the playful and presenting straightforwardly what is deceptive, he "closes" with something that can only cause new beginnings—a question. This, after all, is one answer appropriate for the modern ironist:

> Воспоминанье прихотливо.
> Как сновидение—оно
> Как будто вещей правдой живо,
> Но так же дико и темно
> И так же, вероятно, лживо . . .
> Среди каких утрат, забот,
> И после скольких эпитафий,

---

to Professor John Malmstad of Columbia University for pointing me in the direction of the angel on the Peter and Paul Cathedral. Thanks are due as well to Nina Berberova for corroborating this interpretation.

Note how Khodasevich has removed even the angel's grammatical agency through the use of passive constructions: *otrazhen, oprokinut,* and *otrazhalsia.*

[85] Of all the media available to modern man, the photograph is perhaps by nature the most impersonal and the most open to irony. See, for example, Sontag, *On Photography,* p. 158: "Photography has powers that no other image-system has ever enjoyed because, unlike earlier ones, it is not dependent on an image maker. However carefully the photograher intervenes in setting up and guiding the image-making process, the process itself remains an *optical-chemical* (or electronic) one, the workings of which are automatic, the machinery for which will inevitably be modified to provide still more detailed and, therefore, more useful maps of the real. The *mechanical* genesis of these images, and the literalness of the powers they confer, amounts to a new relationship between image and reality. And if photography could also be said to restore the most primitive relationship— the partial identity of image and object—the potency of the image is now experienced in a different way. The primitive notion of the efficacy of images presumes that images possess the qualities of real things, but our inclination is to attribute to real things the qualities of an image." (Emphasis added.)

Теперь, воздушная, всплывет
И что закроет в свой черед
Тень соррентинских фотографий?   (*SS*, p. 156)

Memory is capricious.
Like a dream, it seems
alive with prophetic truth,
but is just as wild and obscure
and, probably, just as false . . .
Amidst what losses and troubles,
and after how many epitaphs,
now, belonging to the air, will it surface,
and what shall overlay in turn
the shadow of Sorrento photographs?[86]

Sorrento Photographs occupies a unique position in Khodasevich's work. It shows the poet at his best, if not his most typical, and it shows his irony at its most "forbearing" and least bitter. History becomes within its complex framework something chaotic, imprisoning the poet in the time and space of a meaningless present. But art is equally important, for it applies the various lenses and camera angles of memory and imagination to what moves within two distinct dimensions—Russia in the presence of revolution and life abroad in the absence of Russia—achieving the brief focus that, while "capturing" history, is also outside and free of it. In his poetry Khodasevich gradually moved toward what at the level of the word and the image was specific, "realistic," and in turn deliberately unpoetic and ironic. *Sorrento Photographs* indicates, however, that even in his last collection he did not forswear completely the largely Symbolist ideals of his youth. Another world, seen through the details of this one, is a force in his art to the end. And it coexisted, unwillingly as time went on and crowded in, with the poet's irony. Yet in Khodasevich's finest work, of which *Sorrento*

---

[86] Note that the "vision" (*viden'e*) hidden by memory in the poem's opening and rooted in the tradition of a once vigorous culture is now likened to and contained in the "dream" (sno*videnie*).

Photographs is an example, this tense coexistence finds moments of perfect balance, "moving stasis"—the eyes in the storm of revolution and exile. Perhaps it is, or should be, in the contemplation of such moments that Khodasevich's poetry is rescued from the European night falling around it.

7

NIGHTWATCH: 1927-1939

Во мне конец, во мне начало.
Мной совершенное так мало!
Но все ж я прочное звено:
Мне это счастие дано.

В России новой, но великой,
Поставят идол мой двуликий
На перекрестке двух дорог,
Где время, ветер и песок . . .
—Ходасевич, "Памятник"

In me there is an ending and a beginning.
So little has been accomplished by me!
But still I am a firm link:
that joy is given me.

In the new but great Russia
they'll erect my two-faced idol
at the crossing of two roads,
where there is time, wind, and sand.
—Khodasevich, "Monument"

Khodasevich turned away from poetry writing as an active career after 1927. He did not, however, stop writing. That year seems a convenient watershed because it saw the publication of *The Collected Verse*, a summing up of the poetry written during his major period, and his appointment as literary editor of *The Renaissance*, a position he would hold up to his death. The crisis of 1926, brought on by extreme poverty, a relapse of furunculosis, bad relations with the émigré press, and perhaps the nagging awareness that the source of his poetic creativity was running dry, was over. Khodasevich had to get on with the business of living out his life in exile.

One might suppose that following *European Night* Khodasevich's personal life turned suddenly sour and his literary activity became full of defeatism. Yet the sources we have at hand do not bear this out. Khodasevich seems to have felt that he could serve "poetry forever" in a function other than that of poet. And personally, his close relationship with Nina Berberova continued to keep much of its warmth even after their split in 1932; the kindness and unselfish regard of Olga Margolina, Khodasevich's last wife, made the difficult final years more bearable; and the friendship and respect shown Khodasevich by several members of the younger generation of émigré writers, including Nabokov, Weidlé, and Vladimir Smolensky, remained a bright spot in his life to the end. So on this count Khodasevich had little in common with the desperate, ostracized Marina Tsvetaeva of the late 1930s. Professionally, some of Khodasevich's finest articles and books (*Derzhavin*) were written after 1927, and if sheer number of pages is any barometer of intellectual energy, the post-1927 production surpasses the pre-1927 production several times over. In fact, there are those who believe Khodasevich's work as biographer, memoirist, critic, and Pushkinist is comparable, even superior, in quality to his work as poet. Thus, to be sure, Khodasevich did not stop writing. And from the late 1920s until the end of his life he played a leading role in émigré letters and was a major discussant in the debate foremost in the minds of nearly all émigré writers—how is Russian literature in general and Russian poetry in particular to survive in exile? It would be impossible to write an informed account of émigré literature between the wars without pausing over the Khodasevich-Adamovich polemics, for perhaps more clearly than anything else those polemics posed the question of the viability of Russian poetry outside Russia.[1]

---

[1] For the Khodasevich-Adamovich polemics, see G. Fedotov, "O parizh-skoi poezii" (On Parisian Poetry), in *Kovcheg* (The Ark) (New York, 1942), 189-198; G. Struve, *Russkaia literatura v izgnanii* (Russian Literature in Exile) (New York, 1956), pp. 199-222; and R. Hagglund, "The Adamovič-

Still, the last years have a darker cast than any other period of Khodasevich's life. Though by 1927 Khodasevich was growing convinced that writing poetry was no longer an ongoing possibility for him, he was not yet ready to admit that writing poetry in general was a futile enterprise. This accounts, at least in part, for his articles' gathering tone of admonishing teacher and judge of young talent: while Khodasevich's "way of grain" was finished, there was still time to turn his attention to those who were beginning careers. The articles he wrote regularly for *The Renaissance* were not, it is true, comparable to the unannounced visits of the *dusha*. They could be drudgery, a means of survival—one missed feuilleton might play havoc with a tight monthly budget. Poetry, in short, had been a labor of love; now the weekly feuilleton often became simply labor. Yet, it might have seemed fair compensation to Khodasevich, and his last years might have seemed brighter, if he could have shaken free of the conclusion that, in addition to the sense of personal loss, he was living through the twilight of Russian poetry. Clouding his last years was the belief (in some ways exaggerated but no less poignant) that between the past (chiefly the Pushkinian tradition) and the future (a younger generation capable of forging its own identity and passing its own "way of grain") of the national poetry Khodasevich so loved there was no longer a living link.

IN MARCH 1926 Khodasevich and Berberova found their first flat in Paris. 14 rue Lamblardie remained their address until September 1928, when Berberova found them another home on rue des 4 Cheminées, in the Billancourt district. It was at the rue des 4 Cheminées address that Berberova, intrigued by the multifarious émigré life centering around the Renault factory, began to publish her cycle of stories *Biankurskie*

Xodasevič Polemics," *Slavic and East European Journal* 20 (Fall 1976), 239-252.

prazdniki (Billancourt Holidays) in the pages of *The Latest News*. Khodasevich's daily routine at this time had fallen into a certain rhythm. Waking late in the morning, he would spend his days in a combination of activities—visiting the editorial offices at *The Renaissance*, meeting with friends (Weidlé, Terapiano, Knut, Alexandre Bacherac), sitting over a coffee in cafés (the Berry, the ubiquitous Tabac, and—the favorite of these years—La Rotonde on Montparnasse). Often he would drop by to see his sister Zhenya, who by now had also emigrated to Paris. In the evenings he might be invited to the Zaytsevs or the Tsetlins or the Merezhkovskys (he called such gatherings ironically "balls"). Then, returning home in the late evening, he would write long into the night and early morning.

Khodasevich, always high-strung, was particularly bothered by the bustling pace of Parisian life. There was constantly a deadline to meet for the next article in *The Renaissance*. Therefore, as had been his practice in Russia and in the early years of emigration, Khodasevich would find some time (usually during the summer) to escape the city. The choice might be the Southern coast of France (Cannes), in some modest resort area, or as was his preference in later years, the picturesque countryside not far outside of Paris (Versailles, St. Mesmin, Arthies), in some simple country house. Usually friends, such as the Zaytsevs or Bunins, came along. But when he needed a quiet place to work on a project, Khodasevich was apt to go alone. At Chez Yarko in Arthies, for example, in June, and again in October and November, of 1930, Khodasevich did much of his work on *Derzhavin*.[2] Arthies became for Khodasevich what Boldino had been for Pushkin exactly one hundred years earlier—a place to shake off other concerns and give oneself up totally to one's work. As Khodasevich exclaimed to Berberova in a letter dated 29 November 1930: "Here it's wonderful. The weather is awful,

---

[2] It was the nephew of this Yarko, coincidentally, who was found dead from a drug overdose with Boris Poplavsky in 1935.

but it makes one feel very cozy. The most necessary thing for a man—as necessary as air—is quiet."[3]

Efforts to give shape to émigré intellectual life gained momentum in 1926 and emerged in early 1927 as "Zelenaia lampa" (The Green Lamp), a literary and philosophical society organized by the Merezhkovskys. The society took its name from the Petersburg group in which Pushkin had taken part and had its first meeting on 5 February 1927 at the Russian Commercial and Industrial Union.[4] Initially, Khodasevich took an active interest in the society and agreed to make an opening speech on the history of the Petersburg group. He no doubt understood that, at least *in posse*, such a society could greatly benefit those of the younger generation of émigré writers (including Berberova, his wife) who had been forced to leave Russia with only a sporadic education. But Gippius and Merezhkovsky, as was their wont, steered discussions into the open waters of Kierkegaard, Hegel, Nietzsche, and Solovyov, and Khodasevich had little patience for metaphysics on a large scale. Perhaps he felt that Berberova, Ladinsky, Poplavsky, Smolensky, Knut, Chervinskaya, and others should keep to a simpler course of self-expression before taking on such momentous concepts. At any rate, it is difficult to conceive of Khodasevich and Zinaida Gippius existing in a state of peaceful coexistence for any length of time.[5] Khodasevich soon withdrew

[3] Khodasevich's letter to Nina Berberova dated 29 November 1930. (Archive of Nina Berberova, Beinecke Library, Yale. Courtesy of Nina Berberova.)

[4] See Gulliver [Khodasevich and Berberova], "Literaturnaia letopis' " (Literary Annal), *Voz*, no. 618 (11 February 1927); and Temira Pachmuss, *Zinaida Hippius: An Intellectual Profile* (Carbondale, Ill., 1971), pp. 238-246.

[5] For Khodasevich's later negative feelings about Gippius, see his "Eshche o pisatel'skoi svobode" (Some More About A Writer's Freedom), *Voz*, no. 3347 (2 August 1934). For Gippius' later negative feelings about Khodasevich's poetry and criticism see Anton Krainii [Gippius]: "Znak" (Sign), *Voz*, no. 926 (15 December 1927); and "Sovremennost' " (Contemporaneity), *Chisla* (Numbers), 9 (1933), 141-145. See in addition Pachmuss, *Zinaida Hippius*, pp. 271-272. Khodasevich and Gippius carried on a lively corre-

from the society, calling it wryly, as Terapiano recalls, "the mystery of the Trinity at a coffee table."[6]

The clash with Georgy Adamovich came to a head in 1927, although there were signs of a difference of opinion earlier. Thereafter a polemical exchange continued, off and on, until shortly before Khodasevich's death. Now, some fifty years later, the question of this ongoing "debate" needs to be put in perspective. There are those, such as Georgy Fedotov, who claim that in the contest for the establishment of a prevailing voice in émigré poetry Adamovich emerged as the obvious victor. Adamovich's influence among young poets, says Fedotov, was more consistent and lasting, while "Khodasevich's efforts to teach the youth classical mastery [of form] and to cultivate in them the spirit of someone confident in the autonomous value of Pushkinian art came to nothing."[7] And there are others, such as Yury Terapiano, who maintain that Georgy Ivanov, one of Adamovich's allies and a leading source of the so-called "Parisian note" in émigré poetry, was at least partly responsible for shaking Khodasevich's views on his own art.[8] Perhaps such arguments have an element of truth to them, but the conclusion they draw—that the Adamovich/Ivanov faction drove Khodasevich from the stage of émigré letters (Terapiano goes so far as to suggest that Khodasevich's silence as a poet may have been due to a witheringly sarcastic review of his collected verse by Ivanov)—are overstated. To place, as Fedotov does, an equal sign between Adamovich the "poet-critic" and Khodasevich

---

spondence from late 1925 to late 1929, after which time their personal differences seemed to make close contact impossible. Gippius, however, wrote Khodasevich—just a month before his death—a touching letter in which she appeared to bury the hatchet and wished him the best: see Gippius, *Letters to Berberova and Khodasevich*, ed. Freiberger Sheikholeslami.

[6] Iurii Terapiano, *Vstrechi* (Encounters) (New York, 1953), pp. 86-87.

[7] Fedotov, "On Parisian Poetry," p. 190.

[8] Iurii Terapiano, "Ob odnoi literaturnoi voine" (About One Literary War), *Mosty* (Bridges), 12 (1966), 363-375.

the "poet-critic" is only superficially justified. By 1927 Khodasevich was considered by many to be the leading poet of the emigration. He had, and continued to have, a significant influence on the work of young poets both in emigration and in the Soviet Union. Traces of his *ars poetica* can be found in poets as different as Terapiano, Smolensky, Knut, Shteyger, Prismanova, Nabokov, and Georgy Ivanov himself.[9] Even in the Soviet Union, where Khodasevich had become a "nonperson" by the late 1920s, we discover his influence in the early work of Vadim Shefner, Alexandr Gitovich, Vladimir Lifshits, and Anatoly Chivilikhin.[10] In comparison with that of Khodasevich, Adamovich's gift as a poet was much more modest and his artistic influence much more limited. As a critic and spokesman for the younger poets at *Chisla* (Numbers), Adamovich was considered more influential, and his role in this regard, that is, in the *mood* of the poems that appeared in the journal's pages, is probably what Fedotov had in mind when he states that "Adamovich's influence on the young poets was huge."[11] But the idea of tracing the actual poetic manner of Chervinskaya or Shteyger or Poplavsky to an Adamovich-inspired mood of self-absorption and defeatism (could not Khodasevich be equally self-absorbed and defeatist?) appears to rest on shaky ground. That Adamovich brought the younger generation face to face with modern European alienation and loss of values is certain; to translate that awareness of alienation into the question of real artistic influence is more dubious, however. As far as Terapiano's assertion is concerned, one wonders how some harsh remarks by Georgy Ivanov (whose reputation as a major poet was established only in 1931 with the appear-

[9] See Struve, *Russian Literature in Exile*, pp. 318-356. Khodasevich caught Ivanov in an imitation of one of his (Khodasevich's) early poems in "Otplytie na ostrov Tsiteru" (*Embarkation for Cythera*) [a review of Ivanov's book of verse], *Voz*, no. 4080 (28 May 1937).

[10] My thanks to Professor Lev L. Loseff (Dartmouth), the son of Vladimir Lifshits, for this observation.

[11] Fedotov, "On Parisian Poetry," p. 190.

ance of *Rozy* [Roses], his first book of verse written in emigration) could have served, in 1928, as the last straw forcing Khodasevich into poetic silence.[12] Khodasevich could not have been thus "silenced" by Adamovich or Ivanov. The causes for his growing disenchantment run much deeper than personal animosity.

In July 1925 Adamovich devoted an article in *Zveno* (The Link) to Khodasevich's poetry. By way of concluding he opined that, despite its flawless "how," there was something lacking in the "what" of Khodasevich's verse:

And here's the main thing: can one love Khodasevich's verse? At this point I'm overcome with perplexity. Poetry is not instruction, but it still looks down on the world from above. From a height, from a distance, there is no breaking down of the world [into parts], but a "panorama," a re-creation from a "bird's flight." But as for the verse of Khodasevich? It amazes us with the sharpness of its sight, fixedly intense, aimed point blank, but it [also] troubles us with the absence of "wings," freedom, air.[13]

Adamovich only hints at what later he will assail more openly: sophisticated poetic technique in the absence of "wings" (read "Blokian lyricism") leaves him as reader unsatisfied. Curiously, Weidlé would soon use the appellation "wingless genius" (*beskrylyi genii*)[14] to praise Khodasevich and his ironic verse, while Ivanov would turn Weidlé's phrase into an occasion to reduce Khodasevich's stature next to that of Blok.[15] The battle lines were beginning to be drawn.

A few months later, in September 1925, Khodasevich spoke to the question of where real Russian literature now resided—"here or there."[16] The vitality of émigré literature depended on the presence of mature talent (Marina Tsve-

[12] Terapiano, "About One Literary War," p. 371.

[13] G. Adamovich, "Literaturnye besedy" (Literary Causeries), *Zveno* (The Link) (27 July 1925).

[14] Veidle, "The Poetry of Khodasevich," p. 468.

[15] Ivanov, "In Defense of Khodasevich."

[16] Khodasevich, "Tam ili zdes' " (There or Here), *Dni* (Days), no. 804 (18 September 1925).

taeva) and the ability to cultivate new talent (Boris Bozhnev). Yet Khodasevich already feared that émigré literature was losing sight of its mission and that gifted beginners might stray from their inherited culture in the Western European atmosphere: "If the art here is still alive, then it is to a significant degree not *thanks* to the fact that that art is émigré, but *despite* the fact that it is such."[17]

In March of the following year Khodasevich and Adamovich found occasion to cross swords again. The editorial board of *The Link* had decided to sponsor a poetry competition. Three hundred twenty-two poems were submitted, of which twelve were chosen by three judges (Adamovich, Gippius, and Konstantin Mochulsky) and then presented to the public in the pages of *The Link* for a final vote to determine the winners. Khodasevich put little stock in the taste of the reading public, and he further chafed at the fact that there was no way of controlling the number of votes cast by an individual (the balloting blanks appeared in *The Link* and could be bought up and submitted in any number). First prize went to a certain Reznikov, whose metaphor-laden lyric was strongly reminiscent of the then quite popular Pasternak. Khodasevich pointed out that Reznikov's metaphors were too elaborate, heavily realized, often mixed. Were a preference to be made among the twelve finalists, Khodasevich's would have been a more modestly competent poem receiving many fewer ballots than the winner.[18] Adamovich then replied in a subsequent issue of *The Link* that in matters of taste no panel of judges could agree (Khodasevich, quite the contrary, always had a firm concept of what poems were good or bad, what poets, artistically speaking, were better or worse than others), that the taste ("leftist," in this case) of the public was at least instructive, and that Reznikov's poem had, after all, a certain appealing flair

[17] Ibid.
[18] Khodasevich, "Zametki o stikhakh" (Notes on Verse), *Days*, no. 954 (14 March 1926).

to it, "a Byronic sensation of the sea," and was therefore, in Adamovich's view, perhaps deserving of first prize.[19]

With the onset of 1927 the Khodasevich-Adamovich polemics became more explicit and animated. Both men were making quite different cases for the direction that émigré poetry should take in the future and both seemed to be vying, often eloquently and persuasively, for the attention of the younger generation. The year 1927 seemed an ideal time to stake out the dimensions of each camp because that year marked the ninetieth anniversary of Pushkin's death (thus Pushkin was on everyone's mind) as well as the appearance of Khodasevich's *Collected Verse*—the most tangible evidence of his *ars poetica*. Adamovich began by expressing his displeasure at the fact that the "Parisian School of Russian poetry" seemed nothing more than a group of novice poets engaged in bland imitation of Khodasevich. His logic went as follows: no actual school can grow out from under the influence of Khodasevich because Khodasevich is a poet of the first water, completely unique and inimitable; to copy his manner without experiencing the *dukh* (spirit) of his art is a futile, insincere, even blasphemous enterprise; poetry is above all the attempt to say the unsayable, to give expression to an inexpressible content looming somewhere beyond the lines; but, unfortunately, the epigones of Khodasevich are happy to say what is sayable, even as the genuine *golos* (voice) of their teacher eludes them. Adamovich was suggesting that form and content in poetic structure are separable (Khodasevich would say they are homeostatically related). The younger generation, concluded Adamovich, would be better served by taking a poet such as Pasternak for their model: at least with Pasternak, whose "form" may be uneven but whose inner world is richer and more far-ranging, they would not be caught up in the sterile imitation of style,

---

[19] Adamovich, "Literary Causeries," *The Link*, no. 164 (21 March 1926).

and hence would discover their own genuine (however in-articulate) voices sooner.[20]

The mention of Pasternak was, in this year of a Pushkin anniversary, calculated to give the younger generation some-thing to consider. Perhaps the time in which they lived, wrote Adamovich in April, demanded that one turn away from the lapidary simplicity of Pushkin to a poetic form more expressive of the complex problems beseiging modern man:

It seems that our world is indeed more complex and rich than it once appeared to Pushkin. And it seems that one might achieve the verbal perfection of Pushkin with a view of the world that is more introspective, more broadly and deeply penetrating. At any rate, there is in this nothing theoretically impossible. Pushkin's is not the path of greatest resistance. One need not exaggerate the value of a clarity in which all the murk in the world is left unil-lumined. Pasternak has refused the biddings of Pushkin.[21]

Khodasevich seemed to sense that Adamovich had suddenly taken on the role of a modern day Bulgarin and that, over Pushkin's deceptive "simplicity," his apparent lack of "con-tent," the adversary was holding up in praise the flashy ro-manticism of a modern day Benediktov. He immediately retaliated with his sharpest volley yet at Adamovich:

When business at hand concerns Pushkin, we have the right to demand proof and not to trust Adamovich's intuition alone. Here our love for Pushkin and our respect for those who have worked a great deal on Pushkin are offended. Here, finally, our literary (and not only literary) patriotism is offended, for Pushkin is our home-land, "our all." . . . Pushkin's is in fact the path of greatest resist-ance . . . for in the depiction of greatest complexity he takes the way of greatest simplicity.[22]

Of course, Adamovich did not let Khodasevich's criticism go unchallenged. Was there not, he soon answered, some-

---

[20] Adamovich, "Literary Causeries," *The Link*, no. 208 (23 January 1927).

[21] Adamovich, "Literary Causeries," *The Link*, no. 218; quoted in Kho-dasevich, "Besy" (The Devils), *Voz*, no. 678 (11 April 1927).

[22] Khodasevich, "The Devils."

thing "suspicious" in Pushkin's formal perfection? As captivating as that perfection was (more captivating, in fact, than that of Racine or Goethe), was there not something equally appealing in "poor, rhetorical," semantically inexact Lermontov, the psychic exile?[23]

To prove the maladroitness of his adversary's position, both Khodasevich and Adamovich, as often happens to persons embroiled in a debate, were forced to exaggerate, reduce, simplify. Adamovich's subsequent encapsulation of Khodasevich's position—"Gentlemen, write good verses, iambs and trochees, correct and pure rhymes, composition, polish, clarity"—[24] was hardly fair, since anyone familiar with Khodasevich's work (as Adamovich was) would not argue that it consists merely of an insouciant aggregate of well-wrought lines. And Khodasevich's counterattacks on the poetry of the "human document" (chelovecheskii dokument)—what today we might call "confessional" verse—were also at times excessive: surely the work of the younger poets, such as Lidia Chervinskaya, who eventually surrounded Adamovich at Numbers offers more than "ignorance and illiteracy."[25] But that is where the argument took them, willy-nilly, over the next few years. Praising the traditional orientation of the "Perekrestok" (Crossroads) group (Terapiano, Raevsky, Smolensky, Yury Mandelshtam, and others),[26] Khodasevich continued to insist that a poem is, first of all, its words and that, to be a poet, one needs self-discipline, a period of apprenticeship, knowledge of prosodic principles, respect for the written word, a desire to preserve native poetic traditions, an ability to poetically objectify (in Yeatsian terms "to mask") all that is crudely personal.[27] If a genuine voice was hidden

[23] Adamovich, "Literary Causeries," The Link, no. 220 (17 April 1927).
[24] Adamovich, "Zhizn' i 'zhizn' '," (Life and 'Life'), PN, no. 5124 (14 April 1935).
[25] Khodasevich, "Human Document," Voz, no. 1514 (25 July 1929).
[26] See Khodasevich, "Po povodu 'Perekrestka' " (Concerning Crossroads), Voz, no. 1864 (10 July 1930).
[27] For Khodasevich's understanding of "masking," see his "Glupovatost' poezii" (The Stupidity of Poetry), SZ 30 (1927), 281.

in the apprentice, it would surface in time, and Khodasevich encouraged the group to seek innovation and to steer clear of slavish imitation of their teachers (the chief one being Khodasevich himself). Criticizing the Crossroads group and seeing more talent in the "Soiuz molodykh poetov v Parizhe" (Union of Young Poets in Paris),[28] Adamovich proposed that the younger generation turn inward in order to pour forth, in an unmediated fashion, their feelings of accidie, anguish, and uprootedness. It was absurd or, worse, dishonest to preserve intact a poetic tradition indigenous to nineteenth-century Russia in post-World War I Paris. Khodasevich had held the name of Pushkin up "like an icon" long enough;[29] was it not time to bring the émigré cultural community in contact with the work of Proust, Gide, and other European modernists? All values were in flux; the poetic word, à la Tyutchev and the Romantics, could never express everything; and perhaps, after all, there was something higher than what is "artistic" or "literary." Tolstoy, who renounced his own finest art in the name of a higher truth, might be a more proper example for young émigré writers.[30]

The debate progressed along these lines until a point shortly before Khodasevich's death. Because Khodasevich, like Nabokov, did not publish in *Numbers*, the principal outlet in the early 1930s for young émigré writers, it may have appeared as time passed that he fell out of touch with the youth. In this sense Fedotov might be correct about Adamovich's eventual "victory," for at *Numbers* Adamovich did indeed have a large and visible following. But even that may be a simplification. There were always a number of Khodasevich "loyalists," among them Smolensky, Knut, Ladinsky, Yury Mandelshtam (to replace Khodasevich at *The*

[28] See Adamovich's review of the Crossroads group in *Numbers* 2-3 (1930), 239-240.
[29] Adamovich, "Literary Causeries" (17 April 1927).
[30] See Adamovich, "Kommentarii" (Commentaries), *Numbers* 2-3 (1930), 167-176.

Renaissance in 1939), and Nabokov and Berberova, who had—
not without significance for Khodasevich—turned to prose.
Khodasevich never ignored a poet with talent, no matter how
different that poet might be from himself: the many reviews
(some omnibus, others individual) through the 1920s and
1930s of the work of younger poets and the singling out (as
often as not with praise and encouragement as with criticism) of those such as Poplavsky and Chervinskaya are evidence of this.[31] Moreover, Khodasevich felt that his active
criticizing of "bad" poetry was, for the reason that it acknowledged such poetry as worthy of comment, better than
Adamovich's indifference to form and his tacit sponsoring
of the Parisian note (the phrase was apparently coined by
Poplavsky) in émigré verse.[32] Yet, by the end of 1938, just
months before his death, Khodasevich was ready to concede
victory to Adamovich. Importantly, Adamovich had convinced him not of the veracity of his (Adamovich's) views
on the nature of art, the creative process, the form-content
equation, and so on, but of the futility of any attempt to
graft Russian poetry to émigré life. In Khodasevich's mind,
the non-art of the human document now reigned supreme
over the minds of the younger generation, and it was time
to dispense with fulminations:

A genuine human document (be it a diary, letter, memoir, or something of the kind) is nothing more than direct evidence of a psychological fact (or chain of facts). Like any document (including a
photographic snapshot), it must possess only two virtues: genuineness and accuracy. Like any document, it is only material for
further generalizations and conclusions. As material it may serve

[31] See, e.g., Khodasevich's high praise for Poplavsky, in "O smerti Po-
plavskogo" (On the Death of Poplavsky), *Stat'i*, pp. 233-242; and "People
and Books," *Voz*, no. 4153 (14 October 1938).

[32] See Khodasevich: "Novye stikhi" (New Verse), *Voz*, no. 3585 (28 March
1935); and "Zhalost' i 'zhalost' " (Compassion and 'Compassion'), *Voz*,
no. 3599 (11 April 1935). Poplavsky gives a basic outline of the Parisian
note in his "O misticheskoi atmosfere molodoi literatury v emigratsii" (On
the Mystical Atmosphere of Young Literature in Emigration), *Numbers* 2-
3 (1930), pp. 308-311.

the needs of the psychologist, sociologist, historian, artist, etc., but by itself it is not a psychological, sociological, historical, or artistic work. It is a slice of life which, in order to become art, needs to undergo a complex, deep, and in part mysterious transformation called creation [*tvorchestvo*]. From this it is clear that the reverse process, that is, the turning of art into the manufacture of human documents, is, in an artistic sense, illicit, illegal, because it opposes the very nature of the artist. The artist goes from reality to art; the manufacturer of human documents, just the contrary, from art to reality. . . .

Often I have had occasion to polemicize with G. V. Adamovich over the replacement of literature by the fabrication and publication of human documents. I recall that only recently I wrote that we would still wage war. I must confess that such a desire on my part has passed almost completely. It is worth it to battle in order that young talent be led from a path that to me seems incorrect. But what is talent? . . . Does not literary talent consist of one's being able to instinctively find the true artistic path? And does not the fact that one is standing on an incorrect path simply attest the absence of talent? But in that case it is not worth it to struggle, not worth it to preserve talent that does not exist. Once, at the beginning of our arguments, Adamovich wrote that the authors whom I "attacked" were hardly capable themselves of creating something genuine, that their lot was only to leave behind material from which a talented writer of the future would be able with time to make something. At that point such words struck me as too hopeless, even too harsh. Now it seems to me more and more that Adamovich was right and that there was nothing to break lances over.[33]

Though Khodasevich continued to labor for the present and future of Russian poetry, his thoughts in the thirties were turning increasingly to the past. The decade seemed almost to open for him "retrospectively." In April 1930 the staffs of *Contemporary Annals* and *The Renaissance* honored Khodasevich with banquets for his twenty-five years of literary activity. As an announcement in *Rul'* (The Rudder) tells us, "all Russian literary Paris"[34] was present at the affair

[33] Khodasevich, "People and Books," *The Rudder* (14 October 1938).

[34] *The Rudder*, no. 2848 (8 April 1930); see also G. R., "Vladislav Khodasevich," no. 2849 (9 April 1930).

Khodasevich in Paris,
1930.

sponsored by *Contemporary Annals* (over which Bunin presided), and at the dinner organized by *The Renaissance* (the initiative was actually Berberova's) speeches were read by Sergey Makovsky, Kuprin, Weidlé, and others.[35]

But the retrospectivism of the last years found its most eloquent expression in *Derzhavin*, which Khodasevich excerpted and serialized in *Contemporary Annals* (issues 39-42, 1929-1930) and then published as a separate book in 1931. The actual process of writing spread out over two years (from 21 January 1929 to 6 January 1931) and took place in Paris, Versailles, and Arthies. With an almost Keatsian "Negative Capability," Khodasevich seemed to enter body and soul into Derzhavin's life and the epoch of Catherine. Whether describing Derzhavin's early, near ruinous passion for cards (perhaps Khodasevich's favorite pastime), or the "Wild West" atmosphere of the Pugachyov Rebellion, or the penning of the great ode "God,"[36] or the spirited arguments with Cath-

[35] See L. L., "Chestvovanie V. F. Khodasevicha" (The Honoring of V. F. Khodasevich), *Voz*, no. 1776 (13 April 1930).

[36] Mark Aldanov thought that Khodasevich's description of Derzhavin at

erine and other grandees, or the final period of decline and the bittersweet pleasure of providing commentaries to old poems for niece Liza Lvova,[37] Khodasevich continually conveys to his reader the warmth he feels for his subject. Because he had no access to archival material, Khodasevich could add little by way of new facts to Grot's monumental two-volume biography of Derzhavin, and yet his "artistic" biography, through its slightly "archaic" style and syntax (wafting of Derzhavin's eighteenth century), its scrupulous attention to detail, its obvious empathy and sympathy for the character of the poet, manages to weave Grot's scholarly material into living tissue.

What did Derzhavin represent to Khodasevich and why was the modern poet, with his intensely private world, so intrigued by the public-spirited odist? The question is key to understanding Khodasevich's frame of mind near the end of his life, for the rewards received by entering into Russian poetry's heroic past in some ways (though in the end not enough) compensated for a dismal present and increasingly ominous future. Derzhavin was the only poet Khodasevich felt as strongly about as Pushkin: "One could," said Khodasevich in January 1929, as he was beginning work on the biography, "take what is written by Derzhavin and compile a collection of seventy to a hundred poems, and that book

---

work on his ode "God" might be included in an anthology of the finest Russian prose. See M. Aldanov, "Vladislav Khodasevich. Derzhavin," *SZ* 46 (1931), 496-497; mentioned in John E. Malmstad, "The Historical Sense and Xodasevič's *Deržavin,*" in Khodasevich, *Derzhavin* (Paris, 1931; rpt., Munich, 1975), p. xviii n.

[37] The commentaries to old poems that Derzhavin dictated to Liza Lvova were, as John Malmstad has pointed out, not unlike the notes that Khodasevich made to his own poems in Berberova's copy of his *Collected Verse.* "Turning poetry into reality (as he had once turned reality into poetry), Derzhavin was completing his previous creative path, only in a reverse order, and it was as if he were experiencing again the happiness of creation. If one looks at it dispassionately, it is a sad path, and its joys are bitter. But it always warms the heart of a poet which is already growing cold." (Khodasevich, *Derzhavin,* p. 268; mentioned in Malmstad, "The Historical Sense and Xodasevič's *Deržavin,*" p. x.)

would, calmly, confidently, stand beside [the work of] Pushkin, Lermontov, Baratynsky, Tyutchev."[38] In fact, one of the
few occasions when Khodasevich had something negative to
say about Pushkin's taste involved his defense of Derzhavin's significance against the scorn (largely motivated by the
literary politics of the time) of a young Pushkin.[39] Khodasevich admired almost everything about Derzhavin, but most
of all he loved him for those very qualities of mind—resolve,
idealism, certainty about the boundaries of good and evil,
simplicity of soul, faith in God and manifest destiny, duty—
that seemed to be absent in a world eroded by irony, doubt,
and a crisis of values. The *status quo* had become, for Khodasevich, one of Chekhovian impotence, of abulia and ethical hair-splitting, whereas what was needed was Derzhavin's straightforwardness, even his impatience and stubbornness (of which Khodasevich himself possessed a
little):

During Chekhov's time we were dying. Now we have died, crossed
"beyond the border." Chekhov's era was for us what sickness is to
the dying. But if we are fated to be reincarnated (and only for that
are all our prayers, only toward that all our will), then our future
lies not in "Chekhovian moods" but in Derzhavinian action. If
Russia is allowed to be resurrected, then the pathos of its next
epoch, the pathos of our tomorrow, will be constructive, and not
contemplative, epic, and not lyric, masculine, and not feminine,
Derzhavinian, and not Chekhovian.[40]

There was something intriguing about Derzhavin the minister of state and Derzhavin the odist and lyricist: Khodasevich discovered that, thanks to Derzhavin's expansive,
headstrong nature and to the "constructive" (*sozidatel'nyi*)
epoch in which he lived and, most important, to the mysterious symbiosis binding man to epoch and epoch to man,
no split could be found between citizen and artist. Der-

---

[38] Khodasevich, "Song of Igor's Regiment," p. 18.

[39] See ibid., pp. 18, 33; and Khodasevich, "Pushkin o Derzhavine" (Pushkin on Derzhavine), *Voz*, no. 3019 (7 September 1933).

[40] Khodasevich, "O Chekhove" (On Chekhov), *Stat'i*, pp. 129-130.

zhavin's poems to Catherine were not only words, but words that the poet, in his dual role as senator or minister of state, aimed to translate into deeds—laws. Poems and statutes authored by Derzhavin could be equivalent aspects of one civic accomplishment.[41]

Yet, as much as Khodasevich might have been struck by the historical person of Derzhavin, perhaps he was fascinated more (since the poet in him was never far below the surface of the historian) by the shaggy splendor of Derzhavin's poetic language.[42] Derzhavin had found his own voice at a time when the language of Russian poetry was undergoing turbulent growth, and he eventually became, with faith in his own intuition and with characteristic disregard for convention, an integral factor in the linguistic evolution that cleared the way for Pushkin. Of Derzhavin's many bold strokes in the area of poetic form Khodasevich was particularly attracted by his hyperbole, coarseness, sharp stylistic contrasts, range of subjects, delight at "taking to the air" (*krylatost'*: "how Derzhavin loved everything with wings"[43]— Khodasevich, we recall, was accused of being "wingless"). Because he had the strength and insight to break with tradition, Derzhavin was able to make it new: the deflating details and the "irreverence" in matters of tone and diction in the "Felitsa" poems are precisely what gave the tired odic form new life and the "realism" of the nineteenth-century novel its first embryonic movements.[44] And the blending of styles and the russification of classical motifs found in "Zhizn' zvanskaia" (Life at Zvanka) and the later anacreontic verse offer another rich example of the sort of "grafting" that Khodasevich associated with a living poetic tradition.[45] Finally,

[41] Khodasevich, *Derzhavin*, pp. 112-113, 117.

[42] For Khodasevich's treatment of Derzhavin's poetic language, see especially ibid., pp. 82-87, 107-112, 125-128, 211-212, 262-264.

[43] Ibid., p. 288.

[44] Ibid., p. 121.

[45] Ibid., pp. 211-212.

Derzhavin seemed in touch with some poetic tap root; as was his life, so was his art determined by inner necessity, for his, concludes Khodasevich, "is a language that is primordial, creative. It has total creative freedom—the lot of savages and geniuses."[46]

But, as the biographer knew, there was bound to be a waning of Derzhavin's creative and civic energies. Thus, as Khodasevich came to describe the last years of Derzhavin and the inevitable decline that set in, his thoughts must have turned to himself. These final pages, I believe, are as close as the reader comes to an "explanation" of Khodasevich's silence as a poet. Like Derzhavin, Khodasevich had fallen out of touch with the epoch to which he had given his life:

To reflect an epoch is not poetry's task, but only that poet is alive who breathes the air of his century, hears the music of his time. That music may not accord with the poet's ideas about harmony, it may even be repugnant to him, but his ear must be filled with that music, as one's lungs are filled with air. Such is the law of poetic biology. . . . Events had ceased to elicit in Derzhavin that rapid and sharp echoing sound with which his lyre had once been powerful. True, at first one might suppose that the epoch itself was uninspiring. Not for nothing was Derzhavin at odds with it. . . . [Yet while] Derzhavin still recognized all the grandeur of his time, he no longer caught its music. . . . This was not a decline of talent, but of inspiration. . . . Derzhavin had labored much, loved history and Russia, become himself history and Russia, and now he wanted to see and hear those who would be laboring in the future. Perhaps he felt like adopting someone, as a rich man without children adopts a child. Lovingly he filled his home with nephews, all the while searching in poetry for a successor, a *new Derzhavin*, not a second one, an epigone, but precisely a new one, one who in his own time would hear what Derzhavin had once heard in his, who would find new content and new form, bring that artistic innovation which Derzhavin had brought forty years earlier.[47]

[46] Ibid., p. 264.
[47] Ibid., pp. 289-290.

One needs hardly to add that that successor was Pushkin and that the cycle of Derzhavin's "grain's way" was made complete when the schoolboy read his poem—an imitation of Derzhavin—to the old poet at Tsarskoe Selo. As Derzhavin trumpets in the ode on the death of Countess Rumyantseva, he can rise above history—"I am a poet and shall not die." The above passage acquires a special poignancy, however, when we consider that Khodasevich, himself a poet in his waning years, felt that for him and his generation there was no successor in the wings.

Khodasevich's life became especially bleak in April 1932 when Berberova left him. Young and energetic, she felt the weight of her husband's weariness and pessimism to be oppressive, and she feared that her life was in danger of being poisoned along with his. Attempts had been made through vacations to regain strength and resilience for the daily grind, but now she discovered that only when alone was she herself (previously she had been much dependent on Khodasevich). Leaving the flat, Berberova turned from the street to see Khodasevich standing "in the wide open window, clinging

Nina Berberova
in 1932.

to the frame with both hands, in the pose of one crucified, in his striped pajamas."[48]

Khodasevich had loved Berberova more than anyone in his life, so it should not be surprising that his mood after the split became more hopeless than ever before. The new note of despair surfaces most vividly in a letter written to Berberova on 19 July 1932 from Arthies:

My health is tolerable. My mood is gaily hopeless. I think that the last outbreak of illness and despair was caused by my parting with Pushkin. Now, along with my verse, I have given up Pushkin too. Now I have *nothing*. That means it's really time to calm down and try to extract from life what little pleasures it can still offer. But to lofty projects it's time to say a general farewell [a na gordykh zamyslakh postavit' obshchii krest].[49]

Now Khodasevich would never write the biography of Pushkin that many so looked forward to.[50] He seemed to know too much about Pushkin's life and times, to feel that Pushkin's life and art were too complexly intertwined, to generalize: "the master in his declining days is humbly convinced of how endlessly difficult it is to give an impression of even the most insignificant of life's moments."[51] Moreover, the loss of Pushkin was linked in his mind with the departure of Berberova.

There were, to be sure, some bright spots in Khodasevich's last years. His marriage in 1933 to Olga Margolina, whom

---

[48] *Italics*, p. 349; *Kursiv*, p. 403.

[49] Khodasevich's letter to Nina Berberova dated 19 July 1932. (Archive of Nina Berberova, Beinecke Library, Yale. Courtesy of Nina Berberova.)

[50] Khodasevich did write a number of articles about Pushkin's ancestry and youth which he intended to serve as the biography's point of departure, but the project never went farther than that. The articles appeared in *Segodnia* (Today) and *The Renaissance*.

[51] Khodasevich, "People and Books," *Voz*, no. 2956 (6 July 1933). When Khodasevich was asked by Andrey Sedykh (Tsvibak) in 1930 whether he would write a biography of Pushkin to match the biography of Derzhavin, he answered "It will be unbearably difficult to write such a biography. We know too much about Pushkin." (Andrey Sedykh [Tsvibak], "U V. F. Khodasevicha" [At V. F. Khodasevich's], *Today* [10 May 1930].)

Khodasevich and
Olga Margolina in
Longchêne, 1938.

NIGHTWATCH: 1927-1939

Khodasevich had gotten to know better in August and September of 1932 in St. Mesmin (in the Loiret), was happy for both. Though Margolina could not replace Berberova, Khodasevich badly needed someone to look after him, and Olga fulfilled this task cheerfully.[52] When N. V. Makeev, Berberova's second husband, bought a small farm at Longchêne (an hour southwest of Paris) in May 1938, Khodasevich and Olga would come out for pleasant visits. There was, in addition, the appearance of *O Pushkine* (On Pushkin), Khodasevich's expanded and emended version of *Poeticheskoe khoziaistvo Pushkina* (Pushkin's Poetic Economy), in 1937 and of *Necropolis*, his fine book of memoirs, in 1939. Perhaps too much has been made over the years of Khodasevich's "stubborn and humorless" nature,[53] for even at this late date he was capable of genuine humor.[54] In February 1936, for

[52] Portraits of Olga Margolina are found in *Kursiv*, pp. 420-436; and Sylvester, ed., *Valentina Khodasevich and Olga Margolina-Khodasevich: Unpublished Letters to Nina Berberova*, pp. 75-86.

[53] Hagglund, "The Adamovič-Xodasevič Polemics," p. 240.

[54] "No matter how noteworthy a writer, no matter how significant his books, no matter what heights he rises to in his writings, if he has never joked once in his life, never written anything silly or jolly, never shined with an epigram or parody, then I must confess that in the depths of my

example, Khodasevich appeared at the Salle Las Cases to give a benefit lecture (Nabokov, as it turned out, was on the same program, and must have thoroughly enjoyed what his friend was up to): he presented evidence—complete with quotations from manuscripts that in places were glossed as "illegible"—about the life and work of Vasily Travnikov, a gifted, but by chance forgotten poet who wrote at the turn of the nineteenth century. To the great good fortune of Russian poetry, Khodasevich had managed to get his hands on the only extant copy of Travnikov's collected verse (Travnikov had destroyed all other copies because Vladimir Izmaylov, then the editor of *The Messenger of Europe*, mistakenly thinking the author "dead," had published the collection without Travnikov's approval) and was now convinced that Travnikov, and not Karamzin, Zhukovsky, or Batyushkov, was the first to fight with the eighteenth-century "conventions of bookish affectation" and was the logical predecessor to Baratynsky.[55] But the gullible reading public would have to wait in vain for more on the Travnikov discovery—Khodasevich had, with his intimate knowledge of the late eighteenth and early nineteenth centuries, simply invented the whole thing.[56]

---

soul I always suspect such a writer of a hidden lack of talent" (Khodasevich, "Kanareechnoe schast'e" [Canary Happiness], *Voz*, no. 4122 [11 March 1938]). See, in addition, Khodasevich, "Prinoshenie R. i M. Gorlinym" (Offering to R. and M. Gorlin) (*SS*, pp. 225-227), a marvelous travesty written by Khodasevich in 1937: the poet hears of a Maharajah's incurable insomnia and arrives opportunely with the only effective soporific—his articles on Pushkin!

[55] Khodasevich, "Zhizn' Vasiliia Travnikova" (The Life of Vasily Travnikov), *Voz*, no. 3921 (27 February 1936). The first three installments on Travnikov's life are found in *Voz*, no. 3907 (13 February 1936), no. 3914 (20 February 1936), and no. 3921 (27 February 1936). For the Travnikov hoax, see Terapiano, *Encounters*, p. 91; Malmstad, "The Historical Sense and Xodasevič's *Deržavin*," pp. v-vi; and Grigorii Poliak, "Pastish Khodasevicha" (Khodasevich's Pastiche), *Chast' rechi* (Part of Speech), 1 (1980), 193.

[56] See Adamovich's glowing response to the Travnikov discovery ("Travnikov was a most gifted poet, innovator, teacher: it's enough to hear one

Yet by the late 1930s such lighter moments were coming rarely. Khodasevich had reached a state of such bitterness that it was suspected that perhaps he, like Kuprin, would return to the Soviet Union. In a letter written to Berberova on 21 June 1937 Khodasevich, while discrediting the rumors, emerges as a man at the end of his tether:

It is you, my dear, who leave without a word, while I would say goodbye. However, to pose the question on that level is way too premature. It's true that I no longer hide my extreme disenchant-ment in the emigration (in its "spiritual leaders," with some in-significant exceptions); it's true that I have known about Kuprin's impending departure for about three weeks. On the basis of that the "representatives of the élite" have fabricated my rapid depar-ture. Alas, there is no real ground underlying such babble. I have not taken any decisive steps—and don't even know of what they should consist. And most important, I don't know how they would regard such steps in Moscow (though I am sure "in my soul" that if they would take into consideration many important circum-stances, then they would regard those steps positively). At any rate, I would not leave quietly like Kuprin (who has, it is true, fallen into [a second] childhood); I would certainly slam doors, loudly and often, so you would hear after all.

I either sit at home or play cards. Literature, now both the older and the younger, has become absolutely loathsome to me. I preserve remnants of warm feelings for Smolensky . . . and Sirin [Nabokov]. There are two bits of news: it seems Felzen has begun to change his orientation and return to his spiritual homeland, that is, . . . to the stock-market. [The prose writer Anatoly] Alfyorov yesterday wed a fat and ugly musician. The apartment . . . has had the fin-ishing touches put on it, and the newlyweds have left for the moun-tains. In a word, all is evolving along its natural course.[57]

Through his years in emigration Khodasevich had suffered from a variety of illnesses, among them an ear infection, bad

of his poems to be convinced of this"), in "Vecher V. Sirina i V. Khodase-vicha" (An Evening of V. Sirin [Nabokov] and V. Khodasevich), *PN*, no. 5439 (13 February 1936).

[57] Khodasevich's letter to Nina Berberova dated 21 June 1937. (Archive of Nina Berberova, Beinecke Library, Yale. Courtesy of Nina Berberova. Quoted in *Kursiv*, pp. 421-422.)

teeth, and eczema (several of the later letters to Berberova are especially painful to read because Khodasevich's hands were heavily bandaged and consequently his handwriting approaches that of a childish scrawl). The cancer that killed him began to make its presence felt in January 1939. Nina Berberova's description of Khodasevich's final days (written the day of his funeral) is moving in the extreme. Rather than excerpt the description, I shall quote it in full:

He took sick at the end of January 1939. The diagnosis was in part correct, but the treatment was cruel and coarse. At the end of February he was in Longchêne. He was all right. If I were to stay here with you, he said later, I would get better. He said the country would cure him and I began to look for a room for him for the summer somewhere nearby.

Towards the end of March pains began, he became very thin, suffered terribly. There were pains in the intestine and the spine. We feared it was cancer of the intestine.

All of April he suffered cruelly and grew thin (he lost 25 lbs). Sometimes a doctor who lived in the neighborhood would come at night to inject morphine. After this he was delirious. There were three subjects in his delirium: Andrey Bely (meeting with him), the Bolsheviks (they were persecuting him), and I (anxiety about how I was). Once at night he screamed and cried terribly: he dreamt that in an automobile accident I had been blinded. [That year Berberova was learning to drive.]

I came twice a week, but his nerves remained in a terrible state of depression. There were days of continual tears (of kindness, of self-pity, of anxiety). The wallpaper in the room was olive, ashen, the blanket green. Poor, coarse sheets, narrow bed (really a couch). On it he lay, emaciated, long-haired, still smoking a lot. In May he had a bilious attack. His complexion became terrible, from yellow to brownish-green (which was a bad sign). In his face were anguish, torment, horror. He did not sleep at all. He didn't know this might be cancer and didn't actually suspect that he was so seriously sick.

The doctors said that it was necessary to treat him for two weeks in a hospital and make all the possible tests that would aid in establishing a diagnosis. He was taken to the Brousset municipal hospital. It was horrible there: it's impossible to imagine that there can exist such a hell on earth.

Visitors were allowed from 1:00 to 2:00 p.m. We all stood with little bundles (parcels, as in front of a prison) at the gates. At exactly 1:00 p.m. the gates flew open, all ran in whither they had to, so as not to lose precious time. He lay in a glass cage, curtained off from the other wards, neighboring ones, by sheets. A bright hot sun shone in the cage; there was nowhere to turn. Hungry to the point of shudders, he attacked what was brought him (the food was bad in the hospital, and he ate almost nothing there), he joked about himself, and then suddenly lay down, moaned, sometimes cried.

The cot was hard; a second pillow was obtained with great difficulty; hospital linen and a severe prisonlike blanket; and outside, June days which somehow forced their way into the room. He said:

"Tonight I hated everyone. All were foreign to me. Who has not lain on this cot as I have all these nights, has not slept, been tormented, or lived through these hours, that one to me is no one, is alien to me. Only one who, like me, has endured this penal servitude is my brother." Towards the end of the second week it was shown that he had neither a tumor nor stones in the gall bladder, thus the idea of liver thrombosis had to be abandoned. No cancer of the pancreas came to light or was felt (as the doctors put it). It was decided to operate. Why? To become convinced and probably speed up his end.

He returned to his flat, even darker and thinner, overgrown with half-grey shaggy hair. He was happy at my coming, said that the operation was on Tuesday. He didn't think it would be death, he didn't believe in recovery—he himself didn't know what to think, only a shadow now remained of him.

For moments he lay flat on his back and silently stared straight ahead with dark-yellow, greenish eyes. Inwardly something tormented him and he was on the point of tears. N. [V. Makeev] and Olga went out into Olga's room. I remained with him. This was on Friday, June 9th, at 2:00 p.m. I knew (and he knew) that we would not see each other again before the operation.

"To be somewhere," he said, tears pouring, "and to know nothing of you!"

I wanted to say something to him, to comfort him, but he continued:

"I know I am only an obstacle in your life . . . But to be somewhere, in a spot where I would never again know anything about you! . . . Only about you . . . Only about you . . . I love only you . . . All the time about you, day and night about you alone . . . You know . . . How will I be without you? . . . Where will I be? . . . It doesn't make any difference. Only you be happy and well, drive slowly. Now farewell."

I approached him. He started crossing my face and hands, I kissed his wrinkled yellow brow, he kissed my hands, covering them with tears. I embraced him. He had such thin, pointed shoulders.

"Farewell, farewell," he said, "be happy. May God preserve you."

I went out into the hall. Then I again returned to his room. He was sitting on the bed, his head having fallen onto his hands.

On Sunday, June 11th, N. called on him and let him know that he would be operated on not in the Brousset municipal hospital but in a private clinic. His sister [Zhenya] had arranged this. On Monday he was carried there, and at three on Tuesday the 13th he was operated on.

Many of his kind friends helped him financially; some sent him money through a so-called "committee" for him, some came to him and simply gave it to him. His sister did more than anyone else for him. Unfortunately it was too late.

"If the operation is not successful," he said on that last Friday, "*it* will nevertheless be rest."

On Sunday he told N. he would not survive it and they blessed each other.

The operation lasted an hour and a half. The surgeon emerging after it was over, trembling and perspiring, said he had no doubt that it was cancer, but that he had not managed to reach it. He said he had not more than twenty-four hours to live and that he would suffer no more. Right there he gave Olga two stones he had extracted (which the X-rays had not shown!). N. summoned me to Paris and at 7:00 p.m. I entered the ward where he lay.

The nurse said: "He must not suffer." At nine we left. A sort of numbness came upon me. We spent the night in a hotel.

At 7:30 a.m. we were already at the clinic (June 14th). He had died at 6:00 a.m., without regaining consciousness. Before his death he held out his right hand in some direction ("and a flower trembled in it," as he once wrote), moaned deliriously. Suddenly Olga called out to him. He opened his eyes and smiled slightly to her. In a few minutes all was over. In the evening Olga and I cut two locks of his hair. They smelled of eau-de-cologne.

The evening of the fifteenth he was put into a coffin. Olga placed in his hands my baptismal icon of the Virgin of Kazan, which in his last years had hung above his bed. The morning of the sixteenth a van took him from the clinic basement and at 1:45 brought him to the Russian Catholic Church on the Rue François-Gérard, where there were several hundred people and the funeral service was performed. At 2:45 the service ended. I took Olga by the arm. Behind the van that was taking the coffin (in front sat the priest) and was covered with flowers, the cars drifted along. At the Pont Mirabeau (it was a dazzling summer day) it seemed to me there was something even of *relief* in this trip of cars moving somewhere. At the [Billancourt] cemetery gates there was already quite a crowd. At the grave, as is the custom, Olga was handed a spade with sand, then I. I felt a strange deliverance.[58]

IN closing a study of a poet as profoundly ironic as Khodasevich, one wishes to avoid last words and ultimate statements. And yet one also wishes to place the life and work of this remarkable individual in perspective. Khodasevich, it is now safe to say, will be remembered in the history of modern Russian literature for many things: as a memoirist who not only knew those such as Bryusov, Bely, and Gorky, but wrestled with and interpreted the enigmatic core of their personalities as few have done; as a Pushkinist whose work combined superior memory, poetic intuition, and intellectual rigor to produce highly original and often provocative results, results that, though arrived at without access to archives, could be, as Tomashevsky attests,[59] startlingly ac-

---

[58] *Italics*, pp. 364-367; *Kursiv*, pp. 424-430 (the description in the latter is considerably fuller). Pallbearers included Weidlé and members of the Crossroads group—Yu. Mandelshtam, Raevsky, Smolensky, and Terapiano. Russian literary Paris appeared *en masse* to pay last respects: just a brief look at those present yields Adamovich, Aldanov, Annenkov, Berberova, Gippius, Gofman (Modest), Gorlin, G. Ivanov, I. Knorring, Knut, Ladinsky, S. Makovsky, Mamchenko, Merezhkovsky, Odoevtseva, S. Pregel, Prismanova, Remizov, Sirin (Nabokov), Slonim, Felzen, Chervinskaya, Yanovsky, and Zaytsev (the list goes on and on) (see *Voz*, no. 4188 [16 June 1939]; and no. 4189 [23 June 1939]). Eloquent necrologies are found in M. Aldanov, *Russkie zapiski* (Russian Notes), 19 (July 1939), 179-185; N. Berberova, *SZ* 69 (1939), 256-261; and V. Sirin [Nabokov], *SZ* 69 (1939), 262-264. Nabokov has since translated the obituary he wrote in *The Bitter Air of Exile*, eds. Karlinsky and Appel, pp. 83-87 (which volume first appeared as "Russian Literature and Culture in the West: 1922-1972," in *TriQuarterly* 27-28 [Spring and Fall 1973]); he has reprinted it as well in *Strong Opinions* (New York, 1973), pp. 223-227.

[59] See B. Tomashevskii, "Poeticheskoe khoziaistvo Pushkina" [review of

curate; as a biographer whose flair for historicity and whose elegant prose, as if embalmed with the eighteenth century, seemed to bring Derzhavin, Catherine, and their story to life; as an individual who lived through the brilliance and the tarnish of the Silver Age, who witnessed its tragedies and its farces, who himself suffered much both personally and in the name of literature, who ended his life in utter frustration, but who never, with his manifest weaknesses as a person, betrayed that part of him that from the beginning swore allegiance to "poetry forever."

Yet these various aspects of Khodasevich's life and work, demanding of our attention as they may be, are not the "little sun . . . the vestige of [his] soul,"[60] as he once expressed it, that lies at the center of his artistic legacy. That center is, of course, his poetry. As modern poetry, it does not possess the panache of Mayakovsky's rhymes, the "okh" and "akh" of Tsvetaeva's passionate verbal inventiveness, the great "heaviness" and "tenderness" of Mandelshtam's metaphysical "sisters," the immediacy and sprung logic of association that make Pasternak's poetic world, regardless of the tense, break out all over with the present. But within its compass, which is considerably larger than might be first imagined, it has no equal. Its ambivalent, *soto voce*, somehow "unwilling" charm defies the "Pushkinian" epithet that has grown not to enhance, but to corset its reputation.

Khodasevich, in ways that now seem bold, if not iconoclastic, actually went against the grain of the lyric tradition on which he was raised. Irony, at least in its "modern," unstable, ever-questioning guises, is not a concept one generally associates with the dominant strain, righteous, *engagé*, doggedly searching for "truth," of Russian literature. (Not suprisingly, exceptions such as Gogol or Chekhov were often—and still are—misunderstood for the irony in their

---

Khodasevich's *Pushkin's Poetic Economy*], *Russkii sovremennik* (Russian Contemporary), 3 (1924), 262-263.
[60] "Gold," *SS*, p. 39.

works.) If this holds true for prose fiction (would not, for example, any genuine comparison of Joyce and Bely begin with the assumption that the mythological skeleton informing *Ulysses* has no reality beyond its artistic function, while the function of language in *Petersburg* is mythopoetic, aiming outward and, for all the *irony*, taking seriously the ghostly presence of the city and its tradition?), then it does so, *a fortiori*, for Russian lyric poetry—a tradition as close to being purely *lyric* as any in Western Europe. While other countries had several important ironists, including Heine, Laforgue, and Browning, in the lyric tradition prior to the twentieth century, and many afterward, Russia produced no one of stature who consistently questioned, broke in on, challenged, upstaged the assumptions of his lyric "I"—the minor exception of a poet such as Klyushnikov was exposed for this dangerous *refleksiia* (reflection) and duly excoriated by no less than Belinsky.

This aspect of Khodasevich's genius, the yoking of a self-ironizing, multi-voiced speaker with a prosodic profile that is traditional and a lexicon that is disarmingly simple, is finally receiving recognition. Misread, perhaps willfully so, by those such as Adamovich and Georgy Ivanov, Khodasevich's poetry demanded someone like Nabokov—whose own orientation was also toward irony rather than fierce ethical commitment and whose reputation also suffered attack for its "un-Russian'" self-reflectiveness and playfulness (which actually, and *ironically*, went back to Pushkin)—to retrieve it from the neglect that ensued after Khodasevich's death. Not a few have been puzzled by Nabokov's categorical claim that Khodasevich is "the greatest Russian poet that the twentieth century has yet produced";[61] they feel that

---

[61] See, for example, A. Bakhrakh, "Po pamiati, po zapiskam" (Through Memory, Through Notes), *Mosty* (Bridges), 11 (1965), 242-243, who remarks that "such a contentious assertion [on the part of Nabokov] would undoubtedly amaze all lovers of poetry, including, one suspects, even the most zealous supporters of Khodasevich's muse."

this is another case of Nabokov's notorious mystification or *épatage*. But judging by Nabokov's friendship with Khodasevich, by his glowing statements about the latter's poetry from early on, and by the fact that Khodasevich was one of the first and most eloquent to champion the early novels of the *Russian* writer Sirin,[62] one feels certain that Nabokov, according to his lights, was in earnest. If Nabokov eventually found his way into the broader arena of American and European modernist prose, then the beautiful necrology he wrote for his friend was a pledge that the poetry of Khodasevich, the mentor figure Koncheev of *The Gift*, would one day be snatched from its "European night" and ushered into the context of appreciation it deserves.

How will posterity come to view Khodasevich, the symbolist-turned-ironist who fit into no niche during his lifetime and who subsequently, like Mandelshtam, Tsvetaeva, Bulgakov, and other important Russian modernists fully discovered only decades after their deaths, nearly "fell through the cracks" of literary history? To draw a parallel that he himself would probably not have understood, but one that removes him from the vicissitudes of literary politics and perhaps makes him more accessible to the Western reader, Khodasevich is a transitional figure who stands to the modern Russian lyric tradition as does Auden, *mutatis mutandis*, to that of England and America. He is a vital link between Symbolism and post-Symbolism, between the high lyricism and urgently eschatological visions of Blok and Bely, on the one hand, and the gradual foreshortening of that lexicon and those visions by poets, including the so-called Acmeists and Futurists, who rose to prominence in the prerevolutionary years, on the other. Yeats, like Blok, was a major poet long

---

[62] In his reviews of *Contemporary Annals* that appeared in the twenties and thirties, Khodasevich commented enthusiastically on the rise of Sirin's talent. (Like other émigré writers, Nabokov-Sirin serialized many of his works of this period in *Sovremennye zapiski*.) See, especially, Khodasevich, "O Sirine" (On Sirin), *Stat'i*, pp. 245-254.

before the Easter Uprising and the First World War—he called himself one of the "last romantics" and evidently took the appellation seriously; his linking of Maud Gonne with the image of Helen of Troy, the myth of Leda, Irish nationalism, and the eternal return of history suggests obvious parallels, as yet not properly studied, with Blok's merging of Lyubov Mendeleeva, Holy Sophia, Russia, and the return of the Tatar East to the civilized West. During the threat, then presence, and finally aftermath of war in the West and war and revolution in Russia, the Symbolist visions and mystical nationalism of Blok and Yeats were seen by following generations as no longer viable. The appreciation of transcendent culture and of values independent of secular or national history associated with the mature poetry of Eliot and the flair for language and vivid imagination associated with the poetry of Stevens seemed to unite, in the Russian context, in the poetry of Mandelshtam. And the sharp line of vision and pioneering use of free verse forms attributed first to Pound and the Imagists and then, more centrally, to Williams find a Russian corollary in the Pasternak-Tsvetaeva-Mayakovsky constellation, in these "adventurers" whose feats of diction, syntax, rhyme, and rhythm significantly altered the syllabo-tonic verse form on which Russian poetry, since the classic iambic tetrameter of Pushkin, had been based.

Like Auden, another ironist, Khodasevich had to deal with being a post-Symbolist, with living in a world where values, up to and including that of art, were constantly being questioned. (Here we should not forget that Stevens called his works "supreme *fictions*," while for Yeats his works never ceased to be, at some level, supreme *truths*.) Unlike Auden, born in 1907, Khodasevich was not so far removed from the Symbolist ambiance that his evaluation of it could be completely objective or *ironic*, at least in the sense of being disengaged or free from that which one observes or ironizes. If Khodasevich chronicled the ultimate failure of Symbolism, of its attempt to translate art into life, he could still

admire it heroic aspects. Whereas Auden, in his poetic eu-
logy of Yeats, calls the man "silly like us" and his art a cause
that "makes nothing happen," Khodasevich said of Blok that
"It seems that in [him] after all the ideal of Symbolism was
realized: the union of the poet and the man. One might say
(and this would not be simply 'words') that his entire physical being was permeated with poetry. With the end of the
poet there had to follow the end of the physical being as
well."[63] Thus Khodasevich's special blend of lyricism and
irony, of Symbolism and post-Symbolism, was more than
artistic device, though without its form it would have little
meaning. It was his response to all that was being wrested
from him and the literature he had served so well. The stun-
ning music *ex nihilo* of "Ballada" and the superimposed
snapshots, the stereoscopic "before" and "after," of *Sorrento
Photographs* belong to an artist who understood implicitly
the poignant border-crossings, physical, metaphysical, and
historico-literary, confronting him and his generation. And
so, in the final analysis, no other post-Symbolist, including
Gumilyov, understood better the essence of Symbolism and
operated at the cutting edge of two distinct traditions more
masterfully than did Khodasevich.

With Khodasevich scholarship now on the rise, the context
of appreciation anticipated by Nabokov is at last becoming
a reality. In the Soviet Union the poet was nominally "re-
habilitated" in the journal *Moskva* (Moscow) in 1963, and
remains one of the most popular unofficial poets in that
country.[64] After surviving the forties, fifties, and sixties in

[63] Khodasevich, "Neither Dreams nor Reality."
[64] See *Moskva* (Moscow), 1 (1963), 131-135: what is included is a blurb
together with several poems from *European Night*; Khodasevich is worthy
of the Soviet reader's attention because he is a good example of a "poet
unhappy with life in a foreign land." Some fifteen or twenty years ago (see
Weidlé's "Khodasevich from Far and Near," p. 128), plans were made for
an anthology of early twentieth-century poetry to be published by the pres-
tigious *Biblioteka poeta* (Poet's Library) series. There was to be a selection
of Khodasevich's verse as well as an introductory essay by the Soviet scholar

the memory of the émigré community thanks largely to the articles and memoirs of Nabokov, Berberova, Weidlé, Gleb Struve, and others, he has been in the seventies and, now, the eighties reprinted and increasingly studied.[65] Letters and other valuable documents are gradually coming to light.[66] Most encouraging, Robert Hughes and John Malmstad are now in the process of editing a new five-volume collection of his major work. Perhaps therefore, this final quote from Nabokov's necrology suggests better than anything a return to that which causes new beginnings and a constant renewal of our interest:

I find it most odd myself that in this article, in this rapid inventory of thoughts prompted by Khodasevich's death, I seem to imply a vague nonrecognition of his genius and engage in vague polemics with such phantoms as would question the enchantment and importance of his poetry. Fame, recognition—all that kind of thing is a phenomenon of rather dubious shape which death alone places in true perspective. I am ready to assume that there might have been quite a few people who, when reading with interest the weekly critique that Khodasevich wrote for *The Renaissance* (and it should

V. N. Orlov. But these plans were scotched, although the essay ("Na rubezhe dvukh epokh"—On the Border of Two Epochs) appeared in *Voprosy literatury* (Questions of Literature), 10 (1966), 111-143, and was later expanded and collected in V. N. Orlov, *Pereput'ia* (Crossroads) (Moscow, 1976), pp. 144-156. The sense that the ice floe pace of recognition may at last be ready to quicken is suggested by the following: individual poems of Khodasevich are occasionally reprinted in *Literaturnaia gazeta* (Literary Gazette); the poet has now appeared in the *Bol'shaia sovetskaia entsiklopediia* (The Large Soviet Encyclopedia), ed. A. M. Prokhorov (Moscow, 1978), 28:324; and he is quoted anonymously (see Orlov, *Crossroads*, pp. 29-30, who quotes from *Necropolis*, pp. 10-12, and describes the unnamed author as "one of the writers belonging to the youngest generation of Symbolists"), usually a first tentative step toward acceptance.

[65] See the bibliography to this book.

[66] Since 1970 letters by Khodasevich to Gleb Struve, Lev Yaffe, Boris Diatroptov, Georgy Malitsky, Yury Verkhovsky, Mikhail Froman, and Boris Sadovskoy have appeared in print. See the bibliography. His seventy-four letters to Nina Berberova and his one hundred thirty-six letters to Anna Chulkova, which taken together are the best source we have for Khodasevich's life before and after emigration, are now being prepared for publication.

be admitted that his reviews, with all their wit and *allure*, were not on the level of his poetry, for they lacked somehow its throb and magic), simply did not know that the reviewer was also a poet. I should not be surprised if this person or that finds Khodasevich's posthumous fame inexplicable at first blush. Furthermore, he published no poems lately—and readers are forgetful, and our literary critics are too excited and preoccupied by evanescent topical themes to have the time or occasion to remind the public of important matters. Be it as it may, all is finished now: the bequeathed gold shines on a shelf in full view of the future, whilst the goldminer has left for the region from where, perhaps, a faint something reaches the ears of good poets, penetrating our being with the beyond's fresh breath and conferring upon art that mystery which more than anything characterizes its essence.

Well, so it goes, yet another plane of life has been slightly displaced; yet another habit—the habit (one's own) of (another person's) existence—has been broken. There is no consolation, if one starts to encourage the sense of loss by one's private recollection of a brief, brittle, human image that melts like a hailstone on a windowsill. Let us turn to the poems.[67]

[67] Nabokov,"On Khodasevich," in *The Bitter Air of Exile*, pp. 86-87.

SELECTED BIBLIOGRAPHY _____

We have at present no adequate bibliography of works by and about Khodasevich. A complete accounting of such works would run, according to my calculations, close to a thousand: in the research for this book some eight hundred entries have been compiled, and still that list is incomplete for the many prerevolutionary articles and reviews written by Khodasevich under various pseudonyms and appearing in the provincial press. Needless to say, not all of these entries are of equal interest. Hence completeness in this case, unless it were accompanied by some annotation, would only bewilder the uninitiated, while completeness plus annotation would prove too costly in terms of space. The compromise arrived at has as its aim a selected listing of works that is more than basic, but not exhaustive, to a knowledge of Khodasevich's life and art. Those interested in learning more may consult standard (though themselves far from complete) bibliographical sources, including K. D. Muratova, ed., *Istoriia russkoi literatury kontsa XIX-nachala XX veka. Bibliograficheskii ukazatel'* (Moscow-Leningrad, 1963), pp. 419-420, and Ludmila A. Foster, *Bibliography of Russian Émigré Literature, 1918-1968* (Boston, 1970), II: 1,130-1,134. In addition, the bibliographies found in the dissertations by Professors Jane Miller, Philippe Radley, and Richard Sylvester (see below) are helpful.

The bibliographical material given below is divided into two general categories: works by Khodasevich and works about him. Works by Khodasevich are further subdivided into collected works, separate books of verse, books of prose, editions and anthologies, notebooks, published correspondence, translations, and uncollected articles, reviews, memoirs, obituaries, and other materials. The full publication history of Khodasevich's verse can be found in the forthcoming collection of his works under the editorship of Professors Robert Hughes and John Malmstad and therefore will not be duplicated here. Only the first impressions of Khodasevich's translations from Polish are included, and it should further be noted that he occasionally signed his translations under the pseudonym "F. Maslov." Khodasevich wrote literally hundreds of uncollected articles and reviews in his émigré period alone: I have tried to offer a broad cross-section of these, but I have limited the entries where possible to those that have to do with his views on Russian poetry in exile, a topic to which he spoke with special eloquence. Works about Khodasevich have been "reduced" to those that, in my judgment, comment substantively on his life or work. Exceptions have been made—either to add where the commentary is elliptical but still significant (e.g., it belongs to a major figure or is particularly perceptive), or to delete where the commentary is considerable but not necessarily informative (e.g., memoiristic sketches by minor figures that recapitulate clichés or develop the superfluous). Moreover, in a few instances articles have been included that, while not specifically about Khodasevich, proved to be especially helpful in illuminating the background of his life and times.

Abbreviations used in the notes for émigré journals and newspapers are used here as well: *PN* for *Poslednie novosti*, *SZ* for *Sovremennye zapiski*, and *Voz* for *Vozrozhdenie*.

I

COLLECTED WORKS

Sobranie sochinenii. Ed. Robert P. Hughes and John E. Malmstad. Ann Arbor, forthcoming.
Sobranie stikhov. Paris, 1927; rpt. New York, 1978.
Sobranie stikhov. Ed. N. Berberova. Munich, 1961.
Sobranie stikhov v dvukh tomakh. Ed. Iu. Kolker. Paris, 1982.

SEPARATE BOOKS OF VERSE

Molodost'. Moscow, 1908.
Putem zerna. Moscow, 1920.
———. 2nd rev. ed. Petrograd, 1921; rpt. Berkeley, 1977.
Schastlivyi domik. Moscow, 1914.
———. 2nd ed. Petersburg, 1921.
———. 3rd ed. Berlin-Petersburg-Moscow, 1922.
Tiazhelaia lira. Moscow-Petrograd, 1922; rpt. Ann Arbor, n.d.
———. 2nd ed. Berlin, 1923.

BOOKS OF PROSE

Belyi koridor: Ibrannaia proza v dvukh tomakh. Ed. G. Poliak; commentary R. Sylvester. New York, 1982.
Derzhavin. Paris, 1931; rpt. Munich, 1975.
Izbrannaia proza. Ed. N. Berberova. New York, 1982.
Literaturnye stat'i i vospominaniia. Ed. N. Berberova. New York, 1954.

SELECTED BIBLIOGRAPHY

Nekropol'. Brussels, 1939; rpt. Paris, 1976.
O Pushkine. Berlin, 1937.
Poeticheskoe khoziaistvo Pushkina. Leningrad, 1924.
Stat'i o russkoi poezii. Petersburg, 1922.
Zagadki, fairy tale. Petersburg, 1922.

EDITIONS AND ANTHOLOGIES

Bogdanovich, I. F. *Dushen'ka*. With author's foreword and introductory remarks by Vladislav Khodasevich. Moscow, 1912.
Khodasevich, V. F., ed. *Russkaia lirika*. Moscow, 1914.
———. *Voina v russkoi lirike*. Moscow, 1915.
Pushkin, A. S. *Dramaticheskie stseny*. Edited and annotated by Vladislav Khodasevich. Moscow, 1915.
———. *Evgenii Onegin, roman v stikhakh*. Illustrated by M. V. Dobuzhinsky; editing of text by V. F. Khodasevich. Brussels, 1937.
———, and V. P. Titov. *Uedinennyi domik na Vasil'evskom*. Introductory article by Vladislav Khodasevich. Moscow, 1915.

NOTEBOOKS

"Iz chernovikov." *Vozdushnye puti* 4 (1965), 120-125.
"Iz literaturnogo naslediia." Ed. Martin Sixsmith. *Vestnik russkogo studencheskogo khristianskogo dvizheniia* 130 (April 1979), 221-227.
"Iz zapisnoi knizhki Vladislava Khodasevicha (1921-1922)." *Glagol* 2 (1978), 112-121.

PUBLISHED CORRESPONDENCE

Andreeva, I., ed. *Pis'ma V. F. Khodasevicha B. A. Sadorskomu*. Ann Arbor, 1983.
Bernhardt, L., ed. "V. F. Khodasevich i sovremennaia evreiskaia poeziia" [with four letters to Lev Yaffe]. *Russian Literature* 6 (1974), 21-31.
Bethea, D., ed. *Vladislav Khodasevich: The Unpublished Letters to Nina Berberova* [seventy-four letters]. Berkeley, forthcoming.
"Dva neizdannykh pis'ma V. Khodasevicha" [two letters to E. F. Khodasevich]. *Russkaia mysl'*, no. 2760 (16 October 1969).
Hughes, R. P., and J. E. Malmstad, eds. "Towards an Edition of the Collected Works of Vladislav Xodasevič" [with eight letters to B. A. Sadovskoy]. *Slavica Hierosolymitana* 5-6 (1981), 467-500.
Malmstad, J. E., and G. S. Smith, eds. "Eight Letters of V. F. Kho-

dasevich (1916-1925)" [to B. A. Diatroptov]. *Slavic and East European Review* 57 (January 1979), 71-88.

Polianina, S., ed. "Pis'ma V. Khodasevicha k M. Fromanu" [two letters]. *Chast' rechi* 1 (1980), 292-297.

Struve, G., ed. "Iz moego arkhiva" [with three letters to G. Struve]. *Mosty* 15 (1970), 396-403.

Struve, N., ed. " 'Nekropol' ' V. Khodasevicha" [with two letters to G. L. Malitsky and one letter to Yu. N. Verkhovsky]. *Vestnik russkogo khristianskogo dvizheniia* 127 (April 1978), 105-123.

Vishniak, M., ed. "Vladislav Khodasevich" [with thirty-one letters to M. Vishnyak]. *Novyi zhurnal* 7 (1944), 277-306.

TRANSLATIONS

Bodler, Sh. (Baudelaire). "Parizhskii splin." *Voz* (2, 23, and 27 February, 10 May, and 25 October 1928, and 30 March 1929).

Briusov, V., ed. *Poeziia Armenii s drevneishikh vremen do nashikh dnei*. Moscow, 1916.

———, and Gor'kii, M., eds. *Sbornik finliandskoi literatury*. Petrograd, 1917.

———. *Sbornik latyshskoi literatury*. Petrograd, 1916.

Gavalevich, M., and P. Stakhevich. *Pol'skie narodnye legendy o Bogoroditse*. Moscow, 1910.

Gor'kii, M., ed. *Sbornik armianskoi literatury*. Moscow, 1916.

Iaffe, L., ed. *Sbornik 'Safrut'*. Book I. Moscow, 1918.

———. *Sbornik 'Safrut'*. Book III. Moscow, 1918.

Khodasevich, V., ed. *Iz evreiskikh poetov*. Petersburg-Berlin, 1922.

———, and L. Iaffe, eds. *Evreiskaia antologiia*. Moscow, 1918.

———. *Evreiskaia antologiia*. 2nd ed. Moscow-Berlin, 1921.

———. *Evreiskaia antologiia*. 3rd ed. Berlin, 1922.

Kransinskii, S. (Krasiński). *Iridion*. Moscow, 1910.

Makushinskii, K. (Makuszyński). *Mefistofel'*, stories. Moscow, 1913.

Merime, P. (Mérimée). "Federilo." *Voz* (30 March 1929).

———. *Kareta sviatykh darov*. In Merime, *Izbrannye dramaticheskie proizvedeniia*. Moscow, 1954.

Mopassan, G. (Maupassant). *Sem'ia*, stories. Moscow, 1914.

Pshibyshevskii, S. (Przybyszewski). *Adam Dzhazga*, novel. Moscow, 1916.

———. *Deti goria*, novel. Moscow, 1915.

Reimont, V. (Reymont). *Muzhiki*, contemporary tale. Moscow, 1910.

Tetmaier, K. (Tetmajer). *Ianosik Nepdza Lismanovskii*, Tartar tale. Moscow, 1912.

――――. *Marina iz Grubago.* Moscow, 1910.
――――. *Orlitsy,* Tartar stories. Moscow, 1910.

UNCOLLECTED ARTICLES, REVIEWS, MEMOIRS, OBITUARIES, AND
OTHER MATERIALS

"Aglaia Davydova i ee docheri" [article]. *SZ* 58 (1935), 227-257.
"Aisedora Dunkan" [article]. *Voz* (27 October 1927).
"Andrei Belyi" [obituary]. *Voz* (13 January 1934).
"Andrei Belyi. Kreshchenyi kitaets" [review]. *SZ* 32 (1927), 453-
    454.
"Arina Rodionovna" [article]. *Voz* (6 January 1929).
"Bel'fast" [memoir]. *PN* (26 May 1926).
"Beseda" [article/memoir]. *Voz* (14 January 1938).
"Besy" [article]. *Voz* (11 April 1927).
"Blok i ego mat' " [article]. *Voz* (7 and 9 February 1935).
"Blok i teatr" [review of book by N. Volkov]. *Voz* (4 August 1932).
"Bol'shevizm Bloka" [article]. *Voz* (15 November 1928).
"Borodin" [review of biography by Nina Berberova]. *Voz* (24 June
    1938).
"Briusov i Blok" [article]. *Voz* (11 October 1928).
"Bunin. Sobranie sochinenii" [review]. *Voz* (29 November 1934).
"Chaikovskii" [review of biography by Nina Berberova]. *Voz* (21
    May 1936).
"Chelovecheskii dokument" [article]. *Voz* (25 July 1929).
"Chernye predki. Iz knigi 'Pushkin' " [article]. *Segodnia* (25 January
    1937).
"Chisla" [review]. *Voz* (27 March 1930).
――――. *Voz* (7 July 1932).
――――. *Voz* (5 January 1933).
"Dekol'tirovannaia loshad' " [article]. *Voz* (1 September 1927).
"Diadiushka-literator. Iz knigi 'Pushkin' " [article]. *Segodnia* (1
    February 1937).
"Dvadtsat' dva" [review of twenty-two contemporary poets]. *Voz*
    (10 and 17 June 1938).
"Dva poeta" [review of posthumous collections of verse by
    B. Poplavsky and N. Gronsky]. *Voz* (30 April 1936).
"Eshche o kritike" [article]. *Voz* (31 May 1928).
"Eshche o pisatel'skoi svobode" [article]. *Voz* (2 August 1934).
"Fedor Sologub. 'Tiazhelye sny' " [review]. *Zolotoe runo* 2 (Feb-
    ruary 1906), 130-131.
"G. Ivanov. Veresk" [review]. *Utro Rossii* (7 May 1916).

"Glupovatost' poezii" [article]. *SZ* 30 (1927), 278-285.

"Gor'kii" [memoir/article]. *SZ* 70 (1940), 131-155.

"Iazyk Lenina" [article]. *PN* (7 August 1924).

"Igor' Severianin i futurizm" [article]. *Russkie vedomosti* (29 April and 1 May 1914).

"Izbrannye stikhi Briusova" [review]. *Voz* (5 April 1934).

"Juvenilia Briusova" [review]. *Sofiia* 4 (1914), 64-67.

"Kamera obskura" [review of novel by V. Nabokov-Sirin]. *Voz* (3 May 1934).

"K iubileiu K. D. Bal'monta" [note]. *Dni* (6 December 1924).

"Kniga o Briusove" [review of book by N. Ashukin]. *Voz* (9 January 1930).

"Krizis poezii" [article]. *Voz* (12 April 1934).

"Krug" [review]. *Voz* (18 July 1936).

————. *Voz* (14 October 1938).

"Literatura" [article]. *Voz* (14 January 1929).

"Literatura i vlast' v Sovetskoi Rossii" [article]. *Voz* (10, 15, 17, and 22 December 1931).

"Maksim Gor'kii i SSSR" [article]. *Voz* (20 October 1927). (Signed "M.").

"Marietta Shaginian" [memoir]. *Dni* (4 October 1925).

"Marina Tsvetaeva. Molodets" [review]. *PN* (11 June 1925).

"Marina Tsvetaeva. Posle Rossii" [review]. *Voz* (19 June 1928).

"Mladenchestvo" [autobiographical sketch]. *Voz* (12, 15, and 19 October 1933). (Republished in *Vozdushnye puti* 4 [1965], 100-119.)

"Molodost'. Iz knigi 'Pushkin' " [article]. *Voz* (9, 12, 16, and 19 March 1933).

"Molodye poety" [review of collection of verse issued by *Parizhskii soiuz molodykh poetov*]. *Voz* (30 May 1929).

"Nachalo veka" [review of A. Bely's book of memoirs]. *Voz* (28 June and 5 July 1934).

"Nachalo zhizni. Iz knigi 'Pushkin' " [article]. *Voz* (30 April 1932).

"Naedine" [review of V. Smolensky's book of verse]. *Voz* (8 July 1938).

"Na rubezhe dvukh stoletii" [review of A. Bely's book of memoirs]. *Voz* (29 May 1930).

"Ni sny, ni iav'. Pamiati Bloka" [article]. *Voz* (6 August 1931).

"Nizhe nulia" [review of contemporary poets]. *Voz* (23 April 1936).

"Novye stikhi" [review of contemporary poets]. *Voz* (28 March 1935).

———— [review of books of verse by Yu. Terapiano, S. Pregel, and E. Tauber]. *Voz* (18 and 25 July 1935).

"O Bunine" [article]. *Voz* (16 November 1933).

"O Chernikhovskom" [article]. *Evreiskaia tribuna*, no. 13 (189), dated mid-1924.

"O chtenii Pushkina" [article]. *SZ* 20 (1924), 227-234.

"O dnevnike Briusova" [review/article]. *Voz* (7 July 1927).

"O formalizme i formalistakh" [article]. *Voz* (10 March 1927).

"O forme i soderzhanii" [article]. *Voz* (15 June 1933).

"O Gumileve" [article]. *Voz* (19 September 1936).

"O kinematografe" [article]. *PN* (28 October 1926).

"O. Mandel'shtam. Kamen' " [review]. *Utro Rossii* (30 January 1916).

"O. Mandel'shtam. Tristia" [review]. *Dni* (12 November 1922).

"O metsenatakh" [article/memoir]. *Voz* (3 and 17 October 1936).

"O nazhimakh na kritiku" [article]. *Voz* (9 September 1938).

"O novykh stikhakh" [review of books of verse by Yu. Terapiano and L. Lvov]. *Voz* (25 November 1938).

"O pisatel'skoi svobode" [article]. *Voz* (10 September 1931).

"O poezii Bunina" [article/review of *Izbrannye stikhi*]. *Voz* (15 August 1929).

"O pornografii" [article]. *Voz* (11 February 1932).

"O sebe" [autobiographical note]. *Novaia russkaia kniga* 2 (July 1922), 36-37.

"O smerti Gor'kogo" [article]. *Voz* (18 March 1938).

"O sovetskoi literature" [article]. *Voz* (20 May 1938).

"Otplytie na ostrov Tsiteru" [review of Georgy Ivanov's book of verse]. *Voz* (28 May 1937).

"Ot polypravdy k nepravde" [review of A. Bely's book of memoirs, *Mezhdu dvukh revoliutsii*]. *Voz* (27 May 1938).

"O 'Verstakh' " [review]. *SZ* 29 (1926), 433-441.

"Pamiati Bar. V. I. Iskul' fon-Gillenband" [obituary]. *Voz* (20 February 1928).

"Pamiati B. A. Sadovskogo" [obituary]. *PN* (3 May 1925).

"Pamiati Sergeia Krechetova" [obituary]. *Voz* (28 May 1936).

"Parizhskie nochi" [review of D. Knut's book of verse]. *Voz* (10 March 1932).

"Parizhskii al'bom" [article]. *Dni* (30 May 1926).

———— [review of books of verse by N. Otsup and Yu. Terapiano]. *Dni* (27 June 1926).

———— [memoir]. *Dni* (11 July 1926).

"Pered kontsom" [article]. *Voz* (22 August 1936).

"Pis'ma Maksima Gor'kogo k V. F. Khodasevichu." *Novyi zhurnal*

29-31 (1952), 205-214, 189-202, 190-205. (Translated into English by Hugh McLean, with introduction by Sergius Yakobson, in *Harvard Slavic Studies* 1 [1953], 279-334.)

"Pis'ma M. O. Gershenzona." *SZ* 24 (1925), 224-236. (Expanded and republished by Nina Berberova in *Novyi zhurnal* 60 [1960], 222-235.)

"Poetu ili chitateliu" [review of book by N. Shulgovsky]. *Sofiia* 4 (1914), 87-89.

"Poezdka v Porkhov" [memoir]. *Voz* (9 and 16 May 1935).

"Pompeiskii uzhas" [memoir]. *PN* (10 May 1925).

"Po povodu 'Perekrestka' " [review]. *Voz* (10 July 1930).

"Pravo na konflikt" [review of article by A. Makarenko]. *Voz* (30 September 1938).

"Proletarskie poety" [review article on S. Rodov's anthology]. *SZ* 26 (1924), 444-455.

"Pushkin i grafinia Nessel'rode" [article]. *Dni* (25 December 1925).

"Pushkin i Nikolai I" [review article on Count Yu. Strutynsky's notebooks]. *Voz* (14 and 18 February 1938).

"Pushkin, izvestnyi bankomet" [article]. *Voz* (6 and 7 June 1928).

"Pushkin v zhizni" [review of book by V. Veresaev]. *PN* (13 January 1927).

"Ranniaia liubov' Feta" [review of book by L. Sukhotin]. *Voz* (13 April 1933).

"Russkaia poeziia. Obzor" [review of contemporary poets, including V. Ivanov, V. Bryusov, K. Balmont, Yu. Baltrushaytis, S. Gorodetsky, N. Gumilyov, A. Akhmatova, M. Kuzmin, B. Sadovskoy, M. Tsvetaeva, N. Klyuev, I. Severyanin]. *Al'tsiona* 1 (1914), 193-217.

"Severnoe serdtse" [review of A. Ladinsky's book of verse]. *Voz* (19 May 1932).

"S. Ia. Parnok" [obituary]. *Voz* (14 September 1933).

"Sovremennye zapiski" [review]. *Voz* (27 September 1928).

―――. *Voz* (27 October 1932).

―――. *Voz* (29 November 1932).

―――. *Voz* (6 April 1933).

―――. *Voz* (8 June 1933).

―――. *Voz* (9 November 1933).

―――. *Voz* (31 May 1934).

―――. *Voz* (8 November 1934).

―――. *Voz* (4 April 1935).

―――. *Voz* (11 July 1935).

―――. *Voz* (28 November 1935).

———. *Voz* (12 March 1936).

———. *Voz* (8 August 1936).

———. *Voz* (26 December 1936).

———. *Voz* (15 May 1937).

———. *Voz* (15 October 1937).

———. *Voz* (25 February 1938).

———. *Voz* (11 November 1938).

———. *Voz* (22 March 1939).

"Tainye liubvi Pushkina" [review of book by P. Bartenev]. *Dni* (20 September 1925).

"Tam ili zdes' " [article]. *Dni* (18 September 1925).

"Tri pis'ma Andreia Belogo." *SZ* 55 (1934), 256-270.

"Umiranie iskusstva" [review of book by W. Weidlé]. *Voz* (18 November 1938).

"V. Briusov. Sem' tsvetov radugi" [review]. *Utro Rossii* (21 May 1916).

"Viktor Gofman" [memoir]. *PN* (14 October 1926).

"Vo Pskove" [memoir]. *Voz* (24 October 1935).

"V poiskakh kritiki" [article]. *Voz* (14 November 1929).

"V sporakh o Pushkine" [article]. *SZ* 37 (1928), 275-294.

"Zametki o stikhakh. Konkurs 'Zvena' " [article]. *Dni* (14 March 1926).

"Zashchita Luzhina" [review of novel by V. Nabokov-Sirin]. *Voz* (11 October 1930).

"Zhalost' i 'zhalost' ' " [article]. *Voz* (11 April 1935).

"Zheltyi konvert" [obituary for Yu. Aikhenvald]. *Voz* (27 December 1928).

"Zhena Pushkina" [article]. *Voz* (9 December 1938).

"Zhenit'ba Pushkina" [article]. *Voz* (13 February 1930).

"Zhizn' Vasiliia Travnikova" [article]. *Voz* (13, 20, and 27 February 1936). (Republished with commentary by G. Polyak in *Chast' rechi* 1 [1980], 172-193.)

"Zizi" [article]. *Voz* (10 and 12 August 1933).

II

WORKS ABOUT KHODASEVICH

Adamovich, G. "Literaturnye besedy." *Zveno* (27 July 1925).

———. "Literaturnye besedy." *Zveno* (23 January 1927).

———. "Literaturnye besedy." *Zveno* (17 April 1927).

———. "Literaturnye zametki." *PN* (1 July 1937).

SELECTED BIBLIOGRAPHY

Adamovich, G. "Vladislav Khodasevich." *PN* (22 June 1939).

———. "Vladislav Khodasevich. Putem zerna" [review]. *Tsekh poetov* 3 (1922), 60-62.

———. "Zhizn' i 'zhizn' '." *PN* (14 April 1935).

Aikhenval'd, Iu. (under the pseudonym B. Kamenetskii). "Literaturnye zametki" [review of *Schastlivyi domik* and *Tiazhelaia lira*]. *Rul'* (14 January 1923).

———. "Vladislav Khodasevich. Sobranie stikhov" [review]. *Segodnia* (9 December 1927).

Aldanov, M (M. Landau). "V. F. Khodasevich. Derzhavin" [review]. *SZ* 46 (1931), 496-497.

———. "Vladislav Khodasevich." *Russkie zapiski* 19 (1939), 179-185.

Aronson, G. "Tvorcheskii put' Vl. Khodasevicha." *Novoe russkoe slovo* (1, 8, and 15 December 1963).

Bakhrakh, A. "Po pamiati, po zapiskam." *Mosty* 11 (1965), 242-247.

Belyi, A. (B. Bugaev). *Mezhdu dvukh revoliutsii*. Leningrad, 1934; rpt., Chicago, 1966, pp. 249-250.

———. "Rembrandtova pravda v poezii nashikh dnei." *Zapiski mechtatelei* 5 (1922), 136-139.

———. "Tiazhelaia lira i russkaia lirika" [review article]. *SZ* 15 (1923), 371-388.

Bem, A. "Pis'ma o literature." *Rul'* (6 May 1931).

———. "Pis'ma o literature." *Rul'* (2 July 1931).

Berberova, N., ed. "Chetyre pis'ma V. I. Ivanova k V. F. Khodasevichu." *Novyi zhurnal* 62 (1960), 284-289.

———. *Kursiv moi*. Munich, 1972, passim. (Translated by Philippe Radley as *The Italics Are Mine*, New York, 1969.)

———. "Pamiati Khodasevicha." *SZ* 69 (1939), 256-261.

———. "Predislovie." In V. F. Khodasevich, *Literaturnye stat'i i vospominaniia*, New York, 1954, pp. 5-11.

———. "Tri goda zhizni M. Gor'kogo." *Mosty* 8 (1961), 262-272.

———. "Vladislav Khodasevich." *Grani* 12 (1951), 140-144. (Translated as "Vladislav Khodasevich—A Russian Poet." In *The Russian Review* 2 [1952], 78-85.)

———. "Vladislav Khodasevich." *Russkaia mysl'* (15 June 1949).

———. *Zheleznaia zhenshchina*. New York, 1981, passim.

Bernhardt, L. "V. F. Khodasevich i sovremennaia evreiskaia poeziia." *Russian Literature* 6 (1974), 21-31.

Betaki, V. "Pamiati Khodasevicha. K sorokaletiiu so dnia ego smerti." *Kontinent* 21 (1979), 365-370.

SELECTED BIBLIOGRAPHY

Bethea, D. "Following in Orpheus' Footsteps: A Reading of Xodasevič's 'Ballada.'" *Slavic and East European Journal* 25 (Fall 1981), 54-70.

———. "Khodasevich's Blank Verse Narratives: The Pushkin Connection." *Topic* 33 (1979), 3-13.

———. "*Sorrento Photographs*: Khodasevich's Memory Speaks." *Slavic Review* 39 (March 1980), 56-69.

Bitsilli, P. "Derzhavin" [review]. *Rossiia i slavianstvo* (14 April 1931).

Briusov, V. "Debiutanty" [review of *Molodost'*]. *Vesy* 3 (1908), 77-81.

———. "Prodolzhateli" [review of *Schastlivyi domik*]. *Russkaia mysl'* 7 (1914), 19-23.

———. "Sredi stikhov" [review of *Tiazhelaia lira*]. *Pechat' i revoliutsiia* 1 (1923), 70-78.

Brown, C. *Mandelstam*. Cambridge, England, 1973, passim.

Brown, E. J. *Russian Literature Since the Revolution*. Cambridge, Mass., 1982, pp. 346ff.

Chulkova, A. "Vospominaniia o Vladislave Khodaseviche." *Russica* (almanac) (Fall 1982), 275-294.

Chulkov, G. "V. Khodasevich. Schastlivyi domik" [review]. *Sovremennik* 7 (1914), 122-123.

Eikhenbaum, B. "Metody i podkhody." *Knizhnyi ugol* 8 (1922), 13-23.

El'kan, A. "Dom iskusstv." *Mosty* 5 (1960), 289-298.

Erlich, V. *The Double Image: Concepts of the Poet in Slavic Literatures*. Baltimore, 1964, passim.

Fedotov, G. "O parizhskoi poezii." In *Kovcheg*, New York, 1942, pp. 189-198.

Filippov, B. "Vladislav Khodasevich" [review of 1961 edition of *Sobranie stikhov*]. *Grani* 49 (1961), 226-230.

Forsh, O. *Sumasshedshii korabl'*. Leningrad, 1931; rpt. Washington, 1964.

Freiberger Sheikholeslami, E., ed. *Zinaida Gippius, Pis'ma k Berberovoi i Khodasevichu*, Ann Arbor, 1978, pp. 39-109.

Gifford, H. "Vladislav Khodasevich, 1886-1939." *PN* (Winter 1982), 58-61.

Gippius, Z. (under the pseudonym Anton Krainii). "Literaturnye razmyshleniia." *Chisla*, 2-3 (1930), 148-154.

———. "Poeziia nashikh dnei." *PN* (22 February 1925).

———. "Sovremennost'." *Chisla* 2-3 (1930), 311-314.

SELECTED BIBLIOGRAPHY

Gippius, Z. "Znak" [review of 1927 edition of *Sobranie stikhov*]. *Voz* (15 December 1927).

Gofman, V. "Vladislav Khodasevich—Molodost' " [review]. *Russkaia mysl'* 7 (1908), 143-144.

Gor'kii, M. (A. Peshkov). *Literaturnoe nasledstvo: Gor'kii i sovetskie pisateli*. Moscow, 1963, passim.

Grossman, J., ed. *The Diary of Valery Bryusov, 1893-1905* (with reminiscences by V. F. Khodasevich and Marina Tsvetaeva). Berkeley, 1980, pp. 1-32.

Gumilev, N. "Stat'i i zametki o russkoi poezii." In *Sobranie sochinenii*, Washington, 1968, IV, 343-344.

Hagglund, R. "The Adamovič-Xodasevič Polemics." *Slavic and East European Journal* 20 (Fall 1976), 239-252.

———. "The Russian Émigré Debate of 1928 on Criticism." *Slavic Review* 32 (September 1973), 515-525.

Hughes, R. P. "Khodasevich: Irony and Dislocation: A Poet in Exile." In Simon Karlinsky and Alfred Appel, Jr., eds., *The Bitter Air of Exile: Russian Writers in the West, 1922-1972*, Berkeley, 1977, pp. 52-66. (Originally appeared in *TriQuarterly* 28 [1973].)

———, and J. E. Malmstad. "Towards an Edition of the Collected Works of Vladislav Xodasevič." *Slavica Hierosolymitana* 5-6 (1981), 467-500.

Ianovskii, V. "Eliseiskie polia." *Vozdushnye puti* 5 (1967), 175-200.

———. "Polia eliseiskie." *Vremia i my* 37 (January 1979), 165-198.

Ivanov, G. (under the pseudonym "Liubitel' prekrasnogo"). "Buket liubitelia prekrasnogo na grud' zarubezhnoi slovesnosti." *Chisla* 2-3 (1930), 314-317.

——— (under the pseudonym A. Kondrat'ev). "K iubileiu V. F. Khodasevicha." *Chisla* 2-3 (1930), 311-314.

———. "O novykh stikhakh" [review of *Putem zerna*]. *Dom iskusstv* 2 (1921), 96.

———. "V zashchitu Khodasevicha." *PN* (8 March 1928).

Ivask, Iu. "Literaturnyc zamctki" [rcvicw of 1961 edition of *Sobranie stikhov*]. *Mosty* 9 (1962), 187-191.

Karlinsky, S. *Marina Cvetaeva: Her Life and Art*. Berkeley, 1966, passim.

———. "Pis'ma M. Tsvetaevoi k V. Khodasevichu." *Novyi zhurnal* 89 (1967), 102-114.

Lednitskii, V. (Wacław Lednicki). "Literaturnye zametki i vospominaniia." *Opyty* 2 (1953), 152-174.

Malmstad, J. E. "The Historical Sense and Xodasevič's *Deržavin*."

In V. F. Khodasevich, *Derzhavin*, Paris, 1931; rpt. Munich, 1975, pp. v-xviii.

Mandel'shtam, Iu. "Khodasevich o Pushkine" [review]. *Voz* (2 May 1937).

———. "Nekropol' " [review]. *Voz* (17 March 1939).

Mandel'shtam, N. *Vtoraia kniga*. Paris, 1972, pp. 160-162. (Translated by Max Hayward as *Hope Abandoned*, New York, 1974, pp. 140-141.)

Mandel'shtam, O. "Buria i natisk." In *Sobranie sochinenii*, New York, 1971, II, 339-351.

———. "Vypad." In *Sobranie sochinenii*, New York, 1971, II, 228-232.

Markov, V. "Georgy Ivanov: Nihilist as Light-Bearer." In Simon Karlinsky and Alfred Appel, Jr., eds., *The Bitter Air of Exile: Russian Writers in the West, 1922-1972*, Berkeley, 1977, pp. 139-163. (Originally appeared in *TriQuarterly* 27-28 [1973].)

Maslenikov, O. *The Frenzied Poets*. Berkeley, 1952, passim.

Merezhkovskii, D. "Zakholust'e." *Voz* (26 and 28 January 1928).

Milashevskii, V. *Vchera, pozavchera*. Leningrad, 1972, pp. 184-185.

Miller, J. "Creativity and the Lyric 'I' in the Poetry of Vladislav Xodasevič." Ph.D. diss., U. of Michigan, 1981.

Mirsky, D. S. (See Sviatopolk-Mirskii, Prince D.)

Mochul'skii, K. "Vladislav Khodasevich" [review of *Schastlivyi domik* and *Tiazhelaia lira*]. *Zveno* (4 June 1923).

Muratov, P. "Kniga o Derzhavine" [review]. *Voz* (4 April 1931).

Nabokov, V. (in Russian under the pseudonym V. Sirin), ed. and trans. *Eugene Onegin*, Princeton, 1975, passim.

———. "Foreword." *The Gift*. New York, 1970, n.p.

———. "O Khodaseviche." *SZ* 69 (1939), 262-264. (Translated as "On Khodasevich," in Simon Karlinsky and Alfred Appel, Jr., eds., *The Bitter Air of Exile: Russian Writers in the West, 1922-1972*, Berkeley, 1977, pp. 83-87.)

———. *Speak, Memory*. New York, 1970, p. 285.

———. "Vladislav Khodasevich. Sobranie stikhov" [review]. *Rul'* (14 December 1927).

Orlov, V. "Na rubezhe dvukh epokh." *Voprosy literatury* 10 (1966), 111-143. (Expanded and included in *Pereput'ia. Iz istorii russkoi poezii nachala XX veka*, Moscow, 1976, pp. 144-156.)

Osorgin, M. "Knizhnaia lavka pisatelei." *Novaia russkaia kniga* 3-4 (1923), 38-40.

Pachmuss, T. *Zinaida Hippius: An Intellectual Profile*. Carbondale, 1971, pp. 238-246, 271-272, and passim.

Pereleshin, V. "V. F. Khodasevich. Derzhavin" [review of reprint]. *Russian Language Journal* 109 (1977), 213-217.

Petrovskaia, N. "Vladislav Khodasevich. Tiazhelaia lira" [review]. *Nakanune* (25 December 1922).

Poggioli, R. *The Poets of Russia, 1880-1930*. Cambridge, Mass., 1960, pp. 303-308.

Poltoratskii, N., ed. *Russkaia literatura v emigratsii* (sbornik statei). Pittsburgh, 1972, passim.

Poplavskii, B. "O misticheskoi atmosfere molodoi literatury v emigratsii." *Chisla* 2-3 (1930), 308-311.

Pozner, V. *Panorama de la littérature russe contemporaine*. Paris, 1929, pp. 240-245.

Radley, P. "Khodasevich—poet groteska." *Vozdushnye puti* 4 (1965), 256-262.

———. "Vladislav Xodasevič—Poet and Critic." Ph.D. diss., Harvard, 1964.

Scherr, B. "Notes on Literary Life in Petrograd, 1918-1922: A Tale of Three Houses." *Slavic Review* 36 (June 1977), 256-267.

Sedykh, A. (Ia. Tsvibak). "U. V. F. Khodasevicha." *Segodnia* (10 May 1930).

Shaginian, M. "Vladislav Khodasevich. Putem zerna" [review]. *Literaturnyi dnevnik*, Moscow-Petersburg, 1923, pp. 124-127.

Shakhovskaia, Z. *Otrazheniia*. Paris, 1975, pp. 184-187.

Shklovskii, V. *Santimental'noe puteshestvie*. Moscow, 1929, pp. 280-281. (Translated by Richard Sheldon as *A Sentimental Journey*, Ithaca, 1970, pp. 236-237.)

Sixsmith, M. "Vladislav Khodasevich." *Vestnik russkogo khristianskogo dvizheniia* 130 (April 1979), 214-220.

Slonim, M. "Literaturnye otkliki" [review of *Tiazhelaia lira*]. *Volia Rossii* 6-7 (1923), 93-99.

Smith, G. "Stanza Rhythm and Stress Load in the Iambic Tetrameter of V. F. Xodasevič." *Slavic and East European Journal* 24 (Spring 1980), 25-36.

———. "The Versification of Russian Émigré Poetry, 1920-1940." *Slavic and East European Review* 56 (January 1978), 32-46.

Smolenskii, V. "Mysli o Vladislave Khodaseviche" [review of *Literaturnye stat'i i vospominaniia*]. *Voz* 41 (May 1955), 99-102.

Struve, G. "The Double Life of Russian Literature." *Books Abroad* 28, no. 4 (1954), pp. 185-186, 220-222, and passim.

———. "G. Ivanov, V. Khodasevich, i A. Kondrat'ev—Zapozdalye utochneniia." *Russkaia mysl'* (30 January 1969).

————. "Pis'ma o russkoi poezii" [review of *Tiazhelaia lira*]. *Russkaia mysl'* 1-2 (1923), 292-299.

————. *Russkaia literatura v izgnanii*. New York, 1956, pp. 141-146, 185-186, 220-222, and passim.

————. "Tikhii ad" [review of 1927 edition of *Sobranie stikhov*]. *Za svobodu* (11 March 1928).

————. "V. Khodasevich i Georgii Ivanov." *Novoe russkoe slovo* (15 July 1973).

————. "V. Khodasevich o zhurnale 'Vstrechi.' " *Novoe russkoe slovo* (17 June 1973).

Struve, N. " 'Nekropol' ' V. Khodasevicha." *Vestnik russkogo khristianskogo dvizheniia* 127 (1978), 105-123.

Sviatopolk-Mirskii, Prince D. "Bibliografiia." *Versty* 1 (1926), 206-210.

————. *A History of Russian Literature*. New York, 1949, pp. 475-476.

————. "Recent Books on Pushkin and his Times." *Slavonic Review* 1 (December 1922), 475-478.

————. "Sovremennye zapiski" [review of *Derzhavin*]. *Evraziia* (10 August 1929).

————. "Veianie smerti v predrevoliutsionnoi literature." *Versty* 2 (1927), 247-254.

Sylvester, R., ed. *Valentina Khodasevich and Olga Margolina-Khodasevich: Unpublished Letters to Nina Berberova*. Berkeley, 1979.

————. "V. F. Xodasevič in Moscow and Petersburg: A Study of *Putem zerna* and *Tjaželaja lira*, 1914-1922." Ph.D. diss., Harvard, 1976.

Terapiano, Iu. "Ob odnoi literaturnoi voine." *Mosty* 12 (1966), 363-375.

————. *Vstrechi*. New York, 1953, pp. 83-92.

Tomashevskii, B. "Poeticheskoe khoziaistvo Pushkina" [review]. *Russkii sovremennik* 3 (1924), 262-263.

Tsetlin, M. "Poet i Psikheia" [review of 1927 edition of *Sobranie stikhov*]. *Dni* (8 January 1928).

————. "Vladislav Khodasevich." *PN* (3 April 1930).

Tsvetaeva, M. "Geroi truda (zapisi o Valerii Briusove)." *Izbrannaia proza*. New York, 1979, I, 176-220.

————. "Plennyi dukh (moia vstrecha s Andreem Belym)." *Izbrannaia proza*. New York, 1979, II, 80-121.

————. "Tsvetnik." *Izbrannaia proza*. New York, 1979, I, 242-250.

Tynianov, Iu. "Promezhutok." *Russkii sovremennik* 4 (1924), 208-221.

Ul'ianov, N. "Zastignutyi noch'iu." *Svitok*. New Haven, 1972, pp. 34-47.

Varshavskii, V. *Nezamechennoe pokolenie*. New York, 1956, pp. 166-228.

Veidle, V. "A Double-Edged *Ars Poetica*." *Russian Literature Triquarterly* 2 (1972), 339-347.

――――. "Khodasevich izdali-vblizi." *Novyi zhurnal* 66 (1961), 124-140. (Subsequently collected in *O poetakh i poezii*, Paris, 1973.)

――――. "O tekh, kogo uzhe net." *Novoe russkoe slovo* (6 June 1976).

――――. "O tekh, kogo uzhe net." *Novoe russkoe slovo* (20 June 1976).

――――. "O tekh, kogo uzhe net." *Novoe russkoe slovo* (2 October 1976).

――――. "O tekh, kogo uzhe net." *Novoe russkoe slovo* (2 November 1976).

――――. "Poeziia Khodasevicha." *SZ* 34 (1928), 452-469. (Republished as booklet, Paris, 1928.)

――――. "V. F. Khodasevich. Nekropol' " [review]. *SZ* 69 (1939), 393-394.

――――. "V. Khodasevich. O Pushkine" [review]. *SZ* 64 (1937), 467-468.

――――. "Vladislav Khodasevich." *Voz* (3 April 1930).

Vishniak, M. *Sovremennye zapiski. Vospominaniia redaktora*. Bloomington, 1957, pp. 140-146, 201-215, and passim.

――――. "Vladislav Khodasevich." *Novyi zhurnal* 7 (1944), 277-306.

Vygodskii, D. "Vladislav Khodasevich. Iz evreiskikh poetov" [review]. *Vostok* 1 (1922), 115-116.

Weidlé, W. (*See* Veidle, V.)

X. "Sobranie stikhov. Vladislav Khodasevich, stikhi 1913-1939" [review of 1961 edition]. *Mosty* 8 (1961), 335-336.

INDEX

INDEX

INDEX

Library of Congress Cataloging in Publication Data

Bethea, David M., 1948-
Khodasevich, his life and art.

Bibliography: p.
Includes index.
1. Khodasevich, V. F. (Vladislav Felitsianovich), 1886-1939.
2. Poets, Russian—20th century—Biography. I. Title.

PG3476.K488Z59 1983   891.71'3 [B]   82-61355
ISBN 0-691-06559-4